The Work
of
Mara Selvini Palazzoli

The Work
of
Mara Selvini Palazzoli

Edited by Matteo Selvini

Translated by Arnold J. Pomerans

Jason Aronson Inc.
Northvale, New Jersey
London

10 9 8 7 6 5 4 3 2 1

Library of Congress Cataloging-in-Publication Data

Selvini Palazzoli, Mara.
    The work of Mara Selvini Palazzoli.

    Translated in part from Cronaca di una ricerca.
    Includes bibliographies and index.
    1. Family psychotherapy.   I. Selvini, Matteo.
II. Title.   [DNLM: 1. Family Therapy—collected works.
WM 420 S469w]
RC488.5.S45   1988   616.89′156   87-12438
ISBN 0-87668-949-7

The editor gratefully acknowledges permission to reprint portions of the following:

       S. Rusconi and M. Selvini Palazzoli (1970). Il transfert nella coteripa intensiva della famiglia. *Rivista de Psicologia Analitica* 1:159–162, 167–168.
       M. Selvini Palazzoli (1968). Preface to N. W. Ackerman, *Psicodinamica della Vita Familiare* (*Psychodynamics of Family Life*). Turin, Italy: Boringhieri, pp. 10–12.
       M. Selvini Palazzoli (1978). Interview in *Sozialmagazin* 3:32–41.
       M. Selvini Palazzoli (1979). Interview with Klaus Deissler in *Kontext*.
       M. Selvini Palazzoli (1981). Comments on Dell's paper. *Family Process* 20:44–45.
       M. Selvini Palazzoli (1984). Review of *Aesthetics of Change* (B. Keeney, New York: Guilford Press, 1983). *Family Process* 23:282–284.

Manufactured in the United States of America.

Contents

PART TWO

FROM COMMUNICATIONALISM TO EARLY EMERGENCE OF THE GAME METAPHOR

PART THREE

THE CHOICE OF THE BATESONIAN SYSTEMIC MODEL AND THE BEGINNINGS OF INTERVENTIONIST THERAPY

PART FOUR

SELF-STARVATION

PART FIVE

FROM VERBAL TO ANALOGICAL INTERVENTIONISM

Preface

I am convinced that every investigation, when it arrives to consider itself accomplished, is yet on its death-bed. Personally, I consider family therapy based on the systemic model as an investigation which is on its first steps. I mean exactly what Gregory Bateson meant in entitling his book *Steps to an Ecology of Mind*—a sort of signal indicating a direction, a road full of difficulties which will (I hope) attract generations of researchers looking for something completely new.

In our field of family therapy I now feel a danger: the risk of losing the spirit of investigation. I personally have a limited interest in training others in family therapy, especially because of the discomfort I feel in teaching something which should be taught only to people who are disposed to a spirit of investigation.

Unfortunately, the actual reality is very different. I am speaking from my experiences in Italy and in some other European countries. A large number of young people, without any authentic intellectual curiosity, are crowding into the profession of family therapy. There is vast unemployment and a state of diffuse dread, which makes understandable the haste to get *some* tool to do *something*.

Mara Selvini Palazzoli
"Present Imperfect" Address
Don Jackson Memorial Day
San Francisco, 1979

The above quotation nicely states the idea behind this book. Starting in the 1970s, Italy has witnessed a boom in family therapy and a proliferation of schools purporting to train family therapists. This trend has led me to share my mother's mixed feelings: although it is highly encouraging to see basic ideas gain momentum and a wider acceptance, one is terrified to think they may be sold down the river or trivialized. Have we the right to teach students on the basis of experiences that are undergoing continuous clinical and theoretical evolution? Are we justified in telling our students that a viewpoint we ardently espoused only a few months ago now seems to us to be entirely outdated and needs to be discarded? If we take a close, hard look at reality, we find that a considerable number of "family therapy schools," both in Italy and elsewhere, are perfectly willing to present a badly warped image of family therapy to their students in an attempt to allay their fears and gain their confidence. They tout family therapy as a well-established model, and its techniques are held out as a systematic, well-defined set of procedures born out by gratifying experimental results. This, unfortunately, is a dangerous fallacy. The appeal of family therapy lies in its "newness," which applies not only to its being new in its approach and method but also to the underlying epistemology, which requires that the therapist work in a spirit free of prejudice and dogma. This holds true even when a strictly professional goal is at stake. Even the grass-roots practitioner, harboring no special scientific ambitions, can learn more from his own experience and from analyzing his own mistakes than he can from the most influential master of the art. I still remember the whispered insinuations in the halls during a family therapy course I attended: "They're holding out on us; they don't want to let us in on their secrets." This was obviously not so, but I must admit that it was difficult for us to realize that family therapy, at least at our present level of knowledge, simply does not churn out cut-and-dried recipes and procedures to help us. Everyone must tax his own ingenuity and use his creative powers to fill the gaps in his acquired knowledge, without forfeiting methodological rigor.

    An account of the charted course Mara Selvini Palazzoli followed in her research work seems to me to have exceptional didactic value. Not only is Selvini a "self-taught" family therapist, she is *still* teaching herself. Family therapy is both the object of all her endeavors and her finely honed instrument for researching human behavior. A historical account of her progression is therefore appropriate. We can learn from the way Mara Selvini proceeded from psychoanalysis to communications theory, from cybernetics to the paradigm of complexity, from paradox to the typing of "games," all the while devising and developing adequate therapeutic techniques as she went. For the "systemic-relational practitioner" (a clumsy expression, this, but less misleading than "family therapist"), such a study in self-teaching and research should provide an invaluable sounding board for gauging one's own apprenticeship. The book's scope is, therefore, not merely biographical; it attempts to go beyond historic reconstruction, to advocate the adoption of a steadfast research attitude. It identifies with both the liberating joy and the suffering that are part of the heightened awareness and that require constant readjusting of one's sights.

I have collected a number of Mara Selvini's articles and sundry writings spanning more than a decade (1967 to 1978), all of them, except for a few, published in various books and journals and in several languages. I hope it will help the reader to find this material arranged in such a way as to render it accessible to those who otherwise might have overlooked some of it. The collected writings of Selvini and her co-workers published since 1980 will be gathered into a separate volume, on which I am currently working.

The articles have been arranged so as to reflect, in the case of each item, the logical line of thought prevailing at the time it was conceived, regardless of when the article actually first appeared in print. Very often, in fact, for purely technical reasons (the time needed to translate it, edit it, or get it into print), a paper will go to press a full two years before one that was written earlier. This collection comprises some papers not published in Italian and others never published at all. One of the latter is the detailed account of a complete family therapy, conducted following the method of directive paradoxical interventions described in *Paradox and Counterparadox*. The first session of this therapy was published in the Italian review *Terapia familiare*, whereas the paper as it is included here is followed by a chronicle of all subsequent events (six further

sessions) plus the follow-up undertaken six years after this therapy was terminated. A further unpublished manuscript, "From
Family Therapy to Individual Therapy" was originally intended to be the final chapter in *Paradox and Counterparadox*,
but was ultimately left out. Finally, the book contains some
totally unpublished material, gleaned from Selvini's contributions to various seminars and conferences.[1]

In order to render such vastly differing items more lively for
the reader, I have linked them with introductions and annota-
tions. My notes aim to place each separate contribution in its
proper time-related context, enabling comparison both with
work done before and with subsequent developments of the same
theme. I have tried to spare the reader the tedious, unguided
wandering over heterogeneous ground that normally mars the
perusal of such miscellanea. In so doing, I have traced the chronicle of an adventure in research and the story of its undertaking,
and have used Selvini's writings as so many milestones. My own
comments on how Selvini's thought influenced the development
of the art, as well as other considerations of mine, often bring a
present-day focus to bear on the subject matter. This entails
moving back and forth in time and comparing the context in
which the article was originally written with subsequent events,
leading up to the present. Such many-sided comparisons are of
necessity partially incomplete, since I am unable to deal exhaus-
tively with the present for a number of reasons, chief among
which is that much of the research is still under way, so that a
summing-up would be premature at this stage. However, I have
deliberately run the risk of presenting some of the work in
fragmentary form and of switching back and forth from histori-
cal-descriptive material to currently pertinent remarks in order to
avoid the somewhat elegiac flavor usually accruing to "collected
works" and to strive for something more stimulating and dynamic. I hope this book will be used not only as a reference work
in which to look up a given page or article, but as an account to
be read and discussed on its own merits.

[1]Since 1967, Mara Selvini has been directing various teams and researching
family therapy as well as large organizations. The papers published here were
written mainly by Mara Selvini herself, although they were often also signed by her
several associates.

The fact that I am currently a member of Mara Selvini's research team[2] raises the issue of the authorship of the many comments and observations that surfaced during our team discussions. Generally speaking, I have used the first person singular when responsibility for the views expressed is predominantly mine (and in some instances was not shared by Selvini or other research associates), whereas my use of the first person plural indicates that I am voicing points of view discussed and shared by all those concerned.

Matteo Selvini

TRANSLATOR'S PREFACE

Because many of the papers, addresses, and other passages quoted in this book were originally translated into English by a number of translators for a variety of journals, many discrepancies in style and terminology have inevitably appeared. I have thought it best to iron these out in the present edition. The alterations are slight and any errors that may nevertheless have crept in must be blamed on me and not on the original translators.

Arnold J. Pomerans

[2]In 1979, after separating from Luigi Boscolo and Gianfranco Cecchin, Mara Selvini established a new research team with Giuliana Prata. This association ended in June 1985. Starting in 1982, Selvini formed a second research team (with Stefano Cirillo, Anna Maria Sorrentino, and me). Since 1979, Maurizio Viaro, too, has been working as a research associate. Innocenzo Pisano and Lucio D'Ettorre have been part of the team researching large organizations since 1982.

Acknowledgments

The present work is the result of close collaboration with my mother, Mara Selvini Palazzoli.

Most valuable, too, have been the contributions of my two colleagues on the research team at the *Nuovo Centro per lo Studio della Famiglia* (New Center for Family Studies), namely Stefano Cirillo and Anna Maria Sorrentino. To them and to Maurizio Viaro I owe a great debt, regarding both the general approach used in this collection and specific suggestions, not all of which I have been able to acknowledge.

Many other colleagues and friends have helped by reading and commenting on the successive versions of my manuscript, among them Dante Ghezzi, Milena Lerma, Dario Nutini, Carmela Martino, and Patrizia Taccani.

Luigi Boscolo, Gianfranco Cecchin, and Paolo Ferraresi have kindly allowed me to publish their contributions, as has Giuliana Prata, who also offered me valuable assistance during the phase of collecting and translating my material.

Finally, I wish to thank Giuliana Mauro Paramithiotti for her help in producing the various drafts leading to the final manuscript, and Veronica Kleiber for her help in correcting the English version of this book.

CHAPTER 1

The Evolution of
Her Clinical Work

Matteo Selvini

PSYCHOANALYTICAL BACKGROUND AND TRAINING

Mara Selvini was taught in the fifties by Professor Gaetano Benedetti, who used mainly orthodox principles but put special emphasis on the relationship between patient and therapist. That approach, as part of the overall canvas presented by the various psychoanalytic schools, emphasized certain theoretical and clinical trends, while playing down a number of others.

In 1963, the publication of the first edition of *Anoressia mentale* (Selvini Palazzoli 1963) reflected Mara Selvini's interest in the American school of Frieda Fromm-Reichmann and Harry Stack Sullivan, which, though basically in line with orthodox psychoanalysis, introduced new topics into modern psychopathology, above all the study of interpersonal relationships and their consequences in all the circumstances in which such relationships take place (Sullivan 1955).

Many new influences made themselves felt simultaneously, including those of the British school of Fairbairn and Guntrip, who, concentrating on the object relation, opened the way for a theoretical approach that focused attention on transference and above all on countertransference. *A dyadic relational interpretation was thus given preference to one based on the patient's intra-psychic dynamics.* It was precisely this step, first taken under Benedetti and Cremerius, that laid the theoretical groundwork for an even more consistently relational approach.

A good example was the case of Rita (Selvini Palazzoli 1969b), an account of the difficult individual treatment of an anorectic patient; after years of therapy, the crucial disappearance of the symptom was explained *exclusively* on the basis of the development of the patient–therapist relationship. The therapist, in fact, had come to realize that Rita must be allowed to experience her health as an autonomous achievement and not as the therapist's gift.

A third important influence was that of the phenomenologists associated with existential analysis (Binswanger, Buber, Jaspers, Heidegger). This group was particularly concerned with the relationship between man and those he confronts, between *I* and *Thou*,[1] and led Mara Selvini to her first studies of human communication. While orthodox psychoanalysis is concerned with the historical reduction of phenomena, existential analysis stresses the importance of remaining in the present, in the current world of phenomena.

However, these theoretical influences only proved valuable inasmuch as they could be grafted onto the living experience of continuous therapeutic experimentation. For many years, Mara Selvini used individual therapy in her treatment of anorectic patients, and it is quite certain that it was her practical experience much more than theoretical considerations that persuaded her to drop a whole range of orthodox therapeutic procedures. Above all, she discovered that interpretations based on Freudian psychosexual theories had a negative effect on the therapist–patient relationship and were therefore contraindicated: "Unlike some analytical techniques that try to proffer

---

[1]It is from this approach that Mara Selvini took the concepts of confirmation, rejection, and disconfirmation.

direct psychosexual interpretations, this therapy concentrates on the constructive possibilities of the ego rather than on the libidinal drives" (Selvini Palazzoli 1963 [rev. ed. 1974, p. 135f.]).

Referring to the case of Ellen West, described at length by Binswanger (1959), Mara Selvini stressed the "model" failure of the two equations used by Ellen West's Freudian analyst:

1. slender = spiritual; fat = Jewish bourgeois;
2. eating = getting fertilized and pregnant.

The connection between such psychosexual interpretations and the rigidly intrapsychic attitudes of many traditional psychoanalysts is quite obvious.

There is a precise logic in Mara Selvini's cultural and theoretical path. It reflects the development of much of modern psychiatry. But the influences I have just mentioned rendered her particularly open to the early work of Wynne and Singer on communication and also to the contributions of Gregory Bateson and his followers.

Quite plainly, psychoanalysts of various schools, be they strictly orthodox, be they Jungian, Kleinian or Lacanian, would have found this path difficult to follow, inasmuch as their basic theoretical outlook renders them remote from the systemic approach.

THE LEAP FROM THE INDIVIDUAL TO THE FAMILY

Basically, it was clinical dissatisfaction with *the slowness and the poor results of individual psychotherapy* that propelled Mara Selvini toward a radical decision: to abandon individual psychotherapy in favor of a new experimental approach, namely conjoint family therapy.[2]

---

[2]In the early days of family therapy, American psychotherapists coined the term "conjoint family therapy" to refer to family sessions attended by the patient, at a time when it was common practice to arrange periodic encounters with the patient's parents from which the patient himself was excluded (both in individual and in group psychotherapy).

The starting point of the new clinical approach was rather simple: a shift of focus from the intrapsychic characteristics of the individual and his transference or countertransference to communications and relationships in families in which one member requires treatment for a given symptom.

The theoretical approach remained psychoanalytical, but, unwittingly, Mara Selvini had already prepared the ground for a totally revolutionary approach. In the purely practical field, there were three new aspects, of which only the first had a clear theoretical basis.

1. The first new aspect was the enlargement of the field of observation. The object of the investigation was no longer an individual but a group with a history.[3]
2. Though the aim was research rather than professional work, research was done in a professional context. Families were accepted on the basis of what at the time was a most unusual contract: the entire nuclear family agreed to be involved in the treatment of the member having the symptom (which contrasted sharply with the traditional medical treatment of the symptom). The research thus involved a highly specific therapeutic context. *However, research and therapy never clashed*—research was done to induce a change. As Kurt Lewin (1945) has put it, "If you want to know how something works, try to change the way it works" (p. 132). But then therapy, too, aims at change. Both approaches thus had the same objective, and, at least until now, the best therapy has been the best research, and *vice versa*.[4]

[3]The research team directed by Gregory Bateson defined the object of their study as a "natural group with a history." The stress on *natural group* was intended to distinguish the team from official (academic) psychologists who were in the habit of studying relationships and communications in *ad hoc* groups, that is, in groups constituted for the purpose of the experiment and made up of complete strangers (usually university students picked at random).

[4]The systemic therapist, even if he has no ambition to become a great discoverer, remains a research worker, at least inasmuch as he keeps extending his own experience, learns from his mistakes, checks his results, follows them up, and does not confine himself to the use of recipes and established procedures but turns his work into a flow of creative ideas.

On the surface, this fusion of research with therapy does not seem very remote from the Freudian tradition, but in fact the new type of contract rendered the therapeutic context quite different. It is one thing to treat a patient who has asked help *for himself,* and quite another to have a family group that attends therapy for the sake of one of its members, hence with quite different motives. A great many things can be said on this subject, but here I shall confine myself to one brief example, namely the problem of (deliberate) lies and evasions, which is rarely met in individual therapy but which crops up almost inevitably in the course of family therapy, even when it is obvious to one and all that it is never in the client's best interest to lie to his therapist. Evasions and lies in family therapy are rarely directed at the therapist, but generally reflect a desire to keep certain matters from other members of the family.

3. Family therapy as practised by Mara Selvini has, from the very start, involved teamwork in a particular setting: one or two therapists work face to face with the family, while the rest of the team observes and supervises from behind a one-way mirror.[5]

FAMILY THERAPY WITH
A COMMUNICATIONALIST APPROACH

In 1967, Mara Selvini Palazzoli, following what was still a vague concept, founded the Center for Family Studies in an attempt to cross-fertilize original therapeutic experiences with new theoretical ideas. The three basic departures from the psychoanalytical tradition (in which a single therapist works with a single patient who is motivated to cure himself) were not yet fully defined (I have reconstructed them *a posteriori*), and the general therapeutic framework, too, remained that of psychoanalysis. However, the new method and research context opened the way

---

[5]I will be returning to this revolutionary method, which creates a double level of action and observation.

to new ideas from the outset. The first heterodox ideas came from communications theory. The psychoanalytical conception of mental illness began slowly to make way for a new model in which mental illness was treated as *the result of a breakdown in communication.*

During the first four years of her experimental work in family therapy—from 1967 to 1971—Mara Selvini used a double conceptual framework: she gradually and sometimes reluctantly combined her psychoanalytical principles with the new communicationalist ideas. To these she was led by two lines of research. The first was that of Wynne and Singer (1963), who published a paper on the style of communication used by families with a schizophrenic member; the authors stipulate the use of Rorschach protocols and of Thematic Apperception Tests (TAT), both with single members of the family and with both parents. The protocols were not interpreted in the traditional way, i.e., by focusing on the contents of the communication. Instead, attention was paid exclusively to the style and method of communication used in the answers, i.e., the form of the communication. The authors' ability to put together blindly the results of the tests of schizophrenics with those of their parents was thought to be most impressive.[6]

Second, and certainly much more important, was the influence of Gregory Bateson's research work with which Mara Selvini first became acquainted by reading *Pragmatics of Human Communication* (Watzlawick et al. 1967).[7] The starting point

---

[6]It proved impossible to repeat this result during subsequent experiments. Could this difference be due to Margaret Singer's exceptional flair?

[7]In 1952, Gregory Bateson, a British anthropologist and pioneer of the application of cybernetics to the human sciences, received a grant from the Rockefeller Foundation to investigate the general nature of communication in terms of logical levels. In particular, Bateson believed that science is a classification problem and that man himself is a classifying animal who must label the messages he sends and receives. He went on to define a formal analogy between breakdowns in communication and breakdowns in logic: both are caused by paradoxes. Much as Bertrand Russell's discovery of a paradox in Frege's great logical system had threatened the foundations of that system, the paradoxes generated in the multi-layered structure of human communication threaten the foundations of human behavior and cause it to become pathological. Bateson based his research project on the key concept of logical level and paradox, and was able to recruit a research

had been the application of Russell's theory of types to communication, and Bateson's team came up with the following scheme:

$$\text{logical paradoxes} = \text{logical pathology}$$

hence

$$\text{communicational paradoxes} = \text{human psychopathology}$$

From this "abduced" equivalence they were eventually led to the theory of the double bind.

The influences I have mentioned were responsible for the adoption of the *communicationalist* approach by Mara Selvini and her team. They based their study and treatment of families on observations of *communicative styles*. They were chiefly interested in the *clarity* of the messages and hence the ability to metacommunicate, in the method of qualifying one's own messages and those of others (confirming them, rejecting them, or disconfirming them), in the way in which attention is focused, in noting the consistency of the various channels of communication (for example, between the content of the verbal message and the simultaneous emotional tonality), in the existence of contra-

---

team made up of Jay Haley, John Weakland, and William Fry. Haley had previously been involved in social analysis and the psychology of fantasies, above all as expressed in popular films. Weakland, who had originally been a chemical engineer, later turned to anthropology (he was a specialist on China). Fry was particularly interested in the links between humor and logical types. The team at first turned its attention to ethology, and to the work of Lorenz and Tinbergen in particular. In 1954, for financial reasons, the team accepted a grant to investigate schizophrenic communication. The team was then joined by the psychiatrist Don Jackson. In 1956 they published a fundamental essay (Bateson et al. 1956), in which schizophrenia was attributed to an individual's repeated exposure to certain paradoxical messages ("double binds"). Bateson and his team never intended to publish a general account of all the ideas they had formulated during the many years of their collaboration. It was only a few years later, after the breakup of the team in 1962, that Paul Watzlawick, a colleague of Don Jackson (who, in 1959, had founded the Mental Research Institute—M.R.I.—at Palo Alto), together with Jackson and Janet Beavin, began the enormous task of collating the mass of experimental and theoretical material produced by the Bateson team during the ten years of their collaboration. The result was *Pragmatics of Human Communication,* a study of interactional patterns, pathologies, and paradoxes (Watzlawick et al. 1967).

dictions or of logical inconsistencies between levels of communications (paradoxes), in observing such obstructive communicative techniques as straying from the point, evading the central issue, making empty and irrelevant speeches, lying, withholding information, keeping silent, generalizing, giving tangential replies, uttering cryptic and incomplete phrases, making self-contradictions, and confusing the literal with the metaphorical meaning of words.

With the help of communications theory, it was thought possible to elicit from analytical and special studies of the style of family communication the information needed to understand how the identified patient had come to his present pass. Mental disturbance was thus seen as the result of confusion, ambiguity, dissimulation, misinterpretation, contradiction, and paradoxical elements in family communication.[8] It was accordingly thought that all symptoms could be traced back to the particular mode of communication used by the patient's family.

THE DEVELOPMENT OF THERAPEUTIC TECHNIQUES

The 1967–1971 phase is represented in this collection by "The Obsessive and His Spouse," a paper Mara Selvini wrote with Paolo Ferraresi, and by two papers she wrote by herself, namely "Context and Metacontext in Family Psychotherapy" and "Racism in the Family." This was a transitional phase, characterized

---

[8]While retaining its overall communicationalist approach, the Bateson team later abandoned its linear view of causality according to which the patient is a victim of paradoxical messages (the conception underlying "Towards a Theory of Schizophrenia" (Bateson et al. 1956) in favor of a circular conception, according to which the patient shares a dysfunctional network of communication with others, albeit he occupies a special position. In that sense, the patient is not simply a passive victim of the double bind but learns to use this method of communication actively and to "return" the paradoxes. Other authors, including the British psychiatrists Laing and Esterson, by contrast, have retained the linear approach and continue to view patients as victims or scapegoats of their pathological family.

by oscillation between the old and the new, with various approaches on the theoretical and technical planes intersecting and overlapping, often without a clear logical connection between them.

From 1967 to 1969, the main techniques used were based on a mixture of group therapy (passive attitude of the therapist, broken by brief observations of what is happening *in* the group, with no deep interpretations) and classical methods of transference interpretation (the family session being treated as a kind of individual analysis carried out in the presence of the family). However, with the publication of "The Obsessive and His Spouse," and much more markedly still in "Context and Metacontext," the same therapeutic techniques were associated with the communicationalist approach reflected in the therapist's endeavor *to teach the correct method of communication.*

The constant element, the guiding thread of these three tendencies, however distinct from one another, was the belief that the therapist is a teacher, a pedagogue, albeit in a very special sense.

At the end of 1971, the split of the original team and the adoption of the systemic model led to a revolutionary break with the past in two key respects: (1) the therapist's *active intervention* in conducting the session and (2) the abandonment of explanations, the therapist having changed from a teacher to *a catalyst of change.*

This phase, which in the present collection is heralded by "Racism in the Family" and which gave rise to numerous papers (including the case histories of Elisa, Lina, Lisa, and Pia, and transcriptions of contributions to clinical seminars and congresses) culminated in the publication of *Paradox and Counterparadox* (Selvini Palazzoli et al. 1978).

From 1972 to 1978, Mara Selvini's work was largely bound up with the concepts of the pathological paradox and of the therapeutic counterparadox, that is, interventions based on the sending of conflicting messages at various levels. Its prototype is the prescription of the symptom: whereas, on the level of the definition of their relationship, therapist and patient have an implicit contract to work towards the disappearance of the illness, the therapist prescribes the very opposite on the content level. Since homeostasis is tantamount to the absence of change, it follows that every intervention in favor of the *status quo* becomes paradoxical by definition.

CRISIS OF COMMUNICATIONALISM

The communicationalist ideas were far more important on the epistemological plane than on the purely technical one: communications theory was to become the bridge for the introduction into family therapy of the crucial concepts of *system* and *context*. The idea that the transmission of messages by various people was a chain of actions and reactions (feedback) led to the key concept of the self-corrective system; moreover, it became clear that the meaning of messages could not be discovered without reference to a context that served as a matrix.[9]

In this sense, the classical research of Bateson and his group has been an indispensable spur to developing new ideas, new models, and a revolutionary epistemology. Matters are, however, less clear cut when it comes to the clinical and empirical consequences of this line of research. Thus, while the fascinating and disturbing theory of the double bind opened up a new epoch in psychiatry, it could not have led, by itself, to therapeutic applications nor was it borne out by observation of schizophrenic families.

On the clinical plane the key hypothesis of communicationalism was the *association of a mode (style) of communication with the symptoms of the identified patient*. This hypothesis became the basis of a great many investigations: Bateson and

---

[9]In this respect the introduction of the systemic model was not due to von Bertalanffy: the systemic model is part and parcel of the theory of communication from which it was imported into family therapy. Von Bertalanffy's systems theory was, however, responsible for a process of multidisciplinary cross-fertilization. The confrontation of the family system with similar theoretical constructs in numerous other fields had most fruitful repercussions: from biology, for instance, came one of the first and historically important theoretical concepts, that of homeostasis. This multidisciplinary approach has always been characteristic of the work of Mara Selvini and of the entire history of family therapy, at least inasmuch as its roots go back to the work of Gregory Bateson.

Haley showed that double binds and disconfirmations characterized the communications of schizophrenic families; Mara Selvini drew attention to the escalation of rejections in the case of
anorectics; Sluzki and Verón (1976) argued that particular forms
of double binds were responsible for phobias, obsessions, and
hysteria.

In retrospect, we can say that the communicationalist hypothesis did not produce many concrete results and, in fact,
turned out to be sterile. Thus the international literature shows
that, over the past thirteen years, no work of importance has
been done along this road.

This is also reflected in the work of the Selvini team. The
therapeutic methods used to stimulate communication between
members of the family for the purpose of observing it more
closely proved almost totally unproductive in a double sense:

1. Some families with a schizophrenic patient were found
   to communicate in a way indistinguishable from that
   of other families. Moreover, while the communications
   of schizophrenic families in general tended to be rather
   confused and disjointed, this was not true of *all* schizophrenic families. A more interesting discovery was that a
   particular schizophrenic family might be very confused
   at one session yet be a model of clarity in another if
   different themes were discussed, if a new therapeutic
   phase was introduced, or if the composition of the
   group was altered. (Some people in the group may be
   vague or reticent in the presence of members of the
   extended family but can change completely in their absence. The same observation was also made with parents attending sessions first with their children and then
   separately.)

2. In the field of therapeutic interventions, it seemed ineffective, apart from being ingenuous and moralistic, to
   teach these families to communicate clearly.[10] As we
   shall see, Mara Selvini herself, after having experi-

[10]The main advocate of this therapeutic style was Virginia Satir of Palo Alto,
author of the widely read [*Conjoint Family Therapy* (Satir 1964)].

mented with an explicit method of teaching communication in the Satir tradition, also had recourse to more implicit techniques (Selvini Palazzoli 1963 [rev. ed. 1981]).[11]

Moreover, in quite a different scientific context, even the Bateson group realized that the limits of communicationalism had been reached. Actually, the theory of double bind had been elaborated *before* the beginning of their systematic clinical research. The theory of the double bind was, in fact, the result of a mainly deductive speculation based on the work of a group of experts in distinct branches of behavioral science. In 1959, when the phase of pure conceptual elaboration was past and the group raised the problem of more specific applications of the theoretical model to family therapy and to clinical practice, the limits of the communicational model quickly became obvious.

The Bateson team then co-opted Ray Birdwhistell, a communications specialist, but the use of linguistic models and of kinetics did not do a great deal to advance the research.

Later, with the help of special subsidies, a specific research program was initiated to demonstrate and quantify systematic differences between normal and schizophrenic families and hence to distinguish empirically between successions of double binds. Once again an expert, Alex Bavelas, was co-opted to the team, but the project turned out to be a fiasco, as Haley himself was to admit (Haley 1962).[12]

RESEARCH INTO GAMES

In the Mara Selvini research, the crisis of the communicationalist paradigm does not lead to the creation of another all-embracing model. Instead, there followed a series of attempts to arrive at a theoretical definition of family interactions based on

---

[11]See some interventions reported in the last part of Mara Selvini Palazzoli's *Self-Starvation* (1963 [1981 ed.]), none of which produced significant results.

[12]Just as significant was the failure of experimental research into the double bind (Abeles 1976).

the game metaphor, without, however, leading to a clear and unequivocal definition of a new model.

Historically, the game metaphor, as far as family therapy is concerned, was derived from systems theory and especially from the observation that a system never presents its full range of possible moves, but tends to repeat certain phenomena. In other words, a system presents redundancies while imposing constraints on the behavior of its components. All these concepts, derived from the study of communications systems (e.g., telephone networks), were now used as a "map" of family relationships and hence, so to speak, "anthropomorphized." Jackson,[13] in particular, was able to show by means of these redundancies that the system obeys certain rules. It is but a short step from the family as a system with rules to the family game: all that is needed is a change in terminology. Hence to handle systems as games is not innovation for family therapy but has its roots in the 1960s. In the course of time, however, the communicationalist and the systemic concepts, originally fused, began to fall apart: the clinical fruitfulness and the development of systemic concepts is in no way reflected in the development of communicationalist concepts. The latter concepts seem abstract, general, and inefficient on the therapeutic plane. Both Bateson and Haley came up against the limits of the communicationalist model, albeit unwittingly. Haley (1961), in his history of the Bateson research project, explains how both Bateson and he noticed the lack of a theoretical model in the family field.

In the attempt to fill this gap, Bateson adopted von Neumann's theory of games. In so doing, he took important steps: (1) the theory of games lays greater stress on the decisional process than on communicated behavior, and (2) the players can exchange information on distinct logical levels. It follows that this theory is incompatible with that of the double bind. But Bateson, evidently, was more concerned with the search for a theoretical model capable of serving as a reliable "map" of what had been observed in the field. For example, one of his first

[13]See Greenberg's (1977) bibliography. Here I shall not take up the discussion of the descriptivity or prescriptivity of the rules, which preceded the current discussion of the reality/constructivity of hypotheses.

empirical observations (Bateson 1958), the incapacity of schizophrenic families to make decisions and to assume responsibility, seemed to correspond to Von Neumann's model of a game with more than three players incapable of forming stable coalitions.

Much can be said about the merits of the theory of games. Although this theory continues to provide a useful tool, in Bateson's hands, i.e., used as a map for research into schizophrenia, it proved a complete failure. The theory postulates that the players, with completely or partially conflicting interests (zero-sum games or non-zero-sum games), know every possible agreed move and its consequences and also their own objectives. In that case they would have to be omniscient and as such not open to learning. Such characteristics differ too radically from those of human systems, which are capable of developing by trial and error, and hence much less definite and definable in their objectives. No wonder, then, that Bateson's reflections on the theory of games should have produced nothing of value on the clinical plane. Instead, the impetus of renewed research into schizophrenia came above all from Haley's theoretically less elegant hypotheses. Haley (1959) succeeded for the first time in describing the family of the schizophrenic *not merely as a communicative situation but as a system of relations.*

To that end, he introduced five parameters:

1. The mode in which members of the family qualify their own communications;
2. The mode in which members of the family qualify the messages of other members;
3. The problem of leadership;
4. Alliances;
5. The problem of blame.[14]

The first two parameters still fall into the province of communicationalist theory, but the other three involve a deepening examination of the *rules of the system* and hence call for research into *games.* In the 1960s a whole series of systemic

---

[14]Blaming others means denying responsibility for one's behavior and thus pretending to be a pawn of outside forces.

concepts saw the light of day, chief among them structuralist ideas on generation gaps, subsystems, alliances, and external boundaries. Haley (1959) himself put forward similar ideas. With his concept of the perverse triangle, Haley (1964) advanced a most brilliant hypothesis on the possible structural "perversion" of a family system.

Two other fundamental systemic concepts to appear in the fifties and sixties were those of homeostasis (Jackson 1957) and of myths (Ferreira 1966). The work of Mara Selvini presented in this collection, although written years after the pioneering works of Haley, represents an attempt to respond to the very problems with which Haley and other members of the Bateson team were faced. In particular, she readily adopted the signaling system proposed by Haley (1959) and applied it actively first to the families of anorectics and then to the families of schizophrenics. Moreover, in retracing Haley's steps, Mara Selvini was brought up against the shortcomings of the communicationalist ideas and gradually disembarrassed herself of them completely. But she was also brought up against the purist rigidity imposed on analysis by systemic extremism.

For an entire phase, the one immediately following her break with psychoanalysis (1972–1978), Mara Selvini, no doubt feeling a need to affirm a new identity, seized upon all descriptive accounts of family systems that went beyond individual members to embrace the maximum number of actors (all, if possible). This explains her interest in supra-individual concepts, such as the notion of communicative styles, structures, homeostasis, myths, rules, and language and linear epistemology.

More recently, however, clinical experience once again came to guide Mara Selvini's team. Looking back on our therapeutic work we have found that, *at all times*, even when we did not admit it officially, we continued to use intrapsychic hypotheses about the experiences and intentions of individuals. In particular, we have always looked upon the identified patient as a *loser*, one who tries to remedy his disadvantage by developing symptoms, and we have always thought that his behavior is based on feelings of anger and the wish to be revenged or to punish.

In short, we realized that hypotheses on individual behavior were as important as those concerning the system of relationships on which we had mistakenly believed we could rely exclusively. It had become clear that therapy needed maps capable of integrating the various systemic levels: the biological, the individual, the familial, and the social.

A better theoretical approach to this problem, still in its initial phase, has more recently been offered by Crozier (Crozier and Friedberg 1977) in his concept of *actor's strategy.*

> Behind human beings and the emotional reactions governing their everyday behavior the analyst can, in fact, discover *regularities* that only make sense when referred to a strategy. That strategy is therefore nothing other than the *basis, inferred* a posteriori, *of the empirically observed behavior* [p. 48].

Crozier also stresses that even the most binding and coercive system leaves the individual actor a choice between various strategies; even the prisoner in chains can choose between submissive behavior and, say, a hunger strike.

Crozier, moreover, appeals to the game concept because it correlates individual moves with general rules. In other words, games provide a framework for fusing two fundamental arguments: (1) the argument covering the strategy of the actor; and (2) the systemic argument about the connections and limits set to the actor on supra-individual systemic levels.

This definition seems to agree with the spirit of research into family games conducted by Mara Selvini and her collaborators.

For a long time, attempts to argue in terms of games, asking oneself about who plays what game (the famous rules), had been a useful mental experiment, suggesting analogies and comparisons that could not possibly have emerged from either the study of systems of communication or from comparisons with other types of systems.

Asking who is playing what game is tantamount to looking for the "script" on a supra-individual level, in order to determine whether that script is confined to the nuclear family or whether it involves wider systems, such as the extended family, the school, or the workplace. Studying an ongoing game means analyzing myths, beliefs, stereotypes, and the approach of the group (or the hinterland of the game). But what is particularly thrown into relief when we think in terms of games (and what is almost completely obscured by a purely systemic approach) is *the importance of sequences of individual moves*. All attempts to explain behavior are bound to be defective if they prevent the explication of specific aspects of the actor's ideas, tactics, and objectives (when we define his strategy).

This interpretation of the game metaphor, with its appeal to individual strategies, should not be mistaken for a revival of the intrapsychic approach and the abandonment of systemic epistemology. On the contrary, it is only by this approach that a systemic model can be made *consistent* and carried beyond the limits of earlier attempts to parade as systemic hypotheses relating—and rather arbitrarily at that—the symptoms of the designated patient to a unique level: the family microsocial plane. Rejecting this type of family reductionism is *more* than simply enlarging the field of observation to the extended family, to social service agencies, to the socioeconomic context, and so on, i.e., to wider systems containing the family; a truly systemic and ecological conception cannot ignore the fact that every systemic level has its own identity (and its own limits) and hence its own *relative autonomy*. In other words, the dialectical relationship between supra- and infrasystems is based on the interpretation of dependence and independence. Thus, though the political game played at the administrative level of a local health department has independent rules, it is impossible to ignore the games played by the users and their families (conversely, the family game cannot ignore the rules applying at the administrative level). The same argument applies at the family–individual level. The individual plays his game and has an autonomous strategy, even though that game is *indissolubly* bound up with the game played at the family and higher levels. Every level has its own relative autonomy, its partial independence. Cases in point are genetic mechanisms, the physiology of the human body, individuality, and the family. To clarify this point I shall quote Anna Maria Sorrentino (personal communication) referring to the first manuscript in the present collection of essays:

The fact that we consider not only the relational rules of a system constructed in time but also the biological aspects and the intrapsychic motives of the various players does not mean that we consider these motives to be immune to the constant influence of the interactive game: from our point of view it is as true to say that an individual plays a certain game because he has certain motives as it is true to say that he has certain motives, experiences, sentiments because he participates in a given game that allows him to make certain moves only.

I do not wish to assert that every single player always has clearly defined objectives. As I said earlier, few if any players have the omniscient rationality postulated by von Neumann. However, it is essential to look for the aims every player pursues, in however confused a way. Has the identified patient lost the competitive game with his brother? Is the mother always pursuing a spouse who tries to elude or escape from her? Does the brother try to preserve his prestigious role in the family while beginning to resent the extra weight it places on his shoulders? Does the identified patient derive power from being labeled a sick person, but is furious because, despite his intolerable behavior, he fails to oust the hated brother and, indeed, produces the opposite effect? These are just a few hypotheses about the strategy of the individual actors.

Those forms of behavior by close relatives of schizophrenics, which have been classified under the general heading of "failure to define the relationship" since the publication of *Paradox and Counterparadox* (Selvini Palazzoli et al. 1978), have now become the object of a deeper enquiry into what precise strategies serve what precise ends.

If I may take a literary example, our mental progress resembles that of a reader of Dostoyevsky's *The Brothers Karamazov*. At first the reader is taken aback by the pathological indecision of the feminine protagonist, incapable of choosing between her two lovers. Then, as the story unfolds, the reader discovers that she is simply marking time while awaiting the probable but by no means certain return of a third admirer. The full possession of the facts thus helps the reader to understand the hidden meaning of her apparently odd behavior, aimed at maximizing the gains and minimizing the risks.

It follows that, if our research has similar objectives, the sources of useful information cannot stop with the style of communication!

Verbal reports help us to paint a canvas of the "family romance." We delve into the chronology of the events, the time factor, the pragmatic effects of certain types of behavior on various members, and the beliefs and motives attached by these members to their own behavior and problems.

Family therapy and family study start with a hypothesis about the ongoing type of game. The therapist then tries to collect information to verify or refute the hypothesis. The style of communication of individuals and of the entire family has become *just one of the sources of information* needed for testing the hypothesis and has ceased to be a privileged field of observation. Only when we understand what type of game is being played can we determine how verbal and nonverbal communication are used for making various moves on a particular chessboard. Communication is inevitably connected to specific games family members cannot avoid playing. The correct deductive method is to proceed from the complex (the system of relations) to the simple (the message or the series of messages). It is evident that, without some hypothesis about the ongoing game, the analysis of a series of communicative sequences (for example, a family therapy session) has no meaning at all. A detailed analysis of messages will only yield confirmation or clarification if we have a hypothesis on the game.

The adoption of the concepts of *system* and *game* called for a new model in which the eruption of psychopathological behavior is treated as a *move*, and communicational confusions and ambiguities are seen, not as the crux of the problem, but as the direct result of a certain way of playing the social or family game.

This collection of papers reflects the fact that, ever since her first steps as a family therapist, Mara Selvini, while remaining attached to traditional ideas, introduced revolutionary concepts about relational games. It should not be forgotten, however, that the period in which the game metaphor came into its own began in the eighties and is, therefore, later than the period examined in this book.

LATER THERAPEUTIC DEVELOPMENTS

The final part of this collection also bears witness to a later aspect of Mara Selvini's development.

From emphasizing the importance of interventions of the verbal type (paradoxical comments), she went on to pay increasing attention to nonverbal interventions (rituals, simple prescriptions, and ritualized prescriptions). With both approaches, however, the final message of the session was considered to be the decisive moment of the therapy (a technique I have called *interventionist*). The last article of the collection, "Hypothesizing-Circularity-Neutrality," anticipates the transformation characteristic of Mara Selvini's approach from 1978 onwards: the abandonment of interventionism—understood as the identification of therapeutic efficiency with the ritualized transmission on the verbal or analogical planes of a significant message with which the session is concluded and which serves as the "bomb" exploding the old family equilibrium. Instead, Mara Selvini came to give absolute priority (not only for collecting but also for *giving* information) to the method of *conducting* the session and to the family–therapist suprasystem sealed with the signing of a therapeutic contract.

In that sense we may say that, with her renunciation of the belief that the efficiency of the therapy depends on the transmission of specific messages with unsettling effects, Mara Selvini abandoned her last communicationalist illusion.

PART ONE

EARLY EXPERIENCES IN
FAMILY THERAPY AS
A PSYCHOANALYST

CHAPTER 2

The Emergence of the Center for Family Studies

Matteo Selvini

"The First Conjoint Family-Therapy Session" (Rusconi and Selvini Palazzoli 1967) was the first article written by Mara Selvini Palazzoli as a family therapist, or rather, as a pioneer and beginner in this new field of research.

The article appeared four years after *L'anoressia mentale* (Selvini Palazzoli 1963),[1] in which Mara Selvini presented the results of many years of her research into anorexia, at a time when she was still a psychoanalyst and an individual psychotherapist. However, during the years following the publication of that book, Mara Selvini was not satisfied: there was the applause of psychoanalytical and psychiatric circles from all parts of the world, but good clinical results with anorectic patients were hard to obtain. No doubt, it was a great scientific achievement to have brought this crisis to a head by showing up the therapeutic limits of individual therapy: even an acknowledged authority in the field cannot handle more than a few patients—individual therapy is very costly and hence accessible

[1]All quotations are taken from the 1963 Italian edition unless otherwise specified [Ed.].

to only a small circle of patients, and the outcome is not always encouraging. At the time, Mara Selvini was treating some sixty anorectics, and the results, although positive in 60 percent of all cases, did not warrant the enormous expenditure of energy and time. Moreover, many theoretical problems had remained unsolved. Thus no one could tell why, of the hundreds of girls who, following the latest fashion, went on a diet, only some should have been unable to stop and have gone on to become anorectic. The traditional psychodynamic answer, that it is all due to biological constitution and personality structures, no longer seemed convincing.

Mara Selvini was not, however, so much preoccupied with the prevailing theoretical problems—although she had grown rather tired of the tortuous and mechanical nature of the psychoanalytical doctrine—as with the practical aspects of her clinical work. The many long years it took to treat a patient, coupled with the weariness, boredom, and impotence that often accompany the treatment, as well as the enormous discrepancy between the demanding work (both in terms of intellectual effort and in terms of the time required) and the meager results persuaded Mara Selvini to look for a completely new approach.

In 1967 she made the decision to break forever with individual psychotherapy and to found the Center for Family Studies. Her paper (Rusconi and Selvini Palazzoli 1967) was a kind of manifesto setting out the new path that she was about to follow. Many of her colleagues were taken completely by surprise. How could she throw everything overboard just like that? It was an extremely courageous decision, a stone cast into the calm pool of a psychiatric establishment that was totally unaware of the very existence of conjoint family therapy.

In her new project, Mara Selvini first joined forces with Severino Rusconi, a Jungian analyst and an expert on group therapy, with whom she had previously worked in Balint groups.

In this first paper, just as in her next, both written in collaboration with Rusconi, the influence of two events is apparent: Mara Selvini's 1967 visit with the Eastern Psychiatric Institute in Philadelphia, where she met Boszormenyi-Nagy and Framo (two family therapists with a psychoanalytical approach), and her brief stay in Paris in 1968, where she observed the experimental work with the families of psychotic patients organized and directed by the psychoanalyst Michael Woodbury.

The model of her first experiments with family therapy was therefore psychoanalytical. That model was, however, applied in a completely new therapeutic setting and was, moreover, coupled to a fundamentally new idea: the need to extend the field of observation beyond the individual. There was thus a direct correspondence between the new therapeutic setting and the new object of research.

From 1967 to 1970, the revolutionary scope of the new approach was not yet fully understood. It took Mara Selvini several years to appreciate that the family and relational perspective was incompatible with the epistemological approach of psychoanalysis, a theory based on a profoundly individuocentric view of human behavior, aimed at determining the intrapsychic structure and interpreting its functioning in terms of energy balances. The dichotomy between an epistemology based on energy/quantity and one based on information/form (Bateson 1972 [rev. ed. 1973, pp. 21–31]) was certainly acknowledged, but it had not yet been put into focus, and when it was very soon afterward, conceptual clashes became unavoidable.

From 1967 to 1971, the research team at the Center for Family Studies was gradually enlarged. Mara Selvini and Severino Rusconi were joined by Simona Taccani, Gabriele Chistoni, Luigi Boscolo, Paolo Ferraresi, Giuliana Prata, and Gianfranco Cecchin, all having had a protracted psychoanalytical training in Switzerland or in the United States.

These were very difficult years for the Center. Work with families gave rise to very frequent and frustrating failures, and these problems were aggravated by differences among the team about the theoretical model on which the research was to be based: were they to stick to psychoanalysis or were they rather to look into the pragmatics of human communication and into systems theory? Mara Selvini opted for the second alternative, but only after four years of perseverance with the psychoanalytical model.

During this first, pioneering, phase of her family work,

Mara Selvini wrote "Transference in Intensive Family Co-therapy" (Rusconi and Palazzoli 1970), which was published in 1970 but had been written at least two years earlier. This is the only paper in which Mara Selvini deals with theoretical aspects of family therapy from a wholly psychoanalytical point of view.

Examining two distinct problems (the heterosexual couple of therapists and the first minutes of the session), the paper pays particular attention to the transferal process in individuals and families. The very choice of subject shows that this article was written during the initial phase when Mara Selvini explicitly allied herself to a family-therapy group with a psychoanalytical bias (the "reactor analysts" of Philadelphia) and upheld the conceptual cornerstones of that approach, especially transference and co-therapy, as existential models of the adult parental couple. At heart, the paper was nothing but a defense of transference against the attacks of the so-called "systems purists" (the Palo Alto school). The paper made no reference to general communicationalist and systemic formulation; it simply referred to "the homeostatic system," a newly adopted concept which helped to describe the pathological family as one characterized by rigid homeostasis.

In both papers the influences of the psychodynamic approach is quite evident:

1. The interview is conducted in a passive way, the therapists leaving the initiative almost invariably to the family, making the minimum of demands, and showing a high degree of tolerance when presented with confusion and cross-talk (by family members). Such passivity is in sharp contrast with the deliberately strict control of the therapeutic session, reflected, for example, in insistence on punctual attendance of sessions at the set time.

2. The comments involve continuous references to transference, countertransference, and defense movement. For example, Rusconi and Selvini Palazzoli (1967) lay particular stress, among the other defensive maneuvers of the parental couple, on the parents' attempt to gain the therapists' support by speaking in accusatory tones

of the son, Alberto, the identified "characteropathic" patient. "They accuse Alberto because they themselves think they are under attack" (p. 19). Here are two other typical extracts from "Transference in Intensive Family Co-therapy":

It should above all be stressed that the transference phenomenon in intensive family psychotherapy is infinitely more complex than it is in individual analysis. As the reader will have gathered from our account, we were faced not only with a number of individual transferences by different members of the group, but also with a group transference, mainly for the protection of the prevailing system of family interaction. The family, unlike an *ad hoc* group, comes into therapy with its own, already highly structured, system of interactions, which enables it to confront strangers in a compact way, from a position of strength. Personal transference and family transference are thus superposed and overlap. Our customary models have been revolutionized as a result. In strongly homeostatic systems, moreover, the defenses of the relationship with the therapists, or with one of us, can be used, along the transference path, by various members of the family in turn, in "favor" of the shaky member, whenever the development of an intense therapeutic relationship seems to threaten the family *status quo*. Moreover, if there is one predominant experience we have had with married couples in families with seriously disturbed patients (psychotics and characteropathics inaccessible to individual treatment), it has been that of family transference. It must be kept constantly in mind if the imminent danger of rejection or termination of the therapy is to be averted [pp. 161–162].

To achieve profound co-involvement we must do prolonged and hard work. Such co-involvement, in all cases in which it has been detected, emerges during the second year of intense psychotherapy with highly disturbed couples. In these cases, extremely complex, deep changes appeared and proved very difficult to understand at the time when they occurred. Only a discussion between the team at large and the direct observers and the analysis of our own countertransference helped to explain what had happened. Let me quote the case of a couple in which the designated patient originally presented for treatment was the wife, whose obsessional symptom (dypsomania) had resisted all previous attempts to effect a cure. During the treatment of the couple, which the husband had "generously" agreed to join in order to help his wife, his strong sado-disparaging maneuvers directed at his wife became increasingly obvious; the wife, for her part, seemed unable to find any other escape from his intolerable trap than to resort to her recurrent symptom. For a long time we worked almost exclusively on the decoding of the disparaging communications the husband addressed to his wife, but seeing that these efforts were totally counterproductive and that session after session produced a noisy series of quarrels, accusations, and counteraccusations, we decided to change course. The male therapist now took charge of the sessions and during two of them engaged the husband in intimate and sympathetic discussion. At the third session, the wife turned up in a manic state. Whereas, until that moment she had expressed no feelings towards the male therapist, she now started to flirt with him blatantly, asking his opinion of herself and her looks, and giving him to understand that she was in love with him. The meaning of such behavior began to become clear from observations of the husband's behavior: throughout the embarrassing and dramatic transaction between the wife and the male therapist, he, far from looking offended or jealous, as might have been expected, sat back in his armchair, with an amused and contented smile.

When we took cognizance of this fact, we began to realize that, in this couple bound together in oral sadomasochistic symbiosis, the wife, masochistically attuned to the needs of her husband, was unconsciously and desperately trying to leap to his defense. From what she was shielding him became obvious in the next session, during which she was full of tears and dejected, protesting that she had come for the last time. She could not bear it any longer, she had spent a terrible week, had had horrible nightmares. Between sobs, she reported that in one of these she had seen a person in disguise being pursued by armed men. She had fought desperately to protect the disguised person but without knowing why she was doing so.

It then became clear (but was not interpreted) that the wife's flirtation with the male therapist was simply an attempt to take upon herself her husband's transference, thus saving him from becoming aware of it and preventing the therapists from realizing what was happening, even while protecting the terrified husband from becoming involved in a deep relationship with the male therapist.

In other words, even though this phenomenon was never interpreted, understanding its dynamics helped us to chart the further course of the treatment. That is, it became clear to us that, if we wanted to change the pathological interaction of this couple, then we would have to ignore not only the wife's symptom but also the derogatory communications that seemed to cause it and center our attention on the husband as the key element [pp. 167–169].

In retrospect, I would venture a different hypothesis about the treatment of this couple: the treatment seemed to have established a temporary state of equilibrium based on an alliance between the therapists and the identified patient, which meant putting the blame on the husband. The therapists' unforeseen change of tack terrified the patient, who then tried desperately, by reverting to her symptom, to resurrect the lost alliance.

Many of the transference and resistance phenomena described in that article were bound up with the fact that, for many years, the sessions used to be held weekly. Now, with weekly sessions, unless the family breaks off the treatment, they tend to involve the therapist in a game that is clearly reflected in certain phrases. When reported, these more so than the transference reflect the therapists' inability to control the situation or their own involvement in the family game.

3. The analysis of the family proceeds through the study and description of single members based on their presumed intrapsychic characteristics, such as strength, weakness, structure, affectivity, dependence, intelligence, and neurotic inhibitions.

4. The co-therapists are presented as models of adult and mature behavior. This is, in fact, how they were described in the paper on transference (Rusconi and Palazzoli 1970):

The introduction into the family situation of two co-therapists of different sex as a relatively mature couple collaborating in an adult way and mainly active in the here and now, and with their own transferal and countertransferal movements, helps, in our opinion, to bring out attitudes and deep defenses that, once consciously appreciated by the various members of the group, will lead to the break-up of the homeostatic system.

There are, in fact, types of rigid family homeostasis organized into fixed dyadic subsystems, which, in our opinion, are not easily clarified and changed by a single therapist. The latter inevitably becomes the sole object of a most complicated series of transferal projections and countertransferal reactions, very difficult to detect. The therapeutic couple, by contrast, as we shall see, even though it introduces problems of a different kind, allows more highly differentiated projections and an interactive game that is relatively simpler to specify [pp. 159–160].

5. The interpretation of the progress of a session is based more on the therapist's experience than on the study of communications, of relationships, of observable behavior. As an example, here is how the account of the first session with the family of the "characteropathic" Alberto ends (Rusconi and Palazzoli 1967):

As for the therapists, the woman therapist felt anxious and tense at the beginning of the session and saw fit to hide immediately behind her professional role, handling the situation didactically and issuing orders. She noticed that Alberto was looking at her full of admiration, which she considered to be therapeutically useful. She was moved by the parents' anguish and was above all afraid that they might reject the treatment (a form of fear of her own frustration). . . . Together, the therapists seemed to project onto the family their ambivalent views of their own therapeutic "skills" [p. 19].

I have not thought it opportune to quote the two papers in full, because they are typical of an approach and a technique that are completely outdated today. Their main importance is historical, even though, from the didactic point of view, confrontations with the past help to explain the emergence of more up-to-date procedures, which, though they may seem obvious today, are in fact the culmination of a long process of development.

Thus, over and above the five points to which I have just drawn attention, the almost total failure to gather information prior to the first session and the willingness to treat just two members of a family are two examples of a practical approach that seems almost inconceivable today. Remarkably anticipative, on the other hand, was the attention paid to the problem of the referring person.

Returning to the key problem of the passively conducted sessions, I must stress that nowadays we would frown at any therapist's refusal to react to comments, attacks, and disqualifications, at his wreathing himself instead in a kind of "analytic" impenetrability. The modern way is to use active interventions when dealing with the family's responses to direct questions and with their spontaneous comments. The kind of interaction between family and therapist of which Mara Selvini has become a master is much like a normal conversation, far removed from the formal and artificial atmosphere of the psychoanalyst's study and from that of a courtroom. The therapist's activity and procedure must in no way be rigid or forced. The therapeutic relationship must be controlled in such a way as to ensure the order, clarity, and conciseness needed for the maximum flow of information, in a warm and cordial climate of collaboration.

This is not an easy task. Those who have been, or are being, trained by Mara Selvini have discovered that the most difficult skill to acquire is not so much the formulation of hypotheses or of therapeutic strategies as the ability to conduct the session with a delicate mixture of authority and informality.

CHAPTER 3

Criteria for Assessing Family Dysfunction

Matteo Selvini

From 1965 to 1970, Mara Selvini conducted an intense study of the available family-therapy literature. From Guntrip and Sullivan she went on to look at the contributions of various American schools of, and writers on, family therapy (Ackerman, Haley, Bowen, Minuchin, Satir, the Philadelphia school, but not yet Bateson). These readings were the subject of a series of reviews and papers,[1] so many signposts on Mara Selvini's intellectual road. Thus, in discussing the contributions of others, she often linked them to the work she herself was doing during this difficult transitional phase. In particular, her lectures at the Catholic University in Milan reflected her theoretical preoccupations; in fact, her 1967 course on psychoanalytical psychotherapy ended with an account of the writings of Wynne and Singer. These and similar texts on mental disorders in the families of schizophrenics were an ideal bridge between the orthodox approach and the emerging new ideas, for a number of reasons:

[1]Among these I shall single out Mara Selvini's (Selvini Palazzoli 1971) preface to the Italian edition of Gerhild von Staabs's *Der Sceno-Test*. Experiments with that test were an integral part of Mara Selvini's progress from individual psychotherapy to the relational and family approach, and of her search for more effective techniques.

1. While using established techniques (projection tests), attention was shifted from mental contents to the forms and styles of communication.
2. Starting with the individual, an attempt was made to discover correlations and causal links with the family's mode of thinking and communicating.

All in all, these studies combined Mara Selvini's two key ideas of the time: family and communication. However, she remained firmly attached to psychoanalytical theory, simply grafting on systemic ideas (Haley) and homeostatic ideas (Jackson), and not effecting a real fusion.

Nevertheless, the systemic idea had begun to be part of the *theoretical* arsenal of family therapy, but in Mara Selvini's (Selvini Palazzoli 1967) review of the work of Wynne and Singer, she presents the systemic idea in the transactional formulation of Spiegel and Bell (1959).

On the theoretical plane, this meant rejecting the linear claim that the mentally ill are victims of their parents (more particularly of their mothers, as in the case of the schizophrenogenic mother described by Frieda Fromm-Reichmann). On the clinical plane it meant rejecting the concomitant, on the personal level, of the theory of pathogenic parents, i.e., the incrimination of the parents. Mara Selvini had evidently grasped the danger of transforming the therapeutic setting into a court of law. For that very reason, it is surprising to find her propounding, in an article published during the same period (Selvini Palazzoli 1968), the idea of the *sick family*. This concept may have been compatible with psychoanalytical theory, but not with the systemic-cum-game conception Mara Selvini was to adopt more consistently in the following years.

CRITERIA OF FAMILY DYSFUNCTION

The concept of the "sick family" is unacceptable not only on the clinical plane, because of the blame-attaching connotation, but also on the epistemological plane, because of the biomedical formulation. It is in fact quite wrong to speak of a sick (or pathological) family because nothing in their behavior is intrinsically or essentially pathological: all we can say is that their behavior is *undesirable* in terms of certain parameters that we must be very careful to specify with critical discernment and great care.

For that reason, the term *dysfunctional* is more appropriate. Its use leads to a search for the appropriate criteria in three areas:

1. *Subjective family criteria,* i.e., the realization by one or all the members of the family that something has gone wrong.
2. *The therapist's subjective criteria for evaluating his hypotheses,* i.e., criteria of a *systemic-cum-organizational type.* Systemic-cum-organizational criteria apply to a method of family organization that, according to the therapist, respects certain general rules:
    (a) the relationships must be clearly defined;
    (b) the rules, even if implicit, are fixed and must be respected;
    (c) the rules and hierarchical structure (organigram) of the family are not rigid;
    (d) the system is capable of evolving.
    At the Congress of Family Therapy held in Zurich in 1977, Mara Selvini made an interesting contribution at a round table conference on the subject of *What is a normal family?* (a contribution that, unfortunately, has never been transcribed and is therefore as good as "lost"). In it, she maintained that the parallel study of big organizations had taught her that, much as the correspondence between the manifest and the real organigram of, say, a company is a *conditio sine qua non* of its smooth operation, so also the same correspondence is needed in family life. This remark might be mistaken for an endorsement of Minuchin's structuralism when, in fact, it was quite distinct from and diametrically opposed to it.
    Mara Selvini does not believe that there are bad and, so to speak, inherently good organigrams (in which, for example, the parents are parents and the children are children), but only games that respect the

manifest organigram and games that confuse it, showing respect for the rules on certain levels and breaking
them on others. Thus a family in which the son allies
himself with the mother while the father is "married" to
some other member (inside or outside the family) does
not in fact represent a "psychiatric pathology" *if this
arrangement is observed on all levels.* What would be
confusing and pathogenic in the case we have just mentioned is if the mother played down the privileged relationship with her son and oscillated between treating
him as an equal partner and as a filial dependent, according to the games she happens to be playing with her
husband and with her extended family.

Mara Selvini's therapeutic strategy does not, however, involve exposing the incongruencies of the official
organigram in a direct attempt to restore a proper hierarchy. Her therapeutic process follows a different logic:
it is chiefly aimed at the overall, dysfunctional game of
whose moves (tactics) the hierarchic organization is but
one component.

Take the case of a family with a son inclined to
engage in antisocial acts. The wife accuses the husband
of being incapable of handling, and hence an obstacle
to, the education of his children. On the basis of some
remarks, the therapists postulate that she is involved in a
competitive game with her brothers, centered around
their inheritance from a rich, old father. By playing the
unhappy wife she now hopes to elicit her father's sympathy and to receive special treatment. It would have
been quite pointless for the therapists to attack her marital behavior directly, such as maintaining that by running down her husband she was damaging her own
children. Instead, by successfully attacking the competitive game with her siblings, the therapists also succeeded
in restoring the parity of the couple's organigram.

3. *Subjective attitudes of the therapist as part of a given
   cultural milieu, i.e., sociocultural criteria.* This is the
   most arguable and complex of the criteria. The fact that
   some forms of behavior are considered mad or sane,

desirable or undesirable, depends on parameters of the sociocultural context. Who we call epileptic or psychotic could elsewhere be admired as a shaman or charismatic leader.

No one involved with psychiatry can fail to have culturally determined value judgments when defining the aims and the objects of a family. Much as we consider a company in the red or a clinic with a greater than average death rate as mismanaged, so also do we consider as dysfunctional a family that paralyzes the potentiality of its members and detracts from their normal satisfaction with life. Thus we take a negative view of suicides, the idlers, persons who cannot break away from their family of origin, and all other forms of self-damaging behavior. Such general remarks do not, however, imply that, in special cases or seen in a broader perspective, types of behavior normally considered undesirable may not have positive aspects. Thus suicide may be the least painful way out, or in some cases may introduce a form of learning into the system that allows it to change its function. Death cannot be said to be totally negative, inasmuch as it is a complement to life. Death at one systemic level is life at another level, as witness the operation of the food chain.

A psychotic crisis may well lead to important progress and be an enriching experience both for the subject and for his family. A given neurotic symptom can help to restore the balance of the individual and the family. Depression can be a perfectly good physiological response.

It is an inherent feature of every type of psychiatry and of all forms of psychotherapy that it is impossible *not* to try matching sociocultural values with the specific situation of a particular family. In his attempts to match them, however, the therapist can adopt positions ranging from the prescription of a healthy and functional model[2] to the utopias of Laing and

---

[2]The therapist *knows best* what is the right way of life or how a healthy family works. This seems to be the position of Minuchin's structuralist school: to guide clients towards adopting a certain model of the ideal family. Much the same is true of those individual therapists who guide their clients towards *their*, i.e., the therapists', ideas of an adult and mature person.

Basaglia, in which the mentally ill are seen as revolutionaries fighting against a repressive system.

Mara Selvini's approach is quite different; much less dogmatic, she does not proffer any recipes for the good life nor does she sanctify deviants; she simply tries to free victims from an endless, paralyzing game, without suggesting any ready-made alternatives.

Returning to the dysfunctional family, Mara Selvini contends that a particular symptom may not be the result of family circumstances alone; other systems—be they wider or of the same level—may also be crucially involved.

For example, toxicomania can be due to the interaction of individual, family, and peer group within a particular subculture (city, district) with the specific chemicopharmacological effects of heroin. In other words, there is a convergence, a correspondence (in the case of toxicomania) between:

1. A certain intrafamilial game;
2. A given subcultural mode of association adopted by the young (hence, if we like, another game, albeit in a nonfamilial context);
3. The availability of the toxic substance, which depends on international drug trafficking conditions;
4. The particular nature of the chemical dependence produced by heroin that does not allow sudden changes of behavior. Whereas psychotics or anorectics can, if in some way they manage to make up their minds, abandon their symptomatic behavior overnight and start a new life, this door is not open to drug dependents, who need more time and have to go through a transitory phase that is difficult in many ways.

Similarly, anorexia nervosa is not merely the expression of a family game but also of the interaction between a mode of being—extreme slimness—with a particular family situation in an affluent society. This correlation is demonstrated by the absence of anorexia in the Third World, where food is scarce. In other words, we cannot look to the family in an exclusive, reductionist way, attributing symptoms to just one systemic level, but we must consider the individual as a point at the intersection of various systems and supersystems, while not neglecting his particular biological and genetic dimensions.

A PERIOD OF CONCEPTUAL CONTRAST

Mara Selvini's (1968) preface to Ackerman's book reflected a conflict she felt very deeply: Freudian ideas and orthodox Freudian techniques became increasingly difficult to retain in the light of relevant case histories. With anorectics, Mara Selvini had discovered the inadequacy of the orthodox techniques even earlier. Like Ackerman, she was persuaded to try such new paths as family therapy.

In another preface, this time to the Italian edition of a series of papers by the Philadelphia school (Selvini Palazzoli 1969a), she attacked their insistence on reconciling the psychoanalytical with the relational (transactional) model. This kind of insistence was to culminate in the break-up of the first team at the Center for Family Studies. When it occurred in 1971, Mara Selvini opted for rigorous experimentation with the systemic model and began to argue openly against all forms of eclecticism, all attempts at continued reconciliation with psychoanalysis. Her choice of the systemic model led her to take a special interest in certain developments in cybernetics and biology: Ashby, Wiener, von Bertalanffy, and those contributions of the Bateson group that had "filtered" through to her by way of *Pragmatics of Human Communication* (Watzlawick et al. 1967). The resulting framework, however, remained patchy, rather unsystematic, and, above all, remote from her clinical practice. In 1969, the change from family therapy was still little more than a leap in the dark; closer and more coherent links between theory and practice had still to be forged.

As far as the actual contents of the preface were concerned, they were made up of a number of observations that are still highly topical together with others that are now dated and of purely historical interest. Cases in point were the discussion of transference, the call for "a new personality theory," and the endorsement of Whitaker's proposal that future family therapists should have a training analysis involving the entire family. The preface may thus be considered as highly symbolic of Mara Selvini's vacillation between the old and the new. It explains her identification with Searles, who, like her, had determined to take a new approach, quite different from the one based on purely individual and intrapsychic parameters.

Let me give an example of the conflicting influences at work. The reader will note the exaggerated communicationalist account of the approach of the Palo Alto group (Selvini Palazzoli 1969a):

> The Palo Alto group, in fact, formally rejects the contributions of psychoanalytical doctrine, mainly based, as it is, on the complexity of intrapsychic phenomena, and believes that his approach impedes all attempts to view the family as a unit. The Palo Alto group is mainly interested in observing, and in pointing out to all participants, the transactional style they use, focusing attention on "what is happening here and now," that is, holding up to the participants their immediate communications and metacommunications, their possible incongruencies, the typical and recurrent meanings of their interactions, and their changes under stress.
>
> It has been our firm conviction that pathological interpersonal relations are characterized by a marked breakdown in communications. The components of an abnormal family (by which, in accordance with the medical model, we conventionally refer to families presenting one or more members diagnosed as psychiatric patients, including delinquents and sociopaths) do not seem to speak to one another as frequently, freely, explicitly, and clearly as do normal families. Instead, as the experience of family psychotherapy regularly shows, the members of abnormal families tend to suppress, to distort, or to disqualify information, to send ambiguous or allusive messages to make a habit of hiding their feelings and wishes from one another. Often they do not dare to voice pleasure or displeasure honestly. This gives rise to a typical phenomenon in abnormal families, namely silence. Thus, in certain experimental situations—for instance, having agreed to answer a questionnaire collectively—such families will produce longer and more frequent silences than do normal families. The tendency to keep silent, even if interspersed from time to time by inconclusive bickering, is reinforced by the sense of

hopelessness it brings about. It is important to stress that this decrease in the exchange of explicit information between members of the abnormal family is a characteristic function of the entire family group and not of each member separately. This experimental finding is borne out by the therapist's clinical impression: such families seem terrified of destroying the *status quo* of the group, and it is this fear that evidently stops them, both qualitatively and quantitatively, from making explicit statements, especially such as involve revealing oneself, exposing oneself, or putting oneself into the hands of others.

The Palo Alto group accordingly sees its therapeutic task largely in the opening up of intrafamilial communication in and the correction of communicative distortions [pp. 10-11].

A few lines earlier, Mara Selvini (Selvini Palazzoli 1969a) had still supported the psychoanalytic view of family therapy as advanced by Boszormenyi-Nagy:

Intensive family therapy also aims at emotional clarification, and ultimately at the elimination of the translational distortions and unconscious projections in which the unhappiness of many intimate family relationships is rooted. What good is it to confine oneself to showing, for instance in the course of a family interaction, how subtly destructive the communications of a mother to her own daughter are, if the mother cannot be helped to realize emotionally that she is not, in fact, addressing herself to her daughter but to the projected representation of a significant figure in her distant past at whom she now unconsciously hurls back the hurt and frustration she has received? The practice of family psychotherapy had demonstrated beyond a doubt that translations and parataxes are not confined to one's analyst, but occur above all with members of one's own family, one's husband, for example, and one's own children. This phenomenon might originally have dictated the choice of husband by unconscious motives, motives in every sense opposed to the conscious ones and which, because they are unconscious, are all the more dynamic and sources of communicative conflicts and distortions. More tragically still, the children can become the unconscious and confused bearers of the equally unconscious parental projections, so many screens for "images of the past, unsatisfied longings, and scars left by earlier experiences" (Framo).

While all this may be obvious to anyone familiar with psychoanalysis, it indubitably renders the technical approach of the family therapist more complicated and risky.

In fact it is difficult to avoid falling into the subtle trap that is waiting for all whose experience is confined to individual analysis: that of identification with the designated patient, thus isolating therapist and patient from the rest of the group, while proceeding to the analysis of one person or of several members of the family group instead of analyzing the experimental group as a whole.

Now, in the psychotherapeutic treatment of family groups, whenever attention is focused on the total family interaction, it is inevitable to pause in order to examine individuals. However, this is not individual therapy, because it is conducted in the presence of the whole family and in the interests of the family as a whole. Even so, there is an inherent problem, reflected not only in group resistances but also and above all in the feelings that stem from the therapist's traditional training [pp. 11-12].

PART TWO

FROM COMMUNICATIONALISM TO EARLY EMERGENCE OF THE GAME METAPHOR

CHAPTER 4

The Obsessive and His Wife

Mara Selvini Palazzoli and Paolo Ferraresi

. . . Family therapy has specific interactional constants that cannot be described in purely psychoanalytical terms, because the conceptual instruments of psychoanalysis are inadequate to this task. The therapy of the married couple that we will be presenting here will bear out this view, but we should like to anticipate the account by citing one detail as an example.

During the first session, the wife gave us a direct demonstration of her way of experiencing interpersonal situations: every transaction foundered rapidly because she disqualified or negated the content of her own messages. Psychoanalysis would argue that her behavior was obsessive, that the vacillation between her action and its negation was a defense mechanism erected with the help of the superego against libidinal impulses activated by the ego. The ritual of affirmation and negation satisfied the demands of the superego while partly satisfying the pleasure principle as well. Thus when considering a typical ritual act, for instance the lighting and putting out of a match, we would detect, at the level of

M. S. Palazzoli and P. Ferraresi (1972). L'obsédé et son conjoint. *Social Psychiatry* 7:90–97.

the ego, a succession of affirmations and negations that are so many complements to erotic and self-punishing manifestations.

We could also define the husband's behavior with similar interpretative models, but if we do, we shall never be able to escape from an individual frame of reference. The interpersonal exchanges between the couple would then pass completely unobserved. . . .[1]

THE FERRERS

Rodolfo, aged 30, an engineer, employed by big industry.

Sabina, aged 25, a social worker.

They have been married for five years and have a 3-year-old child who, according to the parents, is in the best of health.

It was Rodolfo who originally contacted the psychotherapist (eventually the female co-therapist in the treatment of the married couple) and asked for individual psychotherapy. During the first interview he gave a clear description of his obsessive symptoms (rituals, brooding, double-checking, work dissatisfaction), which had led him, albeit after many hesitations, to plump for "psychoanalysis." His individual suffering and the trouble his way of living and seeing things caused his family had become unbearable. At the end of the interview the psychotherapist concluded that Rodolfo's personality structure, symptoms, level of pain, and motivations were such as to call for the usual type of therapy. However, during the second session, Rodolfo verbalized important anxieties that the treatment might quickly produce an "existential disequilibrium" between himself and his wife. Psychotherapy might lead to the breaking of "ties that have held despite our difficulties." In fact, such sexual problems as premature ejaculation had for some time cut short all sexual relations. The psychotherapist had the impression that Rodolfo's anxiety not only revealed a resistance to the treatment but also a profound fear that therapeutic intervention might destroy the homeostasis of his conjugal system, a homeostasis that was being maintained thanks to his obsessive symp-

---

[1]The paper, from which several passages have been omitted for reasons of space, went on to clarify the systemic nature of a "context of interpersonal exchanges" and stressed that communicationalist analysis was the only way of defining the functioning of a system [Ed.].

toms. In a subsequent discussion with Sabina, the therapist discovered that her attitude mirrored her husband's: "I don't think matters will come to that, but it would certainly be hard to find oneself with a man who is no longer the same, who has lost his character. I should have to get to know him all over again, and God alone knows what might happen then." It was easy to see to what large extent Sabina, a fragile and immature personality with schizoid traits, had taken refuge from her pregenital anxieties in her marriage.

The therapist felt that the analytical treatment of Rodolfo would be a very long, drawn-out affair, probably with very mediocre results, since the transference effects would be seriously limited by the combined efforts of both spouses, allied in the defense of their marital bonds, which, to them, meant preserving the homeostasis on which their very survival seemed to depend. It should be stressed that many failures in the individual therapy of married patients (including the emergence of problems leading to a serious upset of the other partner) can be explained in this way.

The next interview was attended by both partners. The therapist proposed joint psychotherapy following the usual practice of our Center: weekly sessions conducted by a heterosexual pair of therapists. The Ferrers agreed, and the therapy started two weeks later.

We must underline, by the way, that the Ferrers were an exception among our clients because the majority of married couples look to us to resolve conflicts or situations that have already led to gross conjugal crises.

The data collected consist of transcripts of recordings of the first ten sessions, on the basis of which we framed our hypotheses. It is obviously pointless to quote these transcripts here in full; instead we shall try to present a summary of the way the Ferrer couple functioned, based on some of the most significant aspects of the transactions.

The Husband

During the transactions, Rodolfo communicated implicitly that he was seeking no answers, that he had no need for them. When his interlocutors, be they his wife or the therapists, were able to send him significant messages, he would immediately enumerate the various implications, holding out his hands and indicating that none of them frightened him. His behavior suggested that such enumerations satisfied him and that he expected no reply or clarification, either in the form of a confirmation or of a rejection. In fact, however, he was expecting a disqualification. His laborious comments were used to mark time, not to elicit reactions from his interlocutor; he did not expect a reply. In that way he simply communicated that he had no intention of influencing his interlocutor or of imposing rules on their relationship. He spoke, formulated hypotheses but did so exclusively for himself, expected no clarification from others, as if he took it for granted that his interlocutor would remain silent, and signaling a complete lack of interest in what he might be saying. At the beginning of the sixth session, the male therapist was absent. Rodolfo enumerated various possibilities: "Either he is sick or absent for family reasons or else he is hiding behind the mirror to find out how I react to his absence. . . ." He put no questions to the therapist, nor asked which of his hypotheses was the right one. He expected no reactions. One might have believed that he had learned the rules of psychotherapy and knew that the therapist would not tell him the answer, were it not that he adopted the same attitude to his wife, who had no reason to hide herself behind a screen of therapeutic silence.[2]

During another transaction, in the course of which Rodolfo framed hypotheses about his wife (he mentioned her enormous need for him), Sabina's nonverbal response—she calmly removed a few bits of fluff from her skirt—reassured him. He had clearly expected that his comment would elicit no reply. Satisfied on that point, he continued to speak, but now of himself, declaring that his own obsessions were the sole cause of their conjugal difficulties. In that way, Rodolfo was certain to elicit a confirmation from his wife (which in fact came after a few minutes): "It's quite true; it's his fault that things have gone wrong with us." It was the expected

[2]In this connection—and the contrast strikes us as being most illuminating—we would point out that on that very day the two therapists were also due to conduct a group psychotherapy session. The members of the group also put forward various hypotheses on the male therapist's absence, and then asked the female therapist to tell them which was the correct one, taking her silence as a rejection.

and desired response, and ultimately the justification for Rodolfo's existence: he has his place in the relationship with his wife, the only place that the system accorded him but which allowed him to feel that he was alive, that he "exists": he had a nervous affliction, which was responsible for his wife's unhappiness and for his own.

In short, he could experience himself in terms of an unspoken rule of the relationship: "I am the one who is always ill and feels guilty," and of that he invariably received confirmation.

Now Rodolfo could be sure of just two things: (1) of being able to frame hypotheses about what others felt about him, without receiving either confirmations or rejections; (2) of being able to speak of himself as if he were always in the wrong and to receive a confirmation of that fact.

He could then run the risk of sending messages with a positive emotional content. However, he ran that risk up to a certain point only, because he hastened to discredit what he had just communicated in such a way that the interlocutor was left paralyzed, empty-handed, unable to reply. Let us give a practical example.

Husband (to the therapist): I am full of admiration . . . for what you have just said to me. . . . You get me so often . . . yes, admiration. . . . It may, of course, be no more than a passing fancy. . . . As for what you have just said to me, I felt admiration even though I don't really know. . . . In fact a great deal is open to discussion. . . .
Wife (laughs)
Male Therapist: Why are you laughing, Signora Ferrer?
Wife: My husband has just said that he admires you, but that he doesn't really admire you, because he admires lots of people. He also said that he was struck by what you have said, but that your comments were open to discussion, which means that he does not agree with them.

In the course of this transaction, Sabina showed some insight into her husband's mode of interaction, but this fact did not apparently bother Rodolfo, who let his wife's observations go uncommented upon, thus reiterating his wish to treat the whole matter as open to question.

In the same way, when Rodolfo mentioned how faithful he was to his wife, he added that this was a "deep imperative" but immediately added that the whole thing was purely formal, which showed how little value can be attached to his faithfulness. "It's probably just some egocentric need . . . to cling on to something . . . a kind of prop."

Similarly, he discredited all his messages with a clear emotional content, be it negative or positive, to the therapists. In this connection, we shall look at the transactional sequence that occurred during the session following the male therapist's absence. From the outset, Rodolfo communicated to him, by verbal and nonverbal messages, great anger about his absence, but immediately afterwards explained that "all this is the result of what is known as transference, a very common phenomenon in psychotherapy," and, disqualifying his own expression of feelings with an academic tone, he started a lecture that summed up his cursory readings of psychoanalytical literature.

Similarly he interpreted all the therapists' messages in terms of his usual schemes. Thus when the male therapist said he was impressed by Rodolfo's restraint in his confrontations with his wife, Rodolfo disqualified the implicit message of alliance, declaring that this remark "has dealt me a heavy blow, because with that message the therapist has shown me the error of my ways." In short, he communicated that he did not expect a serious reply. His hypotheses about other people's relationships with him had to remain mere abstractions, receiving neither confirmations nor refutations. He imposed no rules on any relationship, but simply endured it. When he painstakingly elaborated his relationship with others he disqualified it by defining it as invalid, formal, egocentric. The deprecatory reply he was bound to receive in the end was the one he had anticipated all along, and it thus fulfilled his expectations.

The Wife

Her ways of relating were so many disconfirmations. Whenever her interlocutor tries to define himself, she, in fact, tells him: "I am taking no notice; you don't exist." We have already mentioned this type of transaction with her husband—when he declared that his wife had need of him, she simply removed bits of fluff from her skirt as if she had not even heard him. Let us now look at one of her transactions with the female therapist:

Female Therapist: I have noticed that you behave as if you were terribly afraid of getting close to people.
Wife (remains immobile and silent for some time, and then says in a gloomy tone): I am thinking about these paintings. I find them rather disturbing. Everything in this room is so anonymous, so impersonal, just as it should be, but these pictures have been deliberately chosen by someone and say a great deal about him.
Husband (raising his voice): This is the most absurd answer I have heard since we first came here.
Woman Therapist: The most absurd? To me it seems quite in your wife's style.
Husband (getting agitated): I wish you realized, Sabina, that you can really let yourself go here. Try to do as I do; I say everything that comes into my head, without embarrassment. It's like a laboratory here. I feel that I am a test tube, do you follow? The relationship between us and them is of a professional type. It is only when a relationship becomes personal that there is the least need to pull down the shutters.

Sabina clearly rejected the female therapist's message; in her reply, instead of expressing her feelings towards her, she stated what she felt about the imagined qualities of the pictures. In so doing, she deliberately ignored the relational content of the therapist's message, disconfirmed it, and thus avoided defining her actual relationship with the therapist. The maneuver was, however, so blatant that it ran the risk of failing miserably. The husband had an inkling of this danger and tried to smooth things over: "You need not bother, my dear, to hide your true emotions. There is no danger since we are no more than test tubes in a laboratory." In saying this, the husband thus disqualified every part of his messages.

The functional communication:

I (Signor Ferrer, author of the message)
AM SAYING SOMETHING (express my feelings)
TO YOU (the psychotherapist analyzing the relationship)

IN THIS CONTEXT (the psychotherapeutic context in which *I* am
the patient and *you* the therapist)

becomes:

I (a test tube)
AM SAYING SOMETHING (communicate the reactions of a test
tube)
TO YOU (the experimenter)
IN THIS CONTEXT (a laboratory, or research project).

The disqualification thus becomes complete, involving as it
does a shift from the therapeutic to the experimental context.[3]
The intervention of the female therapist had caused a conflict
in the internal method of communication of the couple, thus endangering the homeostasis of the system. Sabina's systematic
disconfirmations had a reassuring effect on Rodolfo. The moment
he noticed a technical flaw in the system, he hastened to teach his
wife his own technique of disqualification, in his opinion much
more subtle and effective than hers.

The Functioning of the Couple

The wife totally disconfirms the relational content of her husband's
messages. Occasionally she will pretend to receive them but she
does absolutely nothing to heed them. Everything must remain
uncertain, at arm's length. Let us look at a typical example:

During one of the first sessions, the therapists observed that
Rodolfo took back what he had only just said every time it con-
flicted with Sabina's opinions, thus always siding with her. Sabina
started the next session by declaring that she had been struck by
the therapists' observations. She kept wondering whether she resembled her mother, her grandmother, and her aunt, three domi-

---

[3]It is amusing to note how Rodolfo, certainly without realizing it, had acutely
perceived the correct nature of the context, i.e., of the game the therapists were
playing. These were, in fact, their first experiences in the treatment of married
couples [Eds.].

neering women who had married rather insignificant men (leaving it an open question whether she had been wondering chiefly about being a domineering woman or about having an incompetent husband, or both). Back at home, she had asked her husband whether she resembled these women.

Wife: He said I did not, but his answer seemed unconvincing. It might well have been a white lie.
Female Therapist: In what sense, Signora?
Wife: Well . . . the kind of reply he knew I would like to hear.
Female Therapist: In that case, your husband was of course obliged to say just that. But what if he had said that you did resemble those women?
Wife: I would have packed my bags and left.
Female Therapist: Did he tell the white lie to make you stay?
Wife: Rodolfo simply had to say no; it is very much in his own interest that I remain with him.

Sabina thus explained why her husband could not have given a different reply. The one he gave, however, was unsatisfactory because it could mean one of two things: "You do not resemble those women," but also "I cannot do without you." The ambiguity of the reply thus allowed her to feel dissatisfied and to blame Rodolfo for it.

Rodolfo, caught in a double bind, then came up with a tangential reply:

Husband (putting an end to the transaction): "All such comparisons are impossible because present-day social conditions are quite different from those we had years ago."

The System

Each married partner defines the other as "the one who needs me," thus characterizing their relationship as "a compulsive experience of each other." The system thus maintains its equilibrium through communicative modalities that have an identical pragmatic effect. The husband denies and affirms at one and the same time. In so doing, he robs his wife of any chance of confirmation or rejection. She, for her part, knows perfectly well that her husband never says anything of significance, but she can do little about it, as he invariably anticipates her reaction.

The wife's messages are designed to negate all definitions of the relationship. She accepts the fact that she is excluded and, indeed, encourages it. Faced with her husband's affirmations and the ensuing disqualifications, she never intervenes to make her own decisions known, thus signaling that "things are best left as they are."

When she asks a precise question ("Am I like the other women in my family?"), she disqualifies the reply ("No, you are not") by dwelling exclusively on the compulsive aspects of her relationship with her husband. She knows beforehand everything Rodolfo has to say about their relationship, but his affirmations, quite apart from being predictable, are and have to remain open to doubt.

If we now pass on from the analysis of the communication to an analysis of its effects, we discover that the system provides reassurance so long as the two partners cling to the predictable patterns shaped by their previous systems of learning. The husband comes out of every transaction as the "culprit" (he is obsessive, incapable, neurotic). That is the only identity his wife can grant him, and one that he accepts without reluctance because, for better or worse, it is at least an identity. The wife is reassured by this relational modality because it reflects the fate of all women in her family. She adopts a castrating attitude, does not try to escape her fated identification with the image of a woman without interlocutors, the conquered conqueror of a battle whose outcome is a foregone conclusion.

We now understand why, when we listen to the conversation of this couple, we have the impression of a complete breakdown in communications; everything the Ferrers say to each other seems as expected and superfluous as it is ambiguous. But why do they bother to continue exchanging messages at all? So that they can go on living in a reassuring system in which each partner can reexperience the schemes he has learned in the interactive system in which he has been brought up. The result is a complementary system. Its complementarity is rigid, the position of the members is not interchangeable, and the outcome is dysfunctional. We propose to call family systems of this type "complementary systems with fixed, noninterchangeable positions." In the course of the transactions, the husband always appears in the inferior position (one down) and the wife in the superior position (one up). Their relationship is based on a competition, from which the wife apparently emerges as the winner and the husband as the loser. But since neither is prepared to be the constant loser in the relationship with the other, Rodolfo takes his revenge in the form of a pathological syndrome. It is not he who prevails, but his illness, something much stronger than both he and his wife. Rituals, scruples, and fastidious attitudes determine the rules and fix the laws of their existence. The one in control is therefore the disease. And Sabina, for her part, can submit, not to her husband, but to his "illness."

* * *

COMMENT

The date of publication of this paper (1972) is misleading. The paper was, in fact, conceived in 1969, a phase when Mara Selvini was still guided by psychoanalytical theory and by the psychotherapeutic techniques used in running Balint groups.[4] It was for purely technical reasons that publication was delayed until the end of 1972.

The psychoanalytical bias of the article is combined somewhat incoherently with communicationalist ideas. As a result one gains the impression that there is a disbalance between the aims that were meant to be communicationalist and systemic,

---

[4]The reader will have noticed that the therapists have been conducting these sessions in a passive way, encouraging transactions between the couple and confining themselves to occasional laconic observations on the relationship and the ongoing communications. It is a basic rule with this type of technique *never* to reply to a client's questions, thus systematically "throwing them back" to him [Ed.].

influenced by *Pragmatics of Human Communication* (Bateson et al. 1967), and the actual procedures that tended to slide back into those more typical of the intrapsychic approach, even while involving relational games. Some passages in the paper are strongly reminiscent of the work of Eric Berne: starting with the intrapsychic needs of the actors, an attempt is made to determine how a certain way of entering into a relationship, for instance pairing with a partner having fixed personality traits, can ensure certain psychological advantages. From the paper, it is possible to see what some of these advantages might be: (1) reassurance based on the repetition of schemes learned in one's own family of origin; (2) the acquisition and confirmation—in whatever way—of an identity; (3) defense and escape from neurotic problems and pregenital anxiety.

Thus, when the paper points out that Rodolfo does not take the risk of sending positive affective messages, it seems to be harking back to Berne's view of the game as a means of defense of interpersonal intimacy, or the belief that unconditional emotional confirmation is confined to those who have dropped their neurotic reticence.

The paper, moreover, gives an intrapsychic account of the protagonists (above all of the wife): "Sabina, a frail and immature person, with schizoid traits, has found marriage a haven in which she can take refuge from her pregenital anxieties." *Communicationalist*, by contrast, is the analysis of the couple's relationship (above all of the husband's attitude): Rodolfo expects nothing but disconfirmations, speaks only to himself, does not expect any answer, as if he knew in advance that anything he said would not interest anyone else, speaks, and immediately denies what he has said. The authors use Haley's model of breaking up a message into four facets:

I
AM SAYING SOMETHING
TO YOU
IN THIS SITUATION

which can be disconfirmed in four ways:

IT IS NOT I WHO IS SENDING THE MESSAGE.

THE CONTENT IS ABSURD OR INCOMPREHENSIBLE
(or people talk without saying anything).

I AM NOT SPEAKING TO YOU WHO ARE LISTENING TO
ME.

THE SITUATION IS NOT WHAT YOU THINK IT IS (in
time or in space).

Apart from the theoretical references, which are of historical interest, the reader will have noted the revolutionary introduction of homeostasis on the clinical plane as a basic criterion
of the contraindication of individual psychotherapy and psychoanalysis. This is because defining a couple (or a family) as
homeostatic means emphasizing that the identified patient,
mainly by means of his symptoms, *colludes* with his family *in
keeping the situation unchanged.* It is clear that, inasmuch as
all are on the same plane, the most effective way of exerting an
influence is to look at *all* through the same viewfinder. It then
becomes clear how futile all attempts are to construct with the
patient what not only his own defenses but his entire family
tries to prevent (Selvini Palazzoli and Ferraresi 1972): "The field
of transferal action is seriously restricted by the combined forces
of both spouses allied in the defense of their marital bond"
(p. 111). The use of the homeostasis concept on the clinical
plane thus helped to spread the idea that the family of the
identified patient is unconsciously but profoundly averse to the
success of the treatment.

The final part of the paper is still highly topical thanks to
the relational approach to obsessive neuroses, a subject, incidentally, that crops up quite seldom in family-therapy literature. The
symptomatic member is seen as being "one down" in a married
relationship that is strictly complementary, but, thanks to his or
her obsessive symptomatology, he escapes from the position of
loser, gains major control over the partner, and thus restores
relative equilibrium. This hypothesis reflects a transition and is,
so to speak, a watershed. The argument that each of the married
partners satisfies and protects the needs of the other had made
way for a hypothesis based on the implicit assumption that a

supra-individual systemic level can be relatively autonomous of the intrapsychic level. The result is a *first systemic hypothesis* with a dyadic range[5]: the game is assumed to be played by two people, the married couple.

Finally, the reader will have noticed that the systemic hypothesis is based on the idea of a game with a winner and a loser; here Mara Selvini was patently influenced by Haley.

[5]Although of great historic interest, this systemic hypothesis now seems highly reductive in that it confines the observation to the married couple alone. That does not, of course, mean that the married couple plays no games and that what the paper describes is not very important and widespread, but today it is thought essential to view the couple in the context of their respective families of origin (especially if the couple is as young as the Ferrers) and also to make a careful assessment of the position of the child, even if it does not seem disturbed [Ed.].

CHAPTER 5

Context and Metacontext
in Family Therapy

Mara Selvini Palazzoli

The fundamental importance of the context of all interhuman communication, be it verbal or nonverbal, has recently been appreciated in sociopsychological and sociopsychiatric research and
even in neuropsychology (Benedetti 1969). It was realized that
every communication derives its meaning from the context in
which it takes place, or rather, that the meaning of every communication emerges from the contextual matrix in which it is embedded
and at the same time it defines. Here I intend to appeal to the
contextual principle or law, according to which words, phrases,
statements, and behavior derive their meaning from the situation in
which they are observed, that is, from the particular circumstances
surrounding a person (or persons) at a given moment and influencing his behavior (English and English 1958). There are many
everyday examples of this principle: when a customer enters a
shop for the first time, his relationship with salesmen reflects an
organized system of roles, rules of behavior that are quite different
from those that would ensue if, let us say, the same persons met in
the headquarters of a political party to decide on taking industrial

From *Archivio di Psicologia, Psichiatria e Neurologia*, 1970, 31:203–211.

action. Words, phrases, behavior at a cocktail party would certainly not be the same as those used at a religious service. A context is made up of a precise situation involving a determined end (or intention) and a particular distribution of roles (Ferraresi 1970).

It follows that, as a rule, a given context ought to give rise to attitudes, objectives, and expectations that are in keeping with the contextual situation.

In fact this is often not the case. It is an observed fact that, once a certain communicative context is assumed implicitly or explicitly, *it can be experienced (by some or by all of the participants) as a completely different context.* The communicative fault, the irrelevance, the confusion of meanings will then be the graver, the less the change or distortion of the context is appreciated.

It is a characteristic of every context that it imposes, implicitly or explicitly, a given rule (or rules) on the relationship; consequently, once the context changes, the appropriate rules will change as well.

Let us take the simple case of a round table conference; the very fact that it was called to deal with a certain topic defines the rules. A fixed number of persons, (probably) experts in the field, meet for an agreed purpose: to express their own views and to listen attentively to those of others, in order to make a joint contribution to the subject under discussion. The act of discussing in such cases, even if it obviously involves a dialogic differentiation of oneself from the rest, presupposes a basic attitude of collaboration centered on the issue under discussion. It is, however, a common observation that the *collaborative* context quite often makes way for a *competitive* context. That shift decenters the discussion and turns the original issue into a pretext. One phenomenon that quickly makes its appearance is the increasingly wavering attention of the participants. It is no longer their regular practice to return to the theme under discussion after every diversion; the diversions, far from throwing fresh light on the subject, make way for disorder and obfuscation. In their contributions, each of the participants now tries merely to score points, looks for weak spots to attack, or for arguments supporting his own view, ignoring all the rest. The general interaction easily breaks down into dyads fighting for "one up" positions, the dyadic counterpoints of the "one down" positions and, in my view, characteristic of regression to dyadic violence.

Some time ago the chairman of a panel, who happened to have a sense of humor, cut short a discussion (following the presentation of the participants' individual points of view) that seemed to be freewheeling inevitably towards uproar, irrelevance, and misunderstanding. The chairman proposed starting from scratch but with one difference: seeing that the individual arguments had already been presented, each speaker would try to repeat in the most faithful way possible the account of one of his colleagues, and then the whole discussion would be resumed. The protests and outraged declarations of those who heard their colleagues presenting their own arguments were such as to bring the meeting to a halt. Nothing had been achieved, except that those present had learned that not one of them had really paid attention to anyone else.

The above example struck me as being convincing enough to allow the introduction of the concept of context shift into family psychotherapy.

The first to have drawn attention to the disturbance of the *communicative context* in family psychotherapy was the American team directed by Wynne.

It is well known that Wynne, director of the National Institute of Mental Health in Bethesda, and his collaborators have, since 1954, been engaged in a deep study, involving highly specialized techniques, of the problem of disturbances in interhuman communications, with particular reference to thought and communication failures in the families of schizophrenic patients. In these studies, special attention was paid to failure of attention, i.e., relative inability of families with schizophrenic members to place and maintain in focus ideas, feelings, and particular points under discussion.

Optimum or focalized attention was said to have the following characteristics: it is directed at the focal point, limits awareness of anything that is irrelevant, and is maintained and directed at an objective, to which there is a return after every deviation or change. A conclusion is only drawn after significant comprehension in depth has been reached. As focalized attention is maintained it becomes possible to examine both the wider aspects and also the closer details of a problem. Many preconscious processes of cognition, of memory, and of perception are actively engaged in the pursuit of the chosen aim. The richer the information presented to the attention, the more complex and varied are the possible elaborations and integrations. These characteristics of focalized attention constitute so many ego functions at work in both intrapsychic acts and also in transactional behavior. In respect of the latter, a starting point for verbal and nonverbal communication is needed; both interlocutors must share the same focal point of attention. This ability to share a focus of attention is the fundamental ingredient of an agreed appraisal and shared interpretation; it constitutes a "reality test."

However, as Morris and Wynne (1965) have explained, the sharing of focal points of attention *requires* (*however minimal*) a *context of trust*, trust that the collaboration on a problem can lead to something potentially valid and significant.

Here we come up against the concept of context in which, still following Wynne, we must clarify some aspects.

As soon as two or more persons meet to discuss a problem, they approach it on three levels. (Haley has stressed that the act of communicating intrinsically contains a definition of one's own relationship with the other person; in other words, communication means establishing rules at some level regarding the nature of the behavior involved in that relationship.)

The three levels of approach to a problem in a discussion group are: (1) the immediate responses; (2) the thematic development; (3) the context.

It will be clear that the method used by Morris and Wynne (1965) in this study was based on conjoint-family therapy, the starting point of which is always *a comment by the therapist*, who is presumably accepted into the system in order to work assiduously on the examination and possible solution of the problems besetting the organized system, and seems worthy of the clients' appreciation and respect. Within this system (or set) it seems only right that the clients should respond to the therapist's comments and that they should be prepared to clarify and develop their own ideas, because the therapist has *defined* this process of clarification as the main purpose of the conjoint session. (It should, however, be noted that the therapist lays down the rules of communication and takes responsibility for them, while the other participants simply acknowledge and accept them. This tests the clients' ability to join *deliberately* in a communicative project whose object is suggested by the therapist and jointly explored, clarified, and eventually implemented.

Although the *direct replies* are examined and evaluated, their importance seems to be small and not infrequently deceptive because, although apparently to the point ("How very true! We absolutely must examine this problem! It's precisely as you say . . . !"), they are often followed by thematic developments that are either in conflict with or tangential to the argument.

Great importance must therefore be attached to level 2, the analysis of the *thematic development* of the discussion, and to level 3, the context. Well-developed themes are substantially relevant comments on the point under discussion (or brief expositions) and can usually be brought to a significant conclusion. The complete evaluation of how a theme develops during a discussion is an extremely important factor in analyzing the relevant communication.

But themes are suggested and developed within wider communicative units, namely contextual levels. "By context we understand all those factors that influence communication without normally having to be stated explicitly. . . ."

In our particular case, we speak of a context if the parents and therapists seem to make the same assumptions about the purpose of their meeting, that is, if they agree on the tasks and objectives of family sessions. Without a (contextual) frame of reference shared on at least a minimal level, misunderstandings and communicative breakdowns are inevitable. The worst confusion arises when the participants are unaware of the absence of a common plan or frame of reference, because in that case there is no way out. Such difficulties are much more common than is generally believed—even in individual psychotherapeutic and psychoanalytical relationships.[1]

---

[1] In my view, the difficulties increase further in the personal analysis of prospective young psychoanalysts due to the inherent confusion (in practice, if not in theory) of two distinct conceptual levels: the psychotherapeutic and the didactic. I believe that this situation calls for a systematic study.

However, if the confusion about the scope and contextual structure of the relationship is at least partially understood, then it is possible to correct even the worst misunderstandings in due course. In that case, those who have been at cross purposes become gradually conscious of that fact, and go on to examine their divergent values, premises, and presuppositions.

Bateson has described the failure of communication at the metacommunicative level, characteristic of the families of schizophrenics. Thus some families may be fully agreed at the level of their direct replies and also at the thematic level, but fail to share a contextual framework. In that case, the apparent correspondence of their direct replies and thematic levels tends to compound the confusion, since there is an (erroneous) presumption that they are based on a common context. By contrast, when there is lack of concordance in the direct replies or in the thematic developments, the confusions and the misunderstandings are much more easily identified.

In our own psychotherapeutic work, although conducted no more than episodically with families presenting a designated schizophrenic member, we have found that therapeutic context shifts, as defined by Wynne (see above), seem to be an extremely common phenomenon.

Take a typical context that, in our experience, often ruins the therapeutic setting: namely, the context of a judicial inquiry.

In the context of a judicial inquiry, the rule implicitly defining the relationship not only involves the specification of, and differentiation between, the roles of the investigator and the accused, but is also *a rule of opposed objectives*. The investigator's objective is to "discover"; the defendant's role is to "hide."

In this light, we might consider the indictment of Joan of Arc, and her final handover to the secular arm and to the stake, as the inevitable epilogue to a contextual hiatus. The examiners who expected (and even hoped) that the accused would hide and deny her intentions were exasperated and confused by a prophetic attitude that was, in fact, concordant with the charges. In our more advanced days, her case would surely have been referred to the psychiatric experts. . . .

Still on the subject of a judicial examination, an excellent example of close adherence to the context and of the consequent verbal and nonverbal transactions by inquisitor and victim can be found in those wonderful pages of Dostoyevsky's *Crime and Punishment* that describe the duel between Porfiri, the police inspector, and Raskolnikov, the assassin.

Turning now to context discrepancies in family psychotherapy, we might quote the following common example. The identified patient (often presenting a socially proscribed symptom) sees himself, at the beginning of the session, as the accused, and his family in the role of accusers. The therapists are thus automatically made to play the part of judges. Though they may be determined to repudiate that role, they may fail to make explicit the change from the therapeutic to the judicial context that has taken place. That failure, together with a common tendency to rush into identifying themselves with "the accused," often strips them of their therapeutic role and causes them to seal a further change in context with their behavior: a law court complete with so many counsels for the defense! If the therapists next, warding off the accusation against the identified patient, turn their attention to the parents and their relational problems, it will be the turn of the latter to find themselves in a judicial context, this time no longer in the role of accusers but of accused. On other occasions the shift in context may be more subtle and, if it is not classified, may seriously hamper the entire therapeutic process.

Let us take a typical example drawn from our own experience.

A young husband, bitterly opposed to his wife's wish for a legal separation, appealed to our Center to arrange a series of discussions that might help to clarify the basic problems. The husband seemed determined to try conjoint therapy in an effort to save the marriage at all costs. He was also worried about the future of their only son, a 4-year-old boy. The wife at first demurred but eventually agreed to take part in exploratory talks. In the first sessions the couple, calmly and with great composure, expressed their respective disappointments with the relationship and regrets that it had failed to live up to their early expectations. The therapists, adopting a neutral stance, confined themselves to collecting information and only intervened here and there when expressly asked to do so. This is how things stood at the beginning of the third session:

The husband arrived 20 minutes later than his wife. He did not apologize, nor did he bother to justify his lack of punctuality. He brusquely took off his scarf and coat and flung them on an armchair. In contrast to what had happened in previous sessions, he seemed annoyed. The wife pointed out that there had been a quarrel, "quite different from the usual ones," during the week and that the husband had consulted a lawyer (although he had previously said he would not even entertain that idea . . .).

By punctuating the husband's behavior at the beginning of the session, we were able to clarify the meaning of the messages in terms of the change of context that had just occurred. Evidently the husband, who had promoted the psychotherapeutic experiment, did not in fact feel at home in this context. His lateness, his bad manners, his annoyance at the beginning of the session, directed as so many reproaches at the therapists, communicated his nontherapeutic motivation together with his disappointment at having missed at previous sessions the context he had expected and had so patiently organized: a meeting akin to a conference, paid for by him, in the chambers of two surrogate lawyers specializing in matrimony and obviously happy to side with him, a highly educated and composed man, against his "errant" wife. The wife's subsequent verbal communication confirmed his great disappointment: the husband, abandoning his composed mood, had, after the second session, approached a *genuine* lawyer as a substitute for the incompetents he had to deal with.

If then our basic definition of the therapeutic context includes trust "that working together on a problem can lead to something potentially valid and significant," then the presence or absence of such a context must be continually subjected to checks (metacontexts). By metacontext we accordingly refer to the knowledge and explication of the context: knowledge, that is, of the type of context in which the ongoing transactions take place and from which the participants gather the meaning of such transactions.

"The study of human behavior then shifts from the *inferential* study of the mind (intrapsychic dynamics in the analytical sense) to the *observable* manifestations of the transpersonal relationship" (Watzlawick et al. 1967).

The vehicle of such manifestations is verbal and nonverbal communication.

It follows that the metacontext, i.e., implicit knowledge about the context, is rendered explicit by the metacommunications used by the participants. (The reader is referred to the case we have just described. What do the husband's lateness, his failure to justify himself, and his annoyance communicate? Noting and eliciting such communications, commenting upon them, and discussing their effects on the various participants is precisely what we mean by metacommunication. After all, it is only by communicating about communication and about the context in which it takes place that we endow messages with definable and verifiable meanings.)

Control of the metacontext is an essential aspect of the therapist's role. Ignoring it, as we have noted, leads inevitably to the therapist's discomfiture.

In the case of family therapy, such control is more important and urgent than in any other kind of therapeutic setting. There is no time to correct mistakes—everything proceeds at an incredible speed, even in a single session. Then, irritation, fear, disappointment, a feeling of uselessness combine to persuade all the members of the family to cut the experiment short. This response, experienced many times over, has forced us to take cognizance of this state of affairs.

As a result, we have been led to the discovery that the successful prevention of early failures in family therapy is directly proportional to the attention paid to the context and to the appropriate technical applications. The incontrovertible conclusion is that *to remain bogged down in a confusion of equivocal contexts is tantamount to remaining bogged down in a confusion of meanings*. This conclusion goes beyond the scope of psychotherapy; it holds for all interhuman contexts.

CHAPTER 6

Racism in the Family

Mara Selvini Palazzoli

The objectionable nature of racism is now recognized in many quarters, and the social evil it constitutes is at last being attacked. At the same time, however, family psychotherapists are beginning to learn, from case after case, that a natural social microgroup—the family—structures and stabilizes its own disorders with the help of hereditary biological myths akin to racial ones. It is for this reason that I have ventured to apply a general sociological term to the family, in which the racist phenomenon can, as it were, be studied in *statu nascendi*.

In its 1957 edition, the *Enciclopedia Filosòfica* (Philosophical Encyclopedia) of the Istituto per la Collaborazione Culturale offered the following definition of racism:[1]

From *Archivio di Psicologia, Psichiatria e Neurologia*, 1971, 32:548–557; first English translation published as "Racialism in the Family," *The Human Context*, 1972, 4:624–629.

[1]Here I am concerned only with the general definition; reasons of space prevent me from discussing the particular implications of Marx's dictum: "A Negro is black in all circumstances, but it is only in certain socioeconomic situations that he becomes a slave."

Racism, in general, is the tendency to consider all forms of civilization and culture as manifestations of fixed racial characters. . . . It does not believe in basic racial equality but holds that races differ and are hence of greater or lesser worth: on this belief it founds the dogma of the supremacy of the superior and stronger, and the subjection of the inferior and weaker. . . . Any distinction between fantasy and reality tends to disappear, and the concrete expression of existence assumes a purely biological and racial aspect; hence the indentification of being with race. . . . Because of its essentially mythical character, racism must not be confused with the scientific study of races and of relationships between races or different civilizations [pp. 1886–1887].

What strikes me as being particularly important in this definition is its stress of the mythical nature of racism: it is mythical in an irrational and antiscientific sense, and is moreover collective inasmuch as the underlying myth is "never the product of a single individual but of a people or clan" (*Philosophical Encyclopedia*, under "Myth").

Let me now try to rephrase this general definition, so as to render it applicable to the primary social group, i.e., to the (racist) family:

Racism is the tendency to consider all individuals and all forms of interpersonal behavior as manifestations of fixed biological characters. Once members of a natural group are seen to be genetically diverse, they are automatically endowed with greater or lesser worth. On this belief racism founds the dogma of the supremacy of the inferior and weaker. Any distinction between fantasy and reality tends to disappear, and the concrete expression of existence assumes a purely biological and racial aspect. Existence is identified with certain hereditary characters. Because of its substantially mythical character, family racism must become the subject of a strict scientific analysis based on the relationships and roles that individuals play in the context of the family system.

In fact, much as the characteristics of racism in general are mythical, so also are the characteristics of family racism—both are irrational and antiscientific social attitudes.

The family myth, too, is not the product of individuals, but of a natural group as a whole. As the reader will see below, it forms part of a family system maintained by all its members.

In his now classic "Family Myth and Homeostatis," Ferreira (1963) was the first to offer a systematic account of "family myth," linking its origins, persistence, and development to the homeostatic maintenance of family life. In that article, though he quoted a number of striking examples of the family myth, Ferreira did not refer to the particular myth with which we are concerned, nor, as far as I know, has any other student of family relationships done so.

As used here, [Ferreira explained] the term "family myth" refers to a series of fairly well-integrated beliefs shared by all family members, concerning each other and their mutual position in family life, beliefs that go unchallenged by everyone involved in spite of the reality distortions that they may conspicuously imply. It should be noticed that although the family myth is an important part of the family image, it often differs from the "front" or social facade that the family as a group attempts to present to outsiders. Instead the family myth is much a part of the way the family appears to its members, that is, a part of *the inner image* of the group, an image to which all family contribute and [which], apparently, [they] strive to preserve. In terms of the family inner image, the family myth refers to the identified roles of its members. It expresses shared convictions about the people and their relationship in the family, convictions to be accepted *a priori* in spite of the flagrant falsification they may represent. The family myth describes the roles and attributes of family members in their transactions with each other which, though false and mirage-like, are accepted by everyone in the family as something sacred and taboo, that no one would quite dare to investigate, much less to change. The individual family member may know, and often does, that much of the image is false and represents no more than a sort of official party line. But such knowledge, when it exists, is kept so private and concealed that the individual will actually fight against its public disclosure, and, by refusing to acknowledge its existence, will do his utmost to keep the family myth intact. For the family myth "explains" the behavior of the individuals in the family while it hides its motives. . . [p. 458].

Ferreira's last statement strikes me as being the most important of all: it explains the origins of the taboo against recognizing the existence of the family myth and against discussing it openly. In fact, as the (somewhat maladroit) therapeutic evidence adduced by Ferreira (it should be remembered that his paper was written in 1963, and that family psychotherapy has made great strides since then) and my own experience clearly suggest, the entire group, no less than the individual member who is most strongly under the spell of the myth, is quick to round on the incautious therapist who dares to expose the myth directly instead of allowing it to filter through with the help of more diplomatic tactics. This is because the family myth is not an individual or parental creation—a fact that cannot be overstressed—but a systematic phenomenon, the key to the homeostasis of an entire group. As Ferreira puts it, it acts as a safety valve in moments of stress, and as a kind of thermostat, set off whenever family relationships are threatened with disruption or chaos. The myth thus tends to maintain and even increase the level of family organization, crystallizing behavior patterns and preserving them in the circular and self-corrective manner characteristic of all homeostatic mechanisms.

The need to maintain the myth is part of the wish to maintain the family relationship: hence it is essential that the myth be shared by all the members.

The hereditary biological (or racial) myth, too, serves the homeostasis of the family system; but *while it helps every member to justify his own behavior and that of his near relatives*, it also disguises the *underlying motives*.

Let me now mention a few examples of the racial family myth as I have met it in my work as a family psychotherapist. For the sake of greater clarity, I shall first examine several basic factors.

THE COUPLE AS AN INTERSECTION OF SYSTEMS

When a man and a woman decide to set up home together, they immediately come face to face with a series of problems, chief among them the difference in their family backgrounds. Quite often they are born in different places, their physical characteristics are different, and so are their beliefs, customs, stereotypes, rites, outlook, and values. They differ in their likes and dislikes of things great and small, in their character armor, and quite often even in the way they use or misuse certain words.

From the meeting of such opposites they must forge a new style suited to the new condition. This they will be able to do the more easily the less their communication is hampered by ambivalent ties with their original family (and the more successful each has been in shedding those ties). In fact it is often the partner with the more strongly marked ambivalent ties who seeks to impose on the other partner either a closer relationship with that family, or else certain forms of behavior, habits, beliefs, and so on. Systematically speaking, I agree with E. Jackson that marriage is a fluid relationship between two partners and their individual systems of behavior. The term *systems* is as applicable to marriage as it is to any other institution.

However, the marriage system is complicated by the fact that as soon as one person sets up home with another, the two invariably generate a new system.

When two people get married the most important thing each of them does is to attempt to define the nature of their relationship. Each seeks a working system satisfactory to himself, and would prefer to achieve it without having to change his established behavior patterns. If one or the other partner is to adapt to the new circumstances, it must preferably be the other. Generally each approves of his own behavior, idiosyncracies, and habits, and criticizes those of his partner. For that very reason most marriages show early signs of dissension. Jackson has stressed that the elimination of such friction is hampered by a universal form of behavioral blindness. The individual contributes to the construction of the joint system not only by conscious behavioral efforts but also with that part of his personality that is unconsciously motivated and hence completely hidden from him.

Nevertheless, each of the two partners attempts to mold the relationship, to influence the way in which the joint system functions, and to determine within what limits his or her own behavior is mutually acceptable.

Once a satisfactory system has been established, it tends towards homeostasis. However, the homeostatic tendency proper to every system assumes a particularly rigid character in unsatisfactory and precariously balanced matrimonial systems.

Since such systems are always characterized by a serious

failure in communication (and by an ever growing number of rules as to the points one dare not raise for fear of causing an explosion), one's dislikes, prejudices, and resentment of the partner's family, together with one's disappointment with the marriage partner, can never be brought into the open. This state of affairs can last for years before a new element is brought into the system. But when that element—a child—does appear, the conflict is merely revived and rendered more acute. With the help of the hereditary myth, recriminations now center around the newcomer.

"Whom does he look like?" This universal question, somewhat absurd while its object remains a relatively shapeless bundle of flesh, can produce overt or unspoken answers that may have the most baleful intrapersonal consequences. To express the *essence* of this new human creature, all the parent needs is a *predicate*, a characteristic feature such as a prominent forehead, eyes of a particular shape, small fingers, and so on. This feature is the first of a whole series of characteristics both feared and expected, welcomed and deplored. The child thus becomes part of a system established by his parents (and by the extended family), to which, at first, he contributes no more than his sex and his personal features; but these suffice to construct a myth the moment the system needs it.

Take this example: a slim, fair woman in her forties—the mother of an only child who was diagnosed as a schizophrenic at the age of fifteen—came to ask my advice about family therapy. At the time she was living with her sister, and she hoped that such therapy might help her to return to her husband and son, recently discharged from a psychiatric hospital. Here is the most significant extract from the (recorded) interview:

Mother: I *realized* that I might have an abnormal child when I was three months pregnant. It was then I found out that my husband's sister was insane. He had kept it from me . . . and many other things as well. They come from [a place in the south of Italy] and are quite incredible. The things they do! Let me tell you about them. That sister turned up at home one day, out of the blue. . . . She had a terrible fight with my husband. . . . She was rolling her eyes and screaming. . . . I was terrified from then on. When the baby was born, I could see straightaway that he *took after them* . . . his eyes, his look [*she opened her handbag and took out a snapshot of a baby with dark eyes who simply looked sad to me.*] Look at that expression. . . . He's peculiar. . . . He's *always* given me the creeps.

From the subsequent conversation it appeared that, at the age of 15, the boy had suddenly started to behave in a psychotic manner, causing violent scenes, shouting and grimacing at the mother (but not at the father, in whose presence he would immediately recover his composure, though his speech remained psychotic). Moreover, the son's psychosis was apparently triggered off whenever his housebound mother made contact with her own family, who always insisted that she should leave her husband. It also struck me as highly significant that the mother should have sought the help of a family therapist just when her son had been discharged from a psychiatric hospital. How would she possibly be able to keep staying away from home now that her sick son was back again and in need of her personal attention?

"Whom does he take after?" This question has long since become part of my stock-in-trade during every first family interview. I have learned, however, to put it very cautiously: in a matter-of-fact but courteous way. In the fortunate case of families with several children, it is best to begin with those who show no symptoms, and then to proceed, almost inadvertently, to the one who is said to be ill. I listen to the replies without comment, lest the therapeutic situation degenerate into a series of denials and recriminations.

A young mother telephoned me for an interview to discuss her older daughter, Paola, 4 years old and said to be unteachable. Her younger daughter, 2-year-old Stefania, was no problem at all. I invited both parents to my consulting room. While jotting down the preliminary data for our family file, I noted that the father used slang.

Doctor: "Education?"
Father: "Oh, I just played school for kicks."

At this the wife, a pale, demure woman who refused to take off her fur coat, looked startled.

From the father's account it appeared that he had always been a rebel, though he was unusually practical and had wide interests. At the age of 14, having left his authoritarian father, a craftsman who insisted that the son take up his trade, the boy had worked at dozens of odd jobs, studying hard at night school, and had then received several technical diplomas. He now held an important executive post, earning a great deal of money and studying electronics (which had nothing to do with his present work but which he found fascinating) in his spare time. He seemed highly satisfied with his work and determined to better himself.

The mother came from a provincial town; her parents were teachers. She was a teacher herself and had been working for several years in a nursery school, "even though I don't need to." Paola attended her mother's school and was taught by a colleague. The mother spoke of her little girl in a stifled voice, her eyes filled with tears, but the story she told was remarkable only for its lack of factual information:

Mother: When she was really tiny, I was terribly worried about her energy. It was totally abnormal.
Doctor: Could you give me a few examples?
Mother: I need only tell you that when she was just a few months old she managed to topple over the plastic high chair she was strapped in—she grabbed hold of something, and crashed down, baby chair and all. I keep thinking that she must have damaged her skull. When she was about 2 years old, I took her to have an electroencephalogram; she just wasn't normal.
Doctor: What precisely did she do?
Mother: She never did as she was told and kept throwing the most awful temper tantrums. People kept asking me what was the matter with her. At the seaside, I could never get her out of the water. I wore myself out trying to make her see reason. The encephalogram didn't show anything; I really had been hoping all along that her behavior would be explained by the bang on her head, but no. . . . Then, when she was 3, I took her to my nursery school. I warned my colleague, of course, and told her that the child was very difficult and would have to have special treatment. And now I gather that my colleague, too, is at her wits' end. I was advised to let the child take more

physical exercise so as to get it all out of her system. So now I take her to skating lessons. At the beginning she was enthusiastic. I would stay to watch the lessons with the other mothers. Then one day she talked back to the skating instructress and insisted on doing everything her own way. I told her to do as she was told, and the end result was a scene with the instructor, who took it out on me [she bursts into tears]. . . . She made me look like a fool in front of all the other mothers. It was too much. I just couldn't take any more. So then I decided to call you. She keeps getting worse, more twisted all the time.

Father: As I see it, my wife likes to put up a front: she keeps worrying about what other people will say and wants to be well thought of. I, for one, don't give a damn about other people. And she expects God knows what from Paola, keeps nagging her about her table manners, so now Paola refuses to sit down to meals.

Doctor (turning to the wife): You have a younger child, too, I think? What is she like?

Mother: Oh, a perfectly normal child [her expression changes as she tells how easy it has been to bring Stefania up].

Doctor: Whom does she take after?

Mother (startled): Who?

Doctor: Stefania.

Mother: Oh, she takes after me; she's just the same as me when I was small. Even my mother says so.

Doctor: And Paola?

Mother (voice rising): She takes after him! [She bursts into tears again.] And I just can't take it any longer. I don't want her to be like that. She'll be unhappy all her life . . . a wretch.

Watzlawick (1967) had this to say of the interrelationship of two subjects in a dyadic situation: "One partner does not impose a complementary relationship on the other, but rather each behaves in a manner which presupposes, while at the same time providing reasons for, the behavior of the other . . ." (p. 69).

When the mother first saw her baby daughter's powerful physique (the personal element the child contributed to the relationship), she was deeply alarmed: here she had incontrovertible biological proof that *the daughter took after the husband*. And because she assumed that the child's conduct was equally prede-termined, she at once rationalized her worst fears. The child, for her part, learned to anticipate certain of her mother's behavior pat-terns and behaved in such a way as to justify these very patterns. The symmetrical communication became circular: action and reac-tion reinforced each other and led to a dangerous escalation. The father played an important part in this game as well, since he, too, was convinced that *Paola was like him*. As a result the triadic relationship turned into a perverse triangle: the father established a secret alliance with the daughter, making no secret of his con-tempt for his wife's stereotypes, and providing Paola, who exas-perated him, with his own behavior patterns. Paola now assumed an important function: she had become a vehicle of communica-tion between the parents. On the basis of the myth that Paola "is just like her father," the two could finally engage in open warfare. The mother could attack what to her was the intolerable coarse-ness of her husband (which she wanted to suppress in Paola); the father could strike out at his wife's snobbery (which she tried to impose on Paola).

But, above all, the two could stay together thanks to the child, whence the whole *problem of Paola*.

TWO FAMILY BACKGROUNDS:
THE CONFLICT IN RACIST TERMS

A large family came for family therapy "because of Emilia," a serious case of anorexia nervosa with severe vomiting that had resisted all previous therapeutic efforts.

She was referred to me by a psychotherapist who, after sev-eral discussions with the patient, had come to appreciate the futil-ity of continued individual treatment. My colleague observed that when the girl had finished telling the story of her "difficulties" and therapeutic misadventures, adding quite incidentally that her par-ents were "two very decent people who unfortunately don't under-stand each other," she had lapsed into complete silence and be-came totally unapproachable in her passive despair. When the parents were brought in for the purpose of establishing the girl's family background, my colleague was amazed by their constant bickerings over even the most trivial matters and by the fact that the patient kept intervening in an obvious but, in the event, quite hopeless attempt to pour oil on troubled waters. The girl's comments, which impressed my colleague by their astuteness, fell on deaf ears—the parents were much too busy attacking each other to pay the least attention to the daughter.

This is what I myself gathered during the first family interview. The two parents, both in their fifties, practised the same liberal profession in a small town. His family (whom I shall call the Crippas) were middle-class provincials and preached the old-fashioned virtues: his mother was all for Church, home, and good works, and his father was totally devoted to his job and religious duties.

The wife, by contrast, came from an upper-class family with liberal traditions and contempt for the Church and anything associated with it. (I shall call them the de Marchis). Apparently Signora de Marchi made no bones about her contempt for her son-in-law's humble origins. Signora Crippa, for her part, felt deeply aggrieved when her son informed her that he proposed to marry an undergraduate, who was also an atheist. "How can you even consider marrying into that family? None of them are any good about the house; none of them will ever make decent wives."

The two nevertheless got married, but started at once to vie with each other, to question the other's success and profession. Their two older children, a boy and the patient already mentioned, had "of necessity" to spend a number of years with their maternal grandmother, an extraordinarily aggressive woman who missed no chance of branding the least of the children's lapses as typical of the Crippas. In answer to the question of whom each of the children took after, I was offered an intricate and random pattern of racial attributes, which differed from parent to parent. The boy, for instance, was said by the mother to be a Crippa in certain respects, whereas the father maintained that he was an obvious de Marchi. Only when it came to Emilia were the two in patent agreement: she was a pure-blooded Crippa.

The following is a transcript from the tape of an exchange between Emilia and her mother:

Emilia (leaning towards her mother): Do you remember when I was a little girl? Whenever I was naughty, you would call me a Crippa. But the worst bit was that father would always join in and side with me, even when I was completely in the wrong. . . . So I was always thrown on Daddy's side . . . and yet I loved you very much. . . . I don't know what I would have given . . . but instead I turned against you because you kept telling me that I was a Crippa. . . . And then I didn't know which way to turn. . . . I would a thousand times rather you had . . . squashed me . . . but both together. But all you ever agreed about was that the de Marchis are better than the Crippas.

Mother (who seems quite incapable of appreciating the pathos of her daughter's appeal and adopts a defensive posture): But what could I do when you never talked to me and walked about with a long face for days on end? [She turns to the therapist, relaxes, and adopts the tone of someone who has at last found someone capable of listening to reason]: You see, Doctor, it's typical of the Crippas to be so touchy. You just can't talk to them. They always take offense.

To grasp her meaning, we can perhaps do no better than translate Watzlawick into the traditional language of racism. If you are convinced that someone is a "Negro," and expect certain behavior patterns from him, you will give him good reason to behave just like that. At the same time, knowing that you take him for "a Negro," he will expect certain behavior patterns from you and provide you with reasons for them in his turn.

If we revert to Marx's dictum quoted in the note on page 69, we can now see how easily it can be applied to the family system: "A human being has certain characteristics in all circumstances but it is only in certain family situations that these characteristics turn him into a 'Negro'."

However, on the family stage the drama of interhuman relationships is so intensified as to cast all the actors into a prison in which each adds to the total stagnation. And much as the "Negro" chooses to remain "a Negro" lest he become a "nobody," those who treat him as a Negro will continue to do so for the same tragic reasons.

* * *

REFLECTIONS ON THE IMPORTANCE OF CONTEXTS

Mara Selvini's paper "Context and Metacontext" is a paper devoid of psychoanalytical terminology; it was an early elaboration of the context approach and continues to be of topical interest.[2] The view of "context" presented in that article had a profoundly innovative impact on the systemic views and helped Mara Selvini to go beyond communicationalism toward the game metaphor.

To Watzlawick and colleagues (1967), context is synonymous with "framework" and hence has a spatial and quantitative meaning, as witness such statements as: "A phenomenon remains unexplainable as long as the range of observation is not wide enough to include the context in which the phenomenon

[2]It must be remembered that from 1967 to 1970 Mara Selvini knew of the work of the Bateson team mainly through *Pragmatics of Human Communication* (Watzlawick et al. 1967). But in Watzlawick's book some arguments did not accurately reflect those of Bateson and Haley. Cases in point were the adoption of mathematical analogies (axioms, etc.), of the dyadic nature of the sender–receiver model, of the neobehaviorist approach (black box). Here I cannot enter fully into this question, on which I am preparing a critical study, but wish only to record that a turning point came in 1972, with the publication of Bateson's *Steps to an Ecology of Mind*. New theoretical horizons were opened up; direct reference to Bateson's complex ideas revealed vistas that the more popular writings had often obscured. The "context" idea, with which I am dealing here, was above all brought home to Mara Selvini by "The Logical Categories of Learning and Communication" (*Steps to an Ecology of Mind*, pp. 250 ff.), an essay not published before and, moreover, the result of at least eight years of study and of many corrections and reelaborations. Of particular importance was Bateson's idea of "context marker" and his analysis of the Pavlovian experiment into "experimental neuroses," in which a dog's task of discriminating between an ellipse and a circle is rendered increasingly difficult. Bateson reinterprets this famous experiment in terms of a double bind or of a shift in context (from the rules of discrimination to the rules of chance) (*op. cit.*, p. 267 f.). Bateson's remarks on the evolution of contexts (*op. cit.*, "Comment on Part Two, p. 153 f.) provided yet another impetus [Ed.].

occurs" (p. 20 f.). Paying attention to the context means refusing to isolate the monad emitting behavioral communications.

References to the quality or nature of the context are not entirely missing but are certainly very general. Watzlawick and colleagues (1967) devote just half a page (p. 132) to explaining that context involves two types of factors: (1) institutional, external factors (not further defined); and (2) manifest messages inasmuch as they generate redundancies (or place restrictions on the range of possible responses by the interlocutors).

In "Context and Metacontext" Mara Selvini expanded her ideas on the quality and nature of contexts, which she now clearly perceived as subject to certain sets of rules, for example, collaborative, competitive, judicial. But above all, the concept of metacontext helped her to question the premises and aims of the participants. She thus began to focus, with Crozier, on the problem of the actor's strategic moves.

This was the type of approach that, although still obscured by communicationalism,[3] was already leading Mara Selvini to

---

[3]The most dangerous feature of communicationalist reductionism is the implicit suggestion that there is a clear distinction between healthy and functional communication on the one hand and pathological or dysfunctional communication on the other, when communication is never sane or insane *but always a function of a context (or a game)*. It is not true that clear and direct communication is always functional; indeed, in certain contexts it can be dangerous (or downright idiotic) and generates a symmetrical conflict. Similarly, the incomprehensible intervention of a politician may not be pathological but a useful tactic to achieve certain ends. Here I wish merely to record that the Palo Alto school helped to spread the belief in a kind of *moralism of communication*, according to which healthy communication is clear and direct while unhealthy communication is indirect, ambiguous, and of course paradoxical. This view, of which Virginia Satir has been one of the leading advocates, has transformed some social workers into grotesque preachers and teachers of clear communication, in the mistaken belief that they have hit upon a panacea for all psychological problems. These people are under a grave misapprehension: their simplistic attitude is bound to lead them to such commonplaces as "short reckonings make long friends" and similar platitudes.

It must, however, be pointed out that in her criticism of this type of pedagogical moralism, Mara Selvini, precisely because of her own involvement in communicationalism, failed to stress the contextual aspect (of the game) of communication, dwelling instead on the inefficiency of the verbal channel for obtaining significant messages about relationships. This was no more than a partial truth, because it ignored the fact that messages are primarily moves in a game [Ed.].

ask herself such questions as, "What sort of game are they (or are we) playing?"

The communicationalist error was obvious above all in the interpretation of context shift as a misunderstanding: the paper leads one to conclude that if the various participants in an interaction have different premises about the nature of the context in which they are involved (for example, experiencing it as a therapeutic or as a judiciary context), then a context shift will be generated with consequent ambiguity and confusion. In fact, however, the context shift must be considered a move in a game. Thus if a competitive "war game" is played at the round table conference I mentioned earlier, then the distorted communication (confusion, not listening to one another, lack of attention) is the result of the game and its intensification. Similarly, in the case of our quarreling couple the context shift clearly reflected in the husband's behavior is a move in his game to subject the wife, or in other words, the effect of his fury at not having found the allies he had sought.

The fundamental nature of the context (or of a relational game) resides in the way the actors adapt themselves to it or try to manipulate its institutional rules. A context can rarely be kept within its traditional grooves. There are always "subversive" moves by the actors: the alliance of one against another, attempts to avoid or shift blame, a struggle against the leadership, and so on. In complex human contexts, unlike in games as such, there is no distinction between "playing a game" and "playing with the rules of the game," or as Bateson (1972) puts it so elegantly: "It's like life—a game whose purpose is to discover the rules, which rules are always changing and always undiscoverable" (pp. 19–20).

In the case of our quarreling couple, the husband tried to transform the rule of the therapeutic context (which implies collaboration) into a judicial context, in which the therapist was expected to play the part of a judge sympathetic to the plaintiff's cause, or at least of counsel for the defense. Having failed in his plan to have his wife defined as "mad," he had to backtrack and turn to a "real" lawyer. If we put forward a game hypothesis (in his case, of a symmetrical battle between husband and wife in which the former, finding that he is about to lose out, hunts for allies), then a careful observation of specific communicative sequences (coming late, flinging his coat down on the chair in a bad-mannered way) can help us to confirm or discard the hypothesis. If, by constrast, we start from a detailed analysis of the communication and dispense with the guidance of a relational game hypothesis, then we are bound to end up in utter confusion.

Today, Mara Selvini no longer believes that there is any point in the therapist's metacommunicating about the rules and characteristics of the therapeutic context—explaining that it is not like a trial, that there is no defendant, no struggle—experience having taught her that it is not with explicit messages that the true nature of the context is driven home. For instance, stating explicitly that one does not want to put anybody on trial can implicitly introduce a legal shift of context. It is far better to run sessions in a certain behavioral and nonverbal way by which the family can be made to collaborate in the therapy and to learn the therapeutic rules (Viaro and Leonardi 1982, 1983).

In the paper I am discussing here, *metacontext* and *metacommunication* (the first being a particular case of the second) are clearly part and parcel of the communicationalist model: as we saw with context shift, attention is focused exclusively on the congruency of the communicative mode in use.

Since then, Mara Selvini has dropped the term *metacontext,* defined as knowledge and explication within a given context—knowledge, that is, of the type of context in which the transactions of the participants take place and from which they derive their meaning. She has dropped it, precisely because it dates back to the "pedagogic and communicationalist" period. By contrast, she continues to pay heed to awareness of the nature of the context and also to the extent to which the various participants share that awareness.[4]

As for the shift in therapeutic context, I now tend to view it as involving at least three games: (1) the game played by the family, (2) the game the therapists intend to play with the

---

[4]In other words, what we have here is the problem of motivation in family therapy, of the type of game that has brought the family to seek therapeutic advice [Ed.].

family, and (3) the game the family and/or its individual members want to play with the therapists.

Each of these games has its own stakes. Thus, the following concerns may be at stake in the therapists' game: (1) to effect changes in the clients and thus to strengthen the therapists' professional identity, (2) to come up with new ideas that might confirm the therapists' possible capacity as research workers, (3) to publish papers, (4) to make a living, and (5) to demonstrate the validity of certain techniques to adversaries and competitors.

The problem is complex and would certainly merit an *ad hoc* discussion. It is, however, obvious that it cannot be reduced to a failure in clarifying the nature of the therapeutic context.

Still on the subject of context shift seen as the result of a relational game, I would refer the reader to Paolo Di Blasio's (1981) excellent Chapter 8 in *The Hidden Games of Organizations*, which deals lucidly with the connection between denied coalitions and context shifts.[5]

RACISM IN THE FAMILY:
THE FIRST HYPOTHESES ON FAMILY GAMES

"Racism in the Family," published in 1971, is "Context and Metacontext" in that it attaches great importance to family assumptions, perceptions, and beliefs. While the first of these two papers dwells on perceptions relative to the nature of the context, the second deals with beliefs revolving around heredity.

Despite certain statements characteristic of her earlier, extremely systemic, phase, Mara Selvini now stresses that observable behavior is the only reliable source of information, and she gives this belief the widest possible practical scope. In particular, observable behavior is thought to include those perceptions of oneself and of close relatives that are brought up during family-therapy sessions.

Mental contents, accordingly, are not put aside, or relegated to the famous black box, but are rather (following a

[5]On the subject of context, Mara Selvini delivered an interesting epistemological address to the 1982 Zurich Congress (see Bibliography).

combination of explicit verbalizations and nonverbal forms of behavior) used by the therapists to arrive at important inferences about beliefs and assumptions shared by all members of the family, even though they are not fully aware of that fact. This is precisely what happens with those beliefs that Ferreira (1963) calls *myths.* "Racism in the Family" though, like "Context and Metacontext" devoid of psychoanalytical overtones, contains a new element: *attention is no longer focused on communication.* Instead, as the examples used make very clear, attention has been shifted to the *quality* of the intrafamilial relationship. While the communicative style is ignored, sociocultural data and the history of the family, by contrast, are taken into careful consideration. Admittedly, there was as yet no systematic framing and testing of hypotheses, but *there was nevertheless a first attempt to research the ongoing game.* The greatest technical innovation was the view that such research must be based on an *active* and *directive* therapeutic intervention.

The investigation is focused on the beliefs, myths, and rules of family life and on the way in which all experiential data are used and manipulated by the married couple, by the nuclear family, and by the extended family. The last example cited in the paper can be considered a description of a type of family game: a tug-of-war between a couple enmeshed in the cultural conflict of their respective families of origin. The myth of biological heredity and the consequent self-fulfilling prophecy have placed the daughter in an impossible position, against which she rebels by developing anorexia as her only means of escape from a game in which irrational prejudice dogs her every step.

The observational field has been extended from the nuclear family to the respective families of origin, thus avoiding the dangerous use of an exclusively dyadic approach, still so evident in "The Obsessive and His Wife."

The temperamental element in the behavior of individuals (the vivacity of Paola) is treated as an important piece of information about the system and by no means ignored (as some of Mara Selvini's critics have maintained). The decision to abandon the intrapsychic approach, according to which the family merely serves the individual's inner needs and motivations, must not be considered a failure to appreciate the importance of individuals on the systemic level. The individual and his past, and not just his biological aspects, far from being ignored, are integrated into a multilevel approach, quite distinct from that of traditional psychoanalytical or of behavioral reductionism.

TRANSFORMATIONS OF THE THERAPEUTIC METHODS

A brief passage in "Racism in the Family," likely to pass unnoticed, reflects a major leap in therapeutic technique. Commenting on Ferreira, Mara Selvini stresses the pointlessness of exposing (or rather, explaining) the family myth to those directly concerned:

> In fact, as the (somewhat maladroit) therapeutic evidence adduced by Ferreira (it should be remembered that his paper was written in 1963 and that family psychotherapy has made great strides since then), and my own experience, clearly suggest, the entire group, no less than the individual member who is most strongly under the spell of the myth, is quick to turn on the incautious therapist who dares to expose the myth directly instead of allowing it to filter through with the help of more diplomatic tactics.

This passage put a seal on Mara Selvini's renunciation of explicit therapeutic techniques.

From 1967–1971, Mara Selvini's technical approach passed through the following stages:

1. Adopting group therapy methods of the Balint type, the therapists confine their activity to brief observations and comments on what was happening during the session: "I have noticed that. . . ." In "The Obsessive and His Wife," for example, the therapist remarks on the fact that the husband retracts everything that he has just said whenever it conflicts with his wife's views. During that period, the method of running the sessions involved brief

observations, followed by long silences on the part of the therapists, with the intention of inducing the client, possibly worried by the silence, to speak. The fixed time schedule was rigorously respected, no in-depth interpretations were offered, nor were particular conclusions drawn and voiced at the end of every session.

2. Another brief phase, immediately following and partly overlapping the first, involved recourse to classical psychoanalytical techniques: transference interpretations, either in terms of family relationships (for example, a mother who experiences her daughter as she had once experienced her own mother) or in terms of the client–therapist relationship. Mara Selvini has not published any clinical material covering that phase, perhaps because the results were disappointing. However, the techniques used can be clearly inferred from the various prefaces I have quoted, and also from her "Transference in Intensive Family Co-therapy," a paper I mentioned earlier.

3. A third phase, following and again partly overlapping the earlier two, involved teaching the family to communicate correctly. Disconfirmations and rejections were noted; the therapists would ask the clients to speak in the first person and not abstractly in the third; there was metacommunication on the true nature of the therapeutic context; all ambiguities and confusions were pointed out. Such techniques, already foreshadowed in "The Obsessive and His Wife," and particularly in the detailed analysis of certain interviews, were manifest in "Context and Metacontext" and would continue until 1973, beyond the split-up of the first team, as we shall see in Chapter 16, "The Use of Therapeutic Interventions."

Though the new team (Selvini, Boscolo, Cecchin, and Prata), which was formed at the end of 1971 and to which I referred earlier, retained vestiges of the communicationalist approach, it transformed the old strategy in two ways:

1. The activity of the therapist became very intense. The theme of each session was laid down during a presession, when attempts would be made to get some idea of the nodal point of the problems involved. "Racism in the Family," although preceding the split-up of the old team, anticipated this approach as applied to the problem of biological heredity. In other cases, too, the sessions revolved about such *ad hoc* themes as money problems, adultery, and the role of a prestigious grandfather.
2. Explanatory techniques were relinquished. Four years of experiment were more than enough to discover the futility of explanations, interpretations, and remonstrations: these years had produced most frustrating therapeutic results. From that time onward, Mara Selvini considered the unmasking of myths to be ineffectual, and she resorted instead to indirect techniques. Not only in the case of myths, however, but also with several other hypotheses about the ongoing dysfunction, it became obvious that attempts to display or explain them to the family served little purpose. Instead, research turned into an experimental search for "covert and imperceptible" tactics. Real changes do not spring from abstract understanding.

The basic problem would always be how to go on from a given hypothesis about the ongoing game to a given therapeutic strategy.[6]

This point, merely adumbrated in "Racism in the Family" (but which I would stress as a signpost of this conceptual evolution), would become one of the two key concepts, and perhaps the more interesting one, of *Paradox and Counterparadox* (to which I shall be referring at some length in Chapter 18).

With the rejection of explanatory techniques, the therapist clearly adopts a provocative role: *he becomes a catalyst of change.*

---

[6]For an illustrative example, see pp. 116–118.

TEAMWORK

The basic reasons for this radical transformation of therapeutic techniques must be sought, not so much in the therapists' changed relationship with their clients, as much as in the particular nature of teamwork: there is a very profound relationship between the development of new ideas in family therapy and the complexity of the observational setting that has emerged, to some extent by coincidence. The idea of teamwork in psychotherapy and psychiatry was born before family therapy, but the teams used to consist of therapists working separately and often with a single patient in abnormal situations (that is, in psychiatric institutions or in therapeutic communities). It is perhaps not fully appreciated to what extent family therapy has transformed teamwork: not only has the field of observation been enlarged, not only has it become possible to take a "binocular" view of the family (Bateson 1979, p. 69 f.), i.e., a view shared by the therapist and the supervisor, but the observers themselves have been "multiplied" and charged to observe themselves.[7] And all this happened before the realization that the new approach is in line with the most advanced theories in philosophy and the methodology of science.

It was the great revolution of direct supervision: the creation of a double, simultaneous level of observation (and interaction), that allowed the creation of a self-corrective system much more efficient than the one made up of the single therapist, or even of the dyad consisting of therapist–indirect supervisor used in traditional psychotherapy. The correction of mistakes was speeded up enormously.

The role of the supervisor, which is one of *attentive surveillance rather than of direct involvement*, facilitates valuable observations of the verbal and nonverbal behavior of the family and of the direct therapist and guarantees the *detachment* (the "meta" position) needed to decrease the risk, run by the thera-

---

[7]On this subject, the reader is referred to the writings of Edgar Morin and especially *La Mèthode* (1977), one of the best systematic treatises on order/disorder, organization, and complexity.

peutic team, of succumbing to the dysfunctional models of the family under treatment.

If we look at these developments in retrospect, what can we say about the effect of this particular method of teamwork? The most obvious result seems to have been an enormous saving of time in choosing the appropriate therapeutic models and methods and in conducting the relevant experiments. Thus Mara Selvini and her various teams were able to conduct, in the space of relatively few years, an impressive number of experiments into the best way of running sessions and into the best tactics and strategies.

This type of teamwork produces striking results so quickly because it enables the therapists to observe and correct one another. Everything seems much clearer and much more obvious than it does with indirect supervision.

It never ceases to amaze me why some family therapists continue to work on their own. There is an economic advantage, of course, but on the methodological, and hence also on the ethical, plane the renunciation of the team dimension and of direct supervision can no longer be justified even when practised by the most expert of therapists: therapeutic control of the family becomes too difficult. The isolated family therapist is likely to founder, above all when dealing with identified psychotics.

True, even teamwork poses problems: it introduces a great many variables, so that the therapists are always engaged on more than one front—the game with the family and the game with the therapeutic team (to which, in the public context, we must add the institutional game).

In Mara Selvini's experience, a team of *equals* working in completely independent research centers, without hierarchic superiors or "dependents" (subordinates or pupils), provides the ideal conditions for generating maximum creative freedom. That arrangement has presented indubitable advantages over teamwork behind institutional walls (universities or the public service), and even more so over teamwork in training centers. The history of family therapy has shown that there is a particularly marked incompatibility between research and training: the therapeutic creativity of many great masters was stifled the moment they began to devote themselves systematically to teaching (Haley and Minuchin are two cases in point). And this need not surprise us: once they have become professional trainers of family therapists, their creative ability is diverted into a different field.

PART THREE

THE CHOICE OF
THE BATESONIAN
SYSTEMIC MODEL AND
THE BEGINNINGS OF
INTERVENTIONIST THERAPY

CHAPTER 7

The Turning Point of 1971

Matteo Selvini

At the end of 1971, the conflict at the Center for Family Studies came to a head. One section of the team (Selvini, Boscolo, Cecchin, and Prata) broke away, not only to come down squarely in favor of the *systemic model*, but also to apply it to family therapy *in the most coherent and rigorous way possible, avoiding all eclectic inclusions*. The other section of the team made a different choice.

Mara Selvini very quickly clarified her stand on psycho-analysis, which she summed up in an interview with Dr. Canevaro and published in 1980 in *Terapia familiare*, Buenos Aires.

Canevaro: What can you tell me about your psychoanalytical past? Do you think it was useless or harmful to you?

Selvini Palazzoli: I think it was useful because it taught me not to be afraid of patients, always to pay close attention to what is happening in a patient's relationship with me, to understand my reactions, always to link what happens during a session with what has happened in the previous session, always to look for my own mistakes instead of blaming all failures on the client's resistance.

But it is equally obvious to me that the psychoanalytical approach has impeded the adoption and application of the systemic method. The temptation to interpret, to be more or less didactic, is always strong, but nowadays I am becoming more and more convinced that families must be induced to *do*, before they can be made to *understand*. Insight into one's own condition serves no purpose in itself but can prove useful *after* a revealing experience.

RESEARCH INTO BIG ORGANIZATIONS

The choice of a particular theoretical model, the rupture of links with the past and work with a self-observing team, heralded a period of *exceptional creativity*: while continuing with her family work, Mara Selvini had started her research into big organizations.

This new interest was typical of her unique approach: financial independence (from institutions no less than from pupils in training), which was unusual enough, now became coupled with the abandonment of the specialist view that focuses attention exclusively on the family.

In this connection I can do no better than quote from Mara Selvini's autobiographical "Present Imperfect" address (1979):

> The year 1972 was very important to me for yet another reason. Along with research on families in schizophrenic transaction, I had a chance of engaging in research on big systems. This opportunity was offered to me by a group of former pupils at the Catholic University who, at the end of their course, invited me to lead a research team. The objective was to discover whether the systemic model, which had proved so valuable with families, could also be applied to the study and solution of the problems encountered by educational psychologists.
>
> The work of this team, which lasted for two and a half years, ended with the publication (in 1976) of a book entitled *Il mago smagato* ("The magician without magic"). By that expression we had tried to sum up the strange dilemma of psychologists working in Italian schools, in which all members of the scholastic community (headmaster, teachers, pupils, parents) re-

fuse to be labeled as "clients" yet expect the psychologist to produce magic answers. The efforts of the research team were accordingly aimed at discovering a method that would allow the school psychologist to structure his own professional context.

In 1976, I began to work with a second group, this time composed of psychologists employed in various organizations: in industry, in business, in hospitals, in boarding schools, and in planning and consulting services. General systems theory and cybernetics were applied to the examination of the relational patterns that could be observed in the various institutions, as well as in the interaction between the psychologist and the various subsystems of the organization. I do not wish to speak at length about this research; all I want to say is that our work is now especially aimed at recording *similarities* and *differences* in the phenomena observed in the different types of organization. Concerning the similarities, we have found and described isomorphic redundancies with the same pragmatic effect—the preservation of homeostasis—in widely differing organizations.

As for the differences, the most striking one between big organizations and families was found to be the following: while double binds in big organizations undoubtedly cause some of their members discomfort and unhappiness, they very rarely produce the psychotization we often observe in families. The explanation is that organizations do not give rise to the vital and intense relationships we find in families. In organizations, firing staff is relatively simple and so is resignation. The difficulty of leaving the field thus seems a crucial element of family dysfunction.

Research into the big systems is so interesting because it allows comparisons with the family system. Similarities and differences throw light on both fields of research.[1]

THE EPISTEMOLOGICAL DIMENSION

The singling out of a specific object of research focused the team's attention on the epistemological dimension constituting the basis and connecting tissue of work in the various fields.

The systemic model became the team's theoretical frame of reference. At this point, I must clarify what the systemic model

---

[1]Adapted from the transcript by the translator.

means to Mara Selvini, since there are, in fact, a host of different interpretations of that model. Apart from being in general agreement with von Bertalannfy, Mara Selvini's systemic ideas are mainly derived from cybernetics (Ashby and Wiener) and from the application of cybernetics described by the authors of *Pragmatics of Human Communication*. However, it was precisely during the period under review that she discovered Gregory Bateson, whose great collection of essays, *Steps to an Ecology of Mind* (1972), had just been published in California. As I said earlier, that book proved a great revelation to Mara Selvini, all of whose theoretical ideas were deeply influenced by Bateson[2] until her discovery of Edgar Morin, Michel Crozier, and Niklas Luhmann in the 1980s.

THE SELVINI-BOSCOLO-CECCHIN-PRATA TEAM

When the old team broke up at the end of 1971, Mara Selvini, together with Luigi Boscolo, Gianfranco Cecchin, and Giuliana Prata, decided to adopt the "Palo-Alto" approach of those who at the time were called the "systems purists."

From the material presented below the reader might conclude that Mara Selvini was persuaded to adopt the communicationalist systemic model on purely theoretical grounds, when in fact the impetus had been a practical one: the new research framework (active self-observation by the team, new research object, new therapeutic context, and so on) could no longer be reconciled with the psychoanalytical model and *called for different theoretical horizons*. In Mara Selvini's work, the theoretical structures (the epistemological ones no less than those governing the therapeutic changes) seemed forever "in pursuit" of the new facts brought to light during the continuous experimental search for new solutions, not only in the strictly therapeutic field, but also in self-training, in the organization of a research center, in team work, and so on.

---

[2]On the occasion of the publication of an Italian translation of *Steps to an Ecology of Mind* in 1976, Mara Selvini wrote an interesting critique (Selvini Palazzoli 1977).

In fact, the new team, with great courage, not only opted for the new conceptual model but decided to "go it alone," to learn above all from its own errors and not from other family therapists.

The result was a center quite different from the great majority of family therapy centers that sprang up throughout the western world in the sixties and seventies: many of them made it a habit to co-opt well-known therapists, who introduced their own models and techniques in turn. This had two important consequences: conformism reflecting a wish to imitate the example of these experts, and confusion due to the eclectic mixture of a host of disparate approaches.

Mara Selvini's center was unique in relying exclusively on its own forces and above all in *devoting itself entirely to research*. It was a private center, free of all institutional links, and hence not even subject to the usual professional or teaching constraints: for seven years the four members of the team agreed to finance themselves, taking no money for the three days a week they devoted to the research.

It was a small, isolated, and very compact group that stuck together until 1978, producing an excellent crop of ideas and experiences. Selvini has described the first of these in the following excerpt.

CHAPTER 8

Present Imperfect

Mara Selvini Palazzoli

It was our common decision to adopt the systemic circular model, with particular emphasis on the avoidance of contamination of linear causal models. When at last we began to work with families without any conflicts in the team, we made an amazing discovery. It was as if we had suddenly been given new eyes to see . . . we were getting clever! In this way we learned, through our own experience, to what extent a competitive struggle renders people blind . . . one cannot see anything but one's own struggle to prevail . . . . We went on from moments of discomfort to moments of joy and astonishment at some of the effects our interventions suddenly elicited in families, and that would have seemed quite inconceivable before, particularly in families presenting anorectic patients. During my previous work as an individual psychotherapist, specially skilled in the treatment of anorexia nervosa, it often took me hundreds of sessions to obtain a positive result. But now, working with families, just a single well-centered therapeutic intervention could suffice to produce a radical change!

Excerpts from the address delivered at the fourth Don Jackson Memorial Day, San Francisco, 1979.

THE CASE OF ELISA

I remember a family with a chronic anorectic girl . . . for the first time the team decided that the only possible effective intervention was to declare that the therapist was unable to help. I want to mention this case briefly. It was a middle-class family of five. The parents were of the typical old-fashioned bourgeois type, super-dedicated and supercompetent. Elisa had been anorectic since the age of 13, and could look back on a very sad history of compulsory hospitalizations and individual psychotherapeutic treatments that had regularly failed. The parents then applied for family treatment to our center, having decided, after so many failures, to do every-thing possible to get Elisa a doctor who was considered "the undisputed authority" in the field. When the treatment began, with myself as the treating therapist, Elisa's physical condition was poor, but not disastrous. However, during the treatment, notwith-standing our frantic efforts, her condition gradually worsened, until (when the family arrived for the sixth session) we realized Elisa was on the point of dying. The team discussion after the family session was dramatic. Something drastic would have to be done to save Elisa's life. But what? Gradually, as our discussion proceeded, an idea emerged: we had to shift the focus of attention from the relationship within the family to the relation of the family with the therapist. An escalation had clearly developed: Elisa, trapped between two assumed superpowers—the parents and Doc-tor Selvini—had no other way of keeping both at bay than to stop eating. We were able to reconstruct the story as follows: the super-competent parents, having failed to get Elisa to take food, had hired a supercompetent therapist who, in terms of her mandate, would induce Elisa to eat. Elisa's starvation, accordingly, was a brave but dangerous fight against both parents and therapist. At this point of the discussion, the team could take but one decision: the therapist would have to eat humble pie by confessing her helplessness, without blaming anyone else.

I must confess that this task was not an easy one, but, any-way, I performed it. The parents reacted with expressions of great anguish and despair, Elisa's sisters seemed shocked, while Elisa herself put on a poker-face.

What happened a few hours later, when Elisa went to her grandmother for lunch, hit everyone, ourselves included, like a bombshell. The meal was served. For the first time in many years, Elisa sat down at the table and said in a firm tone of voice: "Now that Doctor Selvini *too* doesn't know what to do, it's up to me to take care of myself." She took large helpings of every dish and ate everything up. Clearly, she had no more enemies to fight with! Six years have passed since. We have had recent news of Elisa. She is very well, goes to the university, and is a good student and a very attractive girl.

Our team has had similar results with many anorectic patients. Each time they took me by surprise, because in my long experience I had never before witnessed such sudden changes.

THE CASE OF LINA

Still more striking were some of our results in the treatment of families with schizophrenic patients. Here is a truly impressive example.

Lina came to us with her father, mother, (paternal) grandmother, and her four brothers and sisters. She was 17, the oldest of five children. We shall call this family the Zanons. They had some standing in the small town of Veneto in which they lived, having run a confectioner's shop for generations. Traditionally, women in the Zanon family were held in unusually high regard and were not expected to work in the shop. They stayed at home, took care of the children, helped the parish priest, visited the sick, and were often asked for advice. But Lina's mother was not a real Zanon; she came from a peasant family. During her first pregnancy, the Zanon grandparents made it clear that they were very keen to have a granddaughter. As soon as Lina was born, Grandmother took care of her. Four children came later, but Lina remained the grandparent's favorite: she was a pretty girl, good at school, and obedient. At 17 she suddenly turned psychotic and presented a catatonic syndrome.

During the first session, Lina adopted a very strange posture, as only catatonic people can. She sat rigidly in her chair, her head twisted far back. The (one-way) mirror showed only the nape of her neck. She looked like a broken doll. We formed the hypothesis that Lina's position in her family was reflected in the posture she adopted during the session. She was trapped between her mother and her grandmother, and she had no way of choosing between the two: she was damned if she did and damned if she did not. The messages she received from both sides were incongruent, of different logical levels.

During the session we carefully checked this hypothesis and found that it was sound.[1] In the team discussion, after the family interview, we took the following decision: for the therapy to work, Lina would have to be placed squarely in only one of the two camps, her mother's. However, we would have to be careful not to be critical of the grandmother. With this goal in mind, we made a paradoxical comment followed by the following prescription:

The Therapist (addressing the mother in a sympathetic tone): "Look, Signora Zanon, we have been deeply touched. . . . What Lina is trying to do is quite wonderful. . . . It's all for your sake, Signora Zanon, for your sake alone that Lina is doing what she does! Let me explain. Lina has all the qualities needed to become a prestigious Zanon woman; like her great-grandmother, like her grandmother, she has beauty, education, good character. . . . But, at a certain moment, she realizes that, to develop these qualities, she would have put you in an intolerable position. You are not a real Zanon . . . she is one . . . and so is her grandmother. . . . How would you have felt with two prestigious Zanon women in the family? That is why Lina decided to stop developing her potential. Look at her now . . . and all this for the love of you. Now we have a prescription for you. From now on, until the next session, you have to take care of Lina personally, you and nobody else. Stay with her as much as possible, feed her, take her to the lavatory, dress and undress her, put her to bed. All this in order to show Lina how grateful you are to her. Do you agree?"

While the therapist was still speaking we could see (and video-tape) Lina's head turning forward ever so slowly. The mother

[1]It should be mentioned that this case was reelaborated in 1979 so that the use of certain terms (hypothesis, etc.) is derived from the theory adopted after the 1972–1975 period [Ed.].

was sobbing. The family came back for the second session a month later. Lina had completely dropped her catatonic behavior.

* * *

VERBAL INTERVENTIONISM

From these two typical examples the reader will have been able to gain some idea of the characteristic therapeutic approach of the new team. As I said earlier, the method of conducting the sessions had become more active, reflecting the team's wish to explore certain areas assumed to be crucial. The key moment, however, was not the beginning of the session. When about an hour had passed, the therapists would interrupt the session and withdraw for a lengthy discussion of the final intervention with the supervisors. The team's maximum effort was concentrated on *contriving* interventions,[2] mainly of the verbal type, with a disruptive effect, like so many bombs exploding the family's philosophy. The relationship of the therapists with the family undoubtedly contains a large antagonistic component, evidence of an "athletic" attempt to beat "the adversary." This does not, however, do away with the other fundamental and indispensable component: the warm collaborative commitment, rich in respect and trust.[3]

Inside the team, by contrast, collaboration is unreserved; the intellectual effort is intense, the climate is lively and bright, and the therapists often enjoy themselves a great deal.

One component that must not be underestimated when

[2]The team's discussion was mainly devoted to the comparison of the various types of intervention and therapeutic strategies; the team was much less interested in reaching an understanding of the family game. With regard to the latter, they often made do with the rather general hypotheses exemplified by the case of Lina [Ed.].

[3]Here, Mara Selvini and her current collaborators disagree radically with the Manichean views of Dell, Keeney, and De Shazer, i.e., with the idea that there is a sharp opposition between aesthetics and pragmatics or between cooperation and challenge. In good family therapy, an intervention will be pragmatically effective precisely because it is aesthetic. Similarly, therapy is efficaciously cooperative because it *challenges* certain family moves and rules [Ed.].

assessing the effects of therapeutic interventions is *ritualization*: the sessions are held in a room with a "technological" atmosphere (telecameras, microphones, one-way mirrors), there are long breaks, and finally a conclusive prescription, often very dramatic in the contents no less than in the telling.

In the case of Elisa, the double interpretation of her symptom—as an interfamily game and as a game between the family and the therapists—was an early example of clinical recourse to the family–therapist supersystem, a departure that was to have extremely fruitful consequences.[4]

Interesting, too, was the intervention in Lina's case: a combination of a paradoxical comment (made to provoke the identified patient)[5] with a structural prescription (in this case not paradoxical) justified by a cryptic and farfetched explanation (in other words, the therapists did not explain their real reasons for the prescription, since doing that would not only have been pointless but would also have meant leveling a dangerous accusation at the grandmother).

This phase is best characterized by the prevalence of provocative paradoxical comments and the sporadic assignment of tasks to be performed at home. In other words, while the first phase was characterized by reliance on the linguistic or verbal channel, the emphasis shifted to any instruments that might help to make the actions, the facts, and behavior "speak" for themselves.

Given the mainly clinical nature of the interventionist experiences (practice, as I have already said, undoubtedly preceding the theoretical elaboration), I can do no better to illustrate the new therapeutic approach than quote Mara Selvini's account of another two cases,[6] both originally presented to the Congress of Louvain of 1975.

[4]See Chapter 27 [Ed.].

[5]It should be noted that the hypothesis concerning the trigger of Lina's catatonia was consistent with the prescriptive aspect of the intervention and not with the paradoxical comment. Evidently and perhaps unconsciously the therapists had postulated that Lina felt hatred towards her mother, who had left her in the care of interfering grandparents [Ed.].

[6]Like the two cases described earlier, these, too, were reelaborated in 1981, and the critical comments reflect this fact [Ed.].

CHAPTER 9

Family Therapy

Mara Selvini Palazzoli

THE CASE OF LISA

This case illustrates a typical dysfunctional interaction between subsystems: individual, family, and school. As we shall see, the crucial therapeutic intervention was based on the therapist's successive operational choices.

A very worried father telephoned me to ask me if he could bring me his 8-year-old daughter, whom we shall call Lisa, because of her anorexia and rapid loss of weight. As always, I tried to elicit as much information as I could during the telephone call, such information, as we shall see, being indispensable for the formulation of hypotheses and hence of operative choices. It appeared that Lisa had lost a lot of weight the year before but had fully recovered in the summer holidays. However, soon after the beginning of the new school year (it was in November) she had had a relapse, this time very much more rapid and worrying. The whole thing, the father explained, seemed inexplicable because

Excerpted from the address presented by Mara Selvini Palazzoli at the Family Therapy Congress, Louvain, 1975.

the girl went to a private school and had an excellent teacher who took a special interest in her. The family was made up of four members, including Lisa's sister, who was two years older. The father described her as an extremely bright and vivacious girl, quite unlike Lisa, who was said to be timid and an introvert. At the end of the telephone call I had to make the first decision: whether to see the entire family or just the parents. For two reasons, I decided to invite the parents alone.

My *first* reason was to make sure that Lisa would not be labeled as a patient. Had she come along to the interview, she would inevitably have been made to feel that "we are going there for your sake."

My *second* reason was to observe the parents' relationship and hence to deduce the relationship between them and their daughter. I had been struck by the news that Lisa's anorectic symptom had spontaneously disappeared during the last summer holidays. I postulated that although her anorectic behavior was rooted in several subsystems, it had been triggered off by the interaction between Lisa and her class at school (teacher and classmates). If possible, I would try to work with the parents without ever seeing the girl.

At my first meeting with Lisa's parents, I found myself face to face with a young couple who behaved in diametrically opposite ways. The father was a successful businessman, worldly, keen on social activities and on sports. The mother was a modest little woman of low social origins, devoted exclusively to her home and evidently accepting a complementary position *vis-à-vis* her husband. In the course of our discussion it became clear that the older daughter was considered a copy of her father, whereas Lisa, the younger, was considered a copy of her mother. For that reason, Lisa, unlike her sister, who went to a public school, had been sent from the first year of primary school (on her father's suggestion and with her mother's consent) to an expensive private school, both parents feeling that she had need of special help. However, enquiring into the details of Lisa's school life, I quickly deduced that she did not, in fact, benefit from her private education. The teacher, drawn into the family rules and probably beset with problems that had nothing to do with Lisa, had come to treat Lisa as a "poor little girl" in need of special care, *thus isolating her from her classmates.*

Periodically the teacher would summon the parents for a discussion, exaggerating her own dedication and the particular care needed to teach a girl who was so inhibited and perhaps a little retarded as well.

At the end of our first meeting, I felt clearly that I was being presented with a combination of three dysfunctions: that of the family, that of the interaction between the family and the school, and that of the class in which Lisa had been enrolled. In the family, the very interaction of the couple reflected the existence and consolidation of a myth, already extended to the second generation: in that myth there was a clear distinction between the strong and the weak, between the bright and the dull, and between protectors and protégés.

In the interaction with the school, the myth and rules of the family system were taken over whole, as unfortunately happens so often. (In Lisa's case, there was also a special reinforcement: *a good girl needing help* is a godsend to any expensive private school.) However it was the third dysfunction, that of the subsystem of Lisa's class at school, which struck me as the trigger of Lisa's symptom. Here she experienced the intolerable climax of the whole chain of dysfunctions: the schoolmistress, turning her into a "case," had isolated her and had deprived her of the support and sympathy of her classmates.

Once I had framed this hypothesis I had to pick the best type of intervention. On which of the subsystems would it be best to act? On the married couple? On the school? On the teacher? Lisa's situation was desperate.

I rejected the idea of intervening with the married couple. The mutual relationship, inasmuch as it was sharply complementary, appeared to me functional enough for the needs of the two partners. Their myth of the strong and the weak did not seem to be downright pathogenic. I accordingly thought it best to explode the myth as it had been extended to the other subsystems. I did, however, reject the idea of intervening with the staff of the private school: there was a risk of becoming bogged down in sterile diatribes and making a bad situation even worse. I preferred to profit from the parents' anxiety, from their concern about Lisa, and to convince them that it was best to transfer the girl immediately to a public school. *I carefully avoided voicing the least critical remarks about the parents*, which is always counterproductive. I praised the father for his parental concern for Lisa and . . . reserved my critical comments for an outsider! The teacher, in her zeal to help Lisa, had adopted false methods, creating an irreparable situation to which Lisa's relapse bore witness. There was no alternative; Lisa would have to be transferred to a public school immediately, regardless of her scholastic shortcomings. To Lisa, the parents had merely to say that they had decided to change school because they had realized that the situation had become impossible. The parents agreed. On the further pretext of economic difficulties, Lisa was transferred to a public school. I advised the parents not to tell the new teacher anything about what had gone before. Within two months of her transfer to the new school, Lisa had not only put on quite a lot of weight, but she was a contented girl and was counted among the best in her class.

During my fourth and last meeting with the parents, I noticed that the mother had changed. She now intervened spontaneously in the transactions and seemed more content and more self-assured. All this confirmed the systemic principle: every part of a system is related to all the other parts, and any change in one part causes a change in all the other parts and in the entire system. Lisa's escape from the range of the weak and the protégés had destroyed the *myth* and rules of the family, no longer divided into two subgroups, and hence had also altered the relationship between the parents, not merely by increasing their insight but also on the level of concrete experience.

The striking success of the intervention calls for some comments.

Obviously the intervention succeeded because the family system was not too rigid and did not have fully crystallized rules. That had, indeed, been the therapist's hypothesis. But the hypothesis could have been proved wrong. For that reason every systemic intervention decided on the basis of a hypothesis about certain functions is nothing but a process of trial and error. The errors, however, are far from useless to the therapist, inasmuch as they supply him with indispensable information for the construction of a new hypothesis about the systemic function he is investigating. The new hypothesis, in its turn, enables the therapist to devise another intervention.

THE CASE OF PIA

We now come to a clinical example that illustrates our method of intervening in the most rigid possible type of family organization: a family with an adolescent anorectic member. As I have said elsewhere, these families are tied down by such fixed rules that they can be compared with a programmed cybernetic machine. Thus the clinical case I am about to describe involves a family so incapable of changing its rules that it reacts with even greater rigidification to all calls for change addressed to it from the outside (the social environment) and to all stimuli from the inside (adolescent changes of a member).

To produce an effective change in this type of family we made use of interventions of the paradoxical type as early as the end of the first session. I must, however, stress that such interventions demand a high degree of skill on the part of the therapist: he must conduct the sessions in such a way as to elicit the greatest possible amount of information about the ongoing types of relationships in the family. As for the intervention itself, it must be carefully analyzed in the light of the theoretical model used, in our case the systemic model.

The family under consideration, whom we shall call the Ferrarinas, was made up of three members, Pia, the identified patient, being the daughter. At the time when the family contacted our Center, Pia was in a hospital ward for gravely emaciated patients. The parents, with the consent of the physician in charge, brought Pia from the hospital to attend the first session. Pia was 17 years old and had been an anorectic for a year.

I now shall sum up the fundamental data collected by the therapist during the first session. The parents were of different social backgrounds. The mother, a factory worker, came from a poor family. The father, by contrast, came from a rich and well-known family in which he had always been the "black sheep," having cut short his studies and having lost enormous sums at gambling tables. To his family, the marriage to a factory worker was another tangible sign of failure. Once married, the two moved into a small apartment, which they owned, holding a mortgage. The family income consisted of the wife's wages and the somewhat chancy earnings of the husband, who had taken a job as a commercial traveler. Gina, the wife, had devoted herself body and soul to her husband's rehabilitation. It was she who found him clients, who encouraged him to work, and brought him back home if he stayed too long in the bar. But quite soon the "gambling demon" resumed its grip on him. One day, when Pia was 6 years old, an eviction order arrived: Augusto, the husband, had lost everything at roulette, including his home. Gina, disheartened but not defeated, found lodgings for herself and her daughter with a lady whose linen she took care of at the end of her factory day. Augusto slept here and there, living hand to mouth. A few years later the family was reunited, but life remained difficult. Augusto did not have a regular income and from time to time he still gambled, although more rarely, and for small sums. As if to make up for it, Pia was a model girl, a great consolation to her mother, who spared no sacrifice to make sure that her daughter lacked for nothing. Pia studied hard for a secretary's diploma.

The period preceding the outbreak of the anorectic symptom was marked by the following events:

Pia, having obtained her diploma, joined a bank and began to earn her living, associated with boys and girls of her own age, and began to go out with them in her free time, sometimes in the evening. The mother invariably waited up for her. The father, now employed as a representative at a very prosperous company, was earning more and handed his wife fairly large amounts of money, but continued to go out almost every night. The wife, for her part, no longer minded; she felt strangely indifferent to her husband's comings and goings. He went out. He didn't go out. To her it was all the same. All her interest was centered on Pia, on the new life that Pia had begun: her colleagues at the bank, her telephone calls, her late nights. It was during that period that Pia, copying some girl friends (who wore tight jeans) began to go on a diet. Her loss of weight became very dramatic, and there was no longer any way of stopping it. . . . In vain the mother implored her, cried, began to cook special dishes. . . .

I now come to the therapist's paradoxical intervention at the end of the first session.

Therapist (turning to the mother): We have all been touched by Pia's concern for you, Signora Ferrarina. It is for your sake that Pia is doing it all. It's because you, Signora Ferrarina, have always been a courageous woman with high moral standards, a woman who stands firm in the face of adversity, who helps others without ever bothering about herself. The story of your life speaks volumes. You have devoted your best years to helping your husband, you have slaved away to make sure your family wants for nothing. Sacrificing yourself for others lends meaning to your life, is your aim. We think that, recently, when things eased up for you (your husband earning enough, his nightly outings no longer causing you suffering, Pia herself having a good job . . .), Pia began to feel, perhaps unconsciously, that a grave threat hung over the family: you might finish up feeling that you had become useless, empty, devoid of reasons to continue the struggle. Perhaps she feared you would become depressed. To avoid that, Pia decided to become anorectic—the best way of making sure that you, Signora, could still feel that you were being a mother, could still feel needed, could still feel in harness. That is why Pia renounced her beauty, her work, and many other things as well. . . .

Mother: But I am ready to commit suicide if only my daughter could become cured! [A dreadful slip, not pointed out by the therapist.]

Therapist: We think that Pia is so convinced of the need to look after you, Signora Ferrarina, that she will continue to behave as she is doing. . . . No one has asked her to do it . . . it is her own free choice, and we respect her for it. . . . [The therapists fix the date of the next session, a month ahead, and take their leave.]

The pragmatic effect of this intervention was immediate. That same evening (the session had been held in the morning) Pia's physician telephoned from the hospital to let us know that Pia had not only eaten the entire evening meal but had even asked for a second helping.

Let us now analyze our intervention.

The parental couple had always had a symmetrical relationship, disguised as a complementary one. The martyred wife had struggled to get the better of her husband and to redeem him by her indefatigable sacrificial presence. The husband, for his part, had fought against the crushing power of the "gambling demon" (an interaction very similar to that of the alcoholic). In a pseudo-complementary escalation, each partner had reinforced the other's behavior. The more efficient the wife was, the more inefficient the husband became and the more of a slave to the gambling demon. When Pia reached full adolescence, started to work, and entered into extrafamilial relationships, the system needed a change of rules. The mother should have renounced her rigid control, and the father should have helped his wife to cope with the new situation, filling the vacuum left by Pia. But the system had become too rigid to change. The mother could no longer renounce her position of supermother; the father had become too marginal a figure to intervene in a constructive way. Moreover, for his own peace of mind, he liked to think that Pia completely filled his wife's life. When Pia communicated a change in the definition of their relationship (she was independent, earned her own living, decided herself what to do with her free time), she was met with anguished rejection by her mother and with cryptic silence by her father.

At this point Pia's learning context sprang into action and suggested an infallible means of putting her mother down without declaring her hostility in the first person. And that is how, just as had happened with her father, a mysterious, deep, indefinable, invincible demon appeared on the scene and gained the upper hand over everyone. In Pia's case it was not a gambling demon but the *demon of anorexia*: "I too would like to eat but I cannot."

Let us now list the fundamental facts underlying all these developments.

When the Ferrarinas appeared at the first session we observed the following phenomena:

1. All members of the family shared the false belief that, by virtue of her symptom, Pia had power over everybody.

2. Pia herself was under the misapprehension that she had assumed power over both her own body and the system.
3. Pia did not declare a hunger strike in her own name but in the name of an abstract entity: her disease.
4. That abstract entity was given a negative connotation: it was thought to be an evil.

Let us now analyze the therapists' intervention:

1. They gave a positive connotation to all forms of behavior they observed.
2. They praised the generosity and the spirit of sacrifice of a mother who had struggled so hard to free her husband from a demon that was stronger than he was, the gambling demon.
3. They defined as good the anorectic behavior of the designated patient, i.e., as an unselfish attempt to act in her mother's best interests.
4. They dethroned the mother from her position of super-mother and conferred on the daughter (for the first time in her life) a maternal role *vis-à-vis* her own mother: her fasting was presented as a means of protecting her mother against depression.
5. They deprived the daughter of her presumed superiority, placing her in a position of inferiority to her new vocation: that of helping her mother.
6. They allied themselves with the homeostatic tendency of the system, temporarily relinquishing any idea of changing it.

But in so doing they had already intervened in favor of a change.

By revising the punctuation and connotation of the observed phenomena, they had introduced a circular view of the reciprocal relationships into the system. As a direct result, the systemic organization was upset, and the old game had to be abandoned.

The first result of this complex intervention, articulated on various levels, was Pia's revolt against her "vocation," so highly praised by the therapists; she dropped her symptom.

Once they had got rid of the symptomatic behavior, the therapists could proceed to the reorganization of the relationships.

To that end, they proceeded step by step: they observed the feedbacks, framed new hypotheses, thought up fresh interventions, tried to steer the family toward new experiences.

In conclusion, I would say that a lecture on the treatment of grave juvenile feeding problems should include an account of the case history of the families presenting patients with severe and disfiguring obesity.

Well, what I have to tell you is discouraging: such families do not present themselves for treatment. Unlike anorexia, obesity is not considered a threat to life, nor a source of guilt. In the two single cases we were able to examine, the failure of the obese subject to adhere to a diet was always helped along by the family who, while criticizing the patient's lack of will power, absentmindedly supplied him or her with the necessary provisions. This is a clear indication that obesity might well serve to maintain family equilibrium. While we should very much like to research such families, we may well have to wait until such time as the idea of family therapy makes further headway in our culture. That research would be very helpful since it would open the way for the relational study of many phenomena that are now labeled psychosomatic illnesses.

* * *

THE IDENTIFIED PATIENT IS NOT A SAINT

Pia's case provides a helpful clarification of the most misunderstood aspect of the fundamental distinction between hypothesis and intervention.

When Pia attained physiological independence, she came up against her mother, a woman incapable of slackening their intense and privileged relationship and of dropping the role of heroic mother, which had become her survival mechanism. Opposition, albeit passive, also came from the father (in the form of a lack of support for Pia), who had used his wife's great devotion to the daughter as a means of escape. Strategically, Pia's anorexia was a move set off by resentment of the obstacles that had been put up in her path and also an attempt to win the game of "putting the mother down" with the help of the same ploy—"It's not me but a force stronger than myself"—that she had seen her father use with such success. Now, though this was our hypothesis, it was not reflected in the intervention, which was, in fact, aimed at repunctuating the meanings the actors themselves attributed to their behavior and to do it in such a way as to challenge and to ridicule that behavior.

Obviously, the therapists did not really believe that Pia wished to sacrifice herself for her mother. The intervention was a paradoxical comment intended to bring out Pia's hostility toward her mother and to challenge the family view of Pia's anorexia.

Mara Selvini never thought that her patients were saints immolating themselves altruistically on the altar of family needs. This fact must nevertheless be stressed since there are many people, especially in the United States, who have mistaken Mara Selvini's paradoxical comments and positive connotations for so many expressions of a belief that the mentally ill nurse a sacrificial philosophy.

The fact that, in presenting his symptoms, the identified patient does not change the game and, indeed, frequently helps to perpetuate it, is not a sign of his benevolence but, on the contrary, reflects a determination not to violate the rules of the family game. In this connection I want to mention a statement by Mara Selvini (made during a discussion in 1983):

> Take the case of an anorectic girl. What a difference there is between an anorectic and a political prisoner who goes on a hunger strike! The rebel who goes on a hunger strike clearly defines the subject of his action, against whom it is directed, and its aim: "I am going on a hunger strike to force you, who wield political power, to change your *definition of your relationship* with my group or nation." The anorectic, by contrast, behaves in quite a different way, defining neither the subject nor the addressee nor the aim. He simply reduces his food intake on the pretext that he has no appetite, that he suffers from nausea or digestive problems, or that he feels bloated. In so doing he

plainly respects the family rule that no one ever takes any step in his own name; the symptom merely strengthens the family organization. This does not alter the fact that the maintenance of the *status quo* is not the result of benevolence on the part of the anorectic.

Every symptom, anorexia, attempted suicide, schizophrenia . . . shows that the situation is felt to be intolerable by the identified patient, who above all wants to punish the others for all the wrongs they have done him.

The fact that such interpretations are anything but arbitrary is borne out by the results of interventions advising patients to persevere: if Lina and Pia had really been filled with benevolence for their mothers (or interested in the homeostasis/ coherence of the system) they would have maintained their symptoms instead of abandoning them as suddenly as they did.

FAMILY RITUALS

The debut of the Center for Family Studies on the stage of international family therapy came at the end of 1974 with the publication in *Family Process* of an article entitled, "The Treatment of Children through Brief Therapy of Their Parents." This article reported a real innovation by the Milan group: the use of *rituals.*

Rituals are prescriptions that change the family rules without any explanations. A family that agrees to adopt a family ritual has an entirely new experience because the ritual proposes rules that differ from the old ones or, rather, contradict them.

Rituals are quite different from such simple prescriptions (or pieces of advice) as changing schools or homes so that mother and son are together less often, for example, but call for behavior at fixed times and in specific places, on one or on several occasions, in clearly defined ways. Family rituals must involve every member of the nuclear family; no one must be excluded.

The conviction that the family must be induced *to do rather than to understand,* which Mara Selvini also mentioned in her interview with Canevaro (see p. 95), not only reflects her abandonment of all parapedagogic or interpretive strategies but also her partial dissatisfaction with paradoxical interventions. True, the latter are not intended to improve insight but to elicit behavioral responses and consequent repunctuations of meanings, but they, too, proceed by way of a purely verbal communicative mode (digital or numerical codes). The invention of rituals thus reflected the new clinical and theoretical demands: to give pride of place to nonverbal communications (analogical and iconic codes). The cases of Tonino and Marella (see Chapter 10) have this in common: much as the change in, and redefinition of, the relationship between the child identified as a patient and the parents was not based on their words but rather on rituals (the contract or the funeral rite), the therapists did not proffer long explanations to their clients: the prescription (and execution) of the ritual was self-explanatory.

CHAPTER 10

The Treatment of Children through Brief Therapy of Their Parents

Mara Selvini Palazzoli, Luigi Boscolo,
Gianfranco Cecchin, and
Giuliana Prata

This is a report on the successful resolution of behavior problems
(encopresis and anorexia, respectively) in two small children
through the brief therapy of their parents. Treatment was based on
general systems theory and the cybernetic model and employed
interventions designed specifically to bring about rapid changes in
family interaction. The course of treatment, as well as the technical
problems arising out of such rapid changes, is discussed below.

Though no comprehensive theory of family therapy has been
put forward to date, it nevertheless seems possible to state a
common denominator: the trend away from the disturbed individual seen as an artificially isolated monad towards the study and the
treatment of dyads, triads, the entire nuclear family and, finally, of
the complex network of relationships in which every family is
embedded. However, beyond this one point of agreement, workers

This article was initially published in *Infanzia anormale* as "Un caso di
encopresi e un caso di anoressia infantile risolti con la psicoterapia breve dei
genitori" ("A case of encopresis and a case of infantile anorexia resolved through
the brief therapy of the parents"). With a few minor changes, the article was then
translated into English by P. Watzlawick (1974) and originally published in *Family
Process* 13:4.

in our fields are known to hold radically divergent views about questions of epistemology and practice, as described comprehensively by Beels and Ferber. These views range from models based on group dynamics in the psychoanalytic sense to role theory, learning theory, games theory, systems theory, and cybernetics.

After various trials and errors, our research team began in 1971 to adopt the theoretical model proposed in the late fifties and early sixties by the so-called Palo Alto Group under Gregory Bateson's theoretical leadership and the extensions of this model developed by Jay Haley in Philadelphia and by the Brief Therapy Center of the Mental Research Institute in Palo Alto. In terms of this model, the family is considered an interacting error-controlled system.

Our procedure is to have two co-therapists meet with the entire family (i.e., all members of the nuclear family actually living together) from the first session onward. The remainder of the team observes the sessions from behind a one-way mirror and after each session meets with the therapists to devise the interventions for the next session. The families are informed of this arrangement.

As a general rule, all sessions are held with the entire family, except when in the course of treatment it seems appropriate to deviate from this rule for the purpose of observing one of the subsystems or of making a specific intervention. In particular, there is one exception to this rule that we consider especially important. It has to do with those parents who seek therapy for behavioral problems in very young children (2 to 4 years old) or in older children who have already been traumatized by numerous medical and psychiatric interventions and are therefore already labeled "sick"—a label we do not wish to tie to them even more firmly. It may be objected that summoning the entire family is in and of itself an implicit communication that the problem is one of the family and not just of the identified patient. It is our experience, however, that the parents often inform their child of the forthcoming first visit with the implied message, "We have to go there because of you." It sometimes also happens that families are referred to us on the strength of some misconception about the center and contact us in the belief that they should "hand over" their youngster for individual treatment.

Since our first contact with the family is usually by telephone, we have set aside special hours for these calls so that we may talk at length and thereby avoid many mistakes and misunderstandings that may otherwise occur due to lack of time. The fact that treatment begins with this first telephone contact can hardly be stressed too much. The member of the team who takes the calls tries to obtain as much information as possible and immediately enters it on a fact sheet. He especially attempts to elicit as accurate a description of the problem as he can, as well as other information about the family's present situation and their real reasons for seeking help.[1]

If the call comes from the parents of a very young child, whose problem, in our view, is almost invariably the expression of a marital difficulty of the parents, or from the parents of a child who has already been traumatized by unsuccessful treatments, we usually invite only the parents to the first session in order to observe their interaction.[2]

During the first visit the therapists collect the information necessary to decide whether they should continue to work with the parents alone or whether the child should participate. In the following two cases, the team decided to continue the therapy with the parents alone. The reasons will soon become evident.

A CONTRACT FOR A CASE OF STOOL INCONTINENCE

An anxious mother called the Center about problems with her youngest child, Tonino, who was 9 years old. Since early child-

[1]This first telephone contact deserves special attention. It enables us to observe, and to note, a number of phenomena: disturbed communication, tone of voice, general attitude, peremptory demands for all kinds of information, immediate attempts at manipulation by requesting a certain date and hour for the interview or by imposing certain conditions, thus attempting a role reversal and making it appear as if the therapists were "looking for" the family. Except for a very few special cases, we have generally found it counterproductive to schedule the family for an emergency session.

[2]Exceptions are those families whose treatment has been discussed beforehand with a referring colleague who is seeing the child in individual therapy. In these cases the families have already been informed by the referring therapist that he considers it necessary for them to meet together for the purpose of observing them as a family group. This is the case, for instance, with autistic children.

hood Tonino had had a moderate encopresis problem that the mother had been prepared to tolerate until recently. The reason she now needed help was that in recent months the incontinence had worsened to an intolerable degree (he "messes his pants" at school almost every day) and the child had developed other "strange" forms of behavior as well, which had finally prompted the teacher to call his mother. Tonino not only entertained his school friends by telling them incredible stories in which he always played the role of the hero and which he firmly insisted were true, but he also "lied" in his compositions. For some time these had been full of grammatical and spelling mistakes, and he had been writing about "things which are neither here nor there."

In the first session the parents brought along two such compositions. In one of them, entitled "An Important Event in My Life," Tonino described with the verve (and the bad grammar) of a sports reporter his overwhelming victory at an imaginary Italian swimming championship for 8-year-old boys, allegedly held in Florence. In the other essay, called "How to Help Others," Tonino described at length his ferocious battle with a wolf during a recent Sunday trip into the mountains. He explained how, alerted by the screams of his oldest brother, he had rushed into a nearby forest and there, after a wild struggle, had managed to strangle this huge wolf that had sunk its teeth into the brother's arm and bitten it off. "That evening," concluded his essay, "I was pleased with what I had done, but somewhat dissatisfied because my brother had lost his arm."

The "mendacious" accounts that had so greatly shocked the elderly teacher thus revealed a Tonino for whom there was no other way of asserting himself. The parents explained that physically Tonino was the least fortunate of their four sons. He was short, puny, cross-eyed, and seemed to have spent a large part of his young life in "mending shops." He had had an operation for his strabismus at an early age and had since been wearing clumsy prescription glasses (which he frequently lost and which the mother promptly replaced with a new pair despite the considerable expense involved). Every week he was taken to an orthoptic specialist to exercise his eyes. He also suffered from a knock-kneed condition and had been made to wear, since the age of 4, heavy orthopedic shoes laced all the way up above his ankles. And now, the mother reported, it had also turned out that his permanent teeth were growing irregularly, and a radical program was under way to have a dentist pull some and straighten out the rest. It goes without saying that with all these treatments and other measures Tonino had been largely deprived of the psychophysical freedom necessary for a child's normal development. His brothers, on the other hand, were all handsome, healthy, and strong boys, especially the oldest (the one who had had his arm bitten off).

The observations of the parents, the description of their relationships with their respective families of origin, and much of what we could intuit about their relationship with Tonino all seemed highly significant. Tonino seemed to have been burdened with a series of problems that the parents had been unable to resolve in their own lives. The mother, still young and attractive, came from a family in which religious observance was pushed to almost fanatical extremes. When she had fallen in love and decided to marry her present husband, she had followed his example of rejecting certain religious practices, whereupon her mother had cursed her, saying that God would punish her: never would living children issue from her womb!

The first three years of her marriage had been spent in increasing anxiety about this curse since she did not, in fact, fall pregnant. After many unsuccessful attempts to benefit from help from specialists, she eventually turned to Padre Pio, a famous miracle healer, and was greatly consoled by him: he told her to go in peace, and children would soon come, like flowers in spring. The prediction turned out to be only too true: she had three sons, with only ten months between one birth and the next. After so much grace, the couple agreed (albeit with a great sense of guilt on the wife's part) to use birth control. But not even that worked: the totally unwanted conception of Tonino followed. With great embarrassment, the mother confessed that at first she had even felt tempted to have an abortion. But eventually she had resigned herself to her fate, hoping for the arrival of a baby girl. Who did arrive, however, but that ugly gosling, Tonino, the result of "grave sins" that called for heavy "retributions." The father, himself homely, puny, and cross-eyed, stated that he saw in Tonino all those negative aspects that made his own life miserable. He came from a broken family in which he had never received any affection and thus not only regretted having passed on to Tonino his own physical defects, but stated he felt a great need to protect and help him and to spare him his own suffering. As a result, he always agreed to whatever steps, regardless of cost, his wife proposed to "mend" Tonino.

At this juncture, then, the latest treatment, orthodontics, was to be followed by yet another and far more dramatic one: psychiatry. It was for this reason that we decided to spare Tonino the additional humiliation and to treat the parents alone. Our expectations were quite optimistic since the marital relationship seemed basically good. The parents appeared to respect each other, to be deeply concerned about Tonino's well-being, and sufficiently motivated to follow any prescriptions the therapists gave them. The chance for a decisive intervention came after the third session. A few days before their next session, the mother called in a state of great anxiety, informing us that she had taken Tonino to his orthoptic appointment and waited for him outside. After a while the ophthalmologist had come out of the exercise room and had asked her to follow her into another office. She told the mother that she was very worried about Tonino's mental state and that he probably needed psychiatric help. It turned out that Tonino had readily sat down in front of the viewer into which she had put slides the child was supposed to describe. What he did see, however, was something totally different, and he insisted that this was what he really saw. Thus, on viewing the last slide, showing a St. Bernard, Tonino looked up at her and stated delightedly, "I see . . . a large flock of colorful birds."

When the parents came to their fourth session, the mother was asked to call the ophthalmologist to find out whether the orthoptic exercises were still indispensable. The answer was no, since the condition had remained unchanged for quite some time and did not seem to be amenable to further improvement. The therapists then decided to have the parents enter into a contract with Tonino that was to be solemnly signed by all three parties. This contract was a kind of barter. The parents were to take Tonino aside and tell him in all frankness that they were fully aware how thoroughly fed up he was with treatment and specialists. They were also aware of the fact that he was now grown up and about to become a man. For this reason they had decided to cancel the appointment with the orthodontist; after all, it was not important for a male to have teeth as regular and perfect as those of the young ladies in toothpaste commercials. They were also willing to replace the special eyeglasses with normal ones and to terminate the sessions with the eye doctor. All this, however, was on condition that Tonino would recognize that he was now grown up and that he would once and for all agree not to soil himself any more. If he accepted these conditions, the contract was to be drawn up by the father and signed by all three of them.

We were told that Tonino did not hesitate for a moment; he immediately accepted the conditions and signed the document with his full signature, i.e., his two Christian names *and* his last name. The contract became valid at once and produced the expected results: the encopresis stopped immediately.

In the following session, and in addition to the terms of the contract, it was agreed that the father would initiate a sports program that was within Tonino's physical capabilities and from which his brothers were to be rigorously excluded. It was also considered necessary for the parents to inform the teacher of these decisions and of their reasons, hoping that Tonino would thus gradually also abandon his exhibitions at school.

Treatment was terminated after the seventh session, and it was agreed that the parents would call us in three months. This they did punctually, informing us that everything was going well. Tonino was very proud to have joined a group of hikers who were training for a mountain camp. This telephone conversation served as our follow-up. If the parents had told us that things were not going well, we would then have taken the entire family into treatment, as the absence of progress would have indicated that we were indeed faced with a more complex and rigid problem than we had originally assumed.

A FUNERAL RITE FOR AN ANORECTIC GIRL

A young married couple requested help for their daughter, Marella, who was 2 years and 2 months old and had been suffering from anorexia for the last six months. The call to us was made by the mother, who sounded anxious but controlled. In this very first contact, she already linked Marella's anorexia with the birth of a baby brother whom Marella had not yet seen. The reason for this was that the baby had remained in the hospital with septicemia, contracted four days after his birth, which had left him severely brain-damaged. Now, seven months later, he was still alive, but there was no hope for his survival. "For Marella he is only a sort of phantom"; this was how the mother literally described the situation. Her request for help followed a sudden worsening of Marella's eating problem. For the last two weeks, she had been on a veritable hunger strike, accepting only very small quantities of baby food and even those few spoonfuls only from persons other than her parents.

In the first session with the parents, their relationship pattern soon became evident: they maintained a complementary relationship in which the husband, whom we shall call Edoardo, clearly held the superior position. He was 30 years old, good-looking, dressed with casual elegance, and came from a wealthy family of local patricians, a large clan comprising four generations, complexly interrelated and headed by a centenarian grandmother. He worked with great indifference in one of the family's several business enterprises, but otherwise devoted every free moment to electronic music, his only real passion. He spent entire days in his music room, recording and composing, neglecting all social relationships and talking very little. He carried on as the "artist," with his head always in the clouds, thus signaling that he was not available for any request, especially not for a practical one.

The wife, whom we shall call Lucia, was extremely graceful and dressed with refined taste. She was emotional and vivacious and tried very cautiously but unsuccessfully to obtain from her hhusband some appropriate recognition of, and reaction to, her feelings. She came from a middle-class family, and it appeared that Edoardo married her more or less out of gratitude for having cured him of impotence. It was quite evident that Lucia tried very hard to adapt herself to the style of the husband's "great" family and to be accepted by them as a full member in her own right, but it also seemed that these efforts were rather unsuccessful.

Lucia was an only child and her parents' marriage was marred by a long neurological infirmity of her father. From adolescence on, Lucia seemed to have assumed the role of "somebody who thinks of everybody else and asks nothing for herself," who was efficient and always there when needed. She had never failed to help her mother, who came to depend heavily on her and demanded that she assume certain functions as head of the family. In keeping with this role, Lucia had also obtained a diploma as a Red Cross nurse.

She had continued to perform this role as a member of the husband's large clan. It was she who would come running when a need arose, who patiently listened to and cheered up the old melancholy aunts, who kept a check on the servants in the family's large country estate where everybody got together during the summer months. All of this was very convenient for everybody, including the husband, but it did not seem to confer any sign of distinction on Lucia. From some indications that emerged during the first session, it appeared that the noble family referred to her at best as "our dear Lucia." In this system of rigid complementarity, Lucia's increasingly frantic attempts to gain the desired recognition only served to reinforce in the members of the clan that very attitude of seignorial condescension that she wanted to change.

Her husband's relationship to her was not very different from that of the extended family. He was certainly not rude, quite the opposite—but he treated her with that slightly annoyed and condescending or amused expression that a grandseigneur would put on when disturbed in his elevated thoughts by the petty preoccupations of his butler.

As a result of this interaction, Lucia had turned all her attention to Marella, employing her usual style of omnipresent helper. The father, on the other hand, treated the little girl as being the mother's exclusive territory. It turned out that Marella had developed the habit of calling him in the shrillest of voices even when he was silently sitting next to her—it seemed that difficult to attract his attention.

The birth of the brain-damaged baby had upset this precarious balance. Marella was separated from her mother for many days, which were spent at her maternal grandmother's, and after the mother returned, Marella saw her disappear every afternoon to spend several hours at the hospital. What was amazing, but at the same time perfectly in keeping with Lucia's role, was that in order to protect Marella she had decided not to tell her about the baby brother's birth, let alone let her see him. She therefore explained to Marella that she went to the hospital to look after the child of a poor friend. "Since Matteo will not live," she said, "there is no need to complicate Marella's life." As far as the members of the clan were concerned, they had almost ignored Lucia's misfortune and after a few telephone calls had shown no further interest in it. Edoardo was certainly upset but could not, or did not want to, show his feelings to his wife.

The sudden worsening of Marella's anorexia, which had seriously reduced her weight, coincided with the family's return from a vacation with the clan. There was reason to believe that this visit had left Lucia exasperated, but she did not dare to say so. In the next session she expressed only her suffering in connection with her husband, who left all the problems and all the decisions to her. The girl refused all food from the parents. It became necessary to take her for every meal to the "little restaurant," i.e., the apartment of the maternal grandmother, who managed to make her swallow a few spoonfuls of mush.

During the three sessions following the initial interview, the therapists showed little interest in the girl's plight and cautiously tried to focus attention on the marital relationship. The spouses, however, appeared extremely defensive and very adept at changing the subject as soon as sensitive arguments were touched upon. The decisive moment occurred in the fifth session. The couple reported that Matteo had died a few days ago and had been buried in the family tomb. The mother, therefore, did not have to go to the hospital any longer, but Marella, whom the mother had again decided to leave in the dark, was eating even less. This time the father also seemed worried. It was obvious to us that the child, with her unusual sensitivity and intelligence, had understood a great deal from the very beginning. Her determination not to eat was now reinforced by this further conspiracy of silence.

We therefore decided to have the parents tell Marella the truth. But mere words would have obviously been insufficient. What was needed was a dramatization, a rite involving all three family members and designed to convey to Marella, who was only at the beginning of the verbal phase of her development, a clear and unequivocal message. Such a rite, it seemed to us, was also indispensable in view of the father's emotional distance, if he was to be involved in a dramatic, emotional experience consistent with that of his wife and daughter. We therefore prescribed that on the following day the official obsequies for the deceased child would take place in the garden of their house: Papa would have to explain to Marella in simple terms everything that had taken place. He had to set out the reasons for the pitiful lie, tell her that she had indeed had a little brother by the name of Matteo and that he had been the very ill baby that Mama had gone to see in the hospital. Now her baby brother was dead; he was no longer there but was buried in the family tomb at the cemetery. But it was important to bury his clothes as well, because Matteo was dead and did not need them any more. The parents agreed to carry out this ritual.

They went into the garden, where Papa dug a fairly deep hole into which, one after the other, Mama slowly laid the baby's clothes. Marella herself took a pair of little shoes and gently placed it on top of them. The parents were quite moved, as if it were a real funeral. Finally the father took the shovel again, filled the hole, and planted a tree on top of it.

That same afternoon Marella was found playing in her room, chewing with great appetite a large piece of bread that she had fetched from the kitchen. Since the phantom was not there any more, there was no longer any need to compete with it by means of eating mush. On the following day, Marella not only ate normally but showed further signs of great improvement. She stopped whining and clinging to her mother's skirts but for many days kept talking almost obsessively about her little brother, as if to reassure herself that it was finally possible to talk about him and to receive an answer. One day she asked her mother why she had never told her that the baby at the hospital was Matteo. When the mother said, "Because he was never here and would never have come home," Marella exclaimed, "But he *was* here, in that big tummy of yours," leaving the mother speechless.

In spite of the confidence the spouses gained through this rapid success (in five sessions), they signaled in various indirect ways that they were not willing, for the time being, to deal with the core problem of their marriage and their relationship with the extended family.

After discussing this in a staff meeting, the team decided to respect their resistance. Our experience had taught us that such joint resistances are insurmountable. Any attempt to meet them head on leads to negative results. One has to be modest and content with the successes achieved with the ostensible complaint. Moreover, in this particular case, we were convinced that by respecting their reluctance we would strengthen their rapport with the therapists, and this, of course, was an indispensable condition for any further course of treatment.

The couple came to see us again six months later. Marella had continued to do very well, and the wall of silence was broken. In this session, it was decided to have the wife meet with one of the co-therapists for some individual sessions to overcome the difficulties of her relationship with her husband's family.

DISCUSSION

The problem of deciding at what point to suspend or terminate treatment is specifically examined by our team in every single case. We have often wondered if it is right and honest to terminate therapy shortly after the identified patient's symptom. Have we perhaps worsened the situation? Have we perhaps deprived the family group of the indicator of its dysfunction? At this juncture we can only say that therapeutic interventions in family therapy do not merely affect one individual but the system as a whole: the disappearance of the symptom is always the expression of a change in the family's mode of interaction. It is, of course, possible that this change may be insufficient to guarantee further improvement. If so, it is up to the team to take that possibility into account and to make allowance for it. In the above-mentioned case, we decided to respect the couple's resistance and in doing so to convey to the spouses an implicit message intended to strengthen their feelings of trust, freedom, and spontaneity towards us. In other cases, we prefer to have the couple call us or come to a session at an appointed date within a few months. By means of this expedient we maintain the family "in therapy" and implicitly assure them of our continued interest and availability.[3]

As far as the technique of our approach is concerned, it should be pointed out that it is not based on the use of interpretation. While our experience may permit us to infer the past causes of a family's present behavior, we do not verbalize this, just as we do not point out to the family members what we see happening in the interviews or what their patterns of interaction are. We keep these observations to ourselves and use them to design our therapeutic interventions. As will have become evident from the above examples, our interventions are of an active-prescriptive kind, and through them we set out to change the interactions of the family as a whole. Obviously, they vary from one family to the next. But how do we go about changing these patterns?

In the course of our research we have discovered a kind of intervention that offers very encouraging results, and we have provisionally called this intervention, to be applied very early in the course of treatment, the *positive connotation*.[4] It consists of approving all observed types of behavior of the identified patient or the other family members, and especially those types of behavior that are traditionally considered pathological. For instance, in the cases we have just described we praised the attitude of the parents as admirable expressions of affection and concern. From sad experience we have learned that criticism of the parents (which,

---

[3]This raises another important question, that of the conclusion of therapy: should one continue with conjoint therapy, or keep the family ostensibly in therapy by means of making appointments in the distant future? Nowadays, with families that come for treatment with a symptomatic child, the alternative of continuing with the treatment of the couple no longer arises: the necessary and sufficient objective is to *extricate* the children from the trap of which the symptom is the most telling expression. Conjugal discord is seen chiefly as a maneuver intended to hold back the children and involve them in a triangular relationship.

If the two generations succeed in going their separate ways, then the conjugal conflict may cease (inasmuch as it has lost its ensnaring effect) or continue in chronic and incurable form, but fundamentally without a threat to either the children or the couple itself [Ed.].

[4]We are quite aware that from a systems-theoretical point of view this term is incorrect. On the other hand, conditioned as we are by the linear-linguistic model, "positive" helps us to make ourselves clear to others, at least until we hit upon a better name. In essence, a positive connotation is nothing but a metacommunication (about the system) serving as a *confirmation*.

incidentally, is "culturally" expected and secretly feared) can have no other effect than to produce indignant and negative reactions or, worse, depressive maneuvers of the "we-have-completely-failed" type, which then reduce the therapists to impotence (Montalvo and Haley 1973).[5]

We do not consider *positive connotation* a ploy or a trick. Quite the contrary, its use has enabled us to go beyond the causal-moralistic bounds of traditional psychiatry. We consider the observable behavior of a family in therapy to be self-corrective and thus tending to maintain the equilibrium of the system. A family who comes into therapy is usually a family in crisis, frightened by the possible loss of homeostasis and anxious to maintain it at all cost. If we were to tell them explicitly that they must change, it would make them form a virtually monolithic coalition the better to ward us off. To be accepted into the family system, we must approve of their behavior, no matter what it is, since it is directed at a more than understandable goal: the cohesion of the family. (Let us mention as an aside that none of our dysfunctional families has ever challenged this point of view.)

Through *positive connotation* we implicitly declare ourselves allies of the family's attempt to maintain homeostasis, and we do this at the moment that the family feels it is most threatened. By thus strengthening the homeostatic tendency, we gain influence over the ability to change, which is inherent in every living system.

Homeostatic tendencies and the ability to undergo change are, indeed, essential characteristics of living systems. Neither is inherently better or worse than the other; rather, the one cannot exist without the other. It is, therefore, not a question of "better or worse," but of "more or less."

Thus, it seems to us that the *positive connotation* is a therapeutic intervention of prime importance in attempts to change a family system. Change does not come about automatically, but rather as a result of a behavior prescription that is accepted and executed (thereby triggering the desired change) precisely because, paradoxically, the therapists have aligned themselves with

[5]In this connection, we feel that the gist of Montalvo's and Haley's (1973) article relates to this fundamental problem, i.e., how to avoid making the parents feel that they are on trial.

the homeostatic tendency. The therapeutic problem presented by each separate case is thus the design of a specific behavior prescription. Invariably, this prescription will be different for every family and will depend on its particular way of conceptualizing its problem.

* * *

POSITIVE CONNOTATION AND
THE PROBLEM OF GUILT

A second important innovation introduced in "The Treatment of Children through Brief Therapy of Their Parents," and examined at greater length in *Paradox and Counterparadox* (Selvini Palazzoli et al. 1978, pp. 55 ff.) is that of *positive connotation*. This intervention differs from the prescription of the symptom already known in psychotherapy (see the so-called *reverse psychology*, Milton Erikson's work, Palo Alto school, et cetera), inasmuch as it prescribes and encourages not just the symptoms of the identified patient, but also the behavior and attitude of all those in his immediate environment.

Today we no longer define positive connotation as an intervention, but rather as a strategy to foster the collaborative involvement of the family by counter-balancing those guilt feelings, especially of the parents, that appear whenever family therapy is indicated.

In our more recent theoretical papers the reader will no longer encounter the concept of positive connotation, which has been incorporated in that of neutrality (Selvini Palazzoli et al. 1980).

From the clinical point of view as well, I have the impression that Mara Selvini now makes less use of positive connotation than her writings from 1974 to 1975 would indicate.

Positive connotation (for example, in association with the prescription of the symptom) is strongly provocative for the patients. While describing them as generous people who sacrifice themselves for the family, we simultaneously present them, implicitly, as puppets. The required effect may also be obtained by negative connotation, which explicitly holds certain forms of behavior up to ridicule and so prevents them.

The choice between one method and another is difficult. It depends on the phase of therapy. Positive connotation may be helpful during the first sessions in order to obtain better cooperation from the family. Explicit criticism is better reserved for the last phase of the treatment when it can provide the final "push," especially if consistent changes have already taken place. In that sense it is also possible that, as the sessions proceed, the therapist's contributions become increasingly explanatory, precisely because the change in behavior that has taken place reflects a change in insight.

The concept of positive connotation was first elaborated in connection with two crucial and closely connected problems: alliances between the therapists and various members of the family, and the attachment of blame (or disapproval). Having to give a positive connotation to the behavior of *all* members of the family already combines the *germ* of the concept of neutrality developed in Mara Selvini's later work.

SHOULDERING RESPONSIBILITY: THE DELICATE BALANCE BETWEEN BLAMING AND WHITEWASHING

The ideas I shall be putting forward in this section reflect the "binocular vision" resulting from comparing my work as a private psychotherapist with the experience of working in a public psychiatric center (Covini et al. 1984).

The practice of family therapy, certainly in the past and sometimes also in the present, often involves blaming of the family for the symptom being presented; the family is *explicitly* held responsible by the therapist. That process can take many different forms; it ranges from Fromm-Reichmann's "schizophrenogenic mother" to the antipsychiatrists' "murderous family," from Satir's "confusion of communication" to Minuchin's "parental failure to play their proper role," to mention just a few.

The experience I gained during those years has taught me that such blame-attachment produces completely negative effects. I was not, of course, the first to arrive at this conclusion: Haley and Montalvo (1973), in a now classic article, went so far as to heap irony on the type of family therapy that reveres traditional forms of child psychoanalysis for its moralistic and accusatory overtones. As Mara Selvini put it, after certain negative experiences in her psychoanalytic and communicationalist periods, she took the road of positive connotation and neutrality, thus joining cultural battle against the accusatory approach to family therapy and, at the same time, against the transfer of the pathological label from the individual to his family.

The indictment (by this legal term I mean open disapproval or accusation) of the parents and of other members of the family has negative effects because it causes resentment of, and lack of collaboration with, or trust in, the therapist, together with symmetrical opposition and the refusal to follow prescriptions in order to satisfy the unspoken desire of making the family therapy fail and hence clearing oneself of the charge: "We too have tried family therapy, but it has served no purpose, because none of this was our fault." No less paralyzing and nontherapeutic is the exact opposite of indictment, namely whitewashing. If a family with an identified patient becomes entrenched in the defensive belief that the patient's suffering has no connection with family relationships (past or present) but is a purely *biological condition* or some mysterious manifestation, then the developmental aspect of the symptom (inasmuch as it is brought to a head by these relationships) will be suppressed; the dysfunctional game is maintained because nothing is called into question and everyone is cleared of any blame. This is in fact the approach of biomedical psychiatry and helps to render the position chronic. It follows that therapy, precisely because it aims at changing the ongoing dysfunctional game, must call into question the behavior of *all* the actors.

Their involvement must not, however, be elicited by indictments, for these merely stimulate defensive rejection and foster the view that the symptom is a purely individual one.

Attaching responsibility is a therapeutic strategy based on

the implicit and carefully measured apportionment of what in common language is called "guilt."

It is evident that family therapy as such, at least in our culture, implies that the patient's problem is caused by a family dysfunction. Even if the term "family therapy" is not mentioned explicitly, the interview establishing a connection between the symptom and the behavior of various members of the family cannot escape inculpating the assembled company. To some extent this fact may be said to convey an important message: the family, faced with their own responsibility, is thrown into a crisis and may thus be propelled into a spontaneous change or into relational therapy.

The families that come to a private family therapy center have very often had serious charges leveled at them and ask for therapy simply in order to be vindicated. The charges do not necessarily come from the outside (from psychiatric workers, for example) but can also be part of the intrafamilial game; for example, a father who is accused by his wife may ask for family therapy not so much because he is anxious to help his son identified as a patient (and who suits him admirably as a ball and chain around his wife's legs) but because he wants to be cleared and have the accusations turned back against his wife.

However, Mara Selvini quickly spotted the danger of building family therapy exclusively on the idea that clients come to be cleared of charges and to seek justification, and she appreciated the need for marking the therapeutic context as a nonjudicial one and for using such tactics as giving a positive connotation to the actions of all members of the family. To obtain true collaboration from the family, the burden of guilt must be lifted. This experience in the private context was responsible for the widespread belief that Mara Selvini looked upon positive connotation not as a specific tactic but as a basic principle of family therapy. That explains why the idea was "exported" into the public mental health sector, where it gave rise to grave errors.

In the public sector it appeared after many frustrating failures that the indiscriminate use of positive connotations was absurd, especially in the early treatment of clients with grave psychotic problems. Their families had gone through the most painful crises, but thanks to the collusion of the biomedical services (hospitalization and sedation, for example), they had been able to ignore any family connection with the problem and to maintain a completely individual interpretation of the crisis ("organic illness," "constitutional," "character," "drug abuse") or even a tacit magical or demoniacal interpretation; in any case, these interpretations had helped to build a very strong line of defense against all possible charges of "contributory negligence" by the patient's family.

Giving the behavior of such families a positive connotation in an attempt to coax them into therapy merely reinforces the users' chronic attitudes developed by medical and social-service routines.

In recent times we have made an experimental study of how such families can be usefully involved in the therapeutic process by being made to *shoulder responsibility* for it. Carefully avoiding all accusations ("It's your fault that he's mad," "The real madmen are you"), we simply stress the fact that family therapy is strongly indicated and so make the family responsible for any possible rejection of the cure and hence for perpetuating their relative's chronic condition. Extreme clarity and strong conviction in proposing family therapy seem the more essential the more the users are opposed to psychotherapeutic interventions either because of their cultural background or because of their family game.

The appropriate message is a very complex one and constitutes the fundamental basis of the therapeutic process. In fact, it implies shouldering a double responsibility:

1. The family members are made to feel participants in the process that has caused one of them to develop a symptom. Such participation implies co-responsibility but no actual guilt, inasmuch as the contribution of each member, though part of the problem, has been quite involuntary—it is an inherent part of a game (and events) not dependent on the good will of the individual actors.

2. The members of the family are held responsible for the outcome of the therapy: their strict adherence to the therapists' prescriptions is crucial to the success of the treatment.

In the early phase of the treatment the stress is laid on the first type of responsibility: the family is accepted for treatment because it is involved in the problem, but at the same time it is absolved from the linear accusation of being its *cause*. *This message must never be explicit* but must take the form of a combination of implicit messages: the statement that family therapy is indicated, the nature of the sessions, the type of intervention, the repunctuations that set off the unconscious sacrifice or "patientification" of a member, or the role of the parents as the child's co-therapists.

As the treatment proceeds, however, the second type of responsibility takes over: the therapist, this time in so many words, underlines how much the success of the therapy depends on strict adherence to his directives.

This definition of the therapeutic process as a double process of delegating responsibility strikes me as a useful means for overcoming a series of difficulties or contradictions that keep cropping up in team discussions. In fact, for some time, Mara Selvini's team had been setting limits to indiscriminate positive connotations: not only as I have said, with certain therapeutic interventions in the public health sector, but also in private family therapy. Thus it was found that negative connotation,[6] sometimes quite explicitly, could help couples in which the symptom was bound up with the arrogant behavior of one of the spouses. In other cases, Mara Selvini Palazzoli used a technique aimed at frustrating dysfunctional games involving flattering or deprecatory attitudes by making satirical remarks directed explicitly against the person using such behavior. In fact, the problem of whether or not negative connotations are needed is badly posed.

[6]Or "patientification," which is different, because it stresses the involuntary nature of the type of behavior involved [Ed.].

The problem is not so much one of either/or as one of more or less, that is, of a delicate balance between elements that invariably occur together. The therapist must avoid open accusations, yet must also make sure that the family does not come to feel they have nothing to do with the condition of the identified patient. In the light of its pragmatic effects, every therapeutic intervention is bound to be a mixture of blame and absolution, of collaboration, and of distrust. The various aspects cannot be dissociated; all the therapist can do is to determine the "dosage" and the choice of an explicit or an implicit approach.

In private family therapy centers it is almost unavoidable to use positive connotations at the start, because the very act of attendance often has an inculpating effect. In the public sector, by contrast, given the great variety of expectations and means of access, determining *to what extent the members of the family feel part of the problem* is a key problem; in fact it is on the basis of that determination that the therapeutic strategy used during the consultation phase of the relationship must be based.

My earlier views (Selvini et al. 1982) notwithstanding, I believe today that the advantages of public psychiatric centers over private family therapy centers do not so much stem from the fact that attending them seems less of an admission of guilt as from the fact that they offer the therapist a chance of working with a fairly unsifted clientele and hence of using the diagnostic and consultation contexts freely for therapeutic interventions (it is only in this sense that I continue to speak of strategies for smuggling therapy through).

Mara Selvini, too, in her private center, systematically defines the first family sessions as consultations needed to decide whether or not family therapy is indicated. Clearly the situation in public psychiatric centers, precisely because of the relative vagueness of the nature of the out-patients' department and the much more varied expectations, leaves greater room for maneuver, that is, for suggesting and deploying a much greater range of interventions.

These advantages do not, however, imply that therapy in the public sector is simpler than it is in the private. In particular, a private family therapy center has the following advantages: (1) a selected clientele (only patients who have been invited to enter into family therapy), (2) the prestige of being referred to a renowned specialist or a well-known center (as against the anonymity of a public clinic), and (3) case histories that, at least within certain limits, are more homogeneous (for example, due to the prevalence of identified patients accompanied by their parents).

The public sector, for its part, offers advantages of a different kind: the intervention often comes at an earlier stage, and the tactics used in accepting the case—no matter what the expectations—are an integral part of the therapeutic strategy, thus obviating one drawback of private practice, where diagnoses and referrals inevitably involve other specialists.

I would like to say one thing more on the subject of guilt. The reader will remember that in the case of Lina,[7] the intervention was based on the wish not to inculpate the grandmother. Why? Because, as we shall see in the case of Sala, structural interventions, designed to remove disturbing members of the family discreetly rather than based on negative connotations, facilitate a *peaceful renegotiation* of the relationships between such persons and the nuclear family. Accusations threaten to fan an intrafamilial conflict, not only by sabotaging the therapy (through the creation of a sworn enemy) but also by impeding all redefinitions and maintaining an (increasingly negative) ambiguous bond with the accused member.

Similar precautions (avoiding the attribution of blame; allowing a peaceful and painless renegotiation of the relationships) must also be taken when it comes to the internal relationships of the nuclear family and to the relationship between them and the therapeutic team: any conflict threatens to "glue" the contenders in the irrational defensive stance they adopted at the beginning.[8]

[7]See pp. 103–105 [Ed.].

[8]Stefano Cirillo, in his valuable comments on the above account, has rightly pointed out that the noninculpation of important members of the extended family is a *tactic* adopted systematically when these members are present at a session; in their absence we often use strategies that inculpate them, for the express purpose of effecting their exclusion and hence of clearly delimiting the boundaries of the nuclear family [Ed.].

HYPOTHESES: SPECIFICITY AND ORIGINALITY

Another important concept merely hinted at in the last lines of "The Treatment of Children through Brief Therapy of Their Parents" is that of the specific nature of every prescription: every prescription must be considered in relation to the particular way in which a given family sees its own problem. It is on this idea that the intervention subsequently, and somewhat misleadingly, described as "counterparadox" is based: a therapeutic strategy or repunctuation used to upset the philosophical or epistemological beliefs of the family. Such repunctuations must be guided by information gathered during sessions but, at the same time, must explain the behavior of the various members of the family in ways that differ radically from the usual view held by the family. The novelty is the different but convincing way of fitting the pieces of the *puzzle*, i.e., of the facts, forms of behavior, and perceptions the family has used or reported.

One of the main criteria in assessing the validity of a hypothesis on a relational game is precisely to confront it with the view of the problem held by members of the family.

Any therapist must start from the assumption that it is essential to prevent the client from continuing to define his problem in a repetitive way, using what punctuations and prejudices he has constructed in the course of time. People requesting psychotherapy have usually exhausted the solutions allowed by *their* view of the problem. The therapist's object is therefore to prevent them from continuing to define the problem in the old way.

If the therapist's hypothesis coincides with the view of the problem adopted by all or some members of the family, then it will be most likely that the therapist's hypothesis is wrong and hence therapeutically ineffective. He will find it impossible to throw the system into disarray (which requires novel inputs); he can only be trapped in perverse alliances and in impotent involvement in, and enslavement to, the dysfunctional rules of the family.

Here I shall not dwell on repunctuation and counterparadox, subjects to which I shall be returning, but merely wish to stress that both are theoretical anticipations[9] of the view that a therapeutic strategy must not be based on observable behavior alone but also on what members of the family say and what the therapists can infer from the members' joint or several ways of viewing their problem and of justifying their own behavior. This is a fundamental advance and highlights the radical difference between Mara Selvini's approach and the neobehaviorism implicit in the concept of the "black box" as developed in *Pragmatics of Human Communication* (Watzlawick et al. 1967).

[9]Similar anticipations were found in "Context and Metacontext" and in "Racism in the Family" [Ed.].

PART FOUR

SELF-STARVATION

CHAPTER 11

Self-Starvation: The Last Synthesis on Anorexia Nervosa

Matteo Selvini

Her new team helped Mara Selvini to make a most encouraging study of families with anorectic patients. These studies led her to the original reflections first published in London in 1974 in a book entitled *Self-Starvation: From the Intrapsychic to the Transpersonal Approach to Anorexia Nervosa.*[1] This book was of striking originality: Mara Selvini, instead of writing a completely new text, accepted the challenge of making the reader privy to her psychoanalytical reflections prior to her break with individual therapy and her leap into family therapy.

Though devoted to anorexia nervosa, the logical and didactic structure of the book was the same as that of the present account; it retraces a clinical and theoretical path step by step. In order to give the reader a better understanding of Mara Selvini's psychoanalytical views I have included in this volume

---

[1]Parts I to III of that book were translated from the 1963 Italian edition of *L'anoressia mentale,* but amplified and reelaborated by Mara Selvini while still using a psychoanalytical approach (from 1963 to 1967). However, Part IV presents the new family approach to anorexia elaborated from 1967 to 1973. *Self-Starvation* has since appeared in various languages: here we need only mention the American edition (New York: Jason Aronson, 1981) [Ed.].

(Chapters 12, 13, and 14) the full text of the most significant chapters of Parts II and III: "The Problem of Death and Suicide in Anorexia Nervosa," "Interpretation of Anorexia Nervosa by the Object-Relation Theory," and "Some Hints on Psychotherapeutic Conduct."

Part IV of *Self-Starvation* is representative of the early phases (1971–1973) of the Selvini-Boscolo-Cecchin-Prata collaboration. It was a predominantly communicationalist period. "The Family of the Anorexic Patient: A Model System" (Chapter 15 in this book) adopts the structure of Haley's famous study on the schizophrenic family, whose title, in fact, it paraphrases. The family of anorectic girls is said to communicate more clearly than the schizophrenic family and to stress rejection rather than disconfirmation; however, in both types of family, no member is capable of taking the lead in his own name.

If we now look at the chapter on the use of therapeutic interventions (Chapter 16 here) we shall find striking illustrations of how communicationalist hypotheses of the type we have already met led to the choice of interventions *based explicitly on teaching the correct way of communicating*, very much in the style of Satir. In that chapter, the section "Interventions into the Problem of Leadership" is cleary based on the view expressed in *Pragmatics of Human Communication* that metacommunication is a source of clarity and hence of mental health.

These and similar assertions are characteristic of the vacillations and contradictions that marked those years. The passages were, in fact, written in 1972–1973,[2] and as early as 1974 Mara Selvini declared in "The Treatment of Children through Brief Therapy of Their Parents"[3] that her approach was not

[2]The manuscript of *Self-Starvation* was sent to the British publishers in the spring of 1973 [Ed.].

[3]Disappointed by the restricted viewpoint of the Italian psychiatric establishment, Mara Selvini had become convinced that it was best to publish as much as possible abroad. Even earlier, she had published "The Obsessive and His Wife" in French, and "Racism in the Family" had been immediately translated for publication in the London journal *Human Context* (4:624–629) in 1972. Mara Selvini herself was the Italian editor of that journal from 1969 to 1975, when *Human Context* ceased publication. One of the problems of publishing original work in Italy was the absence of a suitable journal. Thus Mara Selvini published many of

based on the use of interpretations and that she did not point out their patterns of interaction to families.

Thus, in the same year, Mara Selvini makes two conflicting statements. However, the contents of the articles published in *Family Process* reflect the future research program while the parapedagogical tactics were about to be discarded as the final residue of an outworn strategy.

The process of discarding explanatory techniques while retaining a communicationalist approach was a signpost on the road to an *implicit pedagogy of communication,* in which therapists serve as models of a nonrejecting communicative style while criticizing the communicative incongruities of the family by nonverbal means.

The example of the Crippa family in Chapter 16 is an interesting illustration of this implicit pedagogy of communication. For tackling the problem of internal alliances in the family of anorectics, the communicationalist theories used at the time were gradually combined with research into the specific transactional game involved in such systems. A great many aspects of relational games were explained and examined; attention was drawn to the widespread taboo prohibiting the explicit alliance of two members against a third. One aspect of this general rule is the denied double coalition or hidden double enticement.

In "The Family of the Anorexic Patient" (Chapter 15) Mara Selvini discusses how the patient is forced into an impossible position. She is continually invited to ally herself with the father against the mother, and *vice versa.* Worse still, each of the parents, deeply disillusioned with the other, secretly encourages the patient to make up for the partner's shortcomings. As a result, the patient finds herself playing the role of secret wife and secret

---

her articles in the *Archivio Psic. Neu. Psich.* of the Catholic University, Milan (where she became lecturer in psychology in 1965), an ineffective means of propagating her ideas, at least to the type of reader she tries to address. The problem was solved by publishing regularly abroad, above all in *Family Process,* a journal also read by Italian specialists. Later, the publication of the journal *Terapia familiare,* founded in Rome in June 1977, filled the vacuum in Italy, at least to some extent [Ed.].

husband all at once, dividing her sympathy equally between her parents. Similar hypotheses were also framed in the case of the Salas, which will be described in Chapter 26.

As for the parental couple, one type of symmetrical relationship is the one just described. Mara Selvini states that moralistic partners, who both consider themselves the victims of a compulsory relationship, will inevitably compete with one another for moral superiority, the simplest way of doing this being to appear as the victim. This is a sort of "symmetry through sacrificial escalation."

Another hypothesis is based on the covert paternal seduction of the anorectic daughter. To cope with it, father and daughter are brought face to face for the purpose of unmasking the father's confused messages and eliciting clarifying reactions.

With *Self-Starvation*, Mara Selvini wanted to end her role as specialist in anorexia nervosa, which she felt had become too confining: in 1974 she began to turn her attention to schizophrenia and infantile psychoses. Her specific interest in the family of anorectics waned to the point that her references to the subject were increasingly confined to making helpful comparisons with other dysfunctional types of family organization.

The chapters that follow contain the full text of the chapters just mentioned, as well as the one entitled "The Cybernetics of Anorexia Nervosa" (Chapter 17).

CHAPTER 12

The Problem of Death and Suicide in Anorexia Nervosa

Mara Selvini Palazzoli

Many authors have stressed that anorexics have a strong self-destructive urge; thus Boss (1955) speaks of suicide in "refractive doses" when referring to those patients who, in their innermost selves, refuse absolutely to live as beings of flesh and blood. "They are totally lost to the therapist: using their own method right to the end they allow themselves to evaporate and dissolve."

This highly suggestive interpretation of gradual suicide raises a number of questions. In the first place we must ask ourselves whether the desire for self-annihilation, the suicidal drive of these patients, is conscious, even though dissimulated, or unconscious. In the second place we must determine why, having discovered the apparently intolerable burdens of the flesh (the pressure of physical demands and the body's inevitable decay) they do not put an end to themselves there and then, instead of soldiering on at the price of atrocious sacrifices over many years.

Let me try to answer these difficult questions by drawing on my own therapeutic experience.

From *Self-Starvation*, 1981 ed., pp. 80–83.

From my direct contact with anorexic patients, and from reading their diaries and hearing the confessions of those I was able to cure, I am convinced that not one of them has ever had a conscious wish for annihilation by suicide. (As pointed out on p. 170, the suicide of Anna Maria was in fact unconnected with her anorexia as such.) Nosographically, too, I have never observed anorexics in the kind of depressive state that often leads to suicide, and, in fact, anorexia nervosa patients never deliberately end their lives by direct measures. This, we found, is also reflected in their Rorschach protocols. Moreover, their pathological picture does not even involve an unconscious suicidal wish: psychodynamic studies have shown that their "choice" of emaciation does not serve to remove or displace the real object of their conflict in the manner that common neurotic mechanisms do. It was precisely this bias on the part of many psychoanalysts that was responsible for the failure to cure such patients. Their wish to be thin is perfectly conscious, as is their struggle to keep control of their oral needs and the resulting sense of security, however precarious and unrealistic it may be. No authentic anorexic ever considers her symptom absurd or makes a real effort to eat copious meals; all of them consider their behavior perfectly justified (I am speaking of the prechronic phase, that is, of the phase before various clinical and therapeutic interventions persuade them to *feign* illness).

The true anorexic has a deep and lasting horror of obesity, completely untempered by introspection—it reflects a deliberate decision that must never be renounced. The resulting struggle takes the form of alternate bouts of bulimia and the most stringent fasts, or of unbridled greed and total self-abnegation; but however often the patient succumbs to the demands of the body, her mind is made up that the body can and must be subdued in the long run. But this *type of acarnality is not a death wish*—quite the contrary. It is, essentially, an unrealistic tension and a rejection of existence *qua* living and dying in one's body. More precisely it is a rejection of death as a biological fact, and with it a rejection of aging, corpulence, and existential decay. In short, the anorexic turns her back on the existentially inevitable, on everything that is imposed by, and inherent in, her corporeality.

In two of my cases, the illness appeared quite suddenly after the death of someone they loved, and was preceded by a state of shock and of intense revulsion at the idea of such irreparable loss. In a third case (a probationary nurse) the illness started immediately after her first attendance at an autopsy, for which her rudimentary training had ill prepared her.

This patient, to whom I was the first to give a psychological examination although she had been chronically ill for ten years and had been hospitalized, had never once mentioned this unfortunate episode. It was only when she was given a Rorschach test that she suddenly "saw" an open abdomen and the exposed intestines in many Rorschach cards, thus reliving, and offering associations with, the traumatic experience of the autopsy. "I saw that open abdomen . . . full of stinking bowels . . . and I thought to myself . . . there used to be a soul here . . . and I rebelled!" This patient, who had reached the most extreme state of cachexia (height: 5'2"; weight: 50 lbs) but was still remarkably lively, looked highly skeptical when her doctor told her that she was close to death. She was firmly convinced that she had finally broken through the barrier of physical corruption.

In fact anorexics look upon their possible deaths as so many accidents, but never as something they themselves may be courting. We saw that anorexics, unlike certain psychotics, do not refuse food altogether but merely reduce their food intake to absurdly low levels. Their emaciated bodies are their guarantee that they are winning the fight against passive surrender to greed, so much so that whenever they lost weight for intercurrent reasons (fevers, dental complications, etc.) they pride themselves on this extra loss as yet another victory over their demanding bodies.

These patients play with death like children who think they can disappear by shamming dead. Incapable as they are of facing reality or even, as we shall see, of comprehending their own physical needs, they delude themselves into thinking that they can tamper with their bodies as they please. This I have observed with utter astonishment even in one of my patients who was a doctor, who, in theory at least, was fully familiar with her biological processes and nevertheless treated her own body in the most absurd and antiscientific, and sometimes even magical, way, thus ignoring the most elementary tenets of medical science.

All those who have observed patients in the terminal phase of the disease have been struck by their severe state of psychological regression and their divorce from biological reality. They are in no way depressed or sorry for themselves and do nothing to avert their impending death; but they also take no deliberate steps to hasten their end and show no signs of waiting or hoping for death. This attitude is maintained obstinately and persistently, until extreme organic exhaustion sets in. The accompanying mental state is one of emotional dullness and indifference reminiscent of that of patients debilitated by a long history of chronic organic disease. The suicide of Ellen West described by Binswanger (1959) was an exceptional case: to this unusually gifted woman, death was the mystical personification of salvation from an imprisoned existence, and hence an authentic choice, a *dies festus*. Ellen did not, as Boss (1955) would have put it, trade total suicide for a suicide in *refracta dosi*: to the last she tried bravely to preserve her existence through anorexia, but when, after fifteen years of torment, she came to appreciate the futility of her struggle, she tragically put an end to it.

CHAPTER 13

Interpretation of Anorexia Nervosa by the Object-Relation Theory

Mara Selvini Palazzoli

My psychotherapeutic observations of patients whose capacity to recognize, and distinguish between, body stimuli had been impaired in various ways have convinced me that only a psychodynamic theory based on object relations (particularly on relations with the negative aspects of the introjected object) can make a substantial contribution to the psychopathology of body experience. I was led to this conviction in a very simple way: because all authorities are agreed that the child's original experience with the primary object is a corporeal-incorporative experience, I was persuaded that the incorporation of the negative aspects of the primary object, with the ensuing repression and defense against the return of that object to consciousness, must provide the dynamic foundations of psychopathological body experiences.

In the early phase, the incorporation of the object is inevitable. There is no other way of relating to it. The child's fundamental experiences with his object are body experiences. The experience of goodness and well-being is a body experience, and so is that of

From *Self-Starvation*, 1981 ed., pp. 84–95.

evil and discomfort. Moreover the child can only distinguish himself bodily from his object at a comparatively advanced stage.

We must now discuss what we mean by a child's "good" and "bad" body experiences. This is a point on which the literature is extremely vague. Terms such as oral frustration or poor feeding conditions often recur, but the types of mothers and the different children discussed vary considerably.

I would like to suggest the following general definition of a *good* body experience: to feel one's body, in the relationship with the mother, as a source of predominantly pleasurable sensations, but without premature genital excitation, which, because of its aggressive component, would lead to anxiety. This means treating the child's primary relation with the good object as a pleasant erotization of the cutaneous, mucous, oral, gastric, and passive-motor elements of the body. Only later does the genital aspect come into play, associated with a small amount of aggressiveness (the genital play studied by Spitz). The child, who cannot yet perceive distinct objects, experiences his own body as a good object.

When this process is thwarted by defective emotional relations with that object, a pathological situation arises. In that case the child, because he cannot perceive himself as distinct from the object, may feel his own body as a source of unpleasant or bad sensations. As a result he comes to consider it as bad in itself or else as being inhabited by a bad object.

Psychoanalysis has taught us that personality development is based on the individual's relation with his own body, *from the moment he perceives it as a whole, as existing outside the maternal object. In cases of psychopathological body experience*, the condition of being "outside" is realized in part only. Most of the "bad" experiences of his own body, which the child has met during the incorporative, primary narcissistic, phase of his object relationships, remain immured inside his body. *In these circumstances, all the "bad" experiences he encounters during the subsequent phase of secondary narcissism and later* (disidentification) will be repetitions of the patterns laid down during the primary-incorporative, archaic phase.

In my attempt to account for the patient's "choice" of psychopathological bodily experience, I have emphasized the primary incorporative phase. However, I do not wish to give the impression that I underestimate the importance of all the later interpersonal experiences of childhood, the latency period and adolescence. In different cases they may compensate for, or aggravate, the consequences of the defective primary object relation. The negative consequences of defective interpersonal relations in early childhood on the later phases of development will become apparent in what follows.

On the basis of the above assumptions I suggest the following working hypothesis.

Psychopathological body experiences are a direct expression of a libidinal and aggressive emotional relationship with negative (exciting-rejecting) aspects of the incorporated object.

Let us now consider the bearing of these remarks on anorexia nervosa.

What is the body experience of the anorexic? Should anorexia nervosa be considered a defense against an oral-sadistic impulse? Some writers, under the influence of Melanie Klein, have suggested that the anorexic girl tries, by not eating, to deny her impulse to destroy the primary object; in brief, she tries to repress her cannibalistic impulses. I am rather skeptical of this interpretation. I consider it arbitrary, because it fails to consider the clinical and phenomenologic data that alone can provide a basis for a valid psychodynamic theory.

Patients in a predominantly schizo-paranoid situation with oral-sadistic impulses organize their defenses against a reactivation of their condition by developing either delusional ideas about being poisoned, or fears of not being able to eat, or an actual block against food. This block is completely involuntary and is accompanied by severe irritation, a preoccupation with starvation, and intense feelings of physical damage and decay. Thus one of my nonanorexic patients always carried a bottle of milk with him. He would take advantage of any loosening of his block by taking a few sips from the bottle.

The clinical picture presented by the anorexia nervosa patient is altogether different. She is not the passive victim of a total or sporadic block in her food intake, but reduces it to absurd levels with consistent determination. The most important point is that, once she has consumed food, especially in what, by her standards, are large quantities, she does not feel that her body is being *threatened* or destroyed, but thinks that it has become bloated, ominous, and in the way.

The basic symptoms of anorexia nervosa are therefore: persistent hunger (which is generally disguised and only admitted after long familiarity with the therapist) and a deliberate struggle against it. Hunger pangs may completely disappear in the terminal phases or when excessive starvation and the continuous use of laxatives cause disturbances in the electrolyte balance and lead to ketonaemia.

In short *the body has become a threatening force that must be held in check rather than destroyed.* This is the crucial phenomenon by which anorexia nervosa can be distinguished from similar syndromes. In my view the classic oral-sadistic approach cannot explain why the anorexic should feel after every meal that her body, far from being damaged or threatened, has become intolerably bloated.

This raises the problem of whether the anorexia nervosa patient is afraid of food or of her body. My answer is that she is afraid of her body, and that *she experiences food intake as an increase of the latter at the expense of her ego.*

To the anorexic, *being a body* is tantamount to being *a thing.* If the body grows, the thing grows as well and the "person" starts to shrink. The fight against the body is thus a desperate fight against reification—paradoxically so, because while refusing to be a thing the anorexic fights her battle, not on a spiritual plane, but rather on a purely material one: that of her own body.

Now let us ask how the anorexic acquires this particular experience of her body. In my view she does so by equating it with the incorporated object, namely the mother, in its negative, overpowering aspects, the better to oppose it and to separate it from the ego.

I should like to emphasize that the body of the anorexic does not merely *contain* the bad object but that it *is* the bad object. From the phenomenological point of view, the body is experienced as having all the features of the primary object as it was perceived in a situation of oral helplessness: all-powerful, indestructible, self-sufficient, growing, and threatening. No active aggression enters into the clinical picture or into the patient's dreams: there is an unconscious feeling that the object is far too strong to be destroyed. The result is a dejected feeling of complete helplessness. Liliana, for instance, had the following dream: "I am standing in front of my mother. I would like to do something, but my feet are two bleeding stumps." (Very occasionally a feeble compensatory aggressive fantasy makes its appearance.) She was still a poor and totally helpless child, both biologically and psychologically, when confronting the impervious object. That object did not so much frustrate her *oral* drives and needs as it frustrated the needs of her ego. As another patient, Rita, put it: "I have never been left to experience things in my own way. This is the worst loss anyone can suffer. It leads to emptiness, to a lack of emotional contact with life, to a lack of real vitality, of whatever makes you feel yourself instead of a heavy, shapeless thing."

The typical mother of the anorexia nervosa patient is an aggressively overprotective and unresponsive woman, and as such incapable of considering her daughter as a person in her own right. It is often the parental couple, with its own pathology, or the whole family group, who sabotage the basic needs of the patient's ego, and quite especially the feeling that she is unique, capable, and worthy of respect. My own observations show that the most common basic interpersonal experiences of anorexics are the following:

During infancy the ritual aspect of feeding takes precedence over the emotional relationship with the mother, who derives no pleasure from nursing the child; control prevails over tenderness and joy. Parental stimulation serves to stifle any of the child's own initiatives (Bruch 1961).

During childhood and the latency period, an insensitive parent constantly interferes, criticizes, suggests, takes over vital experiences, and prevents the child from developing feelings of his own.

These pathogenic interpersonal experiences give rise to a paralyzing sense of ineffectiveness pervading every thought and activity (Bruch 1961). Hence, though few anorexics have had to go short of material goods in their childhood, they were nevertheless severely deprived: their spontaneous expressions were ignored or frowned upon, unless they accorded with the mother's possessive ambitions. In the latency period these patients accordingly developed a life style of passive surrender. Their self-awareness, and quite particularly their body awareness, and the feeling of being separate from others and from their expectations were severely impaired.

It is thus—bound to a possessive mother who treats her as a mere appendage and never as an individual deserving uncritical support—that the patient enters adolescence and is faced with what to her is an unbearable traumatic situation. She has to withdraw her libidinal cathexis from the parental figures and to face the difficult problem of establishing new interpersonal relationships. Her body undergoes rapid changes: it is transformed almost beyond recognition and yet it remains her own. She has to discover a new self, which means that she can no longer identify herself with her mother but must play an independent social role. All these problems push her fragile and premorbid personality into a state of depression: she fears that her ego cannot measure up to so many new tasks. If we examine the stage prior to the onset of anorexia—as we should always make a point of doing—we shall invariably discover such signs of ego depression as a transient sense of unreality; boredom; the feeling of being different from others, and especially from one's schoolmates who seem either much more childish or much older; a sense of isolation, and an obscure feeling of helplessness and uselessness. During this prodromic phase, anxiety and depression often go hand in hand with an actual decrease in appetite, which may draw the patient's attention to the problem of food. At this point the depressed ego, faced as it is by impossible tasks, *reactivates* the overwhelming *sense of helplessness* experienced during the infantile period, when the patient was quite incapable of satisfying her own vital needs.

At this point I should like to express my agreement with E. Bibring (1953) that the emphasis should not be laid on oral frustration and the ensuing oral fixation, but on the infant's and child's experience that her ego is totally helpless. This approach

> does not invalidate the accepted theories of the role which orality and aggression play in various types of depression. It implies, however, that the oral and aggressive strivings are not as universal in depression as is generally assumed, and that, consequently, the theories built on them do not offer sufficient explanation but require a certain modification.

We can now try to answer the puzzling question of why it is that anorexia nervosa should occur almost exclusively in the female sex and at about puberty. (The three cases of male anorexia I have studied were not cases of true anorexia nervosa. One quickly developed paranoid delusions. The second entertained hypochondriacal ideas of a psychoasthenic type, centered on the digestive system. The third was the closest to true anorexia nervosa, not least because of his neuromuscular overactivity. This patient, however, had two atypical symptoms: an explicit longing for food, and obvious pride in his condition. Unlike female anorexics, who will invariably tell you that they eat more than enough, this patient would boast about his fasting feats.)

In my view this is due to a process of "concretization." Puberty, as we saw, is a sudden and traumatic experience for the girl. Narcissistic libido cathexis has to be withdrawn from the infantile body and directed towards the new, strange, adult, and rounded body, which, moreover, must be accepted as being part of oneself. This process, that is the separation of one's own body from the maternal object, is, however, impeded by the permanent incorporation of that object. In fact, because of the development of the breasts and other feminine curves, the body is experienced *concretely* as the maternal object, from which the ego wishes to separate itself at all costs. During this transitory phase of pubertal depression, the ego organizes a desperate defense system by splitting itself into two parts, in the hope of averting two major psychic catastrophes: a permanent state of depression and regression to schizophrenia.

The patient considers and experiences her body as one great incorporated object that overpowers her and forces a passive role upon her. Because she builds her defenses at a comparatively advanced stage of psychological development, she is able to make a distinction between identification (an ego function) and oral incorporation (an instinctual process). Psychoanalytical writers usually treat the two processes as closely related if not identical. In the anorexic's defenses, however, they are clearly distinct. The incorporation of the bad object (which becomes one's own body) not only persists, but is reinforced for defensive purposes, for gaining better control of the object. The libidinal parts of the ego remain attached to the object and its needs; as a result of the split, they become detached from the central ego (Fairbairn, see diagram, p. 163). Nevertheless, because the frustrating object is both bad and fascinating, an ambivalent attitude prevails. The central ego, associated with super-ego components, then identifies itself with an ideal that is a desexualized, acarnal, and essentially powerful image. In fact, like hunger, nascent sexuality is reexperienced by the patient as an "inner force" threatening the ego's idealized image.

Whereas, during the premorbid phase, the anorexic sensed unconsciously that the bad object was too strong to be attacked, now that it has been equated with her body, active aggression can be consciously directed towards the latter by starving it of food.

The ego defense that is thus built up is characterized by the rejection of the body as such and of food as a bodily substance. The pathological control of the body is effected by an attitude that I would describe as *enteroceptual* mistrust. Once the body has been equated with the bad, overpowering object, namely with the threatening entity, the logical consequence is distrust of the body and of its stimuli and needs. But, like the bad object, the body is also fascinating and therefore cannot be abandoned or decathected (in which case somatic depersonalization would set in). The body-object must simply be kept under control, not be allowed to swell and grow, must be subjected to hard work and strain. The ego becomes an avenger that transforms its master into a slave. However the slave, too, wields a knout. It is as if the patient says to herself:

> The bad and overpowering object made me a slave by nourishing me: now this incorporated object has become my body and is still trying to enslave me by its demands, by luring me with its hunger, which, once satisfied, makes it even more exacting and irresistible. I must not pay any attention to its signals: hunger, fatigue, or sexual excitement. They are so many tricks the body employs to master me. Whose is the hunger I feel? It is most of all the body's. I must differentiate myself from it, pretend that hunger speaks only for itself and hence is not worthy of my attention. I am here and the hunger is there. So let me ignore it.

In this way, though the patient feels and recognizes the body as her own, she treats it *as if* it were not.

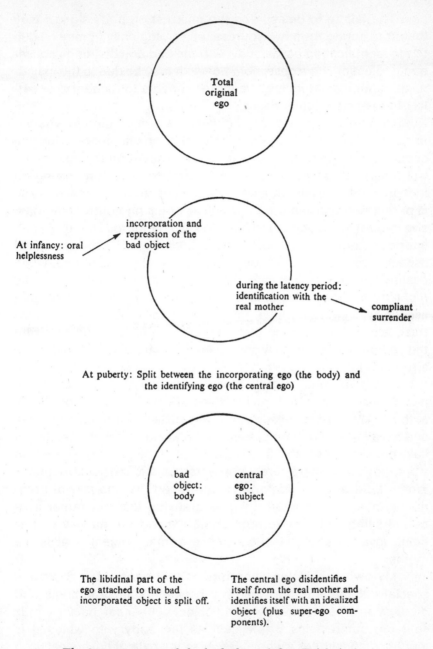

The incorporation of the bad object (after Fairbairn)

The failure to detect, and the mistrust of, body signals may therefore spring from two sources: psychologically, it may be due to the identification of the body with the bad object and its consequent rejection; *neuropsychologically*, it may be due to the maladministrations of an insensitive mother unable to recognize or satisfy her child's original needs.

Certain clinical aspects, however, vary according to whether or not the patient has reached the anal or phallic phase. After the shocking discovery that she is orally dependent on the object, she will resort to starvation as the simplest means of organizing an independent and self-sufficient image of herself. The anal defense is primarily organized around the fear of losing control over passive impulses and objects ("I have to keep dangerous impulses and interfering objects in check"), and reflects more highly organized aspects of the search for power. The reader will recall that, when dealing with that search in anorexia nervosa, I have referred to the *flight from* the passive side of existence. Girls of an intelligent ascetic type prevail in this group. The phallic defenses, by contrast, are built up around the competitive efforts associated with the oedipal situation: the wish to beat the rival, to be admired, to be strong and unvanquished.

The ambivalent attitude towards the bad and fascinating object might also account for fantasies of oral impregnation. Many authors who have studied only a few cases of anorexia nervosa and have found that their patients were afraid of oral impregnation have concluded that this fear is the basis of their illness. In my own work, however, I have rarely come across this particular fantasy. When it did occur, I was always convinced that the fear of pregnancy must not be interpreted as a sexual fear but rather as a sexual symbol of a more frightening experience, namely that of being invaded and distended by the primary object, that is the mother.

My own conclusion, therefore, is that anorexia nervosa is a special defense structure midway between schizo-paranoia and depression. The incorporated bad object neither can be nor ever is split up, but remains whole, just as the body with which it is identified constitutes a whole. Because the patient hovers between schizophrenia and depression, her body experience, too, is ambiguous: it lies half-way between the non-I and the bad I, is both alien and her own, persecutor and persecuted, a destructive non-self invading the self. The patient undoubtedly projects, but defends herself against the schizophrenic catastrophe by projecting the "unacceptable" within the structures of her own personality into her own body. The body thus becomes the persecutor, but a persecutor on whom it is relatively easy to spy and impose controls. This type of projection thus protects the patient from interpersonal delusions and, in a way, preserves her ability to socialize and to relate to the world. Anorexia nervosa is also a safeguard against depression and deliberate suicide. The bad body kept at bay from the self protects the existence of a good, idealized, enhanced, acceptable, and respected ego. No wonder therefore that, just as soon as the anorexic system is organized, these patients shed the depression of the premorbid phase and begin to relate and act against the "object": they become subjects.

The threefold meaning of the anorexic symptom may be schematized as follows:

$$\left.\begin{array}{ll} \text{to retain} & \text{the good} \\ \text{to ward off} & \\ \text{to control} & \text{the bad} \end{array}\right\} \text{object (body).}$$

In order to *retain* the body as the good object, the patient treats it as her own and invests it with libidinal cathexis; there is no somatopsychic depersonalization.

In order to *ward off* the body as the bad object, she keeps it out of the self. The central ego remains worthy of respect, so that there is no depression.

To *control* the body as the bad object, she must keep it at bay. She herself remains in the saddle, the object-world remains good, and there is no schizophrenia.

This schema may well explain the exceptional stability of the anorexic syndrome in the many mild forms that escape the clinician but have an identical structure. In these forms the ego defense is centered on keeping the weight to a fixed minimum that is neither too dramatic nor too dangerous.

I often refer to this minimum jocularly as *the magic weight*. As soon as it is violated, a red warning light seems to flash in the patients' minds. Many so-called recoveries in the wake of various medical treatments are based on this very factor. The *magic weight* adjustment often coincides with the resumption of the menstrual cycle: it provides a minimum level of psychological security for the acceptance of this typical feminine function.

In my view anorexia nervosa is an intrapersonal paranoia (intrapsychic paranoid split). The power motive frustrated in interpersonal relationships is shifted to the intrapersonal structure, that is, to a rigid control of the patient's body. The unacceptable is projected into the body, not into the environment. Can we then speak of an oral syndrome in anorexia nervosa? In a dynamic sense, no. We can merely speak of an oralized aspect of a problem involving the power and worth of the ego. In its primary relationship, the ego has found only three means of psychological survival: (1) preservation of the embodied object (this means that the object is not incorporated in a dependent or anaclitic sense, but embodied and imprisoned for the sake of independence), (2) preservation of the relationship with the other, and (3) preservation of its own power.

The result is a cold, mutilated, and far too often a tragic existence.

CHAPTER 14

Some Hints on Psychotherapeutic Conduct

Mara Selvini Palazzoli

PRELIMINARY STRUCTURAL DIAGNOSIS

Before beginning the psychotherapeutic treatment of anorexic patients it is essential to make a careful assessment of their general state. This puts the therapist on his guard against possible difficulties, and helps to determine the best therapeutic approach to any particular case. In other words the therapist must first decide whether his patient is a stable anorexic without marked mental aberrations, or a bulimic with a severe personality disorder, terrified by the thought of his inevitable food binges and seriously disturbed in his enteroceptive responses, his thoughts, and his powers of communication (see p. 162).

Patients of the first type, provided that their symptoms have appeared fairly recently and that they have not had traumatic experiences, are capable of entering into a valid—albeit ambivalent—relationship with the psychotherapist fairly quickly. They can also accept the fact that they are expected to attend regular sessions, generally up to three a week.

The patients in the second group are much more seriously ill

From *Self-Starvation*, 1981 ed., pp. 118–131.

and also much more difficult to approach: they must be treated with extreme patience and sympathy. Because of their fragile personalities, they are terrified of any kind of intimate interpersonal relationship for which they nevertheless long with passion. With them the therapist must expect constant demands for a reduction in the number of weekly sessions, repeated absences justified in the most childish manner, or requests for a temporary interruption of the treatment. Thus a perceptive colleague, starting the treatment of a gravely ill patient in this second group, realized that the long silence at the end of one of the first sessions was a terrified reaction of the patient to the deep tenderness my colleague felt towards her. This helped my colleague to respond sympathetically when the patient rang up to say that she found the treatment far too upsetting to continue with it. My colleague told her that she quite understood the position but hoped the patient would feel free to call on her services whenever she needed or desired them.

Only in this way can the therapist sometimes initiate a relationship with the patient. In fact some of the gravest cases will often show a marked deterioration to avoid falling into what to them is the fatal trap of an interpersonal relationship with the therapist: because they feel irresistibly drawn into the transference situation, escape into physical symptoms is their only means of preserving their autonomy and their relative independence from what, as experience has taught them, is bound to prove yet another symbiotic and destructive relationship. And as long as the sessions have to be confined to discussion of their grave state of malnutrition, their own secret fears do not have to be brought into the open. . . .

Other patients, fortunately very few in number, will, after a phase of mistrust, enter into a relationship of complete oral dependence on the psychotherapist, interspersed with ambivalent reactions. Since this relationship is bound to be extremely frustrating for them, their physical and mental condition deteriorates dramatically; they "act out" their aggression against the frustrating therapist even while trying to "possess" him. Such cases cannot be helped in the normal way, but must be seen in a hospital clinic. Since I feel it more useful to mention my failures than to dwell on my successes, I shall cite the particularly tragic case of Anna Maria.

Several years ago I imprudently agreed to treat this patient in my consulting rooms, even though I knew that her condition had long since become chronic, that she was poorly educated and in straitened financial circumstances, and that she lived outside the city so that each session involved her in the discomfort of a fairly long journey. The patient, whose anorexia had started at the age of 14 years, had married seven years later, and was 26 years old when I first saw her. Her relationship with her husband, a modest bank clerk who declared that curing his wife was to him "an existential mission," was the exact though veiled replica of her sado-masochistic relationship with her mother.

During psychotherapy she regressed to total oral dependence within a few months. Her need for love and mothering, for symbiotic fusion with the therapist was so pressing that she found the reality of the therapeutic situation altogether unbearable. My repeated assurances that I was fully alive to her deepest need served no useful purpose; her condition deteriorated so dramatically that I was forced to advise her admission to a hospital, which, for financial reasons, had to be in her home town and hence at some distance from me. For several days practical difficulties (quite apart from my own countertransference) prevented me from visiting her. I did, however, keep regularly in touch with her husband by telephone. After the last of these conversations, the husband (as I learned from him later) told Anna Maria rather sadistically that he had gathered from our brief conversations that I was so dispirited about her that I saw no point in treating her any further. Anna Maria then sent me a laconic note: "Signora, since you no longer believe in my cure, I have decided to go to my grave."

As I was hurriedly preparing to leave for her hospital, I received the news of her death.

The husband then came to see me to tell me a secret: Anna Maria had killed herself. At the time she was having a drip of amino acids, and she had heard the repeated instructions that, because of her precarious state, the flow of liquid must be as slow as possible. On her last day the nurse set the drip at minimum flow. When her husband, who was called to the telephone, returned to her bedside he found that the drip bottle was empty and the valve fully opened. Anna Maria died a few minutes later. Her tragic death drove it home to me how essential it is not to start psychotherapy before weighing up the gravity of every case, one's own availability during moments of crisis, and such practical problems as traveling distance, and lack of financial resources. Anna Maria's suicide was clearly unconnected with her anorexia as such: her tragic decision to end her life was the direct result of her belief that she had been abandoned by me.

AGE OF THE PATIENT

Some, but few, cases of true anorexia nervosa can be diagnosed at a relatively early age (9 to 12 years). I myself have dealt with a 10-year-old prepubertal dizygotic twin, whose anorexia was essentially the expression of a desperate search for identity and autonomy in what was a highly complex relationship with her widowed mother and twin sister. In my view such precocious cases should be isolated from their family and placed into more suitable surroundings. If their condition is not too grave or dramatic, they can, for instance, be boarded out with sympathetic friends who are not too closely involved in the family tensions and conflicts. In graver cases it is best to have such patients admitted to a hospital, preferably one with a special ward in which they can be treated firmly but kindly.

The medical staff must be persuaded to adopt a sympathetic but neutral stance, while making sure they are not manipulated or blackmailed by maneuvers of the kind the patient has found so effective at home. The nurses, too, must be prepared for what is in store for them, lest they repeat the mother's mistake of believing the patient is simply refraining from food because she is willful and deliberately trying to cause trouble. In particular they must not keep adding that extra mouthful while coaxing the patient with "Just eat it up as a favor to me, there's a good girl."

With the change in environment and the elimination of direct pressures, such very young and not yet morbidly structured patients will often pass through an acute crisis and abandon their symptom. Psychotherapy proper can then be safely deferred until the patient is more mature.

WEIGHT

Obviously the most promising cases are stable anorexics who seek psychotherapeutic advice soon after the onset of their illness and are still in a passable physical condition. I am firmly convinced that if all anorexics were treated at an early stage, the recovery rate would be almost complete.

Unfortunately the majority of cases only seek psychotherapeutic help when everything else has failed, by which time their condition has seriously deteriorated. In their case the therapist is faced with a dilemma, for he knows perfectly well that at the start his treatment, far from bringing an immediate improvement, does the precise opposite. He must therefore let himself be guided by his own feelings and by his other commitments. Thus whenever I meet the parents of anorexics for discussions I make it a point to take careful note of their attitude toward the patient and of their general emotional state. If the results are sufficiently encouraging, I talk about the expected course of the therapy at some length and stress the likelihood that the patient's condition will deteriorate further and that she may have to be hospitalized, but that it is only if they are prepared to run this risk *with me*, give me time to gain the patient's confidence, and help me to cushion her against the shock of her possible hospitalization in a way that she would feel was neither an imposition nor a punishment, that we can have any hope of success. This process may be the most time-consuming for the therapist, but is, in my view, by far the best for the patient. In some cases, in which I feel I lacked the necessary time, I advised preliminary hospitalization but promised to meet and treat the patient after her discharge. In one very grave case, in which I had to insist on hospitalization after a few dozen sessions, I found that the psychotherapeutic relationship had been irredeemably shattered.

CHRONIC CASES

Patients who have been chronically ill for years, have had to suffer such traumatic experiences as tube-feeding without psychothera-

172 The Work of Mara Selvini Palazzoli

peutic support, and who, as a result, have adopted a definite and irreversible anorexic personality as the only means of preserving their pseudo-autonomy, must, as a rule, be considered incurable. Psychotherapy can nevertheless be attempted, but I myself have succeeded in curing no more than two such cases, and then only after years of hard work and infinite patience. The best one can normally hope to achieve with them is to keep their symptoms more or less under control, and to stabilize them to the level that I like to call the *magic weight*. Once the anorexic personality has crystallized out, the best we can do is to widen the patient's existential horizon and to help her to express her personality more fully. In fact, rather than try to effect a true transformation of the ego by breaking down the patient's defenses, the therapist must content himself with consolidating the existing ego within strictly circumscribed limits.

DEPENDENCE ON THE PARENTS

The psychotherapy of anorexic patients is generally fraught with the same thorny problems that beset the treatment of all adolescents and calls for the kind of awareness described by Anna Freud, Selma Fraiberg, Lampl de Groot, Peter Blos, Leo Spiegel, Irene Josselyn, Eveline Kestemberg, and others. The following facts must be borne in mind especially:

1. The patients are generally minors, and as such economically and otherwise dependent on their parents.
2. The treatment is paid for by the parents, so that the therapist appears a mere hireling of people who often complain of the great expense, thus adding to the patient's guilt feelings, or as someone who turns on warmth and sympathy for financial gain.
3. The patients do not themselves choose psychotherapy. Generally they submit to it because they think the alternative—hospitalization or tube-feeding—is infinitely worse.
4. At adolescence children attempt to escape from the dominance of their elders, yet paradoxically the psychotherapeutic situation seems to resurrect and, indeed, even to increase their dependence on others.

5. Last but not least, because anorexics are afraid of verbalizing their conflicts and negative feelings, they tend to act them out by intensifying their symptom.

The therapist must bear all these points constantly in mind and, during crises, try to draw attention to them in simple and sympathetic ways.

During discussions with the family he must further make it clear that he cannot possibly engage in secret telephone calls or confidential correspondence with them. Nothing must happen without the patient's knowledge; therapy must take place in an atmosphere of absolute trust, not in a conspiratorial climate reminiscent of home. Just how conspiratorial that climate can be was made clear to me by a mother who told me proudly during a preliminary meeting that she had secretly been injecting the stewed prunes that were the only food her daughter would eat with an extract of horse serum and egg yolk. The complicated preparations were all made while the daughter was out, and there was an elaborate system of secret telephone calls from relatives and friends to warn the mother of the girl's imminent return. It is not difficult to see how disastrous the whole atmosphere was for the patient.

As for parental jealousy, one can take it as an axiom that the more indignantly it is denied the fiercer it is. One mother, who had irately "handed" her only daughter, a 14 year old, over to me for therapy, told me that she was washing her hands of her and was highly indignant when I suggested in the most tactful way possible that she had come to feel jealous of me. A year later, when her daughter's attachment to me could no longer be glossed over, she told her to keep my fees and to stay away from therapy. This ruse having failed, she went to the girl's teacher and complained that her daughter was trying to kill her by continuing to visit the odious analyst (forgetting that she herself had originally bullied the girl into coming to see me). The neurotic teacher, who immediately identified herself with the irrational mother, then rebuked the poor girl in front of the assembled school. Fortunately my patient had by then developed so positive a relationship with me that she was able to stand the shock of her public humiliation.

During the second year of the treatment, the unhappy mother realized that the child was also developing more positive feelings towards her father, and to squash these she told the patient that, if it was not for her, she would never have come into the world: the father had insisted on an abortion. When the poor girl stammered this revelation out to me between sobs, I let her cry on (while anxiously searching for the appropriate therapeutic response) and then broke my long silence with: "I think your father was trying to solve a difficult situation in the most realistic way he knew how. He had come to see that he might not make a good father."

THE SCHOOL PROBLEM

Anorexics are intelligent people and set great store by scholastic success. Hence it is a great mistake to take them out of school unless they themselves request it or when their general condition is such as to demand their hospitalization. In some cases, as the therapy progresses, it becomes clear that the only reason why they try to get good marks is that their parents expect it of them, in which case the therapist must help them to discover their real attitude.

THE THERAPIST

I am convinced that the therapist treating anorexia nervosa patients must not only be an able physician but must also have a keen *mens medica*, and this despite the fact that he is not dealing with organic problems. In particular he must guard against the temptation to concentrate exclusively on the psyche and to forget that his patients also *have a body and bodily needs*, thus reinforcing the split between body and mind. In fact some of the patients' psychological debilities are the direct consequence of their physical emaciation or of intoxication.

I have sometimes had to rush patients to hospitals whose sunken eyes or parched lips suggested acute dehydration or chloropenic hyperazotaemia, only to have my diagnosis confirmed by laboratory tests. Thus, when I started treating a patient with an insistent cough which could easily have been mistaken for repressed aggression, I diagnosed tuberculosis, and called for an X-ray which confirmed my fears. In any case, however sound the therapist's medical training may have been, he must, in all serious cases, enlist the help of a competent physician who can keep an eye on the patient's physical condition without interfering with the therapeutic work. As for nonmedical psychotherapists, I believe that, in view of the grave physical state of anorexic patients, they are prone to panic at signs of deterioration that would leave the medical man quite unruffled.

The sex of the therapist must also be taken into consideration: some patients find it exceedingly difficult to be open with male analysts. Moreover, if he is accepted he may, as the therapy proceeds, become a substitute for a weak and neglectful father figure endowed with negative attributes.

To female therapists, by contrast, the patients will quickly transfer their ambivalent homosexual dependence on the mother. This new tie generally upsets them and may greatly complicate the countertransference situation. If the therapist is aware of this fact and accepts the relationship *without interpreting it*, it will gradually develop into a symbolic erotic bond between contemporaries (adolescent friendship, small talk, confidences . . .) and hence help the patient to achieve greater detachment from her mother and eventually to progress to heterosexuality. One of my 16-year-old patients, Sissi, would, during this phase of her treatment, place the photograph or latest letter of a new boy friend on the table between us as a kind of barrier, and then discuss it at length. I would let her rattle on without interruption, and when she eventually dropped the whole charade, I knew her homosexual anxiety had vanished. Quite often, however, the female therapist is seen as a model of complete womanhood with whom the patient can identify herself as an alternative to the mother.

TECHNICAL OBSERVATIONS

In beginning the treatment of particularly grave and emaciated cases the therapist must be extremely realistic. In particular he must warn the patient that the sessions can only be continued if the weight does not fall below a certain minimum. If it does, the patient will have to be hospitalized, a step it would be very much better to avoid. Having said this, the therapist should abstain from further references to the symptom, or from inquiring into the possible use of emetics, laxatives, or enemas, lest he be identified with the patient's parents. Nor should he look suspicious or critical when the patient, as so often happens, asks to go to the lavatory during a session. In this connection Hilde Bruch (1963) has spoken of the constructive use of ignorance. I myself strongly disagree with H. Thomä's (1961) view that it is best to challenge the patient's resistance directly and to bring into the open all the ruses that serve her as so many defense mechanisms. In this connection I can do no better than mention Liliana's confession at the end of her successful treatment:

> I can't tell you how glad I am that you never once harped on the lies and evasions I used at the beginning. Quite frankly, I kept thinking that you must be a bit dim. But then I began to feel an irresistible urge to tell you the truth. Do you remember . . . one day I came to a session and dumped my enema can on your table. To my surprise, you looked neither triumphant nor indignant. You simply said: "Let's try to find out why you still seem to need it." I realize now that you'd known all about it right from the start. But you also knew that, at the time, I had no alternative.

Giving these patients strict orders merely hardens their non-co-operation. Any references to sexual problems not initiated by the patient can also have dire consequences. Moreover, the therapist must take care never to volunteer interpretations of emotions or drives the patient himself thinks degrading—for example, jealousy, rivalry, or aggression.

The parental problem is an extremely delicate one. Some patients will not tolerate the least criticism of their parents, even when they themselves have become increasingly aware of the negative aspects of their home life. In such cases it is always best to sit back while the patient solves the problem at her own pace.

THE CENTRAL APPROACH OF THE THERAPIST

The treatment of anorexics must be specifically directed at strengthening the patients' egos, which they consider totally inadequate and weak. This feeling is masked by a façade of overactivity and diligence. Patients who attend therapeutic sessions for months without removing their overcoats are prime examples of this attitude. No matter what rational justification they may volunteer for their negative behavior, it invariably serves them as an armor against the encroachments of others. For a long time they feel that all interpretations are so many attempts on the therapist's part to display his own efficiency and superior knowledge, and they become even more determined to put him down by taking refuge in their symptom. The omnipotent psychiatrist is the image of the omnipotent parent, an image they are determined to destroy by being "themselves"—not too deep and not too intelligent.

While anorexics are nonconformists in their diets, they are, by contrast, incredibly rigid and conventional in their general outlook and behavior. Their rebelliousness is confined to a struggle with their own bodies. They are puritanical, have a horror of sex (in as much as the subject preoccupies them at all), and are hypercritical of their more uninhibited contemporaries.

These attitudes must never be challenged directly. However, their normally flat and sullen recitations may occasionally be interrupted with a humorous remark, or an optimistic reference to existence in general and their personality in particular, or even to the therapist's own experiences—all of which help to improve the atmosphere of the sessions and pave the way for greater confidence.

Many patients will, during the positive stage of therapeutic progress, make friends with someone of the opposite sex and cautiously test the therapist's attitude towards the new relationship. In general these friendships are rather Platonic but occasionally (in my experience only in the gravest cases of bulimic anorexia) there may be sudden outbursts of promiscuity as the only way to release a vague impulse that is, in fact, a mere substitute for the valid interpersonal relationships that elude these patients. I always warn them against such premature experiences and hold out the promise of more satisfactory relationships when they have reached greater psychological maturity. References to the transference situation are best avoided, not least because the patient finds them too painful. At most there should be fleeting interpretations of such negative transference phenomena as endanger the future of the treatment.

The therapist himself must, however, be constantly aware of his countertransference. Few patients are better than anorexics at driving him into a corner and at provoking all sorts of reactions.

Their obdurate clinging to their symptom, or indeed their physical deterioration in the face of some psychological progress, can arouse feelings of strong aggression in the therapist, often disguised as therapeutic pessimism, and persuade him to order the patient's hospitalization either as a punishment or else for his own peace of mind. Their overt behavior, too, is extremely irritating: they either spend large parts of each session in complete silence, or else disguise their fear of a significant encounter by engaging in an incessant stream of childish chatter. Some of them try to annoy the analyst with continuous complaints, even blaming him for the poor weather; others produce nothing but paeans of praise to their parents, and refuse absolutely to admit the pathological nature of their involvement; yet others, and by far the greatest number, keep voicing endless objections against their families, to whom they nevertheless continue to cling like leeches. In all these cases the therapist is tempted to react with aggressive displays of his superior insight, and these invariably have dire consequences.

What the therapist needs above all is inordinate patience, the ability to wait until the patient produces an authentic feeling or positive action, which can then be used to reveal or strengthen the constructive potentiality of his ego. If the patient starts to put on weight (often by nibbling food on the quiet) and to look healthier, the therapist must take care to turn a blind eye or the patient may mistake his satisfaction for the gloating praises she gets from her mother. Generally menstruation will reappear spontaneously just as soon as the patient's weight is back to normal. The therapist must expect that some patients will hide this happy event from him—some will mention it casually long afterwards, and others may never refer to it at all.

THE TERMINAL PHASE

Once the initial problems have been solved and the patient's ego has been sufficiently strengthened, psychoanalysis proper can be begun. However, this happens far too rarely—only one of my successful cases decided to start analysis (under a colleague) with a view to entering our profession. Most of these patients prefer to terminate treatment as soon as their symptom has been cured, certain that they can do the rest by themselves. Often it is best to agree with them and, rather than arouse their hostility and undermine their self-confidence, to express one's faith in their character.

I want to end this chapter by describing the case of Rita, the most serious anorexic I have ever had to treat.

Rita came to me after two painful and humiliating episodes during which she had been force-fed only to relapse soon afterwards. She showed serious disorders of thought and communication of the schizophrenic type and had enormous difficulties in entering into any kind of relationship with me. I worked with her for five years, during which time she suffered two relapses with a dramatic fall in weight from which she nevertheless recovered without hospitalization. These and several less drastic relapses seemed to occur whenever our relationship was about to become more intimate and hence more threatening to her.

However, during the fourth year of treatment, her persistent ambivalence provoked an even more acute crisis: in the course of a mere fortnight her weight dropped to 61 lbs (height 5'11").

On that occasion she herself asked me to take her to a psychiatric clinic outside the city, where she stayed for three months. Her parents, with whom I had maintained friendly relations throughout this difficult period, while in utter despair, once again expressed their full confidence in me. Though her physical needs were being attended to by capable hands, I made it a point to pay her regular visits and to maintain our rapport. One evening, just as I was taking my leave of her, there occurred something that I can only describe as a breakthrough. Rita had come down with me to see me out. The weather was exceptionally bad, and a gust of wind and snow hit us as soon as we opened the front door.

Rita looked silently at my car across the road, and at the puddle separating me from it. As I was shaking her hand, I saw that her expression had changed: she now fixed me with a strange look, that was both tender and terribly sad.

"*Dottoressina*," she said, shaking her head in anguish, "I have to get better . . . because you believe I can. . . ."

After her release from the hospital, and with the resumption of regular psychotherapeutic treatment, Rita's scholastic and social attainments continued to improve, but her weight remained at the same level it had been on her discharge (88 lbs). This was quite inadequate, though no longer dangerous or subject to sudden fluctuations. She had become deeply attached to me as a person, but had begun to show in a host of different ways that she resented my professional role.

She no longer called me Doctor but Madam, and became depressed as soon as I tried, however tactfully, to interpret her attitude or asked why she had missed a session; she claimed that all such approaches were humiliating and made her feel like a puppet. At the start of one session she made an extremely awkward suggestion and insisted on receiving an immediate reply. She said she had thought about it for a long time; she felt that the compulsory aspects of her attendance had become intolerable but that she lacked the courage to break it all off: her parents, who paid for the treatment, were bound to hear about her decision and would have insisted on her returning to me. She therefore begged me to let her parents continue to pay for three sessions a week, and to allow her to attend only when she herself felt like it. No explanations of her absences were to be demanded.

I was suddenly faced with a dramatic and crucial therapeutic decision: either to analyze and interpret the nature of her request in the orthodox manner, or else to offer Rita a chance of discovering the meaning of her choice for herself and to accede to her request.

I made up my mind there and then that the second alternative was by far the better of the two. It was three months before the summer holidays, and during those three months Rita came to see me three times, always toward the end of the hour allocated to her, thus making sure that I was waiting for her and keeping my side of the bargain we had struck.

I also saw her twice in the street. These meetings were certainly not accidental, though Rita pretended that they were, hurrying to embrace me warmly and then rushing off again.

Shortly before the holidays she came to tell me that she had decided to end her therapy. She had turned into a very beautiful and radiant young woman: she was about to go abroad on a two-year scholarship. On that occasion she spoke only of her plans and said not a word about the past three months. I did not refer to them either, nor did I congratulate her on her appearance—we both felt that no such words were needed.

Rita had decided to take the last steps on her own, and in so doing she had regained her dignity.

CHAPTER 15

The Family of the Anorexic Patient: A Model System

Mara Selvini Palazzoli

In 1968–1969 I made a number of preliminary studies, based on: (1) work with the parents of an anorexic patient, their only child, who had been treated by a colleague; (2) work with the parents of an anorexic patient (Azzurra), whose eventual cure after four years of psychotherapy had caused a grave crisis in the parents' relationship to each other, for which they sought help; (3) work with a young couple, the female partner of which had been a bulimic anorexic since adolescence and who had also become a dipsomaniac after her marriage.

These investigations, the results of which were published (Selvini Palazzoli 1970) as part of *The Child in His Family*, revealed the existence of an *intrapsychic* dynamic. At the time I was still using the old approach I had been taught during my own psychoanalytical training and still lacked the courage to draw the whole family into the psychotherapeutic situation.

However, I was then able to join the Milan Center of Family Studies and to undertake work in a team with the family therapists Luigi Boscolo, Gianfranco Cecchin, and Guiliana Prata. The next three chapters are devoted to the preliminary results of our study.

From *Self-Starvation*, 1981 ed., pp. 202–216.

The idea of doing research into whether or not the families of anorexics show characteristic behavior patterns was suggested to us by J. Haley's (1959) "The Family of the Schizophrenic: A Model System." In this article Haley, basing himself on a study of fifteen families with a schizophrenic member (the study began in 1953 and formed part of the Bateson research project at Palo Alto), put forward a theoretical model designed to describe the family as a unit.

The best method of studying the system of family interaction is to interview the whole family together and to observe them over a fairly extended period of time, in a structured therapeutic context.

From a methodological point of view families with an anorexic member seemed more satisfactory than families with a schizophrenic. This was because schizophrenia, as L. Wynne (1963) has shown, covers a wide spectrum: from transitory catatonic blocks to persistent and organized paranoid delirium and extreme disorganization of a precocious hebephrenic type. It is only recently that Wynne and his collaborators have tried to impose some sort of order into the subject by classifying the various clinical categories on the basis of thought disorders and breakdowns in family communication. Their research has shown that communication disorders in families with a fragmented way of thinking are quite distinct from those found in families with an amorphous way of thinking. The two types of families also seem to differ in internal organization and role allocation, in their ability to communicate, and in their openness to therapeutic help.

By contrast anorexia nervosa, as first described with surprising clinical accuracy precisely one hundred years ago by Gull and Lasègue, is characterized by the appearance of constant symptoms at, or shortly prior to, puberty, generally in girls.

In the psychiatric literature there is wide disagreement as to whether or not the rare cases of male anorexia should be considered authentic instances of anorexia nervosa.

Because we ourselves have only had occasion to study a single family with a male anorexic, we have decided to treat it as an exception, and to defer any discussion of our findings until such time as we have been able to study a representative number of such families.

In family therapy we are not so much interested in the nosographic description of the individual patient as in the diagnosis of the family as a total system, including the therapist. However, since we are still a long way from a satisfactory system of family diagnostics, we continue to classify families in terms of the patient's nosography.

To introduce some order and method, we have based our research on Haley's model, that is, on the following pragmatic axioms of human communication: (1) that it is impossible not to communicate and not to respond to a communication, and (2) that every communication involves at least two levels (a level of content and a level of relationship definition).

We set out to investigate: (1) how the family members qualify their own communications in the particular context of family therapy; (2) how they qualify the communications of other members, and in what circumstances; (3) the problem of leadership in the family; (4) the problem of coalitions; (5) the problem of acceptance, rejection, or shifting of blame among family members when something goes wrong; and (6) the problem of the interaction patterns of the parental couple.

The research was based on the psychotherapeutic study of twelve families. According to our standard practice, all interviews were handled by one male and one female therapist. The interviews were recorded and monitored by other members of the team who, if necessary, suggested alternative strategies.

Our data should be considered preliminary, because of the smallness of our sample and because four families have not yet completed their treatment.

Generally families with anorexic members have a capacity for communication, for focusing their attention, for carrying an argument to its conclusion, and for conveying coherent meanings that is macroscopically superior to that of families with a schizophrenic member.

With a few exceptions, which I shall specify below, our families did not straightaway evince the sense of discouragement, futility, meaninglessness, and chaos that is so characteristic of the families of schizophrenics, nor did they have the fatuous "drawing room" attitude so often exhibited by such families. *Instead there was a clear display of drama and suffering.* The parents made it clear that they were prepared to do anything they could to help the patient, though they often withheld important information in order to maintain a respectable front to which they seemed to attach excessive importance.

HOW THE FAMILY MEMBERS QUALIFY THEIR OWN COMMUNICATIONS

The members of the family of an anorexic patient generally qualify their own communication coherently, verbally no less than nonverbally. They seem to be sure enough of what they say, and of their right to say it, to feel justified in imposing rules on the relationship. The exceptions were some families who, even during relatively relaxed interviews, disqualified their own communications by their concomitant behavior and verbal messages. These were families of anorexic patients whose symptoms had been complicated by violent behavior toward other members of the family (blows, overfeeding of another member, strange or unjustified demands, shouting) or by bouts of bulimia. This would tend to corroborate my Rorschach findings with individual patients. In particular I found that patients suffering from severe bulimic crises displayed thought and communication disorders not present in patients who keep strictly to their reduced diets. Family observations also seem to suggest that major bouts of bulimia go hand in hand with psychotic confusion, violence, and a complete breakdown of family communication.

HOW THE FAMILY MEMBERS QUALIFY THE COMMUNICATIONS OF OTHER MEMBERS

The *rejection* of messages sent by others is extremely common in families with an anorexic patient. Very rarely will one member bear out what another has said, particularly about how he defines himself in the relationship. Contradiction is common. This type of rejection, therefore, does not concern the general invitation to communicate (Axiom 1), which is accepted and reciprocated, but the two levels of the message as such (Axiom 2). In fact it is as if each member of the family reacted to the other's message in the following way:

"I reject the content of what you say, even though I acknowledge your right to say it. And I also reject your definition of yourself (and myself) in our relationship."

Here I can do no better than report a series of brief and typical interactions during an interview of a family of six.

Identified patient: "Our trip to Rome convinced me that I can never have any relationship with my sister, because she does not want it."

Sister: "It's not true that I don't want it. I do everything I can to make it better."

I. p.: "How can you get on with people if you are not sincere. In Rome you never said anything about my vomiting, but when we got back home you told Mother all about it."

Sister: "Well, I was being sincere, at least when we got back. It's you who are never sincere, because you never mention your vomiting to anyone."

Therapist: "Why don't you admit that you vomit up every meal?"

I. p.: "Because I don't vomit up every meal."

Therapist: "Nearly every meal."

I. p.: "Because, to talk about certain things, you need someone who is prepared to meet you half-way. But you [to her sister] aren't prepared to. In Rome you sulked all the time."

Sister: "No, that's not true. I wasn't sulking. I simply said that I wasn't enjoying myself, and then *you* began to sulk. But when I said I wasn't enjoying myself I was simply being sincere, and whenever I'm sincere you get offended."

Mother: "I, too, am at my wits' end with her. If I scold her she says, 'You see, Mother, you've ganged up with the others.' If I'm kind to her, she says, 'You see, Mother, you're handling me with kid gloves, you're not sincere, you've put on your mask again.' But she has never been sincere with me."

I. p.: "You see, Mother, you too keep attacking me."

Mother: "That's not true."

This brief excerpt is typical of the rejection of messages. The rejection, moreover, was undisguised and left no doubt about the position of the speakers *vis-à-vis* one another, and was, in itself, a means of communication or rather of metacommunication.

There are, however, exceptions to this rule. In families with communication disorders more closely related to schizophrenia, there is a much greater tendency to disqualify or even disconfirm the messages of others. This tendency is particularly marked in certain parents to whom it is a matter of great importance to stress the patient's "pathological" state of mind. They tend to discount any messages and even to ignore evident improvements in the patient's behavior or physical health. Thus the parents of one family with whom it had proved quite impossible to communicate during the first four interviews because the daughter kept shouting and being generally aggressive, failed by mutual agreement to acknowledge the subsequent improvement in their daughter's behavior, even when her shouting and aggression had stopped completely. Moreover, at the slightest sign of impatience on their daughter's part, the parents made a great point of expressing their despair to the therapists, implying that she had not really improved. If the daughter herself referred to her changed behavior, they immediately discounted her remarks by reminding her of her abnormal eating habits, and whenever she pointed out that she was eating more, they immediately criticized her general behavior at home.

In such cases communication is of the psychotic type and confusion between past and present is the rule. Thus the parents may preserve absurd forms of behavior on the grounds that they are afraid of triggering off reactions that the daughter has, in fact, long since abandoned.

In another case the patient missed several interviews during which the parents expressed their deep anxiety about their daughter's inadequate diet. The therapists were all the more surprised to find that, on her return to the interviews, the daughter's physical condition had greatly improved. In yet another case the family therapy started after the patient had resumed normal eating habits (she was, in fact, rather obese) only to develop catatonoid symptoms. When we eventually succeeded in reducing these symptoms, the parents put through a highly dramatic telephone call to inform us that their daughter had reverted to a grave form of anorexic behavior, though its consequences proved to be absolutely invisible. What had happened was that the girl was no longer prepared to let them stuff her with food and had decided to eat what and when she liked.

These extreme forms of behavior are, in any case, characteristic of families with marked communication disorders, in which the anorexic symptoms of the patient, as I have already explained, are complicated by such other symptoms as violent forms of behavior and bouts of bulimia.

THE PROBLEM OF LEADERSHIP

One characteristic of these parents, that has also been noted by other authors, including particularly Minuchin (1970) and Barcai (1971), is their reluctance to assume personal leadership of the family. In particular each of the parents feels a need to blame his or her decision on others. Here are a few examples:

Mother: "I don't let her wear miniskirts because I know her father doesn't like them."
Father: "I have always backed my wife up. I feel it would be wrong to contradict her."

Mother: "My husband had decided to spend his holiday by himself in our country cottage [a place she loved herself] but I was simply forced to follow with the whole family and my old parents *on account of my father*. You see, Father wasn't well and he had to be near a doctor [her husband was a doctor]."
Father: "My wife and I never went out because Angela [their elder daughter] protested. Now we have Anna [the i. p.]. How can we even feel like going out?"

The arguments used in the following two examples are even more intricate.

Mother: "Angela came back from school with a peculiar look in her eyes. 'What's wrong with your eyes?' I asked. 'Did you get hit?' She told me that a school friend had applied some brown eye shadow. 'Ugh!' I said, 'how can you put on brown eye shadow? What horrible taste! . . .'"

Therapist: "Were you disgusted by the brown color? Would blue have been all right?"

Mother: "Well . . . the fact is that my husband cannot stand girls who look like painted hussies."

The same mother also produced another gem. Her husband had accused her of living like a recluse. It appeared that the patient, Anna, had for some years been friends with a classmate, Patrizia, and that the two families knew each other.

Father: "But *whom* are *you* friends with? With no one. You have even stopped seeing Patrizia's mother."

Mother: "Well, how could I be friends with Patrizia's mother? You know perfectly well that Angela [the elder daughter] can't stand Patrizia's father."

So the actions of each member are never attributed to personal preferences but to the needs of another member; all decisions are for the good of someone else. This rule applies to the patient's behavior as well, except that her symptoms are so overpowering that she cannot be expected to spare the family. "It is something that happened to her. Nothing can be done about it." *The result is a form of family leadership that is only acceptable because it is pathological. Its subject is not the patient, but the illness.*

THE PROBLEM OF COALITIONS

In my view the system of alliances constitutes the central and most serious problem facing the families of anorexic patients. It is the basis of a large number of secret rules that must never be mentioned or even hinted at and that give rise to a whole series of distorted behavior patterns. However, as we shall see, it may be used to good effect by the therapist. As a typical example I shall now quote the case of a family whom I shall call Bianchi.

The family was made up of the father, a 45-year-old clerk; the mother, a 42-year-old housewife; Flavia, the 17-year-old patient; and Claudio, her 8-year-old and obese little brother. Claudio was obese because his sister forced him to eat enormous meals that she herself prepared for him. In the course of the interviews the behavior of the various members of the family exemplified the taboo against open bipartisan alliances within the family. Thus it appeared that the mother had confided to Flavia that she had only stayed and put up with her husband for Flavia's sake (who consequently owed her a tremendous debt of gratitude). But whenever Flavia herself (often egged on by her mother) dared to criticize her father during the interviews, the mother would immediately rebuke her, which exasperated Flavia and put her even more against her father. When the quarrel between daughter and father had reached its height, the mother, who was sitting beside her husband, would pat his hand in a friendly manner. At this point the whole interaction would come to an end, with the father murmuring, "Let's drop it," and with Flavia bursting into tears. The husband's behavior toward the wife was similar. Whenever he criticized her in the presence of the rest of the family and found someone to back him up, he immediately began to look at his wife affectionately and, at the end of the interview, would help her with her coat (which he did not do normally), thus showing that he had not really meant to run her down.

Again the mother had apparently entered into a secret coalition with Claudio so as to protect him against the enormous amounts of food that Flavia expected him to eat. Thus when she took him to school she would throw away the snacks Flavia had put into his satchel. At the table, on the other hand, she urged him to eat up all the food that Flavia put on his plate, "so as not to make your sister suffer." In the course of the tenth interview the family discussed the arrangements for Claudio's summer holidays. The father said that he was sure Claudio would enjoy himself at a camp with other children. It appeared that the idea had been suggested by Flavia; the mother was convinced that Claudio would be very unhappy and was only prepared to send him to camp "for Flavia's sake. . . ." Flavia then burst into tears, saying that everyone thought her wicked for wishing her brother out of the way. But all she was thinking of was his own good; the boy had to become more independent or else he would end up like her.

The only one not to have been consulted at all was Claudio. Asked by one of the therapists how he felt about going to camp, he promptly gave his mother a questioning look.

Clearly the members of the family behave as if an alliance between any two is a betrayal of the third. They seem to have great difficulty in entering into a two-person relationship; the exclusion of the third strikes them as a grave threat to their pseudo-solidarity—only in the absence of all open alliances can this threat apparently be averted.

Alliance phenomena in families of three are much easier to study than alliance phenomena in larger families, and illustrate the *modus operandi* of the taboo against bipartisan coalitions particularly well. The patient is forced into an impossible position; she is continuously invited to ally herself with the father against the mother and *vice versa*. Worse still, each of the parents, deeply disillusioned with their partner, secretly encourages *the patient to make up for the partner's shortcomings.* As a result the patient finds herself playing the role of secret husband and secret wife all at once, dividing her sympathy equally between her parents.

An excellent example of this situation was provided by Chiara, the only child of a man with refined artistic tastes and an ignorant and loquacious mother. From early childhood Chiara's father had tried to imbue her with a love of art; on Sundays he would take her to visit old churches and museums, while the mother stayed in the car reading the papers. "You for one appreciate beautiful things," her father would say to her, clearly venting his dissatisfaction with his wife. But as soon as Chiara was alone with her mother, she had to fill in all the details of the day's events to make up for the silences of the sullen husband, immersed as he was in his books or his music.

Much the same thing happened to Rosella, the idealized child of a father whose hobbies were sport and ecology. She was invited to join him in the country for horse rides, but also had to take his "place" in bed by the side of her mother, a depressed and drab housewife who shared none of her husband's interests and was far too often left alone.

In the peculiar arrangement, which we have called "three-way matrimony," each member of the family is married to two persons: the mother to her husband and her daughter, the father to his wife and his daughter, the daughter to her mother and father.

The arrangement works fairly well for the parents but not for the daughter, who is expected to share out her attention as fairly as possible, and consequently has no means, or energy, to build up a life of her own or to risk open rebellion on reaching adolescence. Indeed we observed that the daughter generally accepts the role she is expected to play to the point of developing her symptoms precisely when the system is threatened by changes.

Thus, in the two families in which the patient was an only daughter, the symptoms set in shortly after the father, until then fairly detached from the life of his family, made his presence more obviously felt, in one case due to a serious illness, in the other as the result of his disillusionment with politics. The return of the father had quite obviously upset the old equilibrium.

In families with two, three, or four children, the critical factors are much more difficult to identify. However, in a number of families we found that the symptoms appeared after a change in the old system of secret alliances. In some cases, as one of the brothers (or sisters) grew older, he changed his relationship with one or both parents, thus threatening the family equilibrium and the patient's presumed privileges.

However, during the first family session, the interview invariably shows that the patient starts the therapy in a state of isolation from her brothers and sisters; far from being allied to any one, she is secretly detested by all thanks to the privileged position she is rightly or wrongly believed to enjoy in the household thanks to her illness. Here again the patient's fatal loyalty to the older generation not only makes her a stranger to her contemporaries but also makes her play the role of a sort of extra parent, resented by her siblings.

Two-person alliances outside the family are equally frowned upon. Thus when one of our 13-year-old patients made friends with a girl of the same age, Patrizia, and invited her home, the patient's 8-year-old sister immediately set out to turn the relationship into a threesome and succeeded in making friends with Patrizia despite their considerable age difference. The patient found the strain so great that she abandoned Patrizia soon afterwards. In other cases friendships, far from being incorporated into the group, are criticized, often for being too intimate or morbid. There are also cases in which the patient tries to "save herself" by imposing the impossible role of savior on some boy or girl. In several cases the predictable failure of this attempt directly preceded the onset of the symptoms, thus triggering off a family crisis.

THE PROBLEM OF BLAME-SHIFTING

Precisely because every family member effaces himself for the sake of the rest, no one member is really prepared to assume responsibility when something goes wrong. The mothers may blame themselves for their daughter's illness but they promptly invalidate this self-accusation by explaining that they only acted as they did through excess of zeal and devotion (for which they cannot be blamed). If, on the other hand, they are criticized on any concrete point, they either defend themselves hotly or, alternatively, get depressed and declare that they are prepared to leave home if that will improve their daughter's chances of getting better. This apparent spirit of self-sacrifice is a veiled threat to the other members and makes them feel guilty, with the result that they stop voicing any criticisms.

The fathers characteristically speak of themselves as people whose only possible fault may have been to put up with too much for the sake of peace. They consider themselves rational and well-balanced persons and regret that they have never succeeded in making these qualities prevail over their wives' irrational behavior. When one gets down to particulars, however, it always becomes clear that they have so blinded themselves with self-pity as to be totally unaware that their daughter, too, was having difficulties in her relationship with her mother. They seem never to have taken their daughter's part in anything like a courageous or emphatic manner. As for the patient, her attitude, once the symptoms have appeared, is that she can do nothing about them. She realizes that her parents are worried and wishes they were not. But she is now in the grip of an illness that is quite beyond her control and for which she can in no way be held responsible.

THE INTERACTION PATTERNS OF THE PARENTAL COUPLE

Behind the façade of respectability and marital unity the parents generally conceal a deep disillusionment with each other that they are quite unable to acknowledge, let alone resolve.

This failure reflects their ambiguous views of their marriage: while they welcome its gratifying aspects, they deeply resent its compulsory elements. In all the families we have treated to date, the fathers' and mothers' respective view of themselves in the relationship seems to be identical. The mothers see themselves as "Ladies Bountiful," completely dedicated to the good of others. Their rectitude and avowed generosity preclude any criticism of their constant encroachments. They attack anyone who refuses to view them as benefactresses. The fathers, for their part, invariably see themselves as essentially good and decent men. Nothing would induce them to think otherwise. Hence, while the mothers occasionally round on the therapists, the fathers remain respectful at all times. If they are asked to do something, they will do it conscientiously, as if it were homework.

Their blame-transfer maneuvers in the interpersonal relationship are much more subtle than those of their wives: their sad silences are so many fingers pointed at those of whose injustice and lack of comprehension they are the innocent butts. Two moralistic people who both consider themselves the victims of a compulsory relationship will inevitably compete with each other for moral superiority, and the simplest way to do this is to appear to be the victim. Their position in the relationship is therefore of a symmetrical type, but what we have here is a peculiar symmetry: in it one-upmanship serves to prove that one has made greater sacrifices in the cause of duty, respectability, and marital stability than the other. We call this "symmetry through sacrificial escalation."

It is a well-known fact that two marital partners who maintain a rigid symmetrical position in their relationship normally go in search of allies: first of all among their own relatives, and next among friends, advisers or priests, who are asked to take sides, to act as referees in the conjugal jousts and to intervene during moments of crisis. *But this does not happen in the case of our couple that engages in sacrificial escalation in complete secrecy,* because the rule of respectability requires that they appear as an exemplary couple to the outside world. The secret has to be kept from relatives and, *a fortiori*, from social acquaintances, contact with whom is confined to the exchange of conventional courtesies. As a result the system of alliances and the search for an arbitrator are kept within the family and focused especially on the patient, who is secretly encouraged to side with the more persecuted of her two parents. But since each of the parents sees himself in that role, and since the patient depends on them both, she occupies an extremely ambiguous position in the system. This ambiguity is complicated further by the fact that, though the two parents vie for her support, neither is prepared to enter into an open alliance with her since, paradoxically, that alliance would detract from their professed roles of being the more downtrodden of the conjugal pair. In other words the parent who succeeds in winning the alliance of the daughter drops behind in the sacrificial escalation race, and hence loses his moral superiority. For this very reason both parents show striking contradictions in their behavior during interviews. Each seeks the compassion of the daughter and, failing to obtain it, expresses his or her disillusionment, but nevertheless is pained and even indignant if the daughter is too critical of, or aggressive toward, the other.

We have observed this phenomenon time and again. Let me quote just one example: during one family interview, the mother burst into tears while trying to explain her difficulty in communicating with her husband, who was always working in his office, even on Sundays and holidays. Exasperated by the old excuse that he had a lot of professional engagements, she finally said, between sobs: "In that case put a notice on your office door to tell your clients what your working hours are. Then at least I'd know where I stand." Throughout the argument the patient had maintained a detached silence, careful not to side with either parent. At the end of the interview the therapists asked the father to dine alone with his daughter for a certain time, but did not explain the reason for this request. At the next interview the daughter, when describing her meals with her father, mentioned the same painful silences and sense of emotional detachment that her mother had complained of. She did this very delicately, indicating that she did not blame him in any way. The mother at once rose to her husband's defense—her daughter, she said, was expecting too much, whereas she herself had always been content with what little affection she got. In another family the father suddenly expressed anxiety about his wife's long-standing hypertension. "From now on," he said, "she must not be allowed to suffer the least strain." This happened after an interview in which the daughter, with visible anguish, had for the first time succeeded in describing some particularly painful aspects of her relationship with her mother.

The go-between of couples of this type, that is the patient, thus seems quite satisfied to assume a role that is much too difficult for her to play. If she attempts to engage in a real dialogue with her father, he will reject her out of fear, while her mother will reject her out of jealousy. If she gives in to her mother, she is taken over completely as if she were still a baby, and hence rejected as a person; at the same time the father will rebuff her because of her infantile behavior. If she attacks either of her parents, the other immediately rejects her by rushing to his (or her) defense. If, finally, she attempts to abandon the unequal struggle and tries to stand on her own feet, she will, for the first time in her life, find herself opposed by a *united couple*, determined to reject her bid for independence. *In a system where every communication has so high a probability of being rejected, the rejection of food seems to be in full keeping with the interactional style of the family.* In particular it is in perfect tune with the sacrificial attitude of the group, in which suffering is the best move in the one-upmanship game.

CHAPTER 16

The Use of Therapeutic Interventions

Mara Selvini Palazzoli

At this point we think it is opportune to give a brief, preliminary description of some forms of therapeutic intervention that have led to positive changes in the family system of communication and hence in the patient's physical health. Admittedly we have been using these techniques for a relatively short period of time so that no follow-up has been completed. (We are at present drafting a program for the regular follow-up of the families we have treated, and consider such follow-ups essential to the accurate appraisal of our therapeutic techniques. With the last five families we have treated, the system was successfully changed and the anorexic symptom eliminated in less than ten sessions.)

On the other hand we think that by describing even these preliminary attempts to change the system, we may help to shed fresh light on a number of important problems. J. Haley (1971), in a chapter of his book entitled "Approaches to Family Therapy," states explicitly that the fundamental problem of family therapy is one of method. He adds that whereas a beginner would feel happier with a rule of thumb, the experienced therapist realizes that this would, in fact, be a handicap.

From *Self-Starvation*, 1981 ed., pp. 217–230.

Every family has a specific problem that may need a specific therapeutic approach. Hence, rather than try to fit the family to the method, the experienced therapist will seek to devise a method suited to the particular needs of the family. Thus instead of insisting that the whole family attend every session, he may, if he thinks it a tactical advantage, decide to divide the family into subgroups. Some cases may benefit from frequent but short interviews, others from less frequent but longer interviews.

What little experience we ourselves have accumulated in this field leads us to agree wholeheartedly with Haley. In particular, when treating families with an anorexic patient, we have sought to devise modes of therapeutic intervention that take the special characteristics of such families fully into account. Our main aim has been to devise modes of therapeutic intervention that do not depend too much on the imagination, personality, or experience of the therapist. Once we are familiar with the peculiar mode of functioning of this type of family (usually dissimulated and difficult to detect), we are on the lookout for certain patterns and hence in a better position to devise techniques for transforming them.

In particular we have found that with greater experience we have come to intervene much earlier than we used to. We have in fact learned from a host of errors that the state of grace the therapist enjoys in family therapy is rather short-lived. Thus if he fails to fathom certain secret rules of the system, for instance by paying insufficient heed to behavioral redundancies, and hence being unable to change them by concrete directives, he himself may be incorporated into the system and rendered impotent. It is for this very reason that in November 1971 we initiated a research project centered on short-term family therapy. We now believe that the therapeutic cycle should be completed in no more than twenty sessions and even less when it proves easier to obtain a substantial change in the family system and to eliminate the anorexic symptom. The family are, however, told that, they have a "credit" of so-and-so many sessions, which they may or may not use at their discretion in the future.

In our opinion this approach (though still subject to review) goes a long way towards assuaging the family's understandable fears that they will be drawn into protracted treatment with an unpredictable outcome. Moreover, by setting a time limit, we force them to behave responsibly and not with passive acquiescence. The therapists, too, are put on their mettle: they cannot afford to let their attention slip when time hangs over them like the sword of Damocles.

As for the interval between sessions, which was originally fixed at one week precisely, we have since seen fit to vary it as the situation demands. In particular we now tend to lengthen the interval, especially after we have made good contact—we have found that a concrete instruction has a much greater effect if it is left to sink in. The main problem is to set the correct interval for each particular case.

The family members are informed of our technique during the first meeting; they are told that we tape all our transactions, that we work in a team, and that we use a one-way mirror.

The therapeutic observers never intervene personally during the sessions though, when things go terribly wrong, they knock on the door, call one of the "active" therapists out, and suggest a different approach. Strategic decisions are, however, invariably taken by the team as a whole, generally before the session but, in particularly difficult situations, towards the end. In such cases the session is briefly interrupted, while the therapists in charge go into conference with their colleagues. The family is told from the outset that, in the course of the treatment, they will receive a number of directives and that the success of the entire therapy hinges on their implementation.

We invariably see the family as a whole, but may from time to time split them up into different groups, the better to provoke meaningful responses and to stabilize the generation barrier which is usually confused or nonexistent.

Let me now specify some of our techniques that have proved particularly effective.

INTERVENTIONS TO CHANGE THE QUALIFICATION OF COMMUNICATIONS BY OTHER FAMILY MEMBERS

To cope with the highly repetitive pattern of the rejection of messages, we have, as I pointed out earlier, made it a standard practice to work in heterosexual pairs. This calls for a word of explanation.

Sometimes one of the two therapists will join the fray while the other plays the part of the silent observer. After some time the first may find himself reduced to impotence in the face of a whole series of rejections. At this point the second therapist, instead of speaking up in defense of his partner, will continue to play the part of the impartial observer, while "metacommunicating" with his colleague about what is going on. The two therapists eventually agree, taking care to give the behavior of the family a positive interpretation, by arguing that, if every member of the family finds it so difficult to confirm what the therapists say, there must be a good reason for it, and no attempt need be made to change it. On other, more difficult, occasions, we carry this tactic or ploy even further. Thus it has sometimes happened that one of the therapists has been driven by the system into adopting a sharply critical attitude towards one member of the family. It is then observed that the member under attack will defend himself either by rejecting the criticism out of hand or else by making such remarks as: "I must be stupid; I just don't understand." At this point one or several of the other members of the family will often look pleased. The purpose of the whole maneuver is to convince the therapist that with someone so stupid, it is clearly impossible to change the family system. To dramatize the situation the second therapist, who has kept silent until then, now asks his colleague to join him outside for a private talk. After a while the two return. The second therapist now does all the talking. Very calmly he expresses his disagreement with his colleague, and explicitly allies himself with the member of the family under attack. The *rejected* therapist looks duly contrite and, by acknowledging his error, *confirms* his colleague's message. A tactic of this sort has invariably proved highly effective. Not only does it deliver a powerful blow to the system, but it also shows that a couple can peacefully change their respective "one up" or "one down" position in the relationship. I might add that in our dramatizations the final "one up" position has always fallen to the male therapist. This, we think, is therapeutically constructive, not so much on account of the prevailing cultural stereotypes or the fact that we are working with a certain type of family, but by virtue of certain phylogenetic constants from which the distinct gender-roles seem to derive their universal validity. This point, however, requires further investigation and discussion.

In the rare cases in which the entire family group tries to protect the *status quo* by employing disqualifying communications, we have recourse to other tactics. I shall cite the case of a family, which we shall call Crippa, consisting of the parents, both university graduates in their fifties, and four children. The patient, Emilia, was the eldest child. She suffered from chronic anorexia and was extremely emaciated. The crucial intervention occurred at a relatively late stage in the therapy (thirteenth interview), when the therapeutic team at last cottoned on to the defense mechanism used by that family; humor, intelligent, witty exchanges and funny faces. This evasive maneuver was performed with such subtlety, and with so much apparent good will, that it escaped detection for a number of interviews. It was only during a team discussion, in a cheerful and pleasant atmosphere, that one of the therapists, clearly irritated, put his finger on the real problem when he said: "To tell you the truth, I find these interviews awfully boring. I keep asking myself how it is that so intelligent, pleasant and perceptive a family should have a daughter who is starving herself to death." This comment led us to identify the secret weapon with which the family had so skillfully been confusing us, and we decided to disarm it during the next interview.

That session was opened by the patient, who told the therapists of a trip she had taken a few days before with Gianna, her younger sister. She described how disastrous their outing had been and how much she had missed her mother's presence. She said that her sister had been very offhand with her, which was not surprising seeing that "they had set her up on a pedestal and treated her as a model of intelligence and beauty" (from the tape recording).

Therapist: "Who set Gianna up on a pedestal?"
Emilia: "Everyone . . . Granny . . . and . . . Mother. . . ."
Therapist: "Tell me, Emilia, what did your mother and your grandmother think of you when you were Gianna's age?"
Emilia: "That nothing . . . absolutely nothing about me was right."
Father: "Not even her beauty, and believe me, Emilia *was* beautiful!" (He sniggers as if her present condition were a joke.)
Emilia: "Nothing was right. They used to say that my body was misshapen . . . [she sits on the edge of her chair and imitates

a puppet, looking grotesque because of her extreme emacia-
tion] . . . I had flat feet pointing inwards . . . [to her mother]
. . . When I was small you did your best to get me to have . . .
ugly knees . . . legs like a football player's . . . a bottom that
touched the ground . . . quite frightful . . . and a bust . . . that
absolutely defied any bra [gesture]."
(They all laugh at Emilia's funny antics, and egg her on.)
Brother: (grinning) "And what about your nose?"
Emilia: "Ah yes, an enormously thick nose, and my teeth. . . . I had
a very small palate and I always slept with my mouth open so
that I dribbled all over my pillows. . . . My hair, thin and
mousy . . . absolutely ghastly. . . ."
Brother: "You forgot your low forehead. . . ."
Emilia: "Yes, that too . . . good for nothing . . . at school I did get
top marks, but then I had to swot for it all day . . . and all that
time I spent in church. . . ."
Mother: (speaking in dialect, evidently imitating her own mother,
and laughing) "An old bigot just like her father."

(Emilia follows her mother's unspoken command and also breaks
into dialect, imitating her maternal grandmother in an obvious
attempt to divert attention to that [absent] person. Throughout
the entire farce everyone keeps laughing, as if they were discussing happy memories of bygone days. The therapist does not
join in the general merriment but grows visibly sadder; at long last
he cuts into the transaction and addresses the patient in stern
tones.)

Therapist: "Emilia, in these distressing circumstances I can't see
how you could possibly have loved your mother so much, or
why you should have missed her on your recent trip to Rome.
How can you miss someone who had such a low opinion of
you and said all these horrible things about you. . . . I should
have felt terribly resentful in your place."

(Everybody, including Emilia, falls into an icy silence.)

Emilia: (plaintively) "But I thought it was all Granny's fault. . . ."
Mother: Everyone knew what Granny was like . . . no one took her
seriously. . . . Emilia, you weren't meant to believe her. . . ."

Therapist: "How could Emilia fail to believe her? [turning to the patient]. . . . And how did your mother react to Granny's remarks?"

Emilia: "She just laughed. . . ."

Therapist: "Well? Didn't that make it even worse?"

Emilia: (sobbing) "But how could I possibly hate my own mother?"

Therapist: "Whom did you hate?"

Emilia: "Myself! [long pause] I won't be parted from her—if I'd hated her I would have left—but I didn't. . . . I believed every word she said, I talked like her, I was like her, even at school. . . ."

Therapist: "How can you call this love . . . you keep clinging to her and speak of anger and rebellion as if it were love. . . ."

Brother: "That's because *their* family expected one to call it love" (by "their family" he was referring to his mother's family, and, at the same time, betraying a secret rule).

In this transaction we can see clearly that the rejection (clownish antics, laughter) of the dramatic content of the communication was shared by the whole group, including the patient. The therapist's intervention cut short these antics and revealed the true drama they were meant to hide. This kind of intervention is far more beneficial than stopping the entire transaction so as to point out the incoherence of the two levels of communication. In the present case this would have meant robbing a crucial moment of its therapeutic potential.

(It is important to note that in subsequent interviews the family never again displayed this type of behavior so that it became possible to collaborate with them more constructively.)

INTERVENTIONS INTO THE PROBLEM OF LEADERSHIP

When every member of the family has difficulties in stating in the first person what he wants or does not want, then one method of intervention is to metacommunicate the therapists' own observation. In so doing we take care to emphasize the right of every member to have desires of his own and to express them frankly.

Experience has shown that interventions of this type, far from being rejected, very often cause astonishment; no one had realized that he or she was engaging in secret or deceptive maneuvers. On occasion we have asked that, during the interval before the next session, every member of the family should always state what he wants or does not want in the first person, and that one member keep written notes of any failure, including his own, to observe this rule. This forces the family to "metacommunicate" continually even between sessions and hence to reduce obscurity and confusion. Asking family members to state their likes and dislikes in the first person sometimes forces the patient into a paradoxical situation from which he can only escape in one of two ways: by abandoning the symptom or by coming into the open. In the second case it becomes clear that the symptom was used as a form of blackmail and not as a frank expression of the patient's desires.

INTERVENTIONS INTO THE PROBLEM OF COALITIONS

The problem of coalitions is undoubtedly one of the most important in family psychotherapy. Failure to grasp the necessity of intervening into the system of coalitions has caused us quite a few failures, especially during our initial period. Essentially, this type of intervention calls for the intervention of tactics designed to draw father and daughter into a constructive alliance. *This alliance, however, should only be temporary, and great care should be taken that it is not destructive to the mother*, who will otherwise feel excluded and may become depressed or hostile. *The ultimate purpose of this type of intervention is to open the generation gap, so that the daughter may at long last start living her own life.*

This procedure, though easy to explain, is difficult to put into practice. To begin with the system often succeeds in convincing the therapists that the father is in fact totally unreliable. The mother misses no chance to point out her husband's inadequacies where family problems are concerned, and the husband's behavior confirms this view. Moreover, because the daughter often evinces hostility and impatience or expresses fears that it will never be possible to have a meaningful dialogue with him, he, in turn, becomes increasingly reluctant to enter into a bipartisan relationship with her.

In order to surmount these difficulties we have used a variety of tactics and prescriptions, some of which I shall now mention in brief.

In one case, in which the daughter's physical condition was extremely grave and the problem of getting her to eat devolved exclusively on the mother, we thought it essential to compel her detached and Olympian father to become emotionally involved with his daughter. Ostensibly so as to avoid the imminent tragedy of hospitalization, we solemnly proposed that the father alone should take charge of his daughter's meals for some time and that he should eat with her in her room. He was to have the same amount of food as his daughter and to leave whatever she left. Thanks to his extreme self-control, he lost several kilograms before hunger and exasperation finally drove him to have a violent scene with her. The girl had at last got the better of him and had for the first time in her life received a clear and coherent message from him. (Immediately afterwards, she abandoned her symptoms.)

In another case, taking a sympathetic view of the great suffering the patient's refusal to eat caused her mother, we suggested that the mother make the great sacrifice (she was totally "dedicated" to the good of others) of leaving home for a fortnight's holiday. Father and daughter, in their turn, were to make the "sacrifice" of looking after themselves during her absence. By this device we were able to clarify the real nature of the relationship between father and daughter without putting the blame on anyone.

In families with sons and daughters we tried more complex alliance tactics, which, however, proved to be of purely marginal effect unless they went hand in hand with the consolidation of the father's position. When this strategy is successful we invariably end up with intelligent, effectual fathers. *This suggests strongly that the so-called ineffectual father is a product of co-operation between all the members of the system and not an intrapsychic fact.* In this regard I must mention that in one such family the system misled us into writing the father off and conferring his role on one of the sons, in the belief that he would provide a more reliable ally for the patient. We had to acknowledge that this was a further humiliation of the father (required by the system in order to avoid changes).

I should like to add that whenever a temporary alliance between father and daughter is expressly advised by the therapists or tolerated as the unavoidable result of some instruction, the purpose must always be to bring the existence of perverse triangles into the open the better to combat it.

By perverse triangles I refer to *secret* coalitions between one generation and the next against one of the peers. Such coalitions are never acknowledged, and whenever the behavior of the two is such as to betray their secret compact, the betrayal is immediately washed over by metacommunications. The pathogenic structure of the perverse triangle, therefore, does not so much lie in the coalition itself as in the simultaneous denial of its existence and that of the generation gap.

In other words, "there is a certain behavior which indicates a coalition, which, when it is queried, will be denied as a coalition. More formally, the behavior at one level which indicates that there is a coalition is qualified by metacommunicative behavior indicating that there is not" (Haley 1964).

I use the term *coalition* in Haley's sense. By coalition I refer to that process of joint action which is directed *against* a third person, in contrast to an alliance in which two out of three people may openly make common cause.

There is, of course, no reason at all why one of the parents, in our case the father, should not havé a close emotional relationship with his daughter, or even declare that he has entered into a temporary alliance with her against certain of his wife's more intolerable incursions. However, he must guard against the temptation to ignore the generation gap by putting the daughter in his wife's place. Whenever he enters into alliance with her, he must do so for rational and explicit ends.

I would also like to add that, in some cases, our instructions, aimed at bringing father and daughter face to face, far from resulting in a closer emotional relationship, have led to the exposure and elimination of a pathologically ambiguous situation. In all these cases the father, manifestly dissatisfied with his wife, was in the habit of sending his daughter subtle messages, generally of an unspoken kind. It takes an attentive therapist to observe the furtive exchange of ironical glances or the sighs that occur whenever the wife voices one of her usual grievances. It is with the help of such secret messages—so many redundancies—that the father reinforces the daughter's hostility to the mother, insinuating that, if only the mother were not in the way, they would share heaven knows what wonderful mystical experiences. (In this connection I might point out that none of our anorexic patients has ever selected a chair near her father—they usually sit next to the mother or away from the whole group.) In two such cases we issued instructions, without further explanations, that entailed face-to-face encounters between father and daughter long enough to provoke clarifying reactions. Now in both cases our orders were greeted with ill-concealed delight by the daughter, who was no doubt hoping that her father would at last make good the promise of his glances with some sort of beatific dialogue. What happened was the precise opposite.

One of the two fathers, who found himself trapped with his daughter in a small seaside flat for a whole week, shut up like a clam except to break the silence from time to time with: "Wouldn't it be lovely if Mommy were here with us!" and scotched any attempt on his daughter's part to get him to join her in various activities. Everything would have to be deferred until that glorious moment when Mommy would join them! . . .

The other father, who had proved even more underhand in his secret communications with his daughter, was filled with immediate panic by our instructions. As soon as the much maligned wife, whom he had called a simpleton and a gossip, returned home after her prescribed holiday, he burst into tears like a baby (he was the efficient manager of a large business!). In his daughter's presence he pulled his wife close to him and implored her with further tears never to abandon him again, never to make him suffer as he had suffered during her two weeks' absence. During the session following this dramatic scene, we observed that the meaningful glances between father and daughter had come to an end. The father, clinging to his "legal" wife like a drowning man, shouted at the daughter to leave them in peace and to get on with her own life. The wife, so unexpectedly showered with appreciation, rallied to his side, and the daughter, incensed as only a woman can be who has for years been fooled by the wrong man, was for the first time in her life confronted by a fully united couple and made to realize that she could no longer importune them with her own problems.

Such observations are, of course, not new to psychiatry, for they can also be made during individual therapy, and quite especially in the analysis of transference phenomena. What is new, however, is the strategy of trying to bring matters quickly into the open without having to put them into words.

In fact, once we accept a cybernetic definition of the family, that is once we see it as "a self-regulating system obeying certain rules," we are immediately in possession of quite novel therapeutic instruments.

In the two cases I have just described it did not take the therapists long to realize that one of the unspoken rules of the system was *the taboo against seeing the relationship between father and daughter in its true light, and hence against metacommunications about this topic.* Now, had the therapists been imprudent enough to reveal the obvious redundancies in the behavior of father and daughter, and had they metacommunicated these observations to them, they would have been greeted with a series of disqualifications or blunt denials. Nor is that all. Because of our moralistic cultural background, such revelations, though expressed with neutral benevolence, are bound to be treated as so many accusations. The inevitable feedbacks are totally counterproductive and impede therapeutic progress.

Hence therapists and observers must keep their own counsel about their observations and use them to devise an appropriate intervention strategy, that is a set of *concrete* directives intended to explode one of the secret rules responsible for the malfunction of the system as a homeostatic unit. Only when this has been achieved can the therapist begin to intercommunicate about it meaningfully and hope to have his observations confirmed.

INTERVENTIONS INTO THE PROBLEM OF BLAME-SHIFTING

In all our interventions we take great care not to accuse anybody, however, indirectly, and least of all the parents. Even when exceptional circumstances (that are becoming rarer) have forced us to expose a particularly dramatic situation, we have confined our attempts to revealing certain secret rules that stand in the way of honest communication and perpetuate ambiguities and confusion (as when Emilia described her bitter resentment as "love"). Experience has taught us to rely increasingly on the method of *positive connotation*, that is, to attribute constructive intentions to the kind of interpersonal behavior that is commonly described as destructive or injurious. We realize that in using the term *positive* we fall into a linguistic trap, since such antinomies as good-bad and positive-negative have no place in our cybernetic model. But such is the moralistic climate of our age that, to make ourselves understood, we have, for lack of anything better, to continue using the old terms.

To clarify this point I can do no better than mention an actual example of positive connotation that helped us, *inter alia*, to thwart a dangerous maneuver on the part of one of our patients.

The reader may have gathered by now that anorexic patients (and not they alone!) are extremely skillful in presenting their parents in the worst possible light. They often do this by inciting them to act in ways that are bound to be disapproved of by others. If the therapists allow themselves to be caught in this trap, they may seriously endanger the further course of the treatment.

Thus, during the first family interview, one patient skillfully brought the discussion around to her premorbid phase, and quickly succeeded in getting her parents to express antiquated and repressive views on sexual matters that showed them up as old fogeys united only in their determination to thwart their daughter's nascent sexuality. The therapists, far from swallowing the bait, proceeded to make favorable comments on the parents' obvious fascination with their daughter's feminine charms, and on the way in which they had succeeded in driving these charms home to the patient herself. They would certainly not have acted in the way they did had they thought her anything but highly desirable. In fact their assessment of the situation was one with which the patient must have been in full agreement. Why else had she always been so loyal to them and never used even the slightest subterfuge to defy their prohibitions?

As a result of such interventions all members of the family are put on a single plane. This enables the therapist to fit their interactions into the model, which automatically excludes all arbitrary causal punctuations. In fact, in the present case, who is to say which member of the family "caused" the actual situation? Did the parents impede their daughter's sexual development with their fears? Or did the daughter herself start the whole process by signaling her own fears to them in one way or another? The only thing we can see, and quite clearly so, in the here and now of our family sessions is that the entire family collaborates in maintaining the *status quo*, notwithstanding their accusations and counteraccusations, which merely serve to harden self-defensive and rigid attitudes (including the depressive maneuver, especially on the part of the parents, of throwing up their hands in despair so as to convince the therapists that it is quite impossible to change people as set in their ways as they are).

Positive connotation of transactional behavior is to us the golden road for entering, and being freely admitted into, the system, *and changing it in due course. This is no less true of the system as a whole than it is of the patient's symptom.* For it is impossible to prescribe what has previously been criticized. Thus treating the anorexic symptom as a deliberate display of "badness" can only lead to immediate disqualification—the patient will always insist that it is not that she does not *want* to eat but that she simply *cannot.* If, by contrast, we give a positive connotation to the symptom and, in each case, stress the "good" intentions with the help of the particular material offered during the session, we are preparing the way for the paradoxical *prescription of the symptom.* Thus in the case we have been describing we were able, at the end of the very first session, to recommend that the patient (who, in our presence and without being asked to do so, had promised her parents a rapid improvement during her impending Christmas vacation) be extremely cautious in putting on weight. Her emaciation, we explained, was an extremely important protection against a host of fears and dangers with which we fully sympathized. In this way we set up a therapeutic double bind from which the patient could extricate herself only by rebelling against us, which, in the event, meant abandoning her symptom.

This subject of positive connotation is still one to which we have to devote a great deal of further thinking and experimentation, the more so as what is involved is not merely a tactical ploy but also what may turn out to be an important move from a bad to a better epistemology, one that may take us to the very heart of interhuman behavior. We shall deal with the problem in more detail in the following chapter (see pp. 216–222).

CHAPTER 17

The Cybernetics of Anorexia Nervosa

Mara Selvini Palazzoli

Having discussed the analytic approach to families with an anorexic patient, we can now take the final step: a theoretical synthesis based on the cybernetic model.

In systems theory, the family is treated as a whole that cannot be reduced to the sum of the characteristics of its members. What characterizes the family as a system is rather the specific transactional patterns it reflects.

Every family, considered as a transactional system, tends to repeat these patterns with a high frequency and consequently gives rise to redundancies. The latter enable the observer to deduce the rules, often secret and generally implicit, governing the functioning of a given family at a given moment and helping to maintain its stability.

If we define the family as a self-governing system based on rules established through a series of trials and errors, then *its members become so many elements of a circuit in which no one element can be in unilateral control over the rest.* In other words, if the behavior of any one family member exerts an undue influence

From *Self-Starvation*, 1981 ed., pp. 231–241.

on the behavior of others, it would be an epistemological error to maintain that his behavior is the *cause* of theirs; rather must we say that his behavior is the *effect* of past interaction patterns. The study of this type of family transaction is therefore the study of fixed behavioral responses and of their repercussions.

We have spoken of an epistemological error; the latter results from the arbitrary separation of a given behavioral pattern from the pragmatic context of the preceding patterns with which it forms an infinite series.

When I speak of "epistemology" I am not referring to an esoteric discipline reserved for professional philosophers. Every one of us, by his very being in a world he has to share with others, is bound to take a stand *vis-à-vis* his particular mode of existence, and hence to adopt a certain epistemology.

Again, when I speak of epistemological errors or bad faith, I am referring explicitly to a common error of modern Western culture (and hence of psychiatry): the idea that there is a "self" capable of transcending the system of relationships of which it forms a part, and hence of being in unilateral control of the system. For a more detailed analysis, see "The Cybernetics of 'Self': A Theory of Alcoholism," (Bateson 1972).

It follows that even such behavior patterns as reduce the ostensible victim to impotence are not so much stimuli as responses. In other words both partners in the transaction are mistaken—the manipulator who believes in his omnipotence no less than his apparently powerless victim.

But if both are mistaken, where does the real power lie? It lies in the rules of the game played in the pragmatic context of the behavioral responses of *all* the protagonists, none of whom is capable of changing the rules from the inside.

By defining the patient as a pseudo-victim, we are avoiding the blind alley of moralistic psychiatry. It would appear that R. D. Laing and his school, precisely because they have adopted Sartre's distinction between *praxis* and *process*, have fallen into just this moralistic trap. By contrast, if we treat the family as a system in which no one member can hold unilateral sway over the rest, then praxis and process become synonymous. "Persecutor" and "victim" become so many moves in one and the same game, the rules of which neither one can alter from within—all changes depend on strategic interventions from without.

In the particular case of a family with an anorexic patient, we find that the epistemological error of the whole group is that all of them believe that the patient, *because* of her symptom, wields power over the rest and renders them helpless. If we were to take a snapshot during the very first therapeutic session, we should see an anguished expression on the parents' faces, the patient sitting apart from the rest, straight as a statue, pallid and detached, her face showing utter indifference to the others' distress. Her behavior is a clear message, not least to the therapist: "If you think you can get me to break my fast, you'll have to think again. Just look at me: I am nothing but skin and bones and I might easily die. And if death is the price I have to pay for *my power*, then I shall willingly pay it."

This shows that the patient completely misjudges her own situation. To begin with, she is prey to a most disastrous Cartesian dichotomy: *she believes that her mind transcends her body* and that it grants her unlimited power over her own behavior and that of others. The result is a reification of the "self" and the mistaken belief that the patient is engaged in a victorious battle on two fronts, namely against: (1) her body and (2) the family system.

Now this error could not be called a mental illness, were the patient to adopt it voluntarily and were she to declare quite openly that she will take no food until she gets what she wants. This would constitute a rational choice on her part, not a "mental condition." Instead the anorexic sticks rigidly to the family rule that *no one member may assume leadership in his own name*. That is precisely why she derives her powers from an abstraction: her illness. It is the latter that wields power, afflicts her own body and makes others suffer for it. Like every mental symptom, the anorexic symptom, too, is a paradox oscillating between two illusory poles: spontaneity and coercion.

This raises the following problem: does the symptom indicate that the patient does not *want* to eat (spontaneity) or does it rather show that she *cannot* (coercion)? If we take the epistemological view we have just adumbrated, then we must answer both questions in the affirmative. The anorexic herself, however, insists that only the second alternative is correct, that is that she really *cannot eat.*

In dealing with such patients, the psychotherapist must therefore pay careful heed to: (1) the false epistemology shared by all the family members, that the patient is in unilateral control of the whole system; (2) the patient's belief that her *self* (or *mind*) transcends her body and the system, and that she can wage a successful battle on two fronts; (3) the fact that this battle is never waged in the first person, but in the name of an abstraction: the disease for which the patient cannot be held responsible; and (4) the fact that this abstraction is considered "evil" because it inflicts suffering on all concerned.

The therapist must devise his strategies accordingly and, in particular, he must aim at correcting the false epistemology underlying all these phenomena. But how is he to do that? By academic discussions, by communicating his insights, or by critical remarks? If he takes any of these courses, he will, as we have found to our cost, be sent away with a flea in his ear. What he must rather do is, first of all, reduce all members of the system to the same level, that is assign them symmetrical places in the system. Having observed the prevailing communication patterns, and avoiding the temptation of participating in any of the mutual recriminations, he will make it a point, and one that never fails, to approve unreservedly of all transactional behavior patterns he observes. We refer to this type of intervention as *positive connotation*, and the therapist must extend it to even those forms of behavior that traditional psychiatry of psychoanalysis pillories as destructive or harmful. Irritated though he may be by overprotectiveness, encroachment, parental fear of filial autonomy, he must always describe them as expressions of love, or of the understandable desire to maintain the unity of a family exposed to so much stress and the threat of dissolution.

In much the same way he must also lend a positive connotation to the patient's symptom. To that end, he will use what material he has collected to prove that the patient keeps sacrificing herself, albeit unwittingly, for a completely unselfish end: the cause of family unity.

This first and fundamental step in the practice of *positive connotation* is full of implicit messages:

1. The therapist ensures or consolidates his superior position on the hierarchial scale. This is because, in Western culture at least, a disapproving authority casts doubts on its self-assurance (as witness those pseudo-authorities who dispense punishments and prohibitions for the sole purpose of making their presence felt). An approving authority, by contrast, and one, moreover, that explains the motives of its approbation, is clearly one that has no doubts about its rationality.

2. The therapist shows that the entire group is engaged in a single pursuit, namely the preservation of the unity and stability of the family. This connotation, however, introduces an implicit absurdity: how can something so wonderful and normal as family unity exact so abnormally high a price as anorexia?

3. The therapist gently displaces the patient from her customary position to one that is complementary in the game, and, in so doing, alters the respective roles of all the members: he shows that the patient is so sensitive and generous that she *cannot help* sacrificing herself for her family, much as the others *cannot help* sacrificing themselves for the same ends.

4. The therapist keeps stressing the compulsive nature of the symptom ("the patient cannot help sacrificing herself") but takes care to underplay the harmful aspect by defining the symptom as something beneficial to the whole system. At the same time he also defines as "symptoms" the behavior patterns of the other family members (they, too "cannot help themselves" if the family is to stay together) and gives these "symptoms" the same positive connotation.

The way is now open for the decisive therapeutic step: the therapeutic paradox. The symptom, defined as essential to family stability, is *prescribed* to the patient by the therapist, who advises her to continue limiting her food intake, at least for the time being. The relatives, for their part, are also instructed to persist in their customary behavior patterns.

The result is a situation that is paradoxical in several respects, the first of which is quite obvious: the family has consulted the therapist and is paying him for the sole purpose of ridding the patient of her symptom, and all he apparently does in return is not only to approve of this symptom but actually to prescribe it!

Moreover the therapist, by prescribing the symptom, implicitly rejects it as such. Instead, he prescribes it as a spontaneous action that the patient cannot, however, perform spontaneously, and this precisely because it has been prescribed. Hence the patient is driven into a corner from which she can only escape by rebelling against the therapist, that is, by abandoning her symptom. In that case she may return to her next session looking better, only to find that the therapist fails to reprove her—yet another paradox.

A series of such moves proved so successful with three patients during the very first session, that they soon afterwards dropped their symptom. In general, however, we prefer to hasten more slowly. Active tactical interventions designed quite specifically to elicit significant responses from the family have been described in the last chapter, but as our work has advanced, and with it our understanding of the epistemological error responsible for the malfunctioning of such families, we have gone on to devise other tactics.

The most important and effective of these is the one that follows the cybernetic model more closely. It calls for the prescription of family rituals. Let me mention two concrete examples.

The first family to whom we applied the new strategy was not one with an anorexic member, but one with a 6-and-half-year-old son whose aggressive behavior bordered on the psychotic. I mention it here because it is so clear-cut.

The child, whose EEG had shown minimal brain damage, was brought to family therapy when a child psychoanalyst refused to continue his treatment. The child seemed totally inaccessible to psychoanalytic approaches and, moreover, intolerably hostile. After four sessions with the parents, two in the presence of the child, the therapists realized that, apart from being exposed to intense interparental conflicts, the child had been forced into a double bind situation from which he could not extricate himself. Labeled "sick" by the neurologists and having been doctored with massive doses of sedatives, he was treated like a maniac at home and hence allowed to behave in a way that no parents would have taken from normal children, such as vicious kicks at the mother's face as she bent down to tie his shoelaces, lunges with the table-knife, and plates of soup over the mother's dress. By contrast he was invariably treated to long sermons and reproaches about his past misdeeds whenever he behaved like a normal child of his age. The therapists saw quickly that their first move must be the eradication of this double bind situation, and this by destroying the parents' conviction that their child was "mental." But they also realized that they could not achieve this end by verbal explanations, which would have been disqualified there and then. Instead they decided to prescribe the following family ritual: that same evening, after supper, the entire family, consisting of the father, the mother, the patient, his little sister, and the maternal grandmother, would go in procession to the bathroom, the father carrying all the child's medicine bottles and solemnly addressing the following words to his son: "Today we were told by the doctors that we must throw all these medicines away because you are perfectly well. All you are is a naughty child, and we simply won't take any more of your nonsense." Thereupon he would pour the contents of the bottles, one by one and with great ceremony, down the lavatory, all the time repeating: "You are perfectly well." This ritual proved so effective (notwithstanding the mother's fears that the child would kill her without his sedatives) that it led to the disappearance of the aggressive behavior and, soon afterwards, to an amicable solution of the secret interparental conflicts (ten sessions).

Another ritual, this time repetitive, was prescribed to a family with a grave anorexic patient, whom we shall call Nora, and who, during the course of family therapy, had tried to commit suicide so effectively that she had to be resuscitated. This attempt showed that her therapists had made a serious miscalculation: they had focused attention so exclusively on her nuclear family as to miss the secret rule that nothing but good must be spoken of any members of Nora's extended family, a close-knit and powerful clan. It was only during the dramatic session following Nora's suicide attempt that her elder sister dropped some vague remarks about Nora's particularly "difficult" relations with one of her female cousins. Apparently the latter, backed by her mother, and envious of Nora's undoubted good looks, treated Nora with a mixture of affection and great cruelty. Both parents immediately hastened to repair the damage by harping at length on the angelic goodness of the cousin, "a real sister to our Nora." This caused Nora, who had never before mentioned the cousin to us, to speak of her throughout the rest of the session. She had clearly come to distrust her own feelings: if the cousin seemed spiteful and nasty, it was, no doubt, because she, Nora, was herself spiteful, envious, and bad.

In their meeting after the session, the therapists decided to keep their new knowledge to themselves, and not to engage in what were bound to be futile discussions. Instead they decided to prescribe the following ritual.

In the fortnight before the next session, Nora's family would lock the front door immediately after dinner on alternate days and sit around the table for an hour. A clock would be placed in the middle of the table, and every family member, in order of seniority, would have fifteen minutes to vent his own feelings and views, not least about other members of the clan. While any one was speaking the rest must not interrupt, let alone contradict. Moreover, whatever was said at the table must not be discussed outside the fixed ritual hour.

In this case, too, the ritual proved so effective that the treatment could be terminated in a total of fifteen sessions.

We can now explain what precisely we mean by family ritual.

From a *formal* point of view, a family ritual is an action, or a series of actions, accompanied by verbal formulae and involving the entire family. Like every ritual it must consist of a regular sequence of steps taken at the right time and in the right place.

Ritualization may smack of the magical or the religious, but this is not necessarily a disadvantage. It should, however, be stressed that the idea of prescribing a ritual was originally suggested by ethology, and quite particularly by certain intraspecific submission rituals whose sole purpose it is to convey placatory messages. The primary *aim* is to cure the patient with the help of a group engaged in a common task, that is the performance of the ritual.

We have found that the physical enactment of a ritual is

infinitely more productive of positive change than any form of verbalization can hope to be. To return to one of our examples, had we merely told the parents of our little "maniac" that their son was not really ill, and that they must not treat him as an invalid, we should never have effected so rapid a cure. But by uniting the whole family in a carefully prescribed ritual, culminating in the destruction of the child's medicines, to the repeated cry of "You are perfectly well," we were able to introduce a powerful collective motive and hence a new *normative system.* In that sense the ritual may be said to work because it persuades the whole group to strive towards a common goal.

In this connection I must stress the widespread use of rituals in modern China. These do not consist of verbal formulae and slogans to which the individual can turn a deaf ear through selective inattention, but try to foster the idea of social and family co-operation by means of dances, plays, and other public entertainments including, paradoxically enough, a whole range of competitive sports.

The "invention" of a family ritual invariably calls for a great creative effort on the part of the therapist and often, if I may say so, for flashes of genius, if only because a ritual that has proved effective in one family is unlikely to prove equally effective in another. This is because every family follows special *rules* and plays special *games.* In particular, *a ritual is not a form of metacommunication about these rules, let alone about these games; rather it is a kind of countergame* that, once played, destroys the original game. In other words, it leads to the replacement of an unhealthy and epistemologically false rite (for example the anorexic symptom) by one that is healthy and epistemologically sound.

I am absolutely convinced that mental "symptoms" arise in rigid homeostatic systems and that they are the more intense the more secret is the cold war waged by the subsystem (parent–child coalitions). We know that such pathological systems are governed by secret rules that shun the light of day and bind the family together with pathological ties.

In other words psychiatric "symptoms" tend to develop in family systems threatened with collapse; in such systems they play the same part as submission rites play in the animal kingdom: they help to ward off aggression from one's own kind. There is just this tragic difference: the specific human rite, called "illness," acquires its *normative* function from the very malfunction it is trying to eliminate.

At this point I feel that I ought to summarize the central conceptions guiding our recent research, the better to bring out the difference between it and my earlier approach.

We have tried to establish whether or not families with an anorexic patient function as a typical model system that, at a given moment, gives the patient no choice but to take refuge in her anorexic symptom.

As described in Chapter 14 our research had a number of objectives and motives including:

1. Shift of the psychiatric focus of attention from the artificially isolated individual to the wider context of the institutional relationship in which he is involved;
2. My special concern with the problem of anorexia nervosa, thanks to which my services have been sought by a very large number of families with an anorexic member and which has enabled me to accumulate a very considerable body of data;
3. The extremely monotonous clinical picture of anorexia nervosa, which suggested that it ought to be possible to find variables less complex and less numerous than those associated with other psychiatric syndromes, for example, the schizophrenic.

It was mainly the well-known work of Haley (1959) with schizophrenic families that provided us with a methodological research model, or, more precisely, with parameters more suited to describing the family as an interactional system. These parameters are derived from systems theory, the pragmatics of human communication, and cybernetics.

At the Milan Family Study Center our team has been able to study twelve families with an anorexic member, treating each family as a single unit functioning as a system in which:

1. There is a willingness to communicate.
2. Every member of the system generally defines himself in the relationship in a coherent manner.
3. Every member rejects the messages of others (either on the content or the relationship level) with a high frequency. The rejection of food, which the patient finally expresses in her symptoms, seems to be specifically adapted to the interactional modality prevalent in her family: the symptom seems moreover to be specifically attuned not only to the repeated act of rejection, which thus constitutes one "redundancy," but also to another. During the sessions we usually observe that the parents will insist on defining the relationship to their daughter as one between "feeders" and "fed." The daughter, by contrast, will define the relationship in the opposite way, and this precisely through her anorexic behavior, which helps her to gain the upper hand in the fundamental human problem of who defines the relationship for whom. This redefinition is not made by using the first person singular, but in the name of the illness, that is, of a condition that is shrewdly presented in the customary moralistic and sacrificial tone of the family group. This explains why these patients so regularly make it their business to cook for the rest of the family, thus presenting themselves as "feeders."
4. All family members have great difficulty in playing the role of leader overtly.
5. All open alliances of any two against the third are proscribed.
6. No one member will take the blame for anything.

As for the peculiar interactional modality of the parental couple, we have defined it as one of "symmetry through sacrificial escalation."

In chapter 15, devoted to the therapeutic method, we have given a brief account of the techniques designed to change the mode in which anorexic families function. The parameters we have chosen to define the system have also suggested the best tactics for changing it.

The results have proved to be much more rapid and encouraging than those obtained through individual treatment: in the twelve families we have treated, five patients abandoned their symptoms within less than ten sessions; four in less than twenty sessions; and three broke off their treatment because of grave errors on our part.

Not only did the patients abandon their systems, but their families began to function in a new way.

Of course these conclusions are tentative, since only follow-ups can tell us whether the improvements are either lasting or, as we hope, stepping stones on the road to further progress.

With two families we were brought face to face with the problem of a pathogenic interaction between the nuclear and the extended family. In both cases we found it necessary to devise intervention tactics designed to break this pathogenic pattern.

This opens up a new vista based on Watzlawick's claim (1967) that "a phenomenon remains unexplainable as long as the range of observation is not wide enough to include the context in which the phenomenon occurs" (pp. 20-21). In other words, family therapy is the starting point for the study of ever wider social units.

PART FIVE

FROM VERBAL
TO ANALOGICAL
INTERVENTIONISM

CHAPTER 18

Paradox and Counterparadox

Matteo Selvini

From 1972 to 1975 the new team engaged in feverish creative activity. *Paradox and Counterparadox* (Selvini Palazzoli et al. 1978) sums up their therapeutic work with fifteen schizophrenic families.

That book is divided into three parts. Part I deals with the working method and epistemological model used: general systems theory, the contribution of Bateson and the Palo Alto group, and the pragmatics of human communication. Part II is devoted to a theory of schizophrenia. Part III, the longest (it accounts for twelve out of a total of sixteen chapters), presents a broad list of the tactics and therapeutic interventions used by the team.

The main shortcoming of the book is the lack of balance between Parts II and III: between the *generality and abstractness of the theoretical reflections on schizophrenia and the richness and creativity of the therapeutic interventions.*

The approach was still rooted in communicationalism; in the preface schizophrenia is defined as "a particular communication pattern inseparable from the communication patterns observable in the natural group in which it occurs, in our case, the family in schizophrenic transaction" (p. xii). The very title was based on a logico-communicationalist concept, that of the paradox, clearly recalling the classical formulation of the Bateson group. However, as in her earlier writings, Mara Selvini had begun to introduce hypotheses about relational games.

Thus the concept of disconfirmation and the impossibility of defining the relationship are reelaborated in terms of games. The schizophrenic family is defined as "a natural group internally regulated by a symmetry which is exasperated to the point that each member perceives its open declaration as extremely dangerous" (p. 21).

Every member of the family is driven on by a desperate and continuous effort to control the relationship with the rest. Failure does not stop these attempts but on the contrary aggravates them. Such persistence is defined as hubris, an excess of pride. The psychotic nature of this mode of relating to others is bound up with its cryptic and hidden character. There is only one way of avoiding rejection, namely "disqualifying one's own definition of the relationship before the other has the chance to do it" (p. 25). This symmetrical escalation gives rise to a whole series of paradoxes, disqualifications, and disconfirmations. The new approach to schizophrenia thus differed from the original communicationalist one in that it considered communicational dysfunctions the result of a particular symmetrical interaction. In fact, in such early communicationalist writings as the pioneering "Towards a Theory of Schizophrenia" (Bateson et al. 1956) the means of communication (the imposition of the double bind) had been associated either with intrapsychic characteristics (the ambivalence of the mother) or with a particular learning context (the inability to read metacommunicative signals or to label metaphors, for example).

Harking back to the past therefore prevailed over attention to the ongoing game. When the change from communicationalism to the games approach eventually came, it opened up an entirely new road, at the time still unexplored and not fully signposted to this day. However, as we look back at it some ten years later, we acknowledge the remarkable explanatory potential of the new research model.

The ground was thus still untilled: *Paradox and Counter-paradox* cast no fresh theoretical light on schizophrenia. The theoretical part is substantially a reelaboration of the ideas of Bateson, Haley, and Jackson, but applied explicitly to the attempt to define a particular relational game. That definition, however, remained remarkably general and abstract. As a result, the theoretical part is out of balance with the clinical part of the book: the richness, fantasy, originality, and variety of the therapeutic interventions described seem to lack solid foundations. The procedure is one of trial and error applied to the study of the particular relational game played by each of the families under review. The result is an enormous gulf between general ideas about schizophrenic families and the particular games that the various families who were the objects of study and of therapy were assumed to be playing.

THE PARADOX

The lack of continuity between the clinical work and the theory was also maintained in the highly abstract use of the concepts of paradox and counterparadox (Selvini Palazzoli et al. 1978): "As far as paradoxes are concerned, we can say that our research has shown how the family in schizophrenic transaction sustains its game through an *intricacy of paradoxes which can only be undone by counterparadoxes in the context of therapy*" (p. 8) [my italics, Ed.]. Maintaining that the schizophrenic game is characterized by a tangle of paradoxes, the authors tacitly renounced the attempt to probe into its nature, either because they considered it to be too complex or because they realized that every schizophrenic game is distinct and that it is impossible to discover any common denominators beyond the general ones set out in the book. The entire focus of attention was shifted toward counterparadoxes or toward therapeutic tactics likely to produce changes.

The period of *Paradox and Counterparadox* was also the time in which the utmost importance was attached to the conclusions drawn at the end of the session. The book pays relatively little attention to the method of conducting sessions,[1] because that method was considered no more than a preparation for the final intervention. The latter, as I have already said, was highly emphasized, not only by the tone of voice in which it was announced but also by means of a kind of ritualization. All this suggests that the title of the book, chosen for its appeal to the readers' imagination, does not reflect the real contents. The book gives no clear definition of "paradox," nor for that matter of "counterparadox," but presents a whole series of original tactics used to upset the family's assumptions and perceptions. What is so paradoxical about behavioral prescriptions or rituals? Even as far as the therapeutic interventions are concerned, the title seems to ignore the more creative and original idea the Selvini-Boscolo-Cecchin-Prata team was busily developing at the time.

The very use of the word *paradox* is suspect as the authors apply it to their therapeutic interventions; where, for instance, are the two logical levels, the self-contradiction, the double negation, and all the other elements defining paradoxical logic? Only at the cost of marked conceptual contortion can the particular use of the term be justified.

In 1981, in a paper entitled "Some Irreverent Thoughts on Paradox," Paul Dell (1981) was to demonstrate the *theoretical* inconsistency of the therapeutic paradox, pointing out that the term was being applied to a whole series of interventions that were merely unconventional, i.e., that ran counter to the way of thinking (the epistemological assumptions) associated with western culture (and its Aristotelian conception of reality).

Mara Selvini's (Selvini Palazzoli 1981) reply to Dell appeared in the same issue of the journal:

> Even though I am the first author of the book, *Paradox and Counterparadox*, whose title might be considered rather compromising, I cannot share Paul Dell's opinion that a master theoreti-

---

[1]In this respect it should be noted to what extent interactions *between* members of the family were still tolerated or even encouraged for the purpose of closer observation of intrafamilial communication [Ed.].

cian is vitally needed to give a comprehensive explanation of so-called "therapeutic techniques."

This view has developed from another of a more general nature: given the limitations of our minds, the more complex the model we adopt, the more we are forced to make simplifications. The systemic approach, which I have adopted, therefore implies—in respect to an optimum ideal—far more drastic simplifications than those implied by a linear approach.

If we consider the paradoxes that occur in the extreme complexity of human behavioral systems, for instance in the family group, we must realize that in order to understand them fully we must introduce into our analyses not only the variable *time*, as Dell so rightly points out, but also the variable *context*, or, better still, the variable *context marker*. In fact, I believe that in behavioral systems it is largely through a peculiar use of context markers that the paradox derives its paradoxality. For example, the ability to "create confusion" is greatest in families in so-called "schizophrenic transactions." In their communicational style, different contexts or rather different logical levels of context markers are treated as if they were the same thing. We can imagine the intricacy of paradoxical traps (for family members as well as the therapist!) that can arise from this manipulation of context markers. But is it possible for the therapist to unravel such an intricate tangle? In my opinion it is impossible and may well be unnecessary, if the primary purpose of the therapist is to provoke a change of the system.

For that reason, returning to the idea of the need for simplification when a complex model is adopted, we at the Milan Center are gradually moving towards the invention of therapeutic techniques that will permit, so to speak, a giant step forward beyond the daily games of families. Let me give an example taken from the conclusion of a *second* family session:

"Last time, at the end of our first meeting, we told you that we were doubtful as to whether or not we should offer you family therapy. This time we're absolutely certain that family therapy is indicated. Your next appointment is on ——— at ——— o'clock. You (names of children in order of age) stay at home. We'll be expecting you Signor and Signora. . . ."

Is this intervention a real paradox (we have prescribed family therapy yet excluded some members of the family)? This is a question that might well interest Dell, but, to tell the truth, we are not very interested in the answer to the question. What we are interested in is that the family receive information to shake them up because it is totally unexpected, surprising, and produces effects that can be seen in the immediate reactions of the various family members.

Paul Dell, in his paper, mentions the recent confluence of thinking of many authors concerning the importance of the variable *time* in reference to paradox. But I think I see another confluence now common to many outposts of science and art: people are most affected when they expect a certain message and receive instead a message on a totally different level. Consider the case of a film director. He announces a film of a certain type, and therefore the audience expects the appropriate language. His genius derives from the fact that he is then able to invent a totally different language for communicating his primary message.

And here we come to the fundamental concept, the concept of premises, and therefore of expectations, that is so rightly stressed by Dell. It is my belief that what is surprising is surprising precisely because it conflicts with the premises. As family therapists, we must have a closer understanding of the cultural and idiosyncratic premises of a dysfunctional family, the better to thwart them.

Anything predictable is therapeutically inefficient, as we have learned to our cost. Many of the families that come to our Center arm themselves by reading our book *Paradox and Counterparadox*, with the result that many of the interventions described there do not work, regardless of the fact that we always try to adapt them to the specific family context. It is as if they had been immunized. We have had to find other interventions that would work, and when we succeeded in doing that, it was by relying on intuition. Now we have the task of explaining at length what we mean by "the unexpected," which, considering the complexity of systems theory, will certainly not be an easy matter [pp. 44–45].

Critical comments on the consistency and theoretical usefulness of the paradox concept did not, however, diminish the enormous importance of the clinical experiences gained from 1972 to 1978, when Mara Selvini still combined interventionist methods with paradoxical comments. That phase continued for many years until it was gradually superseded by a different approach first developed in 1979 to 1980. Even so, the "confusing" and "surprising" nature of the therapist's comments has remained a fixed element of current techniques, if in a slightly modified form. One of Mara Selvini's last reflections on paradoxical comments is contained in the following extract from an interview she gave Klaus Deissler of the German journal *Kontext* in 1979:

Deissler: Have you been able to make significant follow-up discoveries?

Selvini Palazzoli: That's a very interesting question! We are just in the process of doing follow-up research on the sessions described in *Paradox and Counterparadox*—after many years, that is.

We have made a most interesting discovery: we have found that many patients are now cured who were not yet cured at the end of the therapy; our rate of cures with anorectic patients is approximately 90%—including cases we originally considered as failures. At this moment we are only at the beginning of our control experiments. I have the impression that curing a family with the help of a paradoxical comment is very much like hunting a white whale. We are on a ship, we give chase to the whale, we fire a paradox into his body, and the whale disappears—but with a harpoon inside, and that continues to do its work slowly. In exactly the same way, the paradox in the family continues to do its work; it's far from done at the end of the treatment—it's highly dynamic. If we manage to hit the whale, the harpoon continues to do its work for years and years: it's all most interesting.

Thus we had one case that I recall very well: the family T. with an anorectic girl. The family seemed utterly discouraged. They had just the one daughter, 13 years old. We did a follow-up six years later; the daughter is 19 now. Well, when the family—father, mother, and daughter—first presented themselves, the daughter had been suffering from anorexia for the past four years, that is from the age of 9. She was quite tiny, like a dwarf. At the time I was conducting the session; the family seemed very unhappy about their terribly small girl, about their dwarf. After the session, my colleagues and I concluded that the resistance of that family was so strong as to call for an extraordinary and extremely crude intervention. I accordingly let them know in a very cryptic way that there was every indication that family therapy was called for but that I had decided not to take them on because it was much better for the girl to remain anorectic. For, were she cured and had she started to eat, she would have had to recognize that she was a dwarf, that her bones had stopped growing. I added that after four years of anorexia the skeleton could not possibly go on growing, and that she would always remain stunted. In fact, it would have been far better if she died from anorexia rather than be cured of her symptom and live on as a poor, unhappy dwarf. The family rounded on me with almost savage venom. I said that I was very sorry and I told them to call me again in six months' time; right now I lacked the courage to take on a case that meant facing a dwarf and knowing that, therapy or not, the girl would always remain one. When the six months were over, the family failed to call.

Since then six years have gone by, and two weeks ago, when Giuliana (Prata) was doing follow-up research, her eyes fell on the case of the family T. with the relevant data: a single session, etc. She decided to call the family. The telephone was answered by an irate father, who said as furiously as he might have had the session been held the day before: "Are you Dr. Prata from the Institute of Psychotherapy in Milan? Tell that fine professor of yours, that idiot of a Selvini, tell her that she herself is a dwarf, a fat slob. My daughter has grown 20 centimeters in just one year and has put on 20 kilograms."

She and her family had been cured by the rage I had produced. This shows quite clearly how wrong I would have been to speak of love, sorrow, compassion, etc.; compassion has cured no one so far; something more useful was needed. That family was cured by fury—the father was furious: "Tell her that she herself is a dwarf, a fat slob!"

REFLECTING ON LANGUAGE

The observation and detailed classification of the communicational disturbances peculiar to the family in schizophrenic transaction are undoubtedly an advance in the field of scientific research. For us, however, they were also a source of error as long as we sought to introduce change in the family through correction of such communicational peculiarities: corrections we based on the pointing out of such peculiarities and on encouraging the reformulation of messages in the "correct" way. In other words, we tried to "teach" the family to communicate functionally (Selvini Palazzoli et al. 1978, p. 51)

This comment is important, both as a critique and as a self-critique: it disavows the explicit teaching of correct modes of communication advocated in *Self-Starvation* (and mentioned in my comment on that book). This is how the above passage from *Paradox and Counterparadox* continued:

We also believed that we could fruitfully use the verbal code, mistakenly presuming it to be shared by the family in schizophrenic transaction.

Finally we realized how much our belonging to a verbal world conditions us. In fact, since rational thought is formed through language, we conceptualize reality (whatever that may be) according to the linguistic model which thus becomes the same thing for us as reality.

But language is not reality. In fact, the former is linear while the latter is living and circular. Shands (1971) says that "language prescribes for us a linear ordering of data in discursive sequence. Overwhelmingly and unconsciously influenced by the linguistic method, we then decide and enforce acceptance of the notion that the universe is organized on a linear basis, in cause and effect patterns of general relevance. Since language demands subject and predicate, actor and acted upon, in many different combinations and permutations, we conclude that this is the structure of the world. But we soon learn, in any delicate and complicated context, that we cannot find such a concretely defined order except by imposing it, and we thereafter operate by setting a limit in the middle of a continuous variation, which makes the distinction between 'hypo-' and 'hyper-,' between 'normal' and 'abnormal,' between 'black' and 'white' (p. 32)."

Nevertheless, we are hamstrung by the absolute incompatibility between the two primary systems in which the human being lives: the living system, dynamic and circular, and the symbolic system (language), descriptive, static, and linear.

In developing his species-specific characteristic, language, which is also the tool of tools for the organization and transmission of culture, man has to integrate two entirely different communicational modes: the analogical and the digital. Since language is descriptive and linear, we are forced, in order to describe a transaction, to use a dichotomization or to introduce a series of dichotomizations. The dichotomization which we are forced to use by the very nature of language, requiring a "before" and "after," a subject and object (in the sense of the one who *performs* the action and the one who *receives* the action), implies a postulate of cause and effect, and, in consequence, a moralistic definition. Moralism is intrinsic to language because the linguistic model is linear. . . .

In the case of the family in schizophrenic transaction, where the two communicational levels, the analogical and the digital, are in competition, our linguistic conditioning led us to a series of errors, the most significant of which can be summarized as:

a) conceptualization of the living reality of the family in a linear sense rather than in a systemic-circular sense;

b) judgment of the communicational modes of the family as "mistaken" in comparison to our own, and the consequent attempt to correct them;

c) our basing ourselves almost exclusively on the digital code, that is, on the level of the content of the message, in the attempt to act therapeutically [pp. 51–53].

The objection to interventions involving the explicit teaching of correct modes of communication is here expressed in terms of codes and the linearity of language. Today this seems inadequate: interventions based on implicit (analogical) or explicit incongruencies in communication *do not strike at the basic nodes of the relational games*, but only at one of their expressions. For that reason, not even the implicit method of teaching correct communication is relevant.[2]

In theoretical respects, the most important and original concepts of *Paradox and Counterparadox* are those concerned with the linear nature of language and with the epistemology of the subject-predicate linguistic model. The transition from a linear world view based on causes producing effects unidirec-

[2]Cf. note 3 on p. 82 [Ed.].

tionally to a circular conception in which causes and effects are reciprocal is considered a fundamental step in therapy, ultimately leading to restructuring of the epistemological premises of the family.

In an interview she gave to the German journal, *Sozialmagazin*, Mara Selvini (Selvini Palazzoli 1978) was asked for her views on the politico-social aspects of her new therapeutic approach based on a reevaluation of the analogical code:

> *Question*: Why do you say in your *Paradox and Counterparadox* that your kind of therapy can also be used with working-class families?
>
> *Selvini Palazzoli*: Because we adapt our method to the family. That is to say, we do not hand out pedagogical recipes, we do not make interpretations, we do not offer explanations, we simply stimulate: we research the rules that condemn the family to playing a repetitive game. At this point our intervention takes the form of a prescription, of a ritual, i.e., something they have to do but need not understand. With that approach, the educational level of the family does not matter in the least; a simple prescription can be followed at all social levels.
>
> *Question*: Minuchin, who ran a family therapy clinic in the slums of Philadelphia, said that the most important thing for such families was not reflection or persuasion but experience. What do you say?
>
> *Selvini Palazzoli*: We fully agree with Minuchin that persuasion does nothing but increase the resistance. We have to build the experiences not only of slum families but of all families, rather than give explanations. If at all, explanations can be given after the family has changed, but not before.
>
> *Question*: What are your own experiences with working-class families? Do their problems differ from those of other classes?
>
> *Selvini Palazzoli*: All the families that come to us have very seriously disturbed children, for instance suffering from schizophrenia, infantile psychoses, or grave anorexia nervosa. Faced with such massive family dysfunctions and with such grave symptoms on the part of the designated patient, I can see no difference between working- and middle-class families. I also believe, and here I am expressing a personal view, *that social conditions have no influence on schizophrenia*. This is because the statistical

distribution of schizophrenia is the same throughout the world. The probable explanation is that schizophrenia is a disturbance whose roots are deeply embedded in human behavior. In families with slight disturbances there may well be class distinctions; however, we have no experience of them since we do not work with families of that type.

Question: Class values and norms are also reflected in language. The autonomous individual, as the ideal of the middle classes, is reflected in an "elaborated code"; the importance of solidarity and togetherness to members of the working class is expressed in the "restricted code." Different forms of therapy have often failed because of the resulting difficulties of mutual understanding. In your case that problem does not seem to exist. Why?

Selvini Palazzoli: The explanation is very simple indeed. We believe that we must try to cure the family with minimal use of language. Unfortunately we are not yet there. The pragmatic theory of human communication teaches us that every communication has a context level, often highly coded in verbal language, and a relational level that is mainly expressed through an analogical, nonverbal code. We believe that it should be possible, in therapy, to communicate essentially in the nonverbal mode. We may still be a long way from that ideal, but the linguistic ability of the family does not interest us very much; because we want to understand the game that is being played within the family, we are much more interested in the behavioral modes than in verbal expressions [pp. 32–41].

THE THERAPEUTIC COUPLE

Among the changes that distinguish Mara Selvini's current therapeutic technique from that used from 1972 to 1978, the abandonment of the old insistence on having the sessions conducted by a heterosexual pair of therapists was one of the most important. Today we greatly prefer the interview to be conducted by *just one* therapist. This is a direct consequence of the relinquishment of all therapeutic hypotheses of psychoanalytical or pedagogical origin: it no longer seems important that the therapists should present themselves as adult model figures or as a couple capable of communicating in a healthy way (that is, neither rejecting nor disconfirming).

In *Paradox and Counterparadox* (Selvini Palazzoli et al. 1978), use of the therapeutic couple was justified as follows:

> The use of the therapeutic heterosexual couple is another important aspect of the Institute's work: a more "physiological" equilibrium is established between the two co-therapists, and between them and the family. Moreover, certain redundancies in the initial interaction of the family with one or the other of the therapists can help the team understand certain rules of the family game.
>
> Thus in the case of the family traditionally dominated by women, the members, or certain members, of the family will immediately show a tendency to turn towards the female therapist, apparently ignoring her partner. The use of the heterosexual couple has also helped us to avoid the trap of certain cultural sexual stereotypes inevitably shared by the therapists. In discussing family sessions, we have often observed the completely contradictory impressions voiced by the two therapists in regard to the couple and the tendency to take a moralistic view of the interaction between the two:
>
> "How could he marry a woman like that!"
>
> "What are you talking about? He's the one who provokes her. Didn't you notice? He was even doing it with me!"
>
> Awareness of this phenomenon helped us to adopt the systemic model in the face of a strongly rooted tendency to make arbitrary punctuation and causal interpretations [pp. 10–11].

With regard to the rules of the family game it is impossible to decide whether attachment to the male rather than the female therapist or *vice versa* is independent of the therapist's behavior (or age, name, and so on) and hence a rather ambiguous piece of information. We have found, moreover, that cultural experiences and cultural stereotypes can be identified much more clearly when the co-therapist is engaged in direct supervision behind the one-way mirror.

The main argument against the use of therapeutic couples, however, can be found in Mara Selvini's "Hypothesizing-Circularity-Neutrality: Three Guidelines for the Conductor of the Session" (see Chapter 29).

When a session is largely based on the activity and directivity of the therapist, then the presence of two therapists is unnecessary and only introduces further complications: while one therapist checks on a hypothesis, the other may have to look on idly since, if he intervenes, he may well cross his colleague's path. If he does, the session becomes utterly confused and hard to supervise because two different investigations overlap. Particularly with chaotic and rebellious families, the presence of two active therapists renders control of the session more difficult because the unruly family member tends to break off the conversation with one therapist by turning to the other.

In this area, too, it may be helpful for purely didactic purposes to retrace the road Mara Selvini has traversed.

In fact, a therapist beginning his career may find it very worrying to tackle a family by himself. Thus, if he has a good working relationship with a colleague, he may cope better with an unruly family precisely because he is being backed up.

The problem of the overlap of distinct hypotheses remains but can be partially remedied with frequent exits from the session for the purpose of agreeing on the next move.

THE LAST CONTRIBUTIONS FROM THE *PARADOX AND COUNTERPARADOX* PHASE

The original Italian version of *Paradox and Counterparadox* was published without the last three chapters of the manuscript. Two of these, Chapter 17 ("The Therapists Prescribe the Ultimate Paradox to Themselves") and Chapter 18 ("The Therapists Give Up the Parental Role, Paradoxically Prescribing It to the Members of the Last Generation") were left out because they concerned a family that had been discussed in other parts of the book. It seemed injudicious to base so large a part of the book on a single family, even though that family did so much to stimulate the team's interventionist ideas.

Moreover, detailed and lengthy references to that family seemed undesirable as it seemed likely that family members would read the book. Probably that second reason was the more important, seeing that Chapters 17 and 18 were included in the American edition, which was published by Jason Aronson Inc. in New York in 1978.

"The Therapists Prescribe the Ultimate Paradox to Themselves" (Selvini Palazzoli et al. 1978, pp. 157–162) is really an interventionist flight of fancy, and on rereading it I find that it bears witness to the *excesses* of this therapeutic style.

Chapter 18 (Selvini Palazzoli et al. 1978, pp. 163–171) has more ambitious aims: the description of an entire course of therapy (a series of successive interventions) is coupled to a specific hypothesis on psychosis. That hypothesis can be summed up as follows: the starting point of the psychosis is an incongruous demand directed by both parents to the child: "Only by being a real parent to me can you be a real son to me." (This demand is connected with the competition between the parents.) When that sort of family enters therapy, this incongruous attribution of the parental role also becomes attached to the therapist, accompanied by a symmetrical attempt to enlist him as a judge of who is good and who is bad (a lesson the parents learned from their families of origin). Each spouse is animated by an excessive ambition to receive the palm of victory in the end.

For purposes of therapy, this hypothesis goes hand in hand with a series of moves:

1. Absolute neutrality in face of the increasingly determined attempts by the parents to obtain a pronouncement;
2. Redefinition of the behavior of the identified patient as being sacrificial;
3. When the identified patient abandons his symptom his parents present themselves as a helpless couple;
4. In the closing move of the therapy, aimed at liberating the children and at making the parents play their real part, the therapists abdicate the parental role conferred upon them by the couple and prescribe it paradoxically to the children.

These hypotheses and therapeutic procedures were said to provide a general approach to schizophrenia. In fact, however, they were generalizations based on a small number of cases, and above all on the one mentioned in our example. As her work proceeded, Mara Selvini realized that her suppositions did not lend themselves to being "exported" into other situations. This type of hypothesis, accordingly, was hardly ever used again.

"From Family Therapy to Individual Therapy," which is published here for the first time (Chapter 23), existed in proof form for the Italian edition of *Paradox and Counterparadox* but was left out at the last moment because Feltrinelli's editor was afraid that it might lead readers to confuse individual with family therapy.[3] The decision was probably wrong inasmuch as it encouraged the mistaken view that family therapy is a specific therapeutic technique and not the practical expression of a new paradigm and theoretical model for the study of human behavior.

These three contributions were still bound up with verbal interventionism. To the same conceptual framework—that used in *Paradox and Counterparadox*—there also belongs "The Family of the Anorectic and the Family of the Schizophrenic: A Transactional Study," which is a reelaboration of the paper read by Mara Selvini Palazzoli (1975) at the Fourth Family Therapy Symposium held in Zurich in October 1975. It was republished in Italy in the first issue of *Terapia familiare*. This paper re-echoes the mainly communicationalist approach of the years 1974–1975: mental illness is considered a special mode of communication, based largely on rejection in the case of anorectic families and on disconfirmation in the case of schizophrenic families.

The proposed treatment of the anorectic family is a clear application of some basic concepts first put forward in the last part of *Self-Starvation*. With schizophrenic families, by contrast, the clinical illustrations of Haley's classical concepts seem highly artificial and twisted and indeed a long way behind the more innovative ideas propounded in *Paradox and Counterparadox*.

For that reason, notwithstanding the excellent reception the article had in Italy, I have decided to exclude it from this collection. In fact, although historically interesting, it is likely to cause confusion in the didactic field.

The four chapters that follow have been chosen as the most significant in the book.

[3]The chapter was also omitted from the American edition [Ed.].

CHAPTER 19

Positive Connotation

Mara Selvini Palazzoli, Luigi Boscolo, Gianfranco Cecchin, and Giuliana Prata

The basic therapeutic principle which we call *positive connotation* was initially inspired by our need not to contradict ourselves when giving a paradoxical prescription of the symptom to the identified patient. How, after all, can one prescribe a behavior one has just criticized?

But, if *not* negatively connoting the symptom of the identified patient was easy, we could not say the same about all the behaviors of the other members, especially of the parents, which often appear correlated to that symptom. This traditional view easily leads to the temptation to use an arbitrary punctuation: correlating the symptom to the symptomatic behaviors of the "others," according to a causal connection. Thus it happened, not infrequently, that we found ourselves indignant and angry with the parents of the patient. Such was the tyranny of the linguistic model; such was our difficulty in freeing ourselves of it. We had to force ourselves to fully realize the antitherapeutic consequences of such a mistaken epistemology.

In fact, making a positive connotation of the symptom of the

From *Paradox and Counterparadox*, 1978, pp. 55–66.

identified patient and a negative connotation of the symptomatic behavior of the others is the same as drawing a dividing line between the members of the family system, arbitrarily defining some as "good" and others as "bad," and thereby precluding for the therapists any access to the family as a systemic unity.

It thus became clear that access to the systemic model was possible only if we were to make a positive connotation of *both* the symptom of the identified patient and the symptomatic behaviors of the others, saying, for example, that all the observable behaviors of the group as a whole appeared to be inspired by the common goal of preserving the cohesion of the family group. In this way, the therapists were able to put *all* the members of the group on the same level, thus avoiding involvement in any alliances or divisions into subgroups, which are the daily bread of such systems' malfunction. Dysfunctional families are in fact regularly, especially in moments of crisis, prone to such divisions and factional battles, which are characterized by the distribution of such stereotyped labels as "bad," "sick," "weak," "inefficient," "carrier of hereditary or social taints," etc.

Therefore the primary function of the positive connotation of all the observable behaviors of the group is that of permitting the therapists access to the sytemic model.[1]

But, one may ask, why must the connotation be positive, that is, a confirmation? Can't the same results be obtained through a global negative connotation (rejection)? One could say, for example, that both the symptom of the identified patient and the symptomatic behaviors of the family are "wrong," since they both attempt to maintain the stability of a "wrong" system—"wrong" because it generates pain and suffering. In doing so, however, one would be implying that the "wrong" system should change. And here, we should point out that every living system has three funda-

---

[1]Here it is important to specify that positive connotation is a metacommunication (in fact, the therapists communicate implicitly about the communication of all the members of the system), and therefore a step up to a superior level of abstraction. Russell's Theory of Logical Types postulates the principle according to which whatever includes all the elements of a collection should not be a term of the collection. In metacommunicating positively, that is, in confirming all the behaviors of the members of the collection, one metacommunicates something about the collection and thereby brings about that step up to a superior level of abstraction (Whitehead and Russell 1910–1913).

mental characteristics: (1) *totality* (the system is largely independent of the elements which make it up); (2) *autocorrective capacity* (and therefore the tendency toward homeostasis); (3) *capacity for transformation.*

By implying with a negative judgment that the system should change, one rejects that system, in that it is characterized by a prevalent homeostatic tendency. In doing so, one precludes any possibility of being accepted by dysfunctional groups, which are *always* characterized by this tendency. In addition, one would be committing the theoretical error of drawing an arbitrary dividing line between two of the equally functional characteristics in every living system—the homeostatic tendency and the capacity for transformation—as if the two were opposites, the former "bad" and the latter "good."

In every living system neither the homeostatic tendency nor the capacity for transformation can be judged good or bad, better or worse; each is a functional characteristic of the system, neither of which can exist without the other. Their combination occurs circularly, according to a continuum, substituting for the linear model of *either/or*, the circular model of *more or less*.

All the same, as Shands points out, man tirelessly pursues an impossible state of invariable relations, the "ideal" goal of re-creating his internal universe as completely independent of empirical proofs.

> The process can be seen as moving towards a state of complete independence from the here-and-now of somehow liberating oneself from the insistent physiological necessities of the moment. Scientists and philosophers both seek eternal verities independent of crude biological process. The paradox is that any real attainment of such a state would be incompatible with life for the simple reason that life is a continuously moving, continuously entropy-increasing operation which must continuously be supported by the input of negative entropy ("negentropy" both as energy and information) if the system is to be able to survive. Thus we find the endless paradox of the search for stability and equilibrium even though it is easy to demonstrate that equilibrium and stability are only attainable in inorganic systems, in a limited way at best. Equilibrium is incompatible with life or with learning: forward movement of at least minimal degree is an

absolute requirement for any biological system [1971, pp. 69–70].

Thus the family in crisis, when it comes seeking therapy, is also greatly involved in attaining this "ideal goal," and it would not even come were it not prey to the fear that its equilibrium and stability (defended and maintained against all empirical evidence) were in danger. The difficulties of motivating a family which *does not* feel itself in this danger are much greater.

When we speak of positive connotation, we find ourselves facing a series of contradictions and paradoxes. Earlier we spoke of the necessity of overcoming our linguistic conditioning and its intrinsic moralism. At the same time, to approve and confirm the homeostatic behavior of all the members of the family, we are forced to use language. The very expressions of approval which we use require the use of "moralistic" judgments, the same as if we were using phrases of disapproval.[2]

But it is here that we find ourselves in the paradox of using language to transcend language, and of adopting moralistic behavior in order to transcend moralism, since it is only thus that we can reach the systemic approach in which moralism has no meaning whatsoever.

In other words, by qualifying "symptomatic" behaviors as "positive" or "good" because they are motivated by the homeostatic tendency, *what we are connoting positively is the homeostatic tendency of the system, and not its members.* However, one can approve of certain behaviors of single individuals insofar as these behaviors denote the common intention toward the unity and stability of the group. Through such approval, the therapist not only defines himself as allied with the homeostatic tendency but actually prescribes it.

If we consider the peculiar modes of the family in schizophrenic transaction, we see that the rule of rules of these families is the prohibition of any definition of the relationship. It is as if the

[2]Here we should point out that the nonverbal aspect of our positive connotation is perfectly coherent to the message: it has no sign of recital, irony, or sarcasm. We are able to succeed in this when we are completely convinced that it is indispensable that we ally ourselves to the here and now of the family's homeostatic tendency.

family were metacommunicating to the therapists, "We can stay together only as long as we do not define the relationship. Not defining the relationship is essential to the stability of our system."

Upon reflection, we can see also that the symptom, that is, the psychotic behavior manifested by the identified patient, is, by its very bizarreness and obscurity, an attempt to avoid such a definition. The identified patient, in this sense, *obeys* the rule of rules. But, at the same time, the symptom alludes, in a critical and sarcastic way, as a protest as it were, to a definition of the relationship. In fact, at a higher level of abstraction, a relationship which has been defined as undefinable is, at the same time, defined as untenable.

The identified patient, in this sense, *threatens to violate* the rule of rules. And with this threat, he causes within the group a state of alarm related to the risk of rupture of the status quo.

When the family asks for help, it is seeking the restoration of the equilibrium it enjoyed previous to the outbreak of the symptom. It actually obtains this from traditional psychiatry, since the allusion threatening a new definition of the relationship, that is, a change, is labeled a "sickness" and "treated" as such.

Let us now consider how, and according to which epistemology, we deal with these families when they come to us.

First of all, the therapists make no distinction between the "symptom" of the identified patient and the "symptomatic" behaviors, that is, the peculiar patterns of communication, shared by all members of the family. Do the members of the group in schizophrenic transaction communicate in this way because they don't *want* to communicate otherwise or because they don't *know how* to? To this question we can answer that making a choice would be the same as falling into the illusion of alternatives and would be exactly like trying to decide if the identified patient *can't* or *won't* behave differently. At this point, the therapists "know" one thing only: all the members of the family oppose themselves to any change which presents a danger to their homeostatic ideal, and it is therefore necessary that the therapists ally themselves to this ideal (naturally, for the moment only).

Here we find the therapists doing exactly the opposite of the family. They deliberately ignore the allusive and threatening aspect of the symptom as a protest and invocation to change. Instead they underline and confirm only its homeostatic aspect. Similarly they confirm the behaviors of the other members of the family as striving for the same goal: the stability and cohesion of the group.

In addition to these fundamental functions, positive connotation has two other important interdependent therapeutic functions: (1) to clearly define the relationship among the family members and between the therapists and family without the danger of receiving a disqualification; and (2) to be a context marker, since it defines the context as therapeutic.

In regard to the first point, the family in schizophrenic transaction uses analogic language in contrast to digital language. The transactional patterns of this type of family are characterized by the effort not to define the relationship. Each member refuses to define himself as the one who defines the relationship (and therefore imposes upon the others rules of behavior), just as he refuses the others the right to define the relationship (and therefore to impose rules upon him).

As Haley has shown, and as our own experience has constantly confirmed, the members of the family in schizophrenic transaction disqualify with high frequency all the components of the message: author, receiver, content, and even the context in which it takes place.

In addition to this phenomenon, Haley (1959) has shown two others which are closely related: (a) none of the members of the group is inclined to declare or to truly recognize any leadership within the group; and (b) none of the members is willing to really accept the blame, that is, the responsibility for what goes wrong. We can thus see how the positive connotation transmits, on various levels, a series of messages:

1. The therapists clearly define the relationship between the various members of the family as complementary to the system, that is, to its homeostatic tendency. Finding themselves all in an identical complementary position in respect to the system annuls the hidden symmetric tension present in the various members of the family.
2. The therapists clearly define the relationship between family and therapists as complementary, as they (the therapists) declare their own leadership. This is done not through

a direct and explicit communication, but implicitly through
a global metacommunication which has the character of
being a confirmation.

In doing so, they communicate that they have no doubts about
their own hierarchical superiority. In fact, the authority which
approves and motivates this approval, communicates that it has no
doubts about itself.[3]

As for the context of such a communication, it can be neither
refused nor disqualified by the family members, since it conforms
to the dominating tendency of the system: the homeostatic tendency.

Exactly because the positive connotation is an approval and
not a reproach, the therapists can avoid being refused by the
system. Moreover, the family can for the first time have the experience of receiving an explicit confirmation.

But at the same time the positive connotation implicitly puts
the family in a paradox: why does such a good thing as the cohesion of the group require the presence of a "patient"?

Such a definition of a relationship as described in (a) is
connected with (b): a clear definition of the relationship, as described above, constitutes a marker of the therapeutic context.

To conclude, we can say that positive connotation permits
us to:

1. put all the members of the family on the same level, in that
   they are complementary in relation to the system, without
   in any way connoting them moralistically, thus avoiding
   any drawing of a dividing line between members of the
   group
2. accede to the system through the confirmation of its homeostatic tendency
3. be received in the system as full-right members, since we
   are motivated by the same intention

---

[3]Here we use the word *authority* in the positive sense, as in the latin *auctori-*
tas, which derives from *augere*—to augment (increase, enlarge) the other in the
ontic sense.

4. confirm the homeostatic tendency in order to paradoxically trigger the capacity for transformation since positive
   connotation prepares the way for the paradox, Why should
   the cohesion of the group, which the therapists describe
   as being so good and desirable, be gained at the price of
   needing a "patient"?
5. clearly define the therapist–family relationship
6. mark the context as therapeutic

However, the principle of positive connotation is not entirely
free from difficulties when it comes to its practical application. It
can happen that while a therapist believes he is giving a positive
connotation to all the members of the system, he is making, without realizing it, an arbitrary dichotomization.

This occurred to us in a case dealing with a family of three
generations, the identified patient being a 6-year-old boy diagnosed as severely autistic. In addition to the child and his parents,
the maternal grandparents were requested to take part in the third
session.

From the material gathered during this session it appeared to
us that there existed a possessive and intense attachment on the
part of the grandmother toward her daughter, who, for her part,
had contributed to this attachment by finding various ways of
being in need of maternal help. At the end of the session, we
expressed admiration for the daughter for the sensitivity and kindness she had always shown toward her mother. That this was an
error was immediately brought out by the response of the mother,
who cried, "So then I'm selfish!" Her indignation revealed the
hidden competition between mother and daughter as to which of
the two was the more generous. This error gained us the hostility
of the grandmother and jeopardized the continuation of therapy.

In other cases, we intended to make positive connotations,
which were instead received as being negative. The following case
describes this point.

The family consisted of three members: the father, Mario; the
mother, Marta; and Lionel, 7 years old, who had been sent to us
with the diagnosis of child autism. Considering the intense ties
maintained by this family with its extended family (as happens in
most families with psychotic children), we had requested the pres-

ence of the maternal grandparents at the fifth session. In this session we were able to observe a striking redundancy.

The two grandparents had always been, as a couple, ferociously symmetrical. In their feud, the family had divided into two factions: Marta had been taken over by her father, a violent and possessive man, while Nicola, her younger brother, now in his thirties and married, had always been preferred and overprotected by his mother, a meek and seductive woman.

During the preceding sessions, it had already become apparent that Marta, "having already" the love of her father, had yearned intensely for that of her mother, that is, for the pseudo-privileged relationship her brother had always enjoyed. She declared herself jealous of her brother, just as her husband Mario was. Mario, usually impassive and rigid, became animated only when he protested against his selfish and infantile brother-in-law, who, among other things, did not deserve the gratuitous love showered upon him by his mother. The redundancy which struck us in that session was a statement made by the grandmother over and over again, that she felt strongly inclined to love those who were not loved. She had loved and still loved her son Nicola *only because* her husband had never loved him, but had instead given his love to Marta. Now she felt obliged to love Nicola's wife (poor thing, she was an orphan), and she really loved Lionel, her psychotic grandson, most of all, because she had the impression that Marta had never really accepted him. Ever since he had been born (and here her voice trembled with deep-seated emotion) she had noticed how he had been nursed "as if he were a calf."

It became clear during that session what the moral imperative of that "sweet" grandmother had always been, and still was: "to love the unloved" (an obviously symmetrical move). At the end of the session, the therapists took leave of the family without any specific comment and cordially thanked the grandparents for having so kindly collaborated.

In the next session, only Lionel and his parents were invited. Taking into consideration the material gathered from the previous sessions, we began by praising Lionel for his great sensitivity. He had thought that his grandmother, generous as she was, needed to love only those who weren't loved. Since Uncle Nicola had gotten married six years ago and was therefore loved by his wife and no longer needed his mother's love, Granny was left with no one unloved to love. Lionel had understood this situation perfectly and had realized it was necessary to supply his grandmother with someone unloved whom she could love. Thus, ever since he had been small, he had done everything he could to make himself unlovable. This caused his mother to become more and more nervous, getting angry with him, while Granny, on the other hand, could show infinite patience with him. Only she really loved "poor little Lionel."

At this point in the session, Lionel began to make an infernal racket, banging two standing ashtrays one against the other.

The reaction of Marta was sudden and dramatic: she regarded our statement to Lionel as a sudden illumination of the truth. She added even more to the story by saying that she had actually felt happy when her mother criticized her for rejecting Lionel. "It's true, it's true!" she cried. "I was happy when my mother said I was treating him like a calf. But what can I do now? [wringing her hands] I've sacrificed my son to my mother! What can I do to pay for such a tremendous fault? I want to save my son . . . my poor baby!"

We immediately feared we had made a mistake. In fact, not only had Marta disqualified our definition of Lionel's sacrifice as voluntary by redefining him as *her* sacrificial victim, but she also felt that *she* had been defined by the therapists as the "guilty one" who had sacrificed her child to her mother. In this perspective, Lionel returned once again to his position of victim, and his father, as usual, seemed to find it convenient to remain silent, a spectator to something that really didn't concern him.

At this point, after the suspension of the session and the discussion of the team, the therapists decided to involve the father and to put him back in his position as an active member of the system. Upon rejoining the family, we observed benignly how Mario had, in contrast to Marta, presented absolutely no reaction to our comments.

Therapist: "Our provisional hypothesis is that you also must have some very profound motives for accepting this spontaneous sacrifice of Lionel."

Marta (shouting): "His mother! His mother! Lello [Lionel] is even worse when she's around! She has to convince herself that Mario is unhappy with me! That as a mother I'm a failure! My mother keeps telling me that I'm not patient enough with Lello, but she [the mother-in-law] tells me I'm not strict enough! That's why I get so nervous and yell at Lello! And my husband just sits there. He never defends me . . . look at him!"

Therapist: "Let's all think about this until the next session. In the meantime, let's make it clear that Lionello isn't anyone's victim. [turning to the child] Isn't that right, Lello? *You* thought of becoming crazy so you could help everyone. No one asked you to do so. [turning to the parents] Do you see? He doesn't say anything, he's not crying. He's decided to continue to do just like he's done until now, because he's convinced he's doing the right thing."

As we have already said, our first impression, when faced by the reaction of Marta, was that we had made a mistake. She, while agreeing with our comment, communicated that she felt she had been defined as guilty: she was a bad mother who had sacrificed her son to the needs of her unresolved ties to her own mother. The absence of any reaction on the part of the father strengthened our suspicion that he also had interpreted our intervention in that sense: "Since my wife is the one responsible for Lionel's psychosis, I'm good, innocent, and therefore superior to everyone."

However, in a further discussion we became convinced that our connotation of Lionel's behavior had not been an error, but rather a well-directed move which had uncovered a nodal point. What Marta could not tolerate was the idea that her son was *not* a "sacrificial calf" but rather an active element in the family system and, more than that, in the position of leadership. In disqualifying the active position of Lionel, relegating him again to his role as an object, as a passive victim, Marta was working precisely in favor of the preservation of the status quo of the system. She tried to recuperate her lost position of pseudo-power by defining herself as "guilty" and therefore the *cause* of her son's psychosis.

Her reaction was convenient to Mario, whose presumed superiority in the system consisted in the opposite, that is, in his appearing as the good and tolerant one. To keep their covert competition intact and to perpetuate the family game, it was necessary to put the child back into his role as an object.

For the moment we could do only one thing: put Mario in the same position as Marta by saying that he too was motivated by profound needs to accept the spontaneous sacrifice of Lionel. At the same time, we put Lionel in a position of superiority as a spontaneous interpreter of the presumed needs of the family. Thus we were able to prepare the way for the paradoxical prescription of the psychotic leadership of Lionel.

CHAPTER 20

The Prescription in the First Session

Mara Selvini Palazzoli, Luigi Boscolo, Gianfranco Cecchin, and Giuliana Prata

We have found it useful, and very often necessary, especially in families with psychotic children, to give a prescription by the end of the first session. In some cases, we make an apparently innocuous prescription with various goals:

1. to mark the context as therapeutic
2. to provoke within the family a feedback which indicates compliance and motivation for treatment
3. to limit the field of observation
4. to give structure to the following session

As for the first point, that is, the necessity of defining the context as therapeutic, this is a fundamental point, because this type of family is noted for its ability in disqualifying the context as therapeutic. This occurs both in the talkative and "social" family, which behaves in session as if it were attending a party, as well as in the reticent and withdrawn family.

As for the "social" family, we dealt with one, of "high society,"

From *Paradox and Counterparadox*, 1978, pp. 67–82.

particularly gifted in its fantasy and ability to present at every session a new and imaginative disqualification of the therapy. The beginning of the first session, characterized by a series of giggles and laughter, spirited jokes and word games in response to the attempts of approach made by the therapists, could easily have been entitled "A Typical Afternoon at the Club."

At the beginning of the second session, their mood somewhat dampened by an intervention made by the therapists at the end of the preceding session, the family succeeded in disqualifying the context by posing a series of questions concerning the ideal weight and diet of the identified patient, a slightly obese adolescent girl. We can call this second shift in context "A Chat with Marguerite's Dietitians."

The beginning of the third session was even more fanciful. For ten minutes the family discussed in full, with particular attention to detail, the advisability of attending or not attending the impending funeral of a relative in Liguria.

This we refer to as "A Conference on the Funeral Habits and Customs of Liguria."

As we have stated, the reticent and withdrawn family is no less capable of disqualifying the context of the therapy. Their behavior in the first session is common enough to be described thus: the family sits stiffly in a closely drawn-together group. They fix their eyes upon the therapists with an interrogative expression. Their general attitude is of expectancy and wondering: "Well, here we are, now what do we do?" Looking at them, an outsider would never dream that it is the *family* that has requested this meeting and not the therapists. Their silence and nonverbal attitude is quite clear: "We have courteously come at your kind invitation and here we are to find out what *you* want from us."

Experience has taught us that any interpretation we might make of this attitude of the family only results in a reaction of amazement, negation, and disqualification. Moreover, in attempting to metacommunicate on this behavior, a critical and moralistic connotation would be inevitable. On the contrary, a simple and well thought out prescription, inspired by the redundancies observed during the session, permits us both to avoid any critical or moralistic connotation and to redefine the relationship as therapeutic.

Furthermore, as we have stated in points three and four, such a prescription serves to delimit the field of observation and to give a format to the following session.

In some talkative families, the second session runs the risk of being an exact repetition of the first, *as if* the family had already said everything of importance and could therefore only repeat itself. In receiving a prescription, the members of the family are constrained in the following session to refer in some way to the prescription.

We can give as an example the following case of a family consisting of three members: the two parents and a 10-year-old daughter presenting a psychotic behavior which had begun in her fourth year. The child, although she had been regularly attending a special school for the past three years, had not yet been accepted in the first year of regular elementary school. During the first session, the therapists observed a repetitive phenomenon: if they asked the child a question, her mother immediately responded for her. Without any comment by the therapists on this behavior, the parents spontaneously explained that their daughter couldn't answer because she was unable to construct sentences and was able to utter only isolated words. At the end of the session, the therapists gave to each of the parents a notebook with this prescription: during the week to come the parents were to write down, with great detail and care, each in his own notebook, all the utterances made by the child. They were to be careful to omit nothing, for a single omission could jeopardize the therapy.

This prescription was meant to achieve various goals:

1. to ascertain the willingness of the parents to follow a prescription
2. to provide the little girl a new experience: that of being listened to, and of eventually being permitted to finish a sentence (since her parents, intent on recording every word she said, could no longer interrupt her)
3. to provide the therapists important data
4. to base the following session on the reading of the notebooks, thus eliminating meaningless and repetitive chatter

As a side-note to our main topic, we would like to note the incredible follow-up of this session. In our second session with this family, we discovered in the notebook of the mother sentences which were complete, albeit elementary. But in the notebook of the father we discovered a sentence which was striking when one considered the "dumb" behavior shown by the child. This sentence had been uttered while father and daughter were driving alone in the family car: "Daddy, tell me, do tractors have gears too?" What was even more striking than the content of this sentence was the attitude of the father as he read it. Shaking his head repeatedly, he slapped shut the notebook and looked at us in a bewildered manner, sighing, "Just look what this little girl has to say," as if the recorded sentence were unequivocal proof of her insanity.

At this point we must, however, make clear that even an apparently innocuous prescription could lead to errors, if the therapists failed to take into account and correctly estimate certain behaviors indicative of a particular family organization.

We can see a clear example of this in the case of another family which presented as the identified patient a 6-year-old autistic boy, as well as an apparently healthy 16-year-old daughter. At the end of the first session, we decided to prescribe the recording in a notebook of all the sentences and phrases uttered by the boy. This prescription was to be made, however, to the mother alone, as her husband was a traveling salesman and was to be away on business for the following weeks. Our intention was to make use of this stratagem as a means of separating the couple. The behavior of the family had influenced us to believe (how naive we were!) that by coming alone to the next session, the wife would give us information she dared not give in the presence of her husband. After deciding for these reasons to make this prescription, the therapists rejoined the family to make their final comment and to give the prescription. Upon entering the room, they found the father, who had left his seat, facing them, standing between them and the family with his arms slightly raised at his sides. In other words, he was in the classic defensive position of one whose exclusive possessions are being threatened. Such a clear body message should have warned us of the error we were about to make, but instead we went ahead to invite the wife to come alone to the next session.

The day of that session, we received a call from the husband, saying that his wife could not come, that she was sick in bed. In vain we tried to recuperate this family, but the error proved irremediable.

In other cases, particularly where the family seems not to be motivated, but rather compelled to come by a referring physician, we use interventions intended to put the family in crisis. These are some of the most difficult therapeutic moves and the most exposed to error because these families are firm in their decision to give us as little information as possible.

Such was the case of the Villa family. During the telephone conversation the referring child psychiatrist gave us minimal information concerning the family. Her diagnosis of the five-and-a-half-year-old identified patient was that of child autism. We failed to make further contact with the referring doctor before the first session, thus condemning ourselves to guesswork concerning the family background, which in this case, as we shall see, would have been particularly useful. We did have our transcription of the first telephone contact with the family, made by the mother several months before, requesting therapy.

In this conversation she stated that she had had difficulty in convincing her husband to come to family therapy. She had succeeded in this only because the child psychiatrist, who had been treating their son, Lillo, with medication, had refused to see them again until they had made an appointment at our center. She explained that Lillo's "illness" had begun two years before, immediately after a severe cold. He had changed completely: he no longer played, either alone or with other children. From that time on, he remained quietly in the house, almost as if he weren't there. At times, he cried for no reason. During meals, he had to be fed, since he sat at the table as if in a trance, not noticing the food in front of him. At other times, for no reason at all, he would have tantrums, flinging objects around. In these cases, his mother fed him something and he quieted down.

In the session Lillo had the appearance of a little old man. His skin a faded yellow color, his stomach protruding, he had a sheeplike expression on his face. For most of the session, he remained immobile in an armchair without speaking or responding to any question.

The therapists gathered the following information from the parents. They had married rather late, having met each other at a Catholic matrimonial agency. Neither had had previous sexual experience. They got along immediately, both "simple" and sharing the same ideas. (Here we point out the term *simple*, as it occurred throughout the session ad nauseam.) Their social and cultural level was quite low, and neither had gone past the fifth year in elementary school.

Communicational disturbances of the two were imposing. Any interaction was rendered nearly impossible by continual contradictions and disqualifications. Nearly all sentences were finished with a cryptic "anyway," leaving the therapist who had asked the question with empty hands.

As for their relations with their respective families, it appeared that they had remained relatively distant from the family of the wife, while, on the other hand, they were intricately involved with the family of the husband.

Mr. Villa had lived with his mother and younger sister, Zita, until he was 37 years old. In the same house, which had three stories, lived Villa's two brothers and their wives and children. Both of the brothers had completed technical schools and were economically comfortable.

Nina, the wife, had been well accepted by her mother and sister-in-law, largely because of her "simplicity." To make room for the newlyweds, the mother's apartment had been divided in two by a large closet placed in the central hallway. Until the mother's death, all had gone well, but immediately afterward, Zita had begun to quarrel with her brothers: she wanted to sell them her inherited part of the house (for an exorbitant price) and get out. Nina, who had always tried to please everyone, had been accused by Zita in one of the family arguments, as being the "cause of everything." Nina experienced a tremendous moral shock, and her husband, indignant, couldn't understand how such an unjust accusation could be made of such a sweet and "simple" woman.

Finally, through the intervention of friends, the brothers agreed to pay Zita, who then married and left the family. During this period (preceding Lillo's illness) Nina, depressed and downcast, continually asked her husband to move, and thus get away from the family feud, but failed to convince him. Even after Zita's departure from the field, the relationship between the remaining members of the family remained cold and strained. "The good times were gone forever, when we got together to watch TV in Mama's kitchen." However, in spite of our questions and the answers we received, we had no inkling as to the reason for this coldness. Why had it persisted? Hadn't Zita been the cause of the trouble? Hadn't they all joined together against her? These questions received only vague answers, in the form of the proverb "When you've been burned once, you keep away from the fire." But it was unclear *who* had been burned or *why*.

Lillo's sudden change occurred shortly after Zita's marriage. Our attempts to understand what had happened just before this change were smothered in a mass of contradictions. In the same way, we were unable to discover what the first signs of psychosis in Lillo had been. It was only during this part of the session that Lillo got up from his chair: twice he went to his mother, touching her lightly on the mouth and covering her ears. He never went near his father, who, sitting on the edge of his chair, was on the far side of the room.

In its discussion, the team agreed upon the total lack of motivation in the family to undertake therapy. It was clear that they had withheld important information from us. It would be, therefore, an error to offer them therapy. We felt it essential to define family therapy as being necessary but at the same time, to refuse it, thus pushing the parents to ask for it on their own initiative. But how could we accomplish this?

When the therapists had hinted at the eventual possibility of a change of house, they had met in the couple a wall of resistance: it was impossible, for economic reasons. It was useless to insist on this point. If they could now make up their minds to move, it was clear that they would already have done so. But if the problems of living close to the extended family were really so great, why didn't they leave? Here the best answer we could find was that both were there to get something out of the extended family.[1]

In this complex tactical struggle, Lillo was obviously fully involved. He had most likely received a verbal injunction to be "good" with his relatives and to play with his cousins, while, at the

---

[1]We formulated this hypothesis with the experience we had gained from earlier cases, most often repeated in families with psychotic children. We often found the parents of these children to be imprisoned in a twofold hidden symmetry: that between themselves, and that with some important member in the extended family, from which each of the two competitively hopes to win the laurels of victory, that is, unconditional approval (which will, of course, never occur).

same time, he had received the nonverbal message to keep away from them. Thus placed in a double bind, Lillo had chosen the psychotic solution: keep away from *everyone*.

After this discussion, we decided upon the following therapeutic intervention: we would give the family a letter addressed to the referring doctor, with whom the family had an appointment in two weeks. The letter was not to be a private communication, as is usually the case, but instead was to be read aloud to the family by one of the therapists before handing it over to the father. The letter follows:

Dear Colleague:
     In reference to the case of the Villa famly, we are in complete accordance with your idea of giving the approximately ten sessions of family therapy. However, at the present moment, therapy cannot be initiated due to one factor: the extraordinary sensitivity of Lillo. We say he is a child of extraordinary sensitivity because, already at the age of three-and-a-half, he decided to no longer play with children whose parents did not appreciate his mother. Since, from what we have understood in our first session, we cannot see the possibility of Mrs. Villa's recovering for the time being the esteem she had earlier received from her mother-in-law due to her simplicity, we don't believe Lillo will be able to start playing again and behaving as other children do. Furthermore, Lillo is so sensitive that, in order to offend no one, he doesn't even play by himself. Only when Mrs. Villa will have some idea as to how she can regain the appreciation and esteem of her relatives can we speak of making an appointment for the second session.

The letter, read aloud by one of the therapists, provoked dramatic reactions in Lillo. When the therapist arrived at the phrase "Lillo is so sensitive, that, in order to offend no one . . . ," his face began to wrinkle up. The observers behind the mirror watched him intently. His chin began to tremble, he clamped his lips seeking to control himself, but finally broke into tears. Abruptly he jumped from his chair and threw himself upon his mother, kissing and stroking her. She, receiving his caresses passively, turned brusquely upon the therapists: "But it isn't as easy as you think. How can I make them appreciate me?"

We thus received a feedback of confirmation from both mother and son, although that of the mother was surprising, since she behaved *as if* she herself had given the information referred to in the letter. The father remained in his place on the other side of the room, silent and unmoving.

When the therapists stood up to dismiss the family, Lillo threw himself on the floor, screaming and kicking, directing looks of hate toward the therapists. His parents had to carry him from the room.

Shortly after this session, we telephoned the referring psychiatrist. During this conversation, we received the information that the psychotic behavior of Lillo had begun two years before with a period of acute agitation, during which he uttered at a rapid rate the same words over and over again: "To move, to move, to move." During a diagnostic interview, when asked by the psychiatrist to draw a picture, he had made one of a courtyard full of people. One of these, taller than the others, was separated from the group and inside a cage.

The psychiatrist said that for the past two years she had spoken to the parents about moving. She had even demonstrated, in black and white, that they could afford such a move (obviously they had other reasons for not changing houses!). For our part, we explained the purpose of the letter, that it had been intended essentially as a paradoxical therapeutic intervention: to submit the continuation of the therapy to the realization of an impossible goal: that of Mrs. Villa's regaining the esteem of her in-laws. The paradox lay in the fact that, if the mother was to regain this esteem, therapy would become unnecessary and Lillo would be cured. But, since this was impossible, the family would find themselves at a crossroads: the choice of giving up the therapy or of leaving the field, that is, of abandoning the pretense of recapturing the lost appreciation of her in-laws.

After a month we received a telephone call from the mother, who said that the psychiatrist had found Lillo improved, and had insisted that the family make an appointment for the second session. However, at the moment, this was impossible, for the family was going on a vacation to the seaside for fifteen days. She added: "I know this won't settle anything, but it's the first time we're going away since we got married. Anyway, Doctor, I'm convinced it's all my fault." After another month she called again: "We brought Lillo back to the psychiatrist. She said he's getting better, but that we have to see you again. My husband won't agree because of the expense. I don't know what to do."

After this conversation we again discussed the case and our therapeutic intervention. Regarding the diagnosis, we felt we were dealing with a psychotic depression in a child. Regarding our intervention, we decided that it, in its essential points, had been quite accurate and correct, and had brought about certain desired results. At the same time we were able to discover two grave omissions we had made. The first had been our failure to directly involve the father. We could have, for example, referred to him in the letter as the one who suffered the most for his wife's loss of esteem. Our second omission, the more serious, was that we had not completed the paradoxical prescription at the end of the first session with yet another paradox: fixing an appointment for a second session. This would have been incongruous with our previous statement that it was impossible to continue therapy. Substantially, the point was to do therapy with a reluctant family while defining this as impossible.

When, by contrast, a family comes to us in crisis, of its own will, and not because of the insistence of a referring doctor,[2] we find ourselves in a quite different situation. In such cases, it is often possible, already in the first session, to prescribe the symptom to the identified patient, with surprising results, as long as care is taken to positively connote the symptom in the systemic sense, allying oneself with the family's homeostatic tendency.

One example of this can be found in our treatment of the Lauro family. The appointment for the first session was made with relative urgency (four weeks after the first telephone contact) due to the nature of the case itself as well as to the insistent telephone calls made by the father, who appeared desperate and at the end of his wits.

---

[2]Due to disastrous experiences, we refuse, on principle, to accept a family in therapy as long as any member of that family is in individual therapy. We have seen that in such cases, even if this individual's therapist is in agreement with the family's beginning therapy with us, or is the referring doctor himself, a competitive game unavoidably occurs between the two therapies.

The family had been referred to us by a child psychiatry clinic, where the 10-year-old son had been examined and given a series of psychological examinations. The diagnosis was of acute psychotic syndrome in a subject of high intelligence. The boy had been prescribed and administered heavy medications, but without results. In the first session, the father seemed to be a highly emotional man, a bit flaccid in his appearance. The mother, slim and well-kept, showed, on the contrary, a controlled and aloof attitude. Ernesto, their only son, was tall and overdeveloped for his age, but was striking in his peculiar behavior, which could almost be called farcical. He walked stiffly, slightly bent forward, taking short and hesitant steps like those of a very old man. Seated between the parents at an equal distance from both, he responded to all questions talking "staccato" in a high nasal voice. He used difficult and obsolete words alternated with expressions which sounded as if they came from an early nineteenth century novel. For example, he interrupted his father once with the following phrase: "It is advisable that I now intervene with a clarification so that these gentlemen will not be deceived by appearances."

According to his parents, Ernesto's strange behavior had begun suddenly three months before, after a short visit from an aunt. When she had left, Ernesto had withdrawn within himself, often broke into tears for no reason, and frequently clenched his fists in a threatening way, as if facing some invisible enemy.

While he had always been the best in his class in past years, he was now the poorest student. He wanted to be brought to school by his mother in spite of the jests of his classmates, with whom relations were hostile. He didn't want to go out with his father anymore, because he was afraid someone shooting at his father would miss and hit him instead. In spite of his father's denials and protests, Ernesto insisted that they were always followed by a thin, bearded man. "First I saw him from behind and then we were face to face. Since I'm not subject to hallucinations I recognized him perfectly."

We learned that the couple had lived with the wife's family, which was composed of her father and three older brothers (the mother had died years before). Giulia, Ernesto's mother, had to care for the whole family and was always worn out. When two of the brothers finally married, the Lauro family moved into their own home, and Giulia's father came to live with them. He stayed with them for four years until his death, which occurred when Ernesto was 6 years old. After this death, the family moved again.

Ernesto, according to his parents, had suffered a great deal over the death of his grandfather, to whom he had been very attached. He had always been "smart" for his age, but happy and sociable. After his grandfather's death, he stayed indoors, no longer playing with his friends. He would spend the afternoons after school in his room doing homework or reading encyclopedias. The parents found no complaint in this behavior, as his school work profited from it.

It was only in September, after the visit of his aunt and four years after the death of his grandfather, that Ernesto changed in a sudden and dramatic way. The parents were unable to explain the reason for this change. They could only say that Giulia had had a particularly enjoyable month with her sister-in-law, whom she usually visited in the country during the summer holidays. This sister-in-law had come to town to undergo a series of medical examinations. "It was a happy period because, having always lived only with men, it didn't seem to be true that I was able to stay with another woman, to talk with her about so many things."

The therapists could discover no more than this. They asked what the parents thought about Ernesto's attitude, that is, his way of looking and behaving like an 80-year-old man, and of speaking like someone out of a century-old book. The father said nothing, and the mother answered by saying that Ernesto had always been a precocious child, with a rich and well-developed vocabulary. She admitted, however, that this phenomenon had recently become far more noticeable. At this point, Ernesto interrupted with one of his typical cryptic comments: "This question doesn't surprise me, it doesn't surprise me at all. This has all been pointed out already. I think it's because I don't like summaries [was he referring to the vague and imprecise way in which his parents always expressed themselves?]. I don't ask questions. I read quite a bit. I look for answers in the text. I prefer to read texts."

At this point the two observing members of the team called out one of the therapists. It was clear by now that Ernesto was miming his grandfather. It would be better not to persist in other questions which the family seemed resolutely to evade.

The therapist rejoined the family, and after a few minutes asked Ernesto to tell them about his grandfather, how he had acted. The boy temporized, saying he couldn't remember. The therapist then asked him to show how his grandfather had talked to his mother. After thinking for a few moments, the boy settled himself solemnly in his chair and said: "Oh come on, Giulia, come on" in a tone of benevolent superiority which he accompanied with a gesture which seemed to say: "Cut out the silliness."

After Ernesto had finished this demonstration, the therapist asked him to show how his father spoke to his mother. Ernesto hesitated a bit, then turned to his father saying: "Daddy, I don't want to offend you, but if it can be advantageous. . . ." His father responded with a sign of assent.

Ernesto began in a whining voice: "Giuuulia, Giuuulia . . . I will think about everything. Please now, go take a little nap."

At this point the therapists withdrew to discuss the case with the rest of the team. The two observers remained at the mirror for a few minutes and saw the father agitatedly scold Ernesto: "But why did you say that to the doctors?" To which the boy replied, "So that they'll know that you're good, as good as gold."

In the discussion which followed among the therapists, the prevalent hypothesis was that Ernesto, caught in the middle of an unreconcilable couple, had become aware of some danger immediately after the death of his grandfather. By closing himself up in the house to read and study, he was trying in some way to take his grandfather's place. However, with the arrival of his aunt, the danger of a change, perhaps of a threatening coalition between the two women, must have appeared to him to be much greater.

The team agreed that basically Ernesto was more attached to his father and was convinced of his father's inability to assert himself, to take a masculine role, and to counterbalance the increasing maternal power. To strengthen the homeostasis, Ernesto had resuscitated his grandfather, the only one who had been able to control his mother, to keep her in her place. More than this, for the moment, the team was not able to understand. It was decided, therefore, to close the session with a positive connotation of the behavior of Ernesto, without any criticism of his parents but with a cryptic and nonverbal allusion to a certain fear he had for his father, that is, for his father's possible eventual defeat.

This comment was prepared minutely, not only in its verbal but especially in its nonverbal aspects, because the therapists thought it imperative to avoid naming the mother and the father and their presumed difference of position in the family. The suspicions of the team were immediately confirmed when the therapists rejoined the family, by the change of Ernesto's position: he had pushed his chair closer to that of his father and had moved it somewhat forward, almost blocking him from the therapists' view.

First the therapists announced their conclusion that it was necessary to proceed with family therapy, which would be carried out in ten sessions, at monthly intervals.

Ernesto (always in the voice of an old man): "But your response, what is your response?"

Male therapist: "We are closing this first session with a message to you, Ernesto. You're doing a good thing. We understand that you considered your grandfather to be the central pillar of your family [the hand of the therapist moved in a vertical direction as if tracing an imaginary pillar]; he kept it together, maintaining a certain balance [the therapist extended both hands in front of him palms down, both at the same level]. Without your grandfather's presence, you were afraid something would change, so you thought of assuming his role, perhaps because of this fear that the balance in the family would change [the therapist slowly lowered his right hand, which corresponded to the side where the father was seated]. For now you should continue in this role that you've assumed spontaneously. You shouldn't change anything until the next session, which will be January 21, five weeks from now."

After the delivery of this message, the therapists rose to their feet to see the family out. The parents seemed lost and confused. But Ernesto, after a moment of shock, jumped suddenly from his chair, and, abandoning his octagenarian attitude, ran toward the female therapist, who was leaving the room; grasping her arm, he cried: "And school? You know that at school I'm a disaster. Did you know that? I might get left back. Did you know that?"

Female therapist (gently): "For the moment you're so involved in this generous task you have chosen to carry out, that it's natural you don't have any energy left for school. How could you?"

Ernesto (shouting, with a desperate expression on his face): "But for how many years do I have to repeat the fifth grade until I can make them get along, for how many years? And will I be able to? Tell me!"

Female therapist: "We'll talk about all this on January 21. The Christmas vacation is coming."

Mother (very disturbed): "But I couldn't tell you what happened in September. I wanted to say. . . ."

Male therapist: "We'll talk about all that on January 21."

Father: [disqualified everything by asking for trivial advice].

This first intervention already proved correct in its immediate feedbacks. In the second session we were able to note other changes. Ernesto had given up his old man's behavior, even though he still expressed himself in a literary and dated fashion. For the past two weeks he had been taking advantage of school, and he no longer spoke of bearded men who followed him. These changes permitted us to receive more information and therefore to form new interventions, which in their turn produced new changes and new information. And thus we continued for ten sessions, which resulted in meaningful changes in the couple, and naturally in Ernesto. . . .

CHAPTER 21

Family Rituals

Mara Selvini Palazzoli, Luigi Boscolo, Gianfranco Cecchin, and Giuliana Prata

Another of the therapeutic tactics originated by our team, one which has proved particularly effective, is that of prescribing a ritual to the family. We have prescribed rituals which are to be carried out only once, as well as others which are to be repetitive.

Of the several effective family rituals we have prescribed to date we choose to present one particular example, which had as its goal the destruction of a myth whose existence was created by the members of three generations. So that the reader may have an adequate understanding of this ritual, we shall describe fully the story of the family and of the transgenerational evolution of this myth. In the description of the treatment of the family, certain errors made by the therapists shall come to light, errors which, as usual, were far more instructive than the actual successes. For eventually it was the very understanding of these errors and their feedbacks which led us to the successful prescription of the ritual. Finally, the detailed analysis of the substance and goal of the ritual shall illustrate and explain exactly what we mean by the term. For this case history, we shall give the family the fictional name of Casanti.

From *Paradox and Counterparadox*, 1978, pp. 83–97.

A RITUAL AGAINST A DEADLY MYTH

Our story of the Casanti family begins during the first years of this century, on a large and isolated farm in a depressed area of central Italy. For many generations, the Casantis had sweated a living out of this land, of which they were not the owners, but tenant farmers. The head of the family was the "Capoccia," an iron-fisted worker who based his uncontested authority upon a long tradition of patriarchal rules, which were in fact modeled after those of the feudal era. His wife could have stepped from the pages of *The Books of the Family* written by Leon Battista Alberti in the late 1400s. A tireless and parsimonious worker, she was convinced that the róle of the woman was to serve, give birth, raise children, and never question the superiority and rights of men, having as her only reward her own virtue. She had given her husband five sons. Siro, the youngest, was to become the father of our family.

For these people, when you were born a peasant, you died a peasant. The work was hard, and there was no time for pleasure or holidays. Although the five sons learned to read and write in the village school, they were needed to work in the field. Every helping hand was precious, and no one could be excused; there existed absolutely no alternatives. What else could an ignorant farmer do anyway, but stay with his family and help support it and put away some savings for the common good whenever possible? In unity there was strength, or at least survival. No protests on the part of the sons were tolerated, or even permitted. The only thing was to settle down and join the others.

In the 1930s in the Tuscan Maremma, the patriarchal family was still isolated and considered by its members to present their only assurance of survival and dignity. To leave the family meant emigration and uprooting, without any means or preparation. It meant doing without help and support in case of illness or hard luck. Needless to say, most families, including the Casantis, chose to remain together.

In this culture, a father with sons was fortunate. Not only would he have help in the fields, but he would have daughters-in-law, who, obedient and industrious, would work in the house as well as in the fields. Thus, each of the sons was encouraged to marry early, as soon as he reached the proper age. The bride would come to live with her husband's family, and submit herself to the authority of her father-in-law, her husband, her brothers-in-law, and any sisters-in-law who had preceded her, in that order. The Casantis patterned themselves after this age-old tradition.

The first four brothers had already been married for some time and had settled down to family life when Siro, the youngest, returned from the war. He had been away for several years, from 1940 to 1945, had fought, and had seen many things never dreamt of at the farm. He had also received training as a mechanic and had a truck driver's license. When he was discharged from the army, he returned to the farm, and found himself depressed and estranged. For some time he was unable to get involved in the work, and was treated for mental exhaustion. He gradually readapted himself, and was able to join the others as he had years before.

Soon the "Capoccia" began to nag him. It was time he got married. Two of the daughters-in-law were pregnant, and the family needed a woman who could run the kitchen and care for the livestock. They had already chosen a candidate, the daughter of a neighboring farmer. Siro, however, had other ideas. He remembered Pia, a lovely dressmaker he had met in Florence while serving in the army, and decided to look her up. Pia was not quite as he remembered her. Once lively and gay, she had become wilted and sad. She had been abandoned by her fiancé after years of engagement, and felt her chances for love and romance were over.

Nevertheless, Pia accepted Siro's proposal, going against the advice of her friends and relatives. ("You won't be able to stand that kind of life. You'll see, you'll come back to us soon.") But Pia knew she would never go back. For her, it was almost like going into a nunnery. The Casantis, after much hesitation and doubt about the "city girl," finally accepted her. They understood she was a serious girl and would work hard and never complain.

But times had changed. The family was full of tensions. With the increasing impact of the industrial boom, which had finally succeeded in reaching the most isolated regions of Italy, they began to have contacts with the outside world. They listened to the radio, and going to the market saw all manner of strange things. The daughters-in-law, accustomed as they were to their position in the family as chattels and servants, were amazed when they saw elegant women who smoked and even drove cars! They began to complain of old "Capoccia," who never relaxed his authority, as well as of their mother-in-law, who sided with "her" men. For example, only the men were allowed to go into town on Sundays, while the women were expected to remain home cooking and caring for the livestock. They began to complain about these restrictions, the most courageous actually trying to convince their husbands to leave the farm. But, in the face of this danger, the five sons joined their parents, forming a silent coalition. They, the sons, were the "true" Casantis. It was their responsibility to control the women of the family. There was no place for complaint, expression of dissatisfaction, or jealousy. It had to be clear that there was no inequality in the distribution of jobs and expenses: everything was done with complete equity. And as for the children, it was likewise forbidden to make comparisons, or to express judgments. Rivalry was unthinkable, the children of one were the children of all.

Thus was born the family myth of "one for all and all for one," a myth shared also by anyone who had contact with the family. "No other family in the whole region gets along like the Casantis. Such a big family, and everybody loves each other; no fighting, no bickering. . . ."

Pia, Siro's wife, played a large part in the building of this myth. The last to arrive (and therefore under the authority of all the others), she was considered by her mother-in-law a saint, no small achievement in such a culture. She was the wise one, always the helpful one, the impartial mother of all the children of the clan. In her own children she had been unfortunate, giving birth to two daughters in this family where sons were prized. She treated them with the same care she gave her nephews and nieces, without showing any preference. In fact, in cooking and distributing food, she always served her own children last. Sometimes her daughters found her crying in her room, but when they questioned her, she always answered that she had a headache, or didn't feel well. If her husband, returning from the fields, complained that the hardest work was always left to him, she sought to calm him, telling him that he was mistaken, that the life was equally hard for everyone.

At this point, we can observe how all the characteristics of the family myth, as described by Ferreira (1963), are now present. In the first generation examined by our inquiry, that is, of the "Capoccia" and his wife, we observe the existence of a belief which is still vital in the context of the reality of a patriarchal farming subculture, homogeneous in its isolation: "The survival, safety, and dignity of its members depend on the family. Whoever separates himself from the family is lost."

In the absence of alternatives, information, and confrontations, there is no conflict. But when the second generation, that of Siro and his brothers, reaches adulthood, disruptive tensions begin to appear. The fascist era with its glorification of the grain-growers is over, and democracy, with its political rallies, arrives in even the most isolated villages. The work of the tenant farmer is defined as humiliating and exploited. Industrial culture imposes itself through movies, the radio, markets, and the inevitable contact with people who can "make money fast."

But the Casanti brothers, still led by the old Capoccia, are suspicious. These are all signs of a world gone mad. Their strength is always the old one—to work hard and to be united. To stay together, they must create a myth, a collective product whose very existence and persistence should be able to reinforce the homeostasis of the group against any disruptive influences.

Like all myths, as Ferreira points out, this one "imposes upon its adherents certain limitations which end in gross distortions of reality." In consequence, the myth modifies the perceptive context of the family behavior, in that it supplies ready-made explanations of the rules that govern the relationship within the family. Furthermore, the myth in its content represents a detachment of the group from reality, a detachment which we can at this point call "pathological." But at the same time, this myth constitutes, with its very existence, a fragment of life, a part of reality which confronts, and thus forms, the children born within it.

The myth of the Casantis, by now consolidated and extended to the third generation, survived the death of the Capoccia and his wife, as well as the eventual abandonment of the farm. Toward the end of the 1960s, due to the crisis in the position of the tenant farmer, the five brothers decided to leave the land and transfer themselves to town. They were ex-farmers, uncouth and uneducated. How could they possibly separate, divide their hard-earned savings into minuscule portions? Far better to stay together and found a business which could profit from their common abilities.

They organized a construction company, which immediately profited by the building boom. For the first time in their lives, they had plenty of money: they could begin to enjoy the pleasures of a consumer society. They could live in apartments in town. Here again the myth presided; they all moved into the same apartment building. Although they had separate apartments, their doors were always open to the others of the clan, even to unannounced visits.

With the growth of the third generation, the situation became even more complicated. The myth had to become more rigid, since expectations had changed, and disruptive tensions had become more intense. The petit bourgeois, which made up the society in which the Casantis now found themselves, was fraught with confrontation and competition. Children were compared according to their success in school, their physical attributes, their friendships and popularity. Jealousy and envy occurred with each confrontation. News and gossip flew from door to door; windows became listening posts.

The Casanti myth had rigidified to the extreme. Even the Casanti cousins were true brothers; they shared their joys and sorrows. Together they suffered the failure of another; together they rejoiced in the luck of another. The iron rule, never mentioned, forbade them not only any comment but also any gesture that could be said to be motivated by jealousy, envy, or competition.

When Siro moved with the clan to the city, his daughters were 15 and 8 years old. Zita, the eldest, had always been a tomboy. Dark, stocky, and loving the country and physical activities, she suffered from her new conditions of life. She studied, not because of enthusiasm or ambition, but because it came easily to her. She lived estranged from her surroundings, disappointed in city life, and dreamt only of returning to the country some day. During her sixteenth year, for some months, she manifested an anorectic syndrome, from which she recovered spontaneously.

Nora, the second daughter of Siro, was still a little girl. Completely different from her sister, she passed her days with Luciana, her cousin, who was also her classmate. Nora was closer to Luciana than to her own sister. Luciana may have been skinny and homely, but she was lively and ambitious, and always the first of

her class. Nora, on the other hand, showed no interest in school-
work, and felt no envy at the success of her cousin.

At 13 Nora underwent a dramatic metamorphosis. Always a
pretty child, she became an extraordinarily beautiful girl. Completely different from the rest of the family, she seemed a Madonna
of the Tuscan Renaissance. Her father, Siro, became fiercely
proud of her. He kept in his wallet a photo of his daughter and
showed it to everyone whenever he could. Nora, on the other hand,
seemed hardly pleased by this turn of affairs; in fact, she reacted
nervously to any compliments on her beauty. Together with Luciana and the other cousins and friends, she was urged to go on
outings or to go to dances every Sunday. She returned nearly
every time depressed, without being able to explain why.

In school, things started going badly. Even when she studied,
she was unable to answer the questions put to her. Shortly after
her fourteenth birthday, she suddenly stopped eating. In only a
few months, she was reduced to a skeleton and had to leave
school. Three periods in the hospital, as well as an attempt at
individual psychotherapy, had no effect. Due to the advice of a
local psychiatrist, the family made contact with our Center.

In January 1971 the first session took place. As was our
practice at that time, we made a contract with the family for a
maximum total of twenty sessions. The sessions were to be held
every three weeks or more, according to our judgment. The family
accepted. The trip, due to the distance they had to travel, involved
a great sacrifice. They would arrive after an entire night spent on a
train, only to repeat the trip as soon as the session was over.

At the beginning of the therapy, Siro, the father, was 50 years
old, Pia, the mother, 43. Zita, who was nearly 22, was enrolled in
the University of Siena, but was not taking any courses at the time.
Nora, 15, was a frightening skeleton, five feet nine inches tall, and
weighing seventy pounds. Her behavior was psychotic. Completely removed from what was going on in the session, she limited
herself to moaning, repeating a stereotyped phrase every once in a
while, "You should make me gain weight without making me eat."
We learned that for months she had left her bed only in order to
indulge herself in bulimic orgies, which were inevitably followed by
bouts of vomiting which reduced her to prostration.

The first part of the therapy, which took place in nine sessions, from January to June, was characterized by these outstanding factors:

1. the insistence of the therapists, after the second session, in inquiring into the relationship between the members of the nuclear family and the entire clan;
2. the ironic attitude of the therapists in regard to the myth, and their attempt to attack it openly through verbal clarifications, as well as through naive prescriptions intended to force the family to open rebellion against the myth.
3. the nonsystemic conviction, both linear and moralistic, that the true slave to the myth was the father, and not, as it actually was, all the members of the family;
4. the attempt, obviously unsuccessful, during the sixth and seventh sessions, to call only the three women of the family, hoping that in the absence of the father, they would open up;
5. the failure to point out, as could have been done after the review of the tapes of each session, a peculiar redundancy: every time a member of the family, apparently allied to the therapists, criticized the clan, there was always another member ready to minimize or disqualify what was being said, or to divert the discussion to some marginal topic;
6. the progressive abandonment of her symptom by Nora from the fourth session to the sixth, when she presented herself in flowering physical condition;
7. the suspicion of the therapists that Nora also, with her improvement, was defending the system (which in effect had not changed), and the incapacity of the therapeutic team, on their part seduced by this improvement, to come out of the impasse.

At the end of the ninth session, the therapeutic team decided to halt the treatment, declaring that the goal desired by the family had been reached. Although there still remained eleven sessions, Nora was in excellent condition, and had started work as an apprentice in a beauty shop. In reality, we wanted to sound out the family. If the improvement of Nora was false, the therapists would still have eleven sessions to work with. A telephone appointment to report Nora's progress and to discuss the general state of affairs was agreed upon for the fifth of September.

The call was made punctually by the father. Nora was well, but had given up her work, and tended to stay by herself at home, separated even from her parents and sister. Siro's tone was cryptic, uncertain. He asked the therapists if another session was indicated. The therapists left the decision up to the family, who, although they agreed to discuss the issue and call back, failed to do so.

The team, however, did not expect the dramatic events which followed. Toward the end of October, the father once again called the Center. Nora had attempted suicide and was in a critical ward of the local hospital. They had found her on the bathroom floor in a state of coma induced by alcohol and barbiturates. It being Sunday, she had returned in a depressed state from a local dance where she had met her cousin Luciana. Upon finding herself alone in the apartment, she had profited from the absence of her family by taking this tragic step.

In the session which followed Nora's release from the hospital, the family, by now at the end of its tether, let some important information escape. The father confessed that the clan had shown itself hostile in September to the idea of the family's return to therapy. They felt it was completely useless for Siro to lose valuable time and to spend so much money now that Nora was cured.

Zita, the sister, made an important revelation. Perhaps, in Nora's drama, Luciana had played an important part. During the summer, Nora had confided in her sister that for years she had felt persecuted by her cousin. She had said she was afraid to stay with Luciana, and was nervous and anxious in her presence, even though she didn't know why. But Zita went on to disqualify what Nora had told her, as well as her own revelation of it, by adding: "Maybe this is all only an impression of Nora."

While Nora remained silent, the parents took up the defense of Luciana. She was a true sister to Nora, full of love and concern. In fact they had been struck painfully by Nora's lack of receptiveness, by her reluctance to accept the insistent and affectionate invitations made by Luciana.

But this time the therapists refused to take the carrot offered them. Even if certain members of the family seemed willing to make revelations, the therapists this time had no intention of falling into the same trap. The session was halted while the entire therapeutic team met to discuss the new turn the situation was taking. The errors made in the first sessions had become clear. Going against such an iron-clad myth had served only to strengthen it. Insisting upon change had only succeeded in arousing fears of the breakdown of the system, and had constrained Nora to abandon her symptom in order to reinforce the status quo. In reality, nothing had changed.

Since Nora herself was a participant in the myth, she had ended up by doubting the reality of her own perceptions. How could she dare to think that Aunt Emma and Luciana didn't love her? Perhaps she perceived Luciana as being hypocritical, envious, and evil only because she, Nora, was all of these things.

The team decided, therefore, to refrain from any verbal comment. It was urgent that we invent and prescribe a ritual, making use of the dramatic situation so that it would be followed. At the same time, it was necessary to prescribe the "pathology," that is, the fidelity to the myth, while reassuring the family and putting it at the same time in a paradoxical situation.

The two therapists, returning to the family, declared themselves extremely preoccupied by the dramatic situation, but above all, by the emerging hostility toward the clan, which endangered the accordance and well-being of the whole group. It was of vital importance that nothing escape and of equal importance that the family commit itself to follow the prescription the therapists were about to give. The family, duly impressed, agreed to do so. The prescription was as follows.

In the two weeks that were to precede the next session, every other night, after dinner, the family was to lock and bolt the front door. The four members of the family were to sit around the dining room table, which would be cleared of all objects except an alarm clock, which would be placed in its center. Each member of the family, starting with the eldest, would have fifteen minutes to talk, expressing his own feelings, impressions, and observations regarding the behavior of the other members of the clan. Whoever had nothing to say would have to remain silent for his assigned fifteen minutes, while the rest of the family would also remain silent. If, instead, he were to speak, everyone would have to listen, refraining from making any comment, gesture, or interruption of any kind. It was absolutely forbidden to continue these discussions outside of the fixed hour: everything was limited to these evening meetings, which were ritually structured. As for relations with members of the clan, a doubling of courtesy and helpfulness was prescribed.

The ritual, as can be seen, had several goals:

1. to define the nuclear family as a unit distinct from the clan, substituting for the prohibition, the obligation of speaking clearly about the tabu subjects, while at the same time imposing the keeping of secrecy
2. to give back to Nora her position as a full-right member of the nuclear family
3. to encourage the newborn intragenerational alliance between the two sisters
4. to establish, without explicitly saying it, the right of each member to express his own perception without being contradicted or disqualified
5. to expose any eventual reticent member to the anxiety of silence
6. to prevent, through the prohibition of discussion outside of the evening meetings, the persistence of secret coalitions[1]

The prescribing of reverence toward the clan qualified the therapists as being allied to the family's homeostatic tendencies and placed the family in a paradoxical situation. In fact, they found themselves confronting an unexpected about-face on the part of the therapists in the very moment when they were ready to accept that the clan was endangering their existence and the survival of Nora.

---

[1]The therapists, in fact, did not point out to the family the repetitive phenomenon they had noticed: if a member of the family risked any criticism of the clan, he was automatically and regularly disqualified by another member of the family. By prescribing the ritual in the manner above described, they succeeded in changing exactly the rule which perpetuated this transactional pattern.

The family carried out the ritual and two weeks later presented itself greatly changed. Nora, hardly recognizable, told how much she now understood of the maneuvers of Luciana, who had always made her feel guilty for any success. Luciana was able to do this without commenting openly, by withdrawing into silence, by showing herself as being depressed, by demonstrating a certain coolness toward Nora. It was as if Nora's successes were an offense to Luciana.

Pia, for her part, had "discovered" how much Aunt Emma (Luciana's mother) was consumed by envy to the point of making life impossible for everyone. Siro intervened, saying that Luciana's and Emma's behavior was due to ignorance, not to "badness." Nora replied that she too felt somewhat "bad" to have said what she had of Luciana.

But the rule was broken, and it was finally possible to metacommunicate about it: "Whoever speaks *badly* of his relatives, is *bad*." The therapy had finally touched the system's nerve center and changes followed in great leaps. Once the field was cleared of the myth, it became possible to work with the family's internal problems.

HOW TO DEFINE A FAMILY RITUAL

From the formal point of view, the term *family ritual* refers to an action or series of actions, usually accompanied by verbal formulas or expressions, which are to be carried out by all members of the family. The ritual is prescribed in every detail: the place in which it must be carried out, the time, the eventual number of repetitions, by whom the verbal expressions are to be uttered, in what order, etc.

A fundamental aspect of the family ritual concerned our specific preoccupation with the approach to the family in schizophrenic transaction: how to change the rules of the game, and therefore the family epistemology, without resorting to explanations, criticism, or any other verbal intervention. As Shands (1971) says, the basic idea can never be stressed often enough "that there is a necessarily complete difference between the objective world and the world of symbolic process, between the doing and the

naming, between the level of action and the level of description"
(p. 30). And again:

> The relation between behavior and description is in a certain way
> similar to that which occurs between the circular motion of an
> automobile's wheel and the linear projection that can be de-
> signed on a map to show the path it followed. Behavior is always
> a controlled process of a circular motion (with feedbacks) of
> messages between central and peripheral mechanisms, in which
> the continual input of information from the periphery is at least
> as important as the flow in the other parts of the circle [p. 34].

This agrees with what Piaget showed in his studies of the
epigenetic evolution of the human being:

> The capacity to carry out concrete operations precedes the
> capacity to carry out formal operations; the capacity to "central-
> ize" the perceptive processes precedes the ability to "decentral-
> ize" them, that is to carry out abstract operations. The phase of
> concrete operations is therefore the necessary premise to the
> phase of formal operations. In other words, to arrive at a digital
> code, it is indispensable to have a previous analogic adaptation.
> However, once the individual has arrived at the level of formal
> operations, the two processes, analogic and digital, blend, and
> cannot be distinguished except through a linguistic artifice
> [quoted in Shands 1971, p. 34].

The family ritual, especially in that it presents itself on the
level of action, is closer to the analogic code than to the digital.
This preponderant analogic component is, by its nature, more apt
than words to unite the participants in a powerful collective experience, to introduce some basic idea to be shared by everyone.
One thinks of the widespread use of rituals in the mass education
and conditioning of the New China. Contrary to the slogans, catch-
words, and phrases to which an individual can render himself
impenetrable, rituals are much more successful in introducing, for
example, the basic idea of union, cooperation, and complementarity to the common good. Every ritual becomes valid (in the passage from sign to signal, and from signal to norm) because of its
normative function, which is inherent in every collective action

where the behavior of all the participants is directed toward the same goal.

We can therefore conclude that our prescription of a ritual is meant not only to avoid the verbal comment on the norms that at that moment perpetuate the family play, but to introduce into the system a ritualized prescription of a play whose new norms silently take the place of old ones.

The invention of a ritual always requires a great effort from the therapists, first an effort of observation, and then a creative effort, since it is unthinkable that a ritual proven effective in one family can be in another. It must be specific for one given family, in the same way as certain rules (and therefore a certain play) are specific for each family in a given here and now of its curriculum vitae, which includes, of course, the therapeutic situation. Finally, we want to point out that the prescription of family rituals has proven itself extremely useful also in the treatment of families manifesting types of interaction other than the schizophrenic.

CHAPTER 22

The Therapists Accept
without Objection
a Questionable Improvement

Mara Selvini Palazzoli, Luigi Boscolo,
Gianfranco Cecchin, and Giuliana Prata

This therapeutic maneuver, exemplified in Chapter 21 ("A Ritual Against a Deadly Myth"), consists of our accepting, without objection, an improvement such as the disappearance of a symptom which is, at the same time, not justified by a related change in the transactional patterns of the family system. The suspicion arises that this improvement is no more than a move in which all the members of the family are accomplices, although the identified patient may serve as their mouthpiece. Their common intent is to evade a burning topic and defend the status quo. The main characteristic of such an improvement is that it is sudden and inexplicable, accompanied by a carefree attitude and a certain optimism— *tout va très bien, Madame de la Marquise*—which is in no way substantiated by convincing data. With this attitude, the family implicitly conveys to the therapists its collective intention to catch the first departing train, that is, of getting out of the therapy as fast as possible.

In this case, where it is clear that the family is trying to take control of the therapeutic situation, the therapists cannot lose the

From *Paradox and Counterparadox*, 1978, pp. 113–116.

initiative. A possibility would be to interpret the meaning of this family behavior as a "flight into health." In our experience, however, this would be an error because it implies a critical attitude completely contrary to the principle of positive connotation, and therefore provokes denials and disqualifications or, worse yet, a symmetrical battle. Furthermore, as we have seen in the case of the Casanti family, this urge to flee often follows some therapeutic error or some intervention which, although correct in itself, is premature and intolerable to the group.

Instead, we meet this threat of the family's withdrawal by accepting the improvement without objection, taking to ourselves the initiative of ending the therapy, remaining cryptic and elusive in our attitude.

Since the family has not yet gotten to the point of explicitly requesting termination, but is still involved in the preliminary maneuvers leading up to it, we decide ourselves, from our position of authority, to suspend therapy. The first purpose of such a step is that of always keeping a firm hold on the initiative and the control of the situation, preventing and annulling the move of the "adversary." Our second purpose is directly linked to the terms of our contract with the family: the agreement upon a precise number of sessions. In the face of an inexplicable disappearance of the symptom of the identified patient, accompanied by the attitude of collective resistance described above, we prefer to end the therapy immediately in order to test the authenticity of this "recovery," while having at the same time a number of sessions in "reserve" in case the "recovery" does not bear up under the test of time.

We said that our attitude in this situation is cryptic and elusive. This is because we do not permit ourselves to express in any way our opinion concerning the presumed improvement; nor do we confirm it. We limit ourselves to a simple comment, in which we "recognize" the family's satisfaction with the results of the therapy, and that we have decided the therapy should end with the present session. We stress, however, our obligation according to our contract, to concede to the family upon request the sessions not yet used up, *if* the family should have any need of them.

This therapeutic intervention provokes within the family typical feedbacks, which although they may vary in intensity, bring the family move into the open. One typical response is the question "But what do *you* think?," a question intended to lead us into a discussion of our doubts and objections, which would then be readily disqualified. Instead, the therapists insist that they are basing their decision upon the apparent satisfaction expressed by the family. Thus the family finds itself in the position of being credited for the initiation of a decision which in reality has been taken by the therapists.

Another reaction to this intervention is a sepulchral silence followed by protests and expressions of doubt, uncertainty, and pessimism, and finally an insistence upon making an appointment for another session or obtaining from the therapist at least the solemn promise that an eventual request for an appointment will not necessitate a long period of waiting.

Regardless of the family's reaction, the therapists remain firm in their decision to discontinue the therapy, leaving the family the initiative to request the remaining sessions but with a minimum of time established before such a continuation can be considered. Through such a paradoxical tactic, we are able to annul the threatened sabotage by putting the family in the condition of having to request, sooner or later, the continuation of the therapy.

This type of tactic can also be used with other types of families, for example, with young couples with a patient in early childhood or preadolescence. At times, in such cases, if one is able to obtain the quick disappearance of the symptom of the child, the parents show immediate signs of wanting to escape from the therapy. In this case also, we prefer to avoid any insistence, criticisms, or interpretations. Experience has shown us that such shared resistance is insurmountable. In these cases, we respect the parents' resistance, taking to ourselves the initiative of interrupting the treatment, always leaving open the possibility of an eventual return to therapy. This attitude on the part of the therapists reinforces the parents' sense of freedom in regard to the therapy. Needless to say, the results obtained with the child give them a certain trust in the therapists. In fact, various of these couples have presented themselves after a period of time, to discuss with the therapists their own problems (without the excuse of a child's symptom).

In other cases, while terminating the therapy, we make a telephone appointment or a session within a few months, with the purpose of receiving news and having a follow-up. With this move, we are able to keep the family "in therapy" while we implicitly communicate our continuous interest and availability.

CHAPTER 23

From Family Therapy to Individual Therapy

Mara Selvini Palazzoli

We come now to the treatment of patients diagnosed as psychotic.

The conceptual framework elaborated during family research has suggested several interventions that have proved effective even in individual psychotherapy.

The first of the interventions we shall be discussing here involves a new approach to the psychotic patient in the first phase of psychotherapy. The basic idea is that the therapist must, for the moment, speak out in favor of the prevailing homeostatic tendency. We shall now try to give a summary of this mode of intervention. In the first session the therapist pays a great deal of attention to the patient's relationships so as to discover which types of behavior serve to strengthen the homeostatic tendency. But which homeostatic tendency? Precisely that of the most important relationship system in which the patient is involved.[1] Let us try to illustrate this with an example.

Previously unpublished.
[1]Generally, but not necessarily, that system is the family. However, it should be borne in mind that the same model can also be applied to subjects belonging to other natural groups. I am thinking of the extreme case of patients who have been kept in institutions for years and are hence active participants in the homeostatic game played by the members of opposing factions in the institutional group.

A 19-year-old boy, whom we shall call Lorenzo, presented himself to a therapist in our team for individual treatment. His parents lived apart but kept in touch with each other regularly. The boy, who a year earlier had joined the classical high school and had always done well there, had been playing truant from school for the past few months and had also given up all other activities. Instead he had started to worry obsessively about his inability to understand the *real* meaning of words. He would lock himself in his room for days on end, burying himself in piles of dictionaries, in which he would look up words compulsively every so often, becoming increasingly more perplexed and confused. Often he behaved just like a 2 year old, persecuting his father or mother with a series of interminable and increasingly anguished "whys," which left everybody exhausted and dumbfounded. The parents accordingly decided to send the boy to a psychiatric clinic. However, at the insistence of one of his father's friends, the boy was sent to us instead. The first session produced the following information.

The only male child, Lorenzo, unlike his sister, who was a few years older, seemed forever involved in his parents' conflicts. His whole life had always been planned down to the last detail by his mother, whom he obeyed without question. She, who kept in close contact with her own aristocratic family of origin, systematically and haughtily disqualified every one of her husband's instructions. The father, for his part, though being a fairly prosperous merchant, took his revenge by being stingy with his money and not missing any opportunity to run down the son as the product of an effeminate upbringing.

Faced with the boy's symptomatic behavior and with his history, it was possible to frame a number of different hypotheses.

One could, for example, postulate that the boy, faced with the imminent school-leaving examination, was terrified of having to face the world and of having to shoulder adult responsibilities; or else that he wanted to avoid success because of an oedipal fear of outdoing the father; or again, that by worrying obsessively about the meaning of words, he was symbolically searching for the meaning of his own existence. . . .

If we use the model of the family context, we could also

postulate that the boy was carrying his position in the system of family relationships to an absurd point: someone who knows nothing and to whom everything has to be explained.

In that way he could make a covert protest against the whole system.

In the normal course of events, the analyst considers a host of working hypotheses, ultimately choosing one on the basis of the material produced at the session, of observations, and of his analysis of transference and countertransference phenomena.

In terms of the conceptual framework we have described, however, it was impossible to make any of the above hypotheses, however correct they may have been, the basis of a therapeutic intervention. The reason was that these hypotheses, implicitly disqualifying the homeostatic tendency, did not account for the fact that the subject has always been enmeshed in the prevalent homeostatic tendency of his system, especially at the moment when his symptom erupted. We have, in fact, seen that psychotic behavior erupts under a threat of a change to the familiar transactional system. Every system, and particularly a system involving a schizophrenic transaction, is perpetually in a state of alarm about the possible cessation of the game. The symptomatic behavior emerges suddenly when this state of alarm (for reasons that cannot always be specified) increases.

In the case under discussion, the therapist used the following intervention during the eighth session. Starting from the concrete data supplied by the client, he demonstrated, and then gave a positive connotation of, the respect and sensitivity with which the young man had treated his parents. He said that he had gathered from the young man how vitally important it was for his mother to feel that she was needed by a child who seemed uncertain and in need of a mentor. As he grew older, the young boy had begun to feel, perhaps unconsciously, that his father, too, having now achieved some economic success, had a need to feel, and indeed to be, a real father, in the sense of at least being able to do something for his son. Hence the utter helplessness with which Lorenzo was trying to help everybody: his mother, his father, and perhaps his big sister as well, who, having failed in her studies, might have felt mortified by any success on her brother's part. It was therefore of great importance that Lorenzo should persist with his current behavior, at least for the moment. Any change on his part threatened to throw the whole family into disarray.

This explanation caused an outburst of indignation by the young man: "You are damning me, doctor! I shan't do it a moment longer. . . . I have come here to do something for myself!"

To which the therapist countered that the young man would only be able to do something for himself if he had a strong dose of egoism and did not care for the others. But, having had a charitable attitude since childhood, he must not renounce it point blank; *nor on the other hand could he do so.* In any case, this was certainly not the moment to change. Since the facts showed that he had recently become completely helpless, it followed that he must have sensed that his parents had grown increasingly dissatisfied, had come to feel a basic need to be "real parents." This showed how dangerous changes could be.

During these transactions, the therapist was able to observe that the shriller the boy's voice grew and the more he protested, the more relaxed he gradually became.

At the next session, a week later, Lorenzo said straightaway, and resolutely, how completely he disagreed with everything the therapist had said during the previous session. Only towards the end of the second session, while recounting what had been happening to him, did he add that he had been coping fairly calmly, since, inexplicably, he had had a week of respite from his obsessive ruminations.

The therapist realized that the boy was sending him the following message:

You have been completely wrong. Quite inexplicably, I feel better.

The therapist decided to ignore the boy's deliberate failure to correlate the therapeutic intervention with the improvement, and this for two reasons: (1) not to take up the boy's symmetrical challenge; (2) not to define himself as a champion of the change.

From that moment, the responsibility for the change was vested officially in the client, who was thus forced to protest against certain objections and excesses of caution on the part of his therapist.

The intervention presented here calls for some comments. Psychotic patients invariably put up strong resistance to therapy for at least two reasons.

The first, in the case under discussion, resulted from the fact that the boy's symptoms appeared when his transactional system sounded the alarm in response to changes. In that sense, the allusion to change contained in the psychotic symptoms was a move to which the family system responded by erecting a stone wall. The second reason is that a patient who reports (more or less voluntarily) to a therapist who has agreed to see him has already received an implicit message: that the therapist will "cure" him, and hence induce him to change, because that is his role.

The therapist's support of the homeostatic tendency of the client's system of relationships turns out to be an effective ploy, either because it is paradoxical or else because it avoids the risk of constructing a symmetrical relationship, a source of interminable resistances.

THE PRESCRIPTION OF THE TRANSFERENCE PSYCHOSIS

In other phases of individual psychotherapy, too, the most powerful resistances will often occur. Here we want to stress just one of these: the so-called transference psychosis. In its presence, the therapeutic intervention must be based on the view that the *transference psychosis is a paradox that can only be fought with another (therapeutic) paradox.*

As we said, it sometimes happens that the therapist takes on a patient diagnosed as neurotic by the classical criteria, and that this patient develops a psychotic type of behavior in the course of treatment. The common element, in the many variants of this phenomenon, is an unrealistic (and subtly satirical) overestimation of the therapist in both the good and the bad sense. The therapist becomes the omnipotent parent, the omnipotent lover, the omnipotent persecutor, etc. However, the therapist's alleged omnipotence turns out to be a skillful maneuver to render him impotent. Let us look at a typical example.

A lady in her forties, married and without children, presented herself to a therapist in our team for individual treatment. She had been asked to do so by a colleague who had had her husband in analysis. Once the husband's analysis had been satisfactorily concluded, the wife had developed increasingly severe phobic symptoms. According to the colleague it was easy to infer that the married couple had a ferociously symmetrical relationship disguised as a pseudo-complementary one. It looked as if the husband had used the analysis to gain the upper hand. After a few months of individual therapy, the wife suddenly developed a psychotic erotic transference to her therapist. She tried to cover him with kisses, and declared that she was so desperately in love with him that *she could never be cured unless the therapist requited her love.* She had struggled in vain. . . . Love was stronger than she was.

We can show how this maneuver leads to the radical disqualification of the therapy involving all the essential components of the message: context, sender, receiver, and content.

The maneuver disqualifies the therapeutic context: "We are not in your consulting rooms, doctor, but in the intimacy of your private apartment."

It disqualifies the sender of the message because that sender is not the client, but Eros.

It disqualifies the amorous content of the message by conveying indifference and sarcasm on several nonverbal levels (the client looks untidy and jots down the appointments on a sheet of toilet paper). It disqualifies the receiver of the message, that is the therapist, by insisting that he must render assistance only by *being what he is not*: a lover.

In a situation of that kind it is very difficult for a therapist to escape from the trap, either by interrupting the therapy, or by ordering the client's hospitalization, or even by interpretation.

Most often the therapist will try to interpret the psychotic behavior on a transferal plane.

But however good the interpretation, it comes up against the obstacle of the change in context marker the client has just introduced (from therapeutic to erotic). What must the therapist do then?

To escape from the trap, the therapist must first of all requalify the context, marking it clearly as a therapeutic one. Obviously he cannot do that in an explicit verbal manner. He would immediately be disqualified.

The only means of escaping from the paradoxical situation is that of responding to it in an equally paradoxical way.

Accepting, without pointing them out as such, all the disqualifications, the therapist must give a positive connotation to the psychotic behavior, and indeed prescribe its intensification. To that end, he will rely on concrete data quietly gathered in the course of treatment. Experience has shown that positive connotations and the consequent prescriptions are the more potent the more systemic they are, that is, the more they reflect the overall situation of the meaningful relationships in which the patient is involved.

In the case under discussion, the following intervention led to the rapid disappearance of the psychotic behavior.

Therapist: "I am deeply impressed by what you are doing since, as far as I can gather, you do it all with the intention of reassuring your husband. More than once during the sessions you have expressed your concern for your husband. You have the clear feeling that he has fears connected with your analytic treatment . . . that the analysis might change you, and hence change your relationship. . . . Perhaps there is also an unconscious fear that your husband might have to find himself another woman after the analysis. . . . But by your actions you are showing him that he has nothing like that to fear from your analysis because you are in love with your therapist. At this point it is essential that you persist in your efforts. This month I shall increase the number of sessions so that you can fall more in love with me, thus making sure that your actual analysis won't start."

In other cases the positive connotation and the consequent prescription of the psychotic behavior have had therapeutic effects even if they were applied exclusively to the therapist–patient interaction.

Let us quote the case of Alice, a 32-year-old woman diagnosed as a "borderline" case. She was in individual therapy with a member of our team because of a growing inability to make decisions, which had limited her already poor relational life even further.

After a few sessions, in which she had used very poor but by no means abnormal verbal communication, she suddenly changed. Out of the blue, she began to verbalize incessantly, in an extremely confused manner, alternating between tears and sniggers. She said she was indebted to her mother (who had died more than ten years earlier and with whom she had had an extremely frustrating relationship) for persuading her in mysterious ways to turn to a therapist so full of maternal warmth and so very helpful. But, reading between the lines of her nebulous discourse, the therapist managed to gather that the only result of this *magical* help was to leave her the choice between suicide and prostitution.

Faced with this dangerous maneuver, the therapist decided to intervene immediately. It was just a few minutes before the end of the session. With great feeling, she started to underline how positive it was to feel the need for a relationship with one's therapist that one normally reserves for one's mother. It was, however, essential that Alice give full rein to this vital need. She must think of her therapist continuously, fill her existential void with thoughts of her, and experience her as her mother. If she had any doubts, she ought to ask: "Mamma, what would you do?" while thinking of her therapist.

Alice's reaction to these words was dramatic. She leapt to her feet and covered her stomach with her hands, almost as if she had been dealt a physical blow. Trembling with disgust, she protested that she had been ordered to do something most humiliating. But the therapist sweetly insisted.

Between that session and the next, there was to be a relatively long interval, arranged some time earlier, because the therapist had to attend a congress.

On the appointed day, Alice presented herself punctually. A few hours earlier, however, she had called the therapist's office to check the day and the hour of her appointment. She could no longer remember . . . she wasn't sure. . . . During the session she mentioned that she had had a very worrying time. She had had to make a number of important and unexpected resolutions, which she enumerated one by one. Among other things, she had successfully applied for a job. There was not a sign of her making appeals to her "mamma," nor did the therapist insist. Alice's telephone call had eloquently signaled her change of game.

* * *

RITUALS AND PRESCRIPTIONS

Some time after the publication of *Paradox and Counterparadox*, Mara Selvini and Giuliana Prata used the occasion of a seminar at the Congress of Zurich in 1977 to return to the rules of family relationships and to *the way in which they are expressed unconsciously in nonverbal behavior*. To think that the roles of family relationships have to be learned on the analogical and unconscious levels was the theoretical premise for the prescription of rituals and other modes of behavior: *rituals do not need explanations: all that is required is that the family perform them.* Rituals and prescriptions work on the analogical level and allow a new form of behavior based on a development of the system's latent potential.

"A Ritualized Prescription in Family Therapy: Odd Days and Even Days" (Chapter 25) first introduced the idea of the uniqueness and inimitability of therapeutic interventions. Implicit in the interventionist phase had been the assumption that dysfunctional relational games—for example those played by schizophrenics—were equal and different at one and the same time. Every game was equal in respect to some very general metarules, such as the prohibition of defining the relationship, the high rate of disconfirmation, and the symmetrical hubris. Every game was *different* in respect to the more specific and idiosyncratic rules drawn up by every natural group. We are currently exploring new hypotheses based on the *typing of relational games* rather than on the old and more extreme general/unique polarization (Selvini Palazzoli 1986).

Such typing, in families with an identified psychotic patient, should facilitate the therapist's task of identifying the ongoing game by supplying him with a kind of map.

The research into games can be based on the study of the effects of one and the same prescription in different situations:

this makes it possible to *compare* the reactions of families to the same "input."

"Even and odd days" describes a method of dealing with the relational games played by married couples who continually meddle in and disagree about the children's upbringing. It must be stressed that the underlying prescription, apart from being effective in this type of family interaction, also provides very useful information on *how* the family follows or ignores the prescription.

This particular intervention, however, reflected the influence of the Brief Therapy Center in Palo Alto and of the so-called "problem-focused approach." Today we no longer frame hypotheses that characterize a situation merely in terms of the parents' continuous interference while failing to dwell actively on the position of the identified patient. The parents' interference now strikes us as being just one, albeit a very important, aspect of the game. Today we consider it essential to use a broader hypothesis, and we look upon the type of prescription discussed in the paper as being, though still valid, only of partial use. The Palo Alto group, by contrast, maintains that in terms of systems theory, according to which even a small change in a system has effects on all the other parts, it is quite enough to pay attention to those aspects of the interaction that are directly concerned with the problem, and hence to devise tasks that interfere with the behavioral sequence associated with the symptom.

As for the theoretical basis of the Palo Alto position, it now seems clear that once we surmount the simplistic view[2] of the earliest application of the systemic idea and if we also bear in mind that *systems theory is a set theory*, we shall find that for a small change to produce big effects the system must have very special spatio-temporal parameters. It is certainly not enough to invoke its general character and to claim that a small change can act on the whole, regardless of subsystems, critical thresholds, and temporal cycles.

[2]An oversimplification for which Selvini herself was partly responsible; *cf.* the case of Lisa (p. 110) with the account of the change in the mother [Ed.].

The combination of the systemic model with the concepts of hierarchic structures has always been one of the thorniest epistemological problems. It has particular relevance to the definition of the "status" of the relationship between the family and the therapeutic team.

I shall be returning to this point in my comments on "Why a Long Interval between Sessions?" (see Chapter 27).

CHAPTER 24

From Interpretations to the Prescription of Family Rituals

Mara Selvini Palazzoli and Giuliana Prata

Those family therapists who have adopted the systemic model no longer use psychoanalytic interpretations, which try to trace deviant behavior back to its historical/causal roots. In fact, psychoanalytic interpretations are based on the linear linguistic model and are connected with the linear conception of reality inherent in the cause-and-effect model. But reality should not be confused with linguistic models. Everything that lives is circular in the sense of the word used by cybernetics: every element produces a series of active compensations in response to external perturbations with simultaneous feedbacks to constitute a permanent system of behavioral adaptation (learning). The result is a perpetual process of self-regulation.

The family therapist who adopts the systemic model makes use of two fundamental concepts.

1. According to general systems theory, every time a group of people shares the same life and the same aims for a

Transcript of an address given during a seminar of the Zurich Congress, 1977.

given period of time, that is, forms a natural group with a history—for instance a family, a work team, a religious or lay community—it inevitably develops, after a certain time, typical interactive links that create particular working models. A group becomes static or, on the contrary, creative, depending on these models, which are of course largely independent of the personal characteristics of those who compose it.

2. The configurations of these interactive modes are built up in time through many trials and errors. From these, and from the feedbacks, the members of the group learn the principles of what is permitted and forbidden in their reciprocal relationships.

We can see that the cybernetic model is extremely well adapted to the family: it is possible to consider the family as a *system governed by rules that ensure its relative stability.*[1]

Our experience with systemic family therapy has shown that most of the rules governing the behavior of the family are constructed and operate on the analogical level. This is proved by the fact that those family members whose behavioral redundancies we have studied include among their stock of behavioral instruments responses to analogical messages they are incapable of describing and explaining on the verbal level. We can thus affirm that what we have here is an authentic form of behavior constructed solely on the analogical level.

What follows is a simple, and particularly interesting, example that irrefutably demonstrates the existence of collective family learning in response to an identical signal.[2] A large peasant family reported for their first family therapy session. The family comprised eight members, all of whom lived together: the father, the mother, two sons, three daughters, and the wife of the oldest son.

---

[1]Today, I believe that the function of the rules is above all to limit the range of behavioral choices and hence to reduce uncertainty [Ed.].

[2]We use "learning" and "adaptation" as synonyms, following Ashby's (1954) explanation that learning is adaptation for survival. In the case of a family in crisis, survival can be identified with the maintenance of cohesion.

From behind the mirror the observers noticed a particularly significant pragmatic redundancy, given the great number of participants. Whenever the therapists asked questions about the way in which the sister-in-law was received by the brothers and sisters of the first-born, the mother would withdraw an enormous handkerchief from a purse which she kept close to her feet and silently wipe her mouth. Attentive observation showed clearly that this action invariably had the same pragmatic effect on the family member who happened to be speaking: they faltered in their previously animated speech, grew embarrassed, searched for words, lowered their voice, and finally began to mouth trivialities. To verify this redundancy, the supervisor asked one of the therapists to put the following question to the sister-in-law: "And you, Signora, how do you think you were accepted by this large family and how do you feel in their company today?" The woman replied calmly, and during the therapist–sister-in-law interaction the mother's handkerchief always remained in the purse. This enabled us to postulate that the appearance of the handkerchief was a danger signal used whenever there was talk *about* the daughter-in-law and not when anyone spoke *to* the daughter-in-law.

If, at the end of the session, we had asked those who were inhibited by the appearance of the handkerchief what effect the handkerchief had had on them, we should very probably have been greeted with amazement, embarrassment, or perhaps an "I beg your pardon" or a "What handkerchief are you talking about?" What we had here was, in fact, a specific analogical message, to which all members of the family had learned to reply analogically. This type of analogical behavior has been discussed at some length in the relevant literature, and Mara Selvini had done experimental research into this behavior in nontherapeutic contexts, using such universal signaling codes as frowning. The experiments have shown that the learning of these "universals" bypasses the verbal level (consciousness).

Naturally, this type of learning, too, is governed by the context. Thus it is practically certain that in a different context the mother's handkerchief would not have had any effect on the children. Having said this, we can go on to draw the following therapeutic conclusions:

1. The therapists must try to discover the relational rules governing the dysfunctional behavior of the family by careful observation of the redundancies, remembering that the family cannot metacommunicate about these rules.
2. The family cannot communicate about the rules because they have been constructed, in the course of time, on the analogical level. Consequently these rules cannot be expressed verbally, not because of a ban on metacommunication, but rather because of a genuine inability to produce verbal formulations.

It is on such general considerations that our prescription of family rituals is based. The prescription of a family ritual allows us to eschew all (very often critical) comments on the rules governing the dysfunctional relationships, comments that would have foundered on the rocks of disqualification. What is needed instead is the prescription of an interaction in which new norms have tacitly replaced the old. The performance of a ritual, which consists of a series of actions whose formal aspects are very carefully defined, enables the family to experiment with an interactive modality that not only blocks the habitual interactions but *constitutes an alternative form of behavior* (learning) capable of releasing the latent developmental possibilities present even in more obviously dysfunctional systems.

CHAPTER 25

A Ritualized Prescription
in Family Therapy:
Odd Days and Even Days

Mara Selvini Palazzoli, Luigi Boscolo, Gianfranco Cecchin, and Giuliana Prata

Family therapy that adopts the conceptual systemic model considers the family group as a cybernetic self-correcting apparatus. The transactional patterns characterizing the relationships between the members are structured into the rules under which the members of the system function in their reciprocal relationships. This set of rules, which a family system has contrived to establish in the course of time through random trial and error, determines a kind of program similar to that of a computer: a program that could be detected in the here and now of a family in the therapeutic setting.

Our research has shown that this program is made up of a body of rules operating almost exclusively on the analogical and not on the verbal level. The more dysfunctional the family, the more incongruous are the rules operating on the analogical level with the rules operating on the verbal level. Faced with the discovery of one or more rules sustaining the dysfunction of a family system, the researcher-therapist often yields to the temptation of

First published in *Archivio Psic. Neur. Psich.* 38:293–302 (1977); first English translation in *Journal of Marriage and Family Counseling* 3:3–9 (July 1978).

making these rules explicit by pointing them out to the family, under the widespread illusion that insight by itself can effect change. But the absence of any change within the family will soon convince him/her of the opposite.

On the strength of this conviction, one line of our research in family therapy was directed towards the following aims: (1) to quickly detect the rule or the rules that generate and perpetuate the dysfunction; (2) *to devise prescriptions instead of interpretations* aimed at breaking the rules that perpetuate the dysfunction.

The development of insight can occur after the change has occurred. It is a common experience in family therapy that when awareness precedes change, the family will use it for the purpose of resistance.

Among the various pragmatic prescriptions devised by us to induce change in the family, we consider family rituals to be of particular importance and we have described these in detail in various papers (Selvini 1963 [1974 ed.], Selvini et al. 1974). It is a characteristic and also a disadvantage of these rituals that they cannot be repeated. They are effective only for the specific organization of a certain family in a given here and now of its history and its therapeutic process.[1]

In this paper we shall describe the form, aims, and possible outcomes of a new tactic, which we shall call *ritualized prescription*. The difference between ritual, ritualized prescription, and prescription are as follows: (1) in rituals the formal aspects as well as the content are specified; (2) in simple prescriptions only the content is specified; (3) in ritualized prescriptions only the formal aspects are specified.

We have been applying this last tactic for nearly two years with satisfactory results. The reasons that prompt us to favor ritualized prescriptions are: (1) unlike rituals, they can be repeated in identical ways with the most diverse families; (2) they selectively strike at a ubiquitous dysfunction of couples with one or more disturbed children.

A similar dysfunction in the couple is reciprocal disqualification, which, as we know, apparently concerns the contents, whereas,

---

[1]Whereas in rituals the formal effects as well as the contents are carefully laid down, in ritualized prescriptions only the formal aspects are defined. In simple prescriptions, again, the contents alone are defined.

in reality, it is an escalation involving the definition of the relationship, "I am the one who knows better." Often, there is no harm in this type of escalation, and it might even be stimulating as long as the couple is childless, but serious consequences can arise when children are born. Then the disqualification manifests itself as interference and sabotage of the partner's behavior and of his/her initiatives with the children.[2]

Obviously the efficiency of such a parent—or of a leader in a given situation—is undermined by the negative interference of the other party.[3] The immediate consequence is decisional paralysis; a later one is homeostatic rigidity. If in such homeostatically rigid family systems a child begins to show "symptoms," the type of his symptomatic behavior will be related not only to the mutual interference of the adults but also to the totality of the organizational parameters, rules, and communicational styles.

Putting it more simply, when leadership is assumed by a psychopathic or a schizophrenic subject, it will be based in the first case on the prevalence of the communicational modalities known as *rejection* and *disqualification*, and in the second case on the prevalence of those communicational modalities called *denial, double bind*, and/or *disconfirmation.*[4]

But let us now consider the ritualized prescription, *specifically* devised to block parental interference, whatever type of

---

[2]*Cf.* Rosman and colleagues (1975). This paper presents a brilliant genre painting, worthy of the best Flemish masters, with the help of an account of a meal shared by the therapist with families having anorectic children. In a room in the psychiatric hospital to which anorectic children are admitted, the therapist has a meal served up and invites the whole family of the anorectic to share it. Needless to say, the patient refuses to eat, either toying with the food or else picking at a tiny morsel. The therapist then urges each one of the parents in turn to get the child to eat, booming out that it is his or her responsibility to see that the child gets fed. The problem is thus being presented, not as the problem of a sick subject but as one of the parents' ability to control a stubborn child. While the therapist supports and encourages the attempts of the parent whose turn it is, the other parent is regularly observed to disqualify and discourage the attempts, either crying with pity because the partner is being too violent or sneering at him for being too soft.

[3]A study of macrosystems (schools and business institutions) simultaneously carried out has shown that an antagonistic interference at the top level, for example between headmaster and assistant master, *appears* as a sort of denied complicity towards maintaining the *status quo* (see Selvini Palazzoli 1976, p. 155).

[4]The continued use of such clearly communicationalist assertions during a phase marked by a quite different approach is astonishing [Ed.].

"symptom" the identified patient may show.[5] We shall start by describing and commenting on the form of the prescription and then proceed to analyze its aims.

The interference observed during the session is not pointed out to the family. The therapists carefully avoid either blaming the parents or persuading them to drop the practice. The ritualized prescription appears unexpectedly and is framed, as we shall see, most cryptically, so as to divert attention from the therapist's real goals. Often, under favorable conditions, we try to devise the prescription in a systemic sense, the better to involve all members of the family. To avoid confusion, disqualification, or amnesia, the prescription is dictated at the end of the session to one of the parents (when the therapist is working with the couple alone), to one of the children appointed as recorder, or even to the patient himself.

The essential text of the prescription, on which we shall comment further, runs as follows:

On even days of the week—Tuesdays, Thursdays, and Satur-days—from tomorrow until the next session and at a fixed time between X o'clock and Y o'clock (making sure that the whole family will be at home during this time), whatever Z does (name of the patient, followed by a list of his symptomatic behavior), Father will decide alone, at his absolute discretion, what to do with Z. Mother will have to behave as if she were not there. On odd days of the week—Mondays, Wednesdays, and Fridays—at the same time, whatever Z may do, Mother will have full power to decide what course of action to take with Z. Father will have to behave as if he were not there.

On Sundays everyone must behave spontaneously.

Each parent, on the days assigned to him or her, must record in a diary any infringement by the partner of the prescription that he must behave as if he were not present. (In some cases the task of recording the possible mistakes of one of the parents is entrusted to a child acting as a recorder or to the patient himself, if he is fit for the job).[6]

---

[5]Obviously such prescriptions are based on direct observations of interference during the session or inferred, for instance, from the detailed account the family is asked to give of the day prior to the session. By that tactic we force the wary family to reveal things that they would not have revealed spontaneously (not even when they pay us a sizeable fee).

After dictating the prescription the therapists take leave of the family without any further explanation. The content of the prescription, as may be inferred, is cryptic. In fact, although the temporal factors are specified, nothing is said about how the parents should act. They are left completely free in their decisions.[7]

The prescription is meant to work on different levels. The first consists in changing the rules of the game being played, that is, to prevent interference without actually stating the intention to do so. This allows the family, following the prescription, to have the unusual experience of blocking the usual transactional modalities. On a second level, the idea is to exploit a possible competition between the parents for the therapist's approval. Each will try hard to come out "best." This attempt will shift their attention from the problem of the definition of their relationship to the problem of the contents: "What must I do during the days allotted to me to achieve praiseworthy results?" On a third level, the aim is to obtain a feedback as to whether the family follows the prescription or not.[8]

We have learned that the most dysfunctional families, whose

---

[6]However, as reported here, the description involves a grave error: that of appointing the "healthy" child as recorder. The assignment of that task merely increases his probable "parentification," thus upsetting the family structure. Today we think it best to entrust the job of recorder to each parent in turn [Ed.].

[7]This radically distinguishes our prescription from other, apparently similar, ones (see Lederer and Jackson 1968).

[8]We think it advisable to dwell upon this fundamental concept if only to draw the reader's attention once again to the cybernetic concept of the method of trial and error. According to Ashby (1954): "Adaptation by trial and error is sometimes treated in psychological writings as if it were merely one way of adaptation, and an inferior way at that . . . the method of trial and error holds a much more fundamental place in the methods of adaptation. The argument shows, in fact, that when the organism has to adapt (to get its essential variables within physiological limits) by working through an environment that is of the nature of a Black Box, then the process of trial and error is *necessary*, for only such a process can elicit the required information. The process of trial and error can thus be viewed from two very different points of view. On the one hand, it can be regarded as simply an attempt at success: so that when it fails we give zero marks for success. There is, however, the other point of view that gives it an altogether higher status, for the process may be playing the invaluable part of gathering information, information that is absolutely necessary if adaptation is to be successfully achieved."

Experience has taught us to expect to be asked, during seminars or special courses, how we react when confronted with the failure of a prescription that has not been followed. This shows how much the success aspect prevails culturally over the aspect of *gathering information*. We, too, before gaining enough experience, tended to get angry when a prescription failed, when we should have been concentrating on the feedback.

members include patients diagnosed as schizophrenic, do not follow the prescription or cease to follow it after one attempt only, offering, at the following session and only when asked for an explanation (spontaneously they would not even mention the fact), absurd and childish pretexts. Obviously these families of "big time gamblers" quickly realize how gravely their game would be threatened were they to follow such a prescription. Nevertheless, the first axiom of the pragmatics of communication continues to apply to even these families. It is impossible not to behave, it is impossible not to react; therefore the attempt not to respond is still a clarifying feedback.

By way of illustration we shall now relate the story of a family of four, presenting a patient, Carla, aged 22, who from the age of 14 had been diagnosed as hebephrenic. Attempts to cure her had produced no positive results; discharged after years of wandering from one psychiatric hospital to another, she had recently been kept at home, in a small town in central Italy, with her parents and a younger brother, Livio, aged 14.

The fourth session with this family ended with the prescription we have described above, after the therapists had expressed, in warm terms, their sympathy with its members. In particular, they showed great understanding for the discomfort of the journey, the costs, the sacrifices made by the family to attend the sessions. Still, there was worse to come. It was essential to demand yet another sacrifice: there was work for them to do at home. The therapists first made sure at what time of the day all the family was at home—from 7 to 9 P.M.—and everyone agreed to do as they were asked at that time.

In order to involve Livio, who was showing signs of impatience and irritation, he was asked to act as recorder of the text dictated to him as well as of any transgressions by the parents of the rule "to behave as if he/she were not there" on the days when it was the partner's turn to make all decisions concerning Carla. Carla herself was involved through the implicit prescription of the usual psychotic behavior, which was expressed as follows: "Whatever Carla may do—stay in bed, wander undressed about the house, upset food, break objects, hit or bite—it shall be Father's turn on even days and Mother's turn on odd days, from 7 to 9 P.M., to decide what to do with her."

While Livio was writing down the prescription under dictation, the therapists watched and recorded the immediate feedback. Carla suddenly laughed, not in the usual psychotic way but in short bursts of high spirits, mischief in her eyes, raising her hand to hide her lips, like a schoolgirl caught in the act of playing a joke on her teacher. The father, who up to that time had been impassive, like a dead object, now looked interested and keen. Livio looked satisfied and proud of the role he was playing. The mother, on the contrary, who had first suggested the therapy and had always acted, during the sessions, as the leader of the group, looked sullen and annoyed.

At the next session, about a month later, we were confronted with a talkative family, dwelling at length on the terrible traffic and the difficulties of finding one's way in such a large city. What about the prescription?—asked the therapists. Oh, yes . . . the prescription! . . . Alas, they had followed it on one evening only . . . because Father, he just kept forgetting. . . . But why? Did they not have it in writing? Where was it? (The sheet of paper unexpectedly emerged from Carla's handbag.) And what about Livio? Had he not agreed to keep a diary? What finally seemed to emerge amongst all sorts of contradictions was that Carla, during the past month, had never hit or bitten anyone. But the outstanding fact, which clearly emerged from the general confusion, was the style of the interference, reported by Livio.

On the days when it was Mother's turn, he said, Mother tried to be strict, but Father always interfered, advising Mother to be patient or speaking tenderly to Carla. When it was Father's turn, he just kept silent or, if Carla was being difficult, called out excitedly to his wife: "Elide! Elide! Come along and do something about this girl!"

The climax was reached with the wife's final comment as she pleaded "in defense" of her husband. "He doesn't do it out of spite, poor thing, he just keeps forgetting things . . . simply doesn't think of them" (which means that he is a fool). The husband greeted this "defense" with resigned nods.

However, in spite of the protagonists' efforts to resist the therapy, the fact that the prescription had not been followed allowed the therapists to gain further understanding of the game and also to clarify the immediate feedback noticed at the end of the previous sessions, especially the clouded expression on the mother's face, her sudden looks of annoyance.

A secret family rule was coming to the surface: Carla is Mother's absolute property, and Father must beware of touching her. But clearly he had not given up; instead he undermined his wife's efforts by unobtrusively acting with kindness, with understanding, with the resignation of the poor victim. Thus he passed on to Carla a powerful double bind: "I want so much to have you on my side, for you behave affectionately to me: but you *must not* do it because *I am afraid* of Mother. It would mean disaster for Mother and myself." The prescription, therefore, could not be followed: the father was not allowed to use the time and place allocated to him, or could not, or did not want to.

What the feedback had revealed allowed the therapists to conclude the session with an unexpected, powerful intervention: the breaking up of the group. When the therapists, having discussed the situation among themselves, reentered the room where the family had been kept waiting, the woman therapist turned unexpectedly to Carla, despite the fact that it had never been possible to draw more than a few monosyllables or some vague mumbling out of her. "Next time, Carla, you will stay home with your brother. Mommy and Daddy will come here alone. We shall try to understand why, being so keen and willing, they *have not been able* to follow our prescription."

While the therapists were taking their leave of the family, fixing the time and day of the next appointment, the mother stood on the threshold, crying and complaining about the sacrifices they had to make, about the journey, and Carla's failing to improve. No one in the room had noticed Carla, who in the meanwhile had moved furtively towards the mirror. Only the two observers, speechless with amazement, saw her face, close to the mirror, beckoning to them, while her right hand moved as if shaking hands in a gesture of congratulation and her lips clearly formed the words: "Well done!"[9]

---

[9]The feedback to such phenomena is interesting. Direct observers usually discuss together in order to compare notes, finding it hard to believe they are not mistaken. Many of our colleagues, instead, hearing about this episode, would exclaim: "But then, she was not hebephrenic!," which means that they prefer to believe in the axiom that chronic hebephrenia is incurable, instead of taking into consideration the inadequacy of the therapeutic instruments.

Carla's message, in essence, could be translated as follows: "They play a tough game at home . . . and you've guessed it. . . . Well done! I congratulate you because you, too, know how to play rough."

From this example we may gather that even when the prescription is not being followed, it still provides extremely clarifying feedback.

When the family organization is not extremely rigid and dysfunctional, the prescription is followed with remarkable changes. We have observed cases of parents adopting, in a sense, the other's opposite way of behaving prior to the prescription, but changing it so that, from being opposite, it became similar. It thus happened that in a family where the mother was too protective and the father too detached and ironic, the mother spontaneously assumed the task of disciplining the child, while the father became gradually more interested and active. The effect on the child was almost immediate and highly satisfactory. Once again this shows that to provide parents with advice as to the "right" way of behaving is far too naive a method of approach. They would know perfectly well how to behave with the child if they were not themselves victims of the game. Once the game is up, they cease to be opponents and finally meet on the same ground, as allies linked by a common cause.

* * *

THE PROBLEM OF MOTIVATIONS AND NEEDS

The subject of motivations and needs has always been, and still is, one of the most controversial in the history of systemic research on human behavior. Thus even during the pioneering days of the Bateson group, there was a major dissension on this very point between Bateson and Haley, who accused Bateson of being hamstrung by the traditional view of motivation. Here is how Haley put it when telling the history of their research project:

Bateson also postulates other motivations: that the parents attempt to put the child in the wrong, and that people have an investment in their adaptive behavior and are hurt if that behavior is condemned. Generally, Bateson preferred to assume that people were motivated as had been traditionally assumed: by fear, hate, love, threats of punishment, and avoidance of pain (Haley 1961).[10]

Haley, for his part, preferred to postulate much simpler motives, maintaining that people attempt to regulate, influence, and control what happens in relations with other persons. This model of control (and hence of power) was fiercely opposed by Bateson, who considered that this view of power was *corrupting*.[11]

According to Bateson, even Haley's "motivational theory" and his metaphor regarding the "attempt to control" involve an individualistic approach, that of viewing motivations (or needs) in an *intrapsychic* way.

In 1976 Haley, on the occasion of the (belated) publication of his "History of a Research Project" (Haley 1961), accounted for his contradiction of the systemic model and added an important definition:

> I was trying at that time to shift from the observation of the individual to the observation of a system and to view a power struggle as a product of the needs of a system rather than needs of a person. I still prefer that view and am trying to clarify it. I think it is misleading to say that an individual has an inner need to control other people, just as I think it is naive to postulate an instinct of aggression. When we acknowledge that all learning creatures are compelled to organize (they cannot not organize, just as they cannot not communicate as Bateson pointed out many years ago) and that organization is hierarchical, then we must expect confusions in the hierarchy. At times conflicting levels of hierarchy will be defined, and at times the structure will simply be ambiguous. (For example, when a therapist assumes

[10]The article was written in 1961 but not published until 1976 [Ed.].

[11]In this connection it should, however, be remembered that Bateson slipped in an ethical question when he ought to have remained on the plane of scientific discussion. The echo of the polemic between Bateson and Haley is particularly clear in Bateson's (1960) "Minimal requirement for a theory of schizophrenia." Those interested are referred particularly to the last section entitled "What is Man?" [Ed.].

the posture of an expert and puts the patient in charge of what is to happen, the hierachy is confused.) When the hierarchy is not clearly established, the creatures within it will struggle with one another. An observer watching the action and thinking in terms of the individual as the unit can postulate a drive for power within the person because he is not viewing the situation. I have found it most productive to postulate "needs" in the contexts individuals participate in, and I was groping in that direction at the time of the project [p. 78, n. 1].

These observations, which, incidentally, had few sequels in Haley's later writings, touched upon a fundamental point: maintaining that people try to define their relationships (or, in other words, try to control one another or to limit their respective spheres of influence and power) does not mean postulating an "inner need." To postulate that is to revert to those classical theories of personality that postulate the existence of a primary motivational impetus (Freud: libido; Adler: the will to power; Fromm: needs; psychoanalysis and behaviorism: release of tension, etc.).[12]

If we take a more complex view of reality and consider it made up of systems rather than of individuals, then we must consider the definition of relationships a product of the *needs of the system* and not of the needs of individuals. Every person who comes into the world begins to live in an environment with an absolutely fundamental characteristic: it is an organized system. People cannot interact except on the organizational level to which they belong. As Haley has put it, they cannot help organizing themselves precisely because they cannot help defining their relationships. If the organization is hierarchical then we must expect vacillation and conflict about the definition of the structure of the hierarchy. The definition of the relationship is therefore an individual need inasmuch as it reflects an intrinsic need of systems to create, destroy, and recreate their organization continuously. Nature is organized complexity and hierarchic organization. Hence every organized system is to some degree

[12]When we postulate an "inner need" to choose, the games and relationship approach does not take us much further than Berne. The argument is subordinated to a more or less arbitrary individual metapsychology [Ed.].

hierarchic: its demarcation calls for definitions of the relationship. The problem, therefore, cannot be exclusively viewed, as Haley does, from a structural angle; the needs of the system (e.g., the family) as a sub- and supersystem of various units must also be taken into account. Now, *the needs of systems lie in the premises around which they are organized.*

These premises are convictions, be they inherited or acquired. For example, the fact that whenever the newly born baby cries the mother feeds it is due to an inherited conviction or premise that there must be a complementary feeder-fed relationship between them. Now that relationship, which involves the unconscious premises (inasmuch as they are genetic) of the actors, has an organizational function because the mother–child relationship is a crucially important subsystem in a species characterized by a long period of infantile dependence.

In other cases, or on other possible systemic levels, the organizational premises (or rules) can be acquired. They are thus constructed in a specific way in the course of time. For example, schizophrenic families seem to have the unconscious premise or conviction that there is a need to define the relationship in an ambiguous way and thus to ward off possible rejection. When we say this, however, we do not assume the existence of an intrapsychic characteristic in schizophrenic families, but simply express the "loyalty" of these families to their own relational premises.[13]

In Mara Selvini's work, from 1971 onward, the adoption of the systemic model has led to neglect of motivations and needs; in the main, she seems to allow only such motivations as are of a systemic type, precisely as Haley had suggested.

Hypotheses based on individual strategies remained implicit and, in fact, in their address to the 1977 Congress in Zurich, Mara Selvini and Giuliana Prata adopted—and this was characteristic of that whole phase—Ashby's cybernetic conception: every system is "motivated" by its own survival. That is its only aim and object. Quite clearly, what we have here is a

---

[13]In this sense, I would today reinterpret hubris as a fundamental rule of many psychotogenic games: in the competitive escalation characterizing hubris, none of the actors accepts defeat or thinks of giving way and, conversely, no one boasts about victory lest the others leave the field [Ed.].

collective motivation, one that does not differ from one actor to another.

THE MISUSE OF HOMEOSTASIS

As I have already pointed out, survival for families was identified with the preservation of family cohesion. In other words, the aim of family organization was said to be the preservation of *homeostasis*.

That type of motivational theory strikes me today as being far too one-sided and simplistic.

That oversimplification, however, has historical reasons: during the phase when the systemic approach was still incipient, Mara Selvini's attitude to monadic metapsychologies was highly critical. The research programs hinged on the absolute necessity of abandoning all attempts to focus attention on individuals. At the same time, however, her long psychoanalytical training had predisposed Mara Selvini—as it had many other family therapists—to adopt thought patterns that proved difficult to abandon. Thus, as we saw in "The Obsessive and His Wife," the systemic intentions were belied by the clinical approach. This explains the great enthusiasm for concepts that seemed to lend themselves to describing the family as a whole. It also explains the exclusive interest not only in motivations for survival and homeostasis, but in everything that might have such characteristics, such as the style of communication, the properties and rules of the system, the family myth, the hierarchic structure, and relations with the outside.

In retrospect, the uses made of the concepts of homeostasis and homeostatic function seem most exaggerated. One has the impression that the "theoretical prejudice" led to a "projection" onto the family of the view that everything is dominated by fear of the slightest change. The systemic formulation of the rigidity of "pathological" families (Jackson 1957) had undubitably been a milestone in family therapy, or rather a springboard for the leap from the individual to the family as a microsocial entity. As often happens with great novelties, the initial "model" effect was so strong as to turn the model into a universal fact. The symptoms, the myths, the disconfirmations—in short, nearly everything that happened in families—were all said to be in the service of homeostasis.[14]

As I have pointed out in the first chapter, present research, which has not been able to solve the problem of motivation, tends to link those general and collective aspects that we define as systemic to the analysis of the strategies used by various actors. In this attempt individual and systemic motivations were both integrated in the game metaphor.[15]

OPEN QUESTIONS ON THE GAME METAPHOR

In family therapy research, the game metaphor has been used in many different ways as a model of family relationships:

1. The observation of the redundancies of a system facilitates its description in terms of *rules*: from rules to games is but a brief step (Jackson and the Palo Alto school).
2. Games are context markers. The statement, "This is a game," if expanded, takes the form, "The actions in which we are engaged do not mean what the actions *for which they stand* would mean." What we have here is an analysis of communication in terms of metalevels expressed in analogical ways (cf. Bateson 1972, p. 150 ff.).
3. The theory of games as a method of studying decisional behavior aimes towards the maximization of gains (von Neumann).

[14]It should be noted that the recent repetition of the same "fashionable" approach based on the substitution of "coherence" for "homeostasis" does not strike me as a great improvement. The only difference is the replacement (as Paul Dell has done) of the biological and mechanistic view of homeostasis with a more cognitive one. In other words, the accent seems to have shifted from behavior to beliefs (as factors for maintaining the *status quo*), which seems to be nothing really new, as Mara Selvini's relatively early writings on the subject demonstrate (not to mention the more classical writings of Paul Watzlawick first presented in Watzlawick and co-authors (1974).

[15]In this connection see Anolli (1981), which deals with the relationship between the self-knowledge the psychologist needs and the type of game played in organizations [Ed.].

All three have been superseded by the current definition of games as means of combining systemic with strategic arguments (see Chapter 1). The cybernetic model of rules or games is unable to define the strategies of individuals and can only formalize *purely* systemic equilibria. Bateson's game theory, though brilliant, is reductive because of its communicationalist foundations. Von Neumann's theory, as we said, cannot be used because of the omniscience it attributes to the players.

Nevertheless, current research into games is profoundly influenced by the historical antecedents. At the same time there has been a fourth decisive influence: thinking in terms of games leads one to compare family relationships with real games, even borrowing their terminology: hence the comparisons with games such as chess, poker, and bridge, and such terms as "move," "tactics," "strategy," "hide," "feint," "bluff," "win," "loss," "hand."

The comparison with real games, together with Haley's contributions (the concepts of control and power) and with von Neumann's theory of games have led us to define the game metaphor in competitive terms: *family relationships are shaped as relationships between victors and losers, between those who gain an advantage and those who have to pay the price.* Victory is the maximization of control over others or the attainment of certain objectives considered to be advantages.

Competitive interpretations of the game metaphor have been in vogue outside the field of family therapy as well. Thus the psychoanalyst Eric Berne (1964) has done interesting research on the typing of games and has retained the game metaphor, interpreting games as the search for social and psychological advantages.[16]

Crozier, a sociologist and an expert on organizations, also uses the gain metaphor to describe the strategy of the actors, and so does Mara Selvini, as we saw in many of the articles in this

[16]The most important of these are said to be inner psychological advantages and, in fact, Berne's theory is subordinate to psychoanalysis: intrapsychical needs are considered the foundations of the game itself. A paradigmatic example is the woman with a phobic fear of social display situations married to an authoritarian husband who keeps her locked up at home. The game she plays with her husband thus confers an internal psychological advantage on her: it stifles her phobia [Ed.].

collection, starting with "The Obsessive and His Wife," in which she uses the metaphor of competitive games to explain a particular relationship between married couples. Among her collaborators, Maurizio Viaro has recently made an attempt to give an explicit account of the game concept:

> The game concept is increasingly being bound up with the "pursuit of ends by strategies subject to constraints." Therapeutic prescriptions are seen as so many instruments for providing the therapist with information: they reveal what the parent couple prefers above the patient's cure. For example, the mother may refuse to execute the prescription out of consideration for "mamma's darling" and the father out of respect for his own mother. On this type of *evidence*, produced during the session, the therapist reconstructs the strategies, postulates how the patient has been "played," and so on. With the help of this collection of retrospective hypotheses, the therapist then tries, amidst the confusion of the data offered during the first session, to discover the road that he believes might lead somewhere.
>   His central concepts are: aims, gain/loss, negotiation.[17]

The model of games played for gain remains one of the most important maps of our research; there are, however, growing doubts about the excessively rigid use of the competition metaphor. According to Mara Selvini:

> We need to appreciate that in games there is the hope of winning but also the fear of losing. Certain games can only be organized around a threat: "Heaven help you if. . . ." The schizophrenic game must have neither losers or victors, because it must be "perpetual," that is, it must never end.[18]

In classical competitive games the positions are clear, quantifiable, and perfectly defined. But things are quite different in the "unstructured" interhuman game: the aims are vague and changeable. It is quite impossible to make comparisons with the rational lucidity of the poker player. The stakes do not have the simplicity of money but are represented by much hazier satisfac-

[17]Maurizio Viaro, personal communication, December 1983 [Ed.].
[18]Mara Selvini Palazzoli, personal communication, December 1983 [Ed.].

tions, such as confirmations of various types, emotional appreciation, affirmation of one's own point of view, and reassurance about one's own identity and importance.

Beyond that, the concepts of victory and gain are full of pitfalls: there is, for example, the danger of generalizing the validity of a map that is specific to contemporary western civilization, and may not even include important aspects of that civilization. Bateson's polemic with Haley on *power*, far from being incidental, was of crucial historical and cultural importance. As Bateson remarked, his own views were bound up with eastern ideas and particularly with those of Zen Buddhism.

In this area, recent reading has stirred up many doubts in me. Roger Caillois (1967), in his socio-psychological analysis of games, has introduced an interesting classification of games into four categories:

1. *agon*, meritocratic games in which the bravest wins;
2. *alea*, games based on pure chance, in which luck decides;
3. *mimicry* (or simulation), imitative games, from childish dressing up to dressing for the stage;
4. *ilnix* (or vertigo), states involving loss or deformation of consciousness; from rides on a roller coaster to drunkenness.[19]

The third and fourth categories, simulation and vertigo, suggest the *existence of games in which there are neither winners nor losers. Can such games provide us with a better model than competitive games?*

Might we not be justified in thinking that human beings tend to copy "roles" and "scripts" they have encountered in their own learning context or discovered in their meetings with a new environment or culture?

---

[19]It is characteristic of these four types of game that their *specificity* is maintained in various contexts, e.g., in family life, friendship, work, religion, and art. We, by contrast, are more interested in true games (with precise structures and rules) as models of family relationships.

What distinguishes true games from the game of life is the impossibility of keeping the levels separate. To play a family game with certain rules cannot ever be separated from playing with these rules (or playing to change these rules) [Ed.].

Similarly, might not the "vertigo games" be aimed at altering one's own state of consciousness to produce violent sensations?[20]

Is it possible to conceive of the existence of games with oneself?[21]

An imitative game is played for the purpose of obtaining functional pleasure, of resurrecting favorite models, of retracing learning steps or recapturing past moments, of imagining that one is different from what one really is, of negating negative aspects of one's present life.

There is thus a host of explanations, but it would seem that none of them can be expressed in terms of gains over others.

In conclusion, I can see a parallel between psychotherapeutic practice and theoretic systematization: the deficiencies of clinical research into the typing of family games corresponds to a lack of definition of the theoretical status of the game concept. I hope that further research will be able to throw fresh light on all the outstanding questions.

---

[20]If we could presume that certain roles are copied and that certain sensations are sought because, in the learning context, they have proven to be *winning* activities, then we should be entitled to subsume the game metaphor under the heading of gain [Ed.].

[21]I certainly do not advocate following Berne in interpreting games as a search for intrapsychic advantages, as "cures" for neuroses, because that would be tantamount to reintroducing the old idea of the primacy of intrapsychic phenomena [Ed.].

CHAPTER 26

A Systemic Course of Family Therapy

Mara Selvini Palazzoli

I have been asked from many quarters for a detailed account of the *steps used* in a therapeutic intervention.[1] Only in that way would the nature of paradoxical interventions or of the prescribed rituals be brought out from the context of the interactions involved in the team's work with the family, in the team's discussions, and in the team's hypotheses and their practical application. In an attempt to meet these requests (which cannot, of course, be fully done without films), I shall here try to give a verbal account of all the sessions and the related team discussions involved in a complete course of family therapy. To that end I have transcribed the notes

Previously unpublished.

[1]In the second issue of *Terapia familiare* (December 1977) Mara Selvini Palazzoli, Luigi Boscolo, Gianfranco Cecchin, and Giuliana Prata gave an account of the first of a series of family-therapy sessions. Mara Selvini then decided to write a fairly full account of all the subsequent sessions as well (more fully than she normally does in the personal notes she keeps of every session). The idea was to publish a book covering several complete courses of therapy, every session being described as soon as it was over, including possible anticipations, hopes, and regrets by the team, and not revised in any way lest the account be influenced by the results of the treatment. The project, however, did not proceed beyond the one case, which explains why it remained unpublished.

taken more fully than usual immediately after every session, without any subsequent amendments or revisions.

The decision to report a course of therapy "as it comes" was based on three considerations: (1) to recapture each session just as the team saw and recorded it at the time; (2) to avoid being influenced by knowledge of the final outcome of the therapy; (3) to give a concrete demonstration of the practical application of our latest methods.

THE SALA FAMILY

The Sala family, which had been settled for generations in an agricultural-cum-industrial zone south of Milan, comprised four members. Mario, the father, was a 42-year-old bricklayer. Desiderata, the mother, the same age, now a housewife, had been employed for several years in a small factory but had given her job to Antonella, her daughter, when the latter was old enough. Antonella, now 17 years old, was the identified patient. Fabrizio, the younger child, was 11 years old and reluctantly attended first year of an intermediate school. When the Sala family contacted our

---

This is the only complete example of an entire course of therapy conducted in the paradoxical and interventionist style (it also contains an early account of the method of running a session examined more closely in "Hypothesizing-Circularity-Neutrality," which was published in 1980 and with which the present collection is concluded).

With respect to the so-called paradoxical interventions, I should like to reemphasize that these are not based solely on hypotheses about relationships but also on intrapsychic hypotheses involving the intentionality of the identified patient in at least two ways: (1) the identified patient is convinced that his symptoms have conferred on him enormous powers over his entire family; (2) the identified patient is angry with everyone, and particularly with those he feels have betrayed him (in the case under discussion the mother ostensibly betrayed the patient to his grandmother) or deceived or defeated him, and uses his symptomatic behavior to "make them pay for it."

The so-called paradoxical intervention is intended to provoke the identified patient in such a way as to upset his linear convictions radically: (1) his subjective feeling of power is redefined as total subordination (sacrifice) to the needs of the "traitor" and of the entire family; (2) more specifically, the patient's anger is converted into solicitude and protectiveness.

In short, the paradox has a double effect: it unmasks the ongoing game or certain of its aspects, and it challenges the intrapsychic convictions of the identified patient [Ed.].

center by telephone, Antonella had been an anorectic for five months. Her rapid and dramatic loss of more than fifteen kilograms in two months had led to four hospital admissions but with no effect. A colleague at the local psychiatric hospital, discharging Antonella, had then persuaded the family to ask for family therapy. Some time after their telephone call, our center let the family know the date of their first session. Antonella was in such a state of emaciation (weight 32 kg, height 1.75 m) that there was good reason to fear for her life. The family chart, based on data collected from the mother by telephone, contained some interesting facts.

It appeared that the couple had lived for the first four years of their marriage with the wife's parents. One of the therapist's observations was that the mother did not seem to be particularly anxious.

The First Session

In the time set aside for team discussion (which we have before every session), the family chart was read out loud and discussed. On the basis of the relevant data, no less than of general experience of family therapy, the team agreed on the following strategy for the session (except for changes to be made "on the spot"):

1. Not too much time would be devoted to listening to the family's predictable account of Antonella's anorectic behavior, admissions to hospital, medical examinations (as tedious as they were sterile). Instead, the team would make careful observations of the attitude of the various members of the family (paying particular attention to the apparent indifference of the mother).
2. A careful investigation would be made of the family's relationships past and present with the husband's and wife's respective families of origin (referring to the note about the four years spent with the wife's parents).
3. Antonella's "premorbid phase" would be explored in the systemic way, that is, the team would try to establish not only what had happened *to* Antonella but also what had gone on *in the environment of* Antonella during the months prior to the eruption of the symptom (referring to

the note about Antonella's acute and dramatic emaciation, which, as we knew from our experience, must have been triggered off by some incident).

When the therapists entered the room set aside for the session, they found the parents and Fabrizio seated close to one another while Antonella sat apart. Antonella, her face resembling a skull because of the projection of her cheekbones and the angle of her jaw, sat rigid as a statue. Her delicate features and tall stature suggested that she must have been a beautiful girl. The mother, in a tone that at times was downright fatuous, began the account of Antonella's unforeseen illness and of her numerous and fruitless admissions to hospital. The father, embarrassed, only intervened at the therapists' request. Fabrizio seemed barely interested. The whole climate of these transactions was relaxed.

The therapists then passed on gradually to Point 2 of the agreed strategy and began to investigate the relationships with the extended families for the purpose of eliciting significant data and possible redundancies. The father, the first-born of four sons, seemed greatly attached to his old mother, who lived in the same village and whom he visited frequently. Desiderata, his wife, was, according to him, very attached to her parents, who had given her her first name because she was their only girl, much longed for after eleven boys! After she married, she had persuaded her husband to live with her parents. There they remained for four years before moving into a home of their own. The therapists delicately inquired into the reasons for the move, and at this point Desiderata began to look upset and burst into tears. It appeared that it was the husband who had instigated the move out of regard for his mother, who did not like to visit him "because he was living in someone else's house." Desiderata added that she suffered a great deal from this move because, though her mother was a very fussy woman, she had felt "backed up" in her parents' home. Moreover, Grandmother Teresa had been very attached to Antonella and very sad to lose her.

During these transactions the team noted an extremely strong redundancy. Desiderata, who had not shown any emotion in describing her daughter's condition, burst into tears every time her mother was mentioned.

Having elicited this extremely important fact, one of the therapists decided to pass on to Point 3, that is, to the systemic investigation of the premorbid phase. However, he made the mistake of doing so with too stark and direct a question: "What happened to the family during the months before Antonella's illness?" The mother's fatuous "Oh, nothing special . . . the same old thing" was not contradicted by anyone. The other therapist then decided to proceed in a more indirect way. She turned to Antonella and asked her, full of concern, about her work in the factory. Did she like it there and had she made any friends?[2] Antonella, unbending a little, replied in a calm tone, mentioning walks with some workmates. "Did you perhaps also take a liking to a boy?" asked the therapist in a friendly tone. Suddenly the atmosphere grew extremely tense. The mother changed her position, coughed, the father lowered his head, and Fabrizio looked around with a sly look.

"Yes," replied Antonella calmly, "when I was 15 I found myself a boy, Franco, but I didn't tell anyone at home. No one knew about it." Fabrizio, sniggering behind his hand, said that he had known about it but that he had kept quiet about it on Antonella's orders.

When the family had eventually come to know, they had disapproved strongly. Antonella was too young. Here Desiderata broke into tears again, saying, "My mother would have liked Antonella to do as I did, wait for the right age . . . and she said that Franco was unreliable and lazy and that we shouldn't let them go out by themselves. . . ."

It emerged that Antonella's anorectic behavior first appeared when she was forbidden to go on holiday with a girlfriend because there was the danger that she might see Franco. This was the start of Antonella's admissions to hospital. The final act of the drama came three months later: Franco was involved in a drunken revel in a bar, which culminated in a striptease. Accused of obscene be-

---

[2]The tracking of family events in chronological order is fundamental—"Let the calendar speak," as M. Bowen rightly insists.

One must, however, remember that families, and especially the more dysfunctional, are most unlikely to present themselves on a silver platter. Amnesia, displacements, confusions of dates, and negations are the usual rewards of anyone asking direct questions, which moreover mark the context as an inquisitorial one.

havior in a public place, Franco had been arrested and he was now awaiting trial.

At this point Desiderata again burst into tears, saying that Grandmother Teresa would now be suffering twice over: because Antonella didn't eat and again because of Franco's shameful behavior. And she was all alone, too, had been a widow for the past three years. . . .

The therapist then asked Antonella how she felt. Would she drop Franco if he was found guilty? Antonella replied that she and Franco needed each other, but ended in a whisper, "I am all mixed up now, and I have made up my mind to die."

The father, when asked, said that as far as he could tell Franco's had just been a boyish prank. If he took his punishment and Antonella still wanted the boy, then he for one would not stop her.

The mother, by contrast, insisted that she would feel too ashamed to sit down with someone who had been to jail.

The therapists closed the interview and left the room, asking the family to wait while they had a discussion with the rest of the team.

Before the end of every family therapy session we invariably hold a team discussion to agree on the way of bringing the session to a conclusion (comments, prescriptions) likely to have a therapeutic effect.

This task, hard at all times, is particularly difficult at the end of the first session, which, in our case, usually involves a pronouncement on whether or not family therapy is indicated (we shall see how experience has taught us to use this pronouncement, too, for therapeutic ends).

During the team discussion, we review the observed behavioral sequences—spontaneous or elicited by our interventions— and try to combine them in such a way as to bring out the salient facts. On the basis of the latter, we then try to frame a hypothesis: *what systemic game is being played*? It is on this that we base our intervention.

At the end of the session just described, we came up with the following salient facts: (1) the redundancy of Desiderata's tears every time her mother was mentioned; (2) Desiderata's indifference to her daughter's suffering, which she plainly considered less worrying than the pain inflicted on her old mother, either by her husband's decision to move, or by Antonella's association with Franco; (3) the apparently marginal roles in the life of the family played by the father and Fabrizio.

The game seemed centered on the three women: Grand-mother Teresa, who had very precise views about everything her granddaughter could or could not do; Desiderata, who cared only for her mother; Antonella, who was wedged between an unap-proachable mother and a grandmother who said that she loved her but who sided with Desiderata against her in the name of "moral-ity."

Antonella's anorectic symptom, which appeared after she was forbidden to arrange her holiday as she would have liked, expressed the failure of Antonella's attempt to redefine her rela-tionship with her grandmother and with her mother in a symmetri-cal way: "In this house it is I who decides." The symptom, the final move in the game, nailed Antonella down in the illusory belief that she had redefined the relationship, had seized power: "No one can manage to feed me." But in reality the power was vested in the game, whose rule everyone obeyed: it is forbidden to take deci-sions in one's own name. In fact, the "subject" of Antonella's anorectic behavior was not herself but the illness that prevented her from satisfying her most elementary needs, just like the "mo-rality" that prevented Grandmother and Mother from acceding to Antonella's wishes (much as "concern for his mother," who could not possibly visit him in other people's houses, had forced the father to move house years earlier).

Antonella's anorexia, being an illness, did not, however, change anything at all. Grandmother Teresa continued to hold the nodal point in a systemic game that caused her to suffer twice over: because Antonella still wanted Franco ("that villain who made her ill")[3] and because Antonella was ill. Antonella *ought* to have turned her back on Franco and *ought* to get better so as *not to make her grandmother suffer so much.*

However, in dysfunctional systems no one ever metacom-municates on the absurdity of such pretenses, the level on which

---

[3]This delusion was based on a confusion of dates. In fact, Antonella's ano-rexia had started four months before the "villainy" that led to Franco's arrest.

the pretence is expressed being exclusively analogical. Having framed their hypothesis on the ongoing game accordingly, the team tried to arrive at a formulation with which to conclude the session.

Because of the family's poor educational standard and the probability that our conclusion would be misinterpreted, we decided to convey it on paper, written in very simple language.

This paper was read out aloud by one of the therapists, so that we could observe the immediate reactions. The text went as follows:

Report on the first session with the Sala family

> The specialist has decided that family therapy is strongly indicated, considering that Antonella's life is in danger and that there is a good chance of curing her. But we are worried about a very grave risk. And that risk involves Grandmother Teresa. For if Antonella should be cured, there is the threat that she would see Franco again. And that might cause her grandmother great shame and terrible sorrow, more terrible even than if Antonella were to die from her illness.
>
> At the next session (14 December 1976) we must discuss this threat to the grandmother.
>
> The therapeutic team

As the reader can see, the conclusion of the session sprang directly from the hypothesis we had framed. *However, it was paradoxical and hence therapeutic.*

In fact, once they had understood the game, the therapists did not divulge it, interpret it, criticize the family for playing it, nor say that they wished to change it. On the contrary, they acted as if they wanted to make sure it went on. But, in doing so, they covertly destroyed one rule of the system: they metacommunicated about the game, they put it in the open, they emphasized it the better to render it unacceptable.

And in what way did they render it unacceptable? By talking about the indication of family therapy and the chance of its being successful, while adding that it was this very success—Antonella's cure—that rendered the therapy dangerous. Dangerous to whom?

To Grannie Teresa, whom the therapists assumed to hold the nodal point. They said explicitly that though Antonella's illness and, hence, her impending death were a source of great suffering to Grannie Teresa, Grannie would suffer even worse from an infraction of the imperatives of "morality" and the consequent dishonor.

In making this declaration, the therapists also stood Antonella's secret belief on its head: they pointed out that, with her anorexia, far from punishing her grandmother, Antonella was, in fact, protecting her from far greater sorrow.

With their declaration, moreover, the therapists also stood on their head a number of stereotyped value judgments (connotations) of our cultural system: (1) they declared that the *illness* was "good" rather than "bad" (inasmuch as it benefited the grandmother); (2) they argued that the *therapy*, if it led to Antonello's cure, could turn "good" into "bad" (inasmuch as it posed a threat to the grandmother).

The paradoxical communication reached its climax in the therapists' comments about the next session; before deciding on therapeutic steps, they would have to discuss the threat to the grandmother.[4]

In short, the therapy involves disclosing the apparent reason why there is some hesitation in proceeding with it.

Finally, we must not forget an essential characteristic of the intervention at the end of the session, namely that it is in the nature of a "trial": an input into the system that *cannot help* eliciting an output, namely more or less clarifying feedbacks (either immediately or later). These feedbacks provide us with so many verifications of our hypothesis. If the hypothesis should prove wrong, then we must formulate a different hypothesis. After this brief digression, we shall return to the last few minutes of our session and describe the immediate reactions.

[4]The reader not used to our methods might think that this was a *true* program to be followed in the second session. In fact, it was just a challenge issued for the purpose of involving the family. Thus, had the family refused to continue, they would implicitly have admitted that they were afraid of the dangers of the therapy, i.e., they would have had to acknowledge that they needed Antonella's illness. However, quite often there is little or no need to refer to the dangers during the next session because the family produces very powerful reactions and thus determines the real content of the second session.

The therapists rose. The mother did not protest, thus indicating that she was resigned to the fact that Antonella must die to spare her grandmother a major disappointment. It was the father who stepped forward to take charge of the written instructions. Antonella remained impassive and silent, while Fabrizio left the room in a hurry.

In our notes we noted these immediate reactions together with our expectations.

We expected an aggressive comeback from the father, and we hoped there would be some signs of rebellion from Antonella, whose interests we had paradoxically put second to those of her grandmother (just as the family system did). In that way we had prescribed its own dysfunction to the system.

The Second Session

Since the first session is always of great importance, we have reported it at great length. The remaining sessions will be described more briefly.

During the two-week interval between the sessions we received no telephone calls. The family turned up punctually and took their seats in the same order as they had done at the first session.

In the presession we had agreed to look very carefully into the behavior and belated feedbacks set off by our earlier intervention.

During the session, we noticed straightaway that Antonella's physical appearance had improved appreciably. The mother, looking depressed and wan, announced that Antonella had started to eat, albeit with a great effort and no real appetite. Antonella even got up at night to get something to eat or drink, which worried them because they were afraid she might eat too much.

This type of behavior is typical of the parents of anorectics, who believe that only the food handed out *by them* is any good and thus define their position in a relationship in which they rigidly maintain their role of supercompetents.

It appeared that, on returning from the last session, Antonella had insisted on making straight for her grandmother's house to show her our report. Her mother had told us (in tears) that the grandmother had wept and that she had finally uttered these memorable words: "All I want is for Antonella to be cured! . . . After all, there are many Francos about! . . ."

During the second session, too, Desiderata burst into tears every time her mother was mentioned—a significant redundancy. Completely absent, however, was the father's anticipated aggressive reaction. Asked for his views about our report, he digressed, mumbling that the grandmother was now an old woman and that she didn't have much longer to live.

To determine the father's position in the family more accurately, one of the therapists then had recourse to a tactic that invariably yields information.

He asked for a detailed description of the way in which the family had spent the previous day. From the answer, it emerged that the father had stayed with the family only for the half hour it took to eat the evening meal. He spent the rest of his free time with friends, playing cards in the local tavern, something he had done ever since the first days of his marriage. His wife had never objected. "She likes it best with her mother: men around the house are just a nuisance to her."[5]

After the interview the therapists left the room for a team discussion. From the observed feedbacks the team was able to elicit three fundamental points:

1. Antonella had started to eat again, though with some effort (probably a sign of her resentment that the therapists

---

[5]This type of behavior, which in bourgeois circles would be an important sign of marital dysfunction, was of little importance in the present case, since it is a cultural phenomenon. Again, the failure of our prediction about the father's aggressive comeback had a cultural explanation (see Bott [1971]). The Sala family can be classed among those defined by Bott as "families with a close-knit network." These are families, usually working-class, who have been living in one and the same place for several generations. Married couples belonging to such families keep up, even after marriage, their close links with their parents, friends, and neighbors, favored in this case by topographical vicinity. Marriage is simply superposed on the old relationships. Both husband and wife satisfy many of their personal needs in external relationships, so that their emotional investment in the marriage relationship is smaller than it is in relatively isolated families ("families with a loose-knit network"). As Bott observes, external relationships can prove useful to the nuclear family in case of need but they can also interfere with conjugal solidarity.

should have put her welfare second to that of her grandmother).

2. It was Antonella who had rushed to show her grandmother
   our report after the first session (a probable sign that she
   did not reciprocate her grandmother's affection).

3. Desiderata continued to cry every time there was talk of
   her mother (a probable sign of frustration due either to the
   attention her mother paid Antonella, or else to the fact that
   Antonella, as her husband had done in his day with his
   decision to move out, was *forcing* her to displease her
   mother).

We then postulated that the grandmother needs Antonella
who needs her mother who needs her own mother. The result was
a circular chase in which no one meets.

On the basis of this hypothesis we agreed that the intervention at the end of the second session ought to involve Desiderata in
her role of one "who suffers whenever her mother suffers." And
from what did Grandmother Teresa suffer?

Evidently she suffered from the fear of losing her granddaughter (with whom she played a game of hide-and-seek that
kept them close). Having learned that Antonella had started to eat
again (Point 1), we decided to advise great caution, thus paradoxically prescribing the anorectic symptom to the girl for the good of
her mother, whose love was confined to her own mother.

It was agreed that our carefully prepared—this time verbal—
comment should be conveyed by the female therapist (in keeping
with the rules of groups in which the women have the say), who
would address Antonella with affection and warmth.

Female Therapist: Today, Antonella, we were told that you are
forcing yourself to eat. But we must ask you to be sensible
and not to drop your anorexia at one fell swoop. (Pause.) And
why? Because, apart from being worried about your grandmother, we have become even more worried about your
mother. Let me explain. You told us that, when she heard
about our report, your grandmother said, "All I want is for
Antonella to be cured," and we believe her. She was telling
the truth! We think that you are everything to your grandmother; you are like the sun to her! (*Desiderata bursts into*

tears.) But if you, Antonella, were cured and suddenly turned into a beautiful girl once again, then there is the danger that you might leave home, lead your own life . . . like so many other girls. . . . But your grandmother is so attached to you, wants to have you near her . . . if she were ever to lose you she would suffer terribly. . . . And that is why we are so worried, because your mother would suffer a lot as well. . . . We have seen (speaking with emphasis) that your mother only suffers when your grandmother suffers (Antonella looks daggers at her crying mother). And so be sensible, Antonella; maintain your anorexia a little bit longer. For the next session we shall also invite your grandmother (*cordially*). We want to get to know her, hear what she has to say, as well. . . . (*All signal their agreement by nodding. The therapists rise and take their leave of the family*).

The Third Session

During the presession, we read the minutes of the last session and, seeing that Grandmother Teresa was to be present this time, we agreed to treat her with the utmost respect and to pay her maximum attention during the session. We would also try to provoke, and pay the utmost heed to, acts connected with the relationships between the grandmother and the various members of the family, with particular attention to possible repetition of such redundancies as Desiderata's sobs. We also thought it important to hear Grandmother Teresa's version of the events preceding Antonella's anorexia.

During the actual session we first took note of the seating arrangement of the various members. This time Antonella had changed her place and had sat down beside her father in the row occupied by members of the nuclear family, while the grandmother sat a little apart, in the chair occupied by Antonella during the previous two sessions.

Fabrizio   mother   father   Antonella

                                          grandmother

Desiderata started straightaway by speaking about Antonella. She mentioned that she was eating again, but that after meals she made scenes, saying that she was in despair because she had eaten, that she felt blown-up and pot-bellied. She threatened suicide, and indeed had picked up a knife from the table and had held it to her throat. It had all come to a head the evening before, in the presence of the grandmother, who had been persuaded to sleep in their house because they had to leave early in the morning for the session. Antonella said nothing and offered no explanations: she only suggested that some crisis had taken her by surprise.

Grandmother Teresa, a tiny old woman, very lively and in no way embarrassed by the unusual situation, entered spontaneously into the discussion and spoke of the sudden change her granddaughter had undergone within a few months. She used a very picturesque dialect. What had become of this affectionate darling girl, the pearl among all her grandchildren, the pet, who had lived with her and Grandfather until she had gone to school (that is how we learned that Desiderata, after her move to the village, had put her daughter in her mother's care for a good two years) and then, although she had gone back to live with her parents, did not miss a single day to bicycle over to keep her grandmother company, to help her with the housework, even doing the washing. . . . And then, for months, Antonella had been so weak that she could not even get on her bicycle. . . . She hardly ever saw her these days. . . . And not even Desiderata, forced as she was to look after her daughter, with all the crises she had had. . . .

It emerged that Grandmother Teresa rented an isolated farmhouse a few kilometers from the village. She had two rooms for herself, the rest of the house being occupied by one of her sons, his wife, and two little boys. The son, however, lived there only in a manner of speaking, because a year ago he and his wife had been taken on as school janitors, a post with some accommodation. They only returned to the farmhouse to sleep, and on Sundays they went to the wife's parents.

And so she was alone, quite alone, and when the sun set her heart ached, and she cried with loneliness until she went to sleep. At this point, Desiderata cried a little and said that her brother had a nerve to treat his mother in this way! "But how come? Were there no other sons?" asked the therapists. "Was there no one else to take care of Grandmother?" At this point, the atmosphere grew tense.

Grandmother Teresa assumed the air of a Greek tragedy queen. She said that she had had to struggle all her life, what with a husband who, poor fellow, did little work, to provide for her twelve children—eleven boys followed by Desiderata. Three had died, and all the other eight were married, thought only of their own families, and had forgotten all her sacrifices. . . . Only Desiderata had been left, and now she, too, could do little, what with her sick daughter. She could not go to live with her only daughter and son-in-law because they had no room; they were too crowded. Suddenly Desiderata declared that if only there were room she would gladly have taken her mother in. The husband, asked if he would agree, assented without conviction, adding that it was quite impossible, however. The grandmother would need a room of her own. The therapists proposed various solutions. Would it not be possible to move to a house with an extra room, asking for a contribution from the other eight brothers? The grandmother shook her head, looked gloomy, and said that all men were selfish. . . . At this point Desiderata, for once without crying, burst out that it was high time to tell the truth: Mother was a troublemaker who had quarreled with all her daughters-in-law; to keep the peace everyone had to dance to her tune. Taking her in would mean giving her a special room because she can't bear watching television and a hundred other things besides. . . .

The grandmother did not argue but shrewdly changed the argument by remarking that she had never been able to get used to the television. The therapists had gathered enough and did not press the point. Instead, they asked the grandmother about the episode with Franco, Antonella's boyfriend. The grandmother was quite adamant: she has never interfered, had never said a thing about the boy, whom in fact she didn't know; she had always kept her counsel and left the girl's parents to deal with the matter. . . . No one contradicted her, except for the eloquent looks the members of the nuclear family exchanged, and the convulsive sniggers of Fabrizio, who covered his face.

At this point, the therapists rose and left the room for a team discussion. The two observers lingered for a moment behind the mirror. They saw Fabrizio get up to ask his mother for sweets and for money to go to the cinema in the afternoon. The two of them had a playful argument in which the father, too, intervened. Antonella looked on without comment. The grandmother, bent in her chair, kept her eyes fixed to the ground. She seemed excluded, isolated.

The salient facts elicited during that session were: Desiderata seemed to nurture an intense hostility towards her mother. Calling her a troublemaker who had forfeited the good will of her sons and of her daughters-in-law seemed to have served just one purpose: to remind her mother that she, Desiderata, was her old mother's sole support, a role that, in this type of culture, fell to her inevitably because she was the only female child. By moving in with her mother after marriage she had tried to reconcile her new life with her old role. But the compromise had worked only for a few years: her husband, unwilling to put up with his mother-in-law's "trouble-making," had decided to move.

She had then made a new compromise, really a kind of barter: lending Antonella to the grandmother. The little girl, obliging and affectionate, would take over the role of looking after the old woman, filling the void left by Desiderata. That had been many years ago now; Antonella had still been a little girl. . . . Meanwhile Fabrizio had been born and Antonella, though brought back by her parents, continued to perform her task. Every day she would visit her grandmother, keep her company, lend a hand, perhaps, in her childish way, to find compensation for certain changes she had noticed in her parents' relationship with Fabrizio. Her adolescence and her relationship with Franco upset the equilibrium, so laboriously established. Antonella now went out with Franco and no longer went to her grandmother's house as often as she had in the past. Moreover, the uncle who lived with Grandmother Teresa had found work from which he returned home late at night with his wife and children. Desiderata would probably have to make daily visits to her mother's house.

Everything conspired together because *everybody* was against the least change in Antonella. She simply had to revert to what she had been so that everything could return to what it had been. This turning back of the clock suited the grandmother perfectly for obvious reasons; it also suited the father, who did not like to find his wife anxious, tired, late with the meals, and thinking about nothing but her mother; it suited Desiderata, deeply involved as she was in the conflict with her mother, a woman forced to live the way she did because of her difficult character and whose care seemed to have fallen entirely on Desiderata, riddled with guilt feelings and afraid of the mutterings of the people in the village.

On the other hand, none of those involved in the game told Antonella that she ought to revert to her old self so as to cover up the interactive problems no one had been able to solve. (The reader will have noticed that we use the active verb "tell" as a matter of fact, rather than "could not tell" or "would not tell").

Since it is perfectly clear that if the problem had been stated explicitly, that is, if everyone had metacommunicated in the first person about his own needs and his own motives for wanting Antonella to revert to what she had been, Antonella herself might have communicated in the first person about her own needs and her own motives without having recourse to her symptom. Then there might have been a more peaceful family discussion of all the problems against a background of a clear and reciprocal definition of all the relationships.

Short of this, a family crisis of the kind we have been describing was bound to reinforce the ongoing game and the consequent flow of negative feedbacks.

Antonella, held prisoner in the game, ended up feeling that she was the victim of a conspiracy, of violence directed against her by all members of her family, and she reacted with anorexia, that is, with an undeclared—i.e., nonmetacommunicated—hunger strike.

Her secret and mistaken response was to accuse everybody, to punish all. But instead of wreaking such vengeance she was defined as sick and taken to a hospital. She had become someone who suffers and makes others suffer.

On the basis of these assumptions the team decided to devise and then to prescribe a family ritual. The aim of that ritual would be: (1) to force the members of the family to do what they have never done, i.e., to metacommunicate face to face on certain aspects of their relationships, and to define these; (2) because doing that would not produce any results by itself, the therapists would have to present their ritualized metacommunication *in a cryptic and paradoxical form.*

It was decided to exclude the grandmother from these rituals. She would be thanked handsomely for her collaboration and discharged.

We shall now describe what happened next.

The therapists returned to the family and, addressing Grandmother Teresa, thanked her warmly for having accepted the invitation to attend the session and for her help.

Then they turned to the father and told him that, in a few days' time, he would be receiving a registered letter with instructions that every member of the family must solemnly pledge himself to follow.

They then fixed the date of the next session, to be attended by the nuclear family alone.

The next day they mailed a letter containing a second envelope with the following instructions:

Family task
    Next Tuesday night, when the family has assembled for the evening meal, Father will open the envelope in which he will find three folded sheets of paper, bearing the word Father, Mother, and Fabrizio respectively. Each one, in that order, first the father, then the mother, then Fabrizio, will read his own paper aloud. After having read it, no one will make the least comment. Antonella will ensure that the task is carried out meticulously.

The several sheets of paper bore the following messages:

Father
    Dear Antonella, I want to thank you for never going out of the house because that way you have kept Mother at home.

Mother
    Dear Antonella, I want to thank you because, with your eating problem and your wish to die, you have allowed me to cut down on my visits to Grandmother without feeling that I am an ungrateful daughter.

Fabrizio
    Dear Antonella, I want to thank you for keeping Mother so busy with looking after you that I have been left to do as I please.

While the first two messages were the direct result of the conclusions we mentioned, we must explain the message to Fabrizio. It was added for three reasons: (1) because of the desire to prescribe a systemic ritual that involves every member of the nuclear family; (2) because of the observation by the supervisors (behind the mirror) of the intimacy between Fabrizio and his mother once the therapists had left the room; (3) because of the justified suspicion that Antonella believed her symptoms somehow threatened her brother's privileged position in their relationship with Desiderata.

Meanwhile, the tactful dismissal of the grandmother and the announcement of the impending letter containing the instructions seemed to be greeted with general relief and satisfaction.

The team was inclined to attribute this relief to the fact that Grandmother Teresa had been treated with kid gloves but nevertheless excluded. As for the reactions to the ritual, we anticipated that Antonella's symptomatic behavior would cease once she was no longer being treated as a clinical case and the discussion had become focused on the real problem: what to do with an old and troublesome grandmother who lived alone in an isolated farmhouse, and whom no one, although feeling guilty and ungrateful, had the least wish to take into their own home. We did not reject the possibility that the rituals might, at the end of the agreed interval, present us with a family who had discovered an alternative solution to the grandmother problem, the more so as it was not on paradox alone that we had based our trust in a change. In fact, during the session, we had made ample use of an implicit educational message: we had very courteously invited the grandmother to collaborate with us, had treated her with great respect and sympathy, and had then excluded her completely.

Developments during the Interval between the Third and Fourth Sessions

Three weeks after the third session the mother telephoned.

She told us that Antonella was eating but that she was acting up terribly. During one scene she had overturned the table and chairs and had even bitten her, leaving a mark. She had turned against Fabrizio, saying that he was stupid and spoiled. Alarmed, Desiderata had wanted to take her to the hospital neurologist and ask him for sedatives, but Antonella had refused. Antonella's "fit of nerves" had started after she had read the sheets of paper. Desiderata was contacting us by telephone to find out why. She was told to be patient until the next session.

Two days before that session, Desiderata called us again. She was distressed. Antonella had turned yellow, she had viral hepatitis; she had been admitted to the hospital as an urgent case and would have to stay there for several weeks. The doctors had explained that the hepatitis was the result of a blood transfusion administered during her earlier stay in the psychiatric hospital. Desiderata said she was terribly reluctant to postpone the session because she had wanted to hear why Antonella had turned so viciously on Fabrizio. In the end, however, Antonella had calmed down, eating better, especially the cakes Desiderata had been baking. She was putting on weight and had become quite a beauty. But now Antonella was anxious again; she hated hospitals and didn't want any of that meat they were giving her. Desiderata took her cakes baked with oil, which was good for the liver. She asked us very anxiously if we could fix the next session right after Antonella was discharged. Finally she wanted to know if she, her husband, and Fabrizio should go to the hospital every Tuesday and read the sheets of paper out loud. She was told to suspend that task, was promised a session, and asked to convey the team's best wishes to Antonella.

The Fourth Session

This session was held soon after Antonella's discharge from the hospital. More than two months had passed since the last session. In the *presession* we looked through the mirror to observe the family's seating arrangement. This time Antonella had sat down beside her father and mother, while Fabrizio, a little paler and thinner than the last time, had sat down at the other end of the room.

Antonella   father   mother

Fabrizio

We decided not to spend too much time on the hepatitis and to concentrate instead on the reactions to the ritual we had prescribed at the end of the third session.

The family greeted the therapists' entrance with cordial

smiles. The mother had bright eyes, as if she were welcoming dear friends after a long separation. Antonella, looking most charming although she had lost a little weight, had completely changed in appearance and behavior. She had cut her hair very short (a "trendy" cut), looked elegant, moved with grace, often smiled and spoke with an animated expression. "She is cured!" commented the supervisors behind the mirror, congratulating each other, "and it's thanks to the therapy!" This view was not shared by the direct therapists, who had the distinct impression that Antonella was merely acting out a symmetrical challenge to them. In fact, despite the cordial welcome, the atmosphere very quickly became tense. Desiderata said suddenly that Antonella had not wanted to come because she needed no further treatment. After a few digressions, the therapists asked what the various members of the family had thought about the sheets of paper they had been asked to read. At once, there was a kind of courtroom atmosphere. Desiderata had thought nothing, nor had Antonella. Only Fabrizio (a great deal more alert and intelligent than he had been at previous sessions) said that he had gathered he would be allowed to play outside all afternoon.

The father, by contrast, muttered with emphasis, "I thought that the sheets of paper were meant to calm Antonella." The therapists commented that this remark seemed a little strange, seeing that Desiderata had called them to say that Antonella had grown even more nervous after the reading of the sheets. The mother then decided to speak up. It was true. Antonella had turned wicked. Then she had calmed down a bit but continued to bait Fabrizio, who, to tell the truth, had turned naughty as well. Desiderata had had to beg him to stay outside playing with his friends, not to enrage Antonella. She had chased him out even when it was raining! Antonella was eating quite well, especially in the evenings. She ate the cakes Desiderata had baked for her. But in the morning she would complain and make scenes because of the weight in her stomach. Still, if there was no cake she was hurt and complained that no one cared about her. And she insisted on going out to work, against Desiderata's express advice. For the past two days she had been working in a new factory, on trial, and certainly she was wearing herself out.

"And how are things with Grandmother Teresa?" the therapists asked. This time it was Antonella who replied. "I look in on her every day; Franco takes me on his motorcycle, and Grandmother is happy. Franco has been released and his lawyer thinks everything will turn out fine." Fabrizio intervened at this point, saying that he, too, went to see his grandmother quite often, because he now played on a football ground near her. But his grandmother wasn't too pleased because she always asked, "Why don't you send me your mother?" Desiderata broke in to explain. It was quite true. She didn't visit her mother all that often because something had happened. Her brother had lost his job, was looking for another one, and he also needed more room. In the house he shared with Grandmother he had only two rooms and he needed three. Grandmother was not prepared to give up one of the two she occupied. And so there were continuous and ferocious quarrels with the daughter-in-law, and Grandmother wanted Desiderata to come and tell her why she always took their part. But Desiderata didn't want to get mixed up in it; she didn't want to quarrel with her sister-in-law, and that's why she kept out of the way.

This time the redundancy—Desiderata's bursting into tears every time she mentioned her mother—had disappeared; instead Desiderata had adopted a somewhat more aggressive tone. "I am sick of killing myself for Mother's sake," she said in dialect. "Enough is enough! I have let her drive me mad long enough! She wants a hundred and one things, and whatever you do is no good. Last year, when she had bronchitis, I kept changing her pillows. One was too hard, another too soft . . . then the oil, and even the salt, had to be of a certain type. . . . She nearly drove me mad! And now she keeps attacking my brother and his wife . . . because they leave her alone such a lot!"

The outburst went on for some time, the therapists listening with obvious sympathy. Then Antonella intervened quietly with an unexpected suggestion. "For me the obvious thing is to take Grandmother into our house." Fabrizio was of the same opinion: "Then the fighting with Auntie would stop. I'll sleep on the couch in the kitchen, and Grandmother can have my bed." "And what about the television? When will you be able to see the television, you idiot?" Desiderata shouted at him. "You know that she doesn't like it! . . ."

"Best put her in the old-age home," Father said in conclusion, shrugging his shoulders.

During the *team discussion*, we referred to the difference between the optimistic assessment of Antonella's behavior by the supervisors and the less sanguine view of the direct therapists, who had noticed a well-disguised challenge in Antonella's attitude. The general course of the session proved the therapists right.

She had, in fact, appeared as an elegant, gracious, smiling, almost seductive girl. She had taken pains to find herself a job two days before the session. But she had been reluctant to come and had no desire to meet the therapists. And why not?

The most likely hypothesis was the following:

Antonella was convinced that she had seized control of the system. She had detached her mother from her grandmother, she had had the better of Fabrizio, she had been allowed to go back to her Franco (who was received by the grandmother with full honors because he brought the beloved Antonella to her every day); in short she now ruled the roost. The *status quo* suited her to perfection.

But why her subtle challenge to the therapists?

Because in those sheets of paper they had treated her as a poor fool, with whom everybody could do as they pleased. After a period of confused rage (she had had plenty of time to think in the hospital bed) she had decided that she'd show those rotten therapists. . . . And so she turned up looking beautiful, gainfully employed, with a boyfriend, and with just enough "anorexia" to threaten any who dared to contradict her. . . . And she was good, too, much better than Mamma, because she went every day to look after her grandmother.[6] But in the meantime she had made a plan: to throw the ball of caring for the poor old grandmother back into her mother's court. Fabrizio sided with her because he, too, was fed up to his back teeth with paying unwelcome visits to Grand-

---

[6]This was an interesting hypothesis on the *strategy* of the identified patient. The next therapeutic intervention was accordingly designed to *rebalance* the *relationship of forces* within the family, in accordance with the general therapeutic objective to renegotiate relationships in such a way as to place all members in a tolerable dynamic situation and to prevent the emergence of incongruous hierarchies, here exemplified by Antonella's "characteropathic" leadership [Ed.].

mother Teresa at the behest of his mother, who didn't want to go there herself.

But one essential fact stood out plainly: *Antonella was treating her mother exactly as Grandmother Teresa had done.* That business with the cake was much like the story with the pillows! Grandmother had been a good teacher, had founded a school, "the academy of those who can never be pleased."

From all these findings there gradually emerged the hypothesis on which we would base our next intervention. It was essential to deliver a quick blow to Antonella's dominance before it became crystallized. And that intervention would have to be along the paradoxical line of positive connotation.[7]

Therapist (turning to Antonella): In this session we saw how much you have done to help your mother. A splendid effort, even though it has borne no fruit so far. . . . In the first session, we all saw that your mother was desolate. She kept crying because of her problems with Grandmother, who repaid her badly, kept accusing her, and was never content. But what do we see today? Your mother doesn't cry any more about your grandmother, visits her rarely, does not interfere in her quarrels. And who has done all this? You, Antonella! No one else! Your own sensitivity made you realize that in order to help your mother break free from Grandmother Teresa, *you had to take your grandmother's place and to copy her in every particular.* "Casting out devils with Beelzebub," as the saying has it! And so you, Antonella, started to play the grandmother at home. With the cakes, for example. If Mamma didn't bake them for you, you took umbrage. And when she did bake them, you told her off because they gave you a stomachache.

[7]Here we have yet another demonstration of the mobilizing and dynamic character of systemic family therapy. For example, in our experience, a paradoxical intervention quite often causes an anorectic to abandon his or her fast and engage in psychotic behavior instead. That shift is often connected with his relationship to the therapists. Stopping the therapy in such cases would have disastrous results. It is therefore essential that the therapists keep a firm hand on the situation and use a new intervention that renders such behavior impossible. In Antonella's case, after the brief phase of fury caused by our notes, she faced us with the threat of consolidating her "characteropathic" type of leadership.

And so you too could never be satisfied. But your mother now has no time to think of Grandmother, and she no longer cries. She is better. And we, who have been so worried about your mother, are much less worried now.

Desiderata was completely bewildered, could find no words. She kept looking from the therapist to her daughter and back again. The latter, impassive like a poker player, "cashed in" without saying a word.

No obvious reaction came from either the father or from Fabrizio.

The date of the next session was then fixed.

Once the family had left, the team had a lengthy discussion. There was some disappointment. One of the therapists cast doubt on the effectiveness of the intervention. Various predictions were voiced.

What would Antonella do?

The supervisors thought that she might continue to torment her mother, now with their permission. In that case, however, the intervention would have been a mistake.

But why should Antonella continue to plague her mother?

The team came up with the hypothesis that her mother was a pseudo-fugitive who never defined her relationship with anybody, a woman who signaled to her husband, "I am thinking of my mother," who signaled to her mother, "I am thinking of my husband," who signaled to her daughter, "I am thinking of Grandmother," who signaled to Fabrizio, "I am thinking of your sister," and who now signaled to all and sundry, "I am thinking of my dear therapists, I always think of them, I wait for nothing but the session, and I keep calling them so that they can explain things to me."

Perhaps that was also why Antonella was hurrying to get better, why she had not wanted to attend the session, why she wanted to gain complete control over her mother.

We wondered if Antonella would turn up for the next session. The general feeling was that she would stay away. In that case it would be obvious that we had made a mistake.

But what mistake? We decided to hold a special team meeting

to go over the entire session. It was then that we noticed a grave omission, that we had ignored an unexpected new factor: the alliance between the two children in wanting to ask the grandmother to stay with them despite the trouble to which that would put them. We wondered whether this might not be more than a vendetta, perhaps an attempt to liberate themselves from an unpleasant duty by handing the grandmother squarely back to their parents. Without this omission, that is, had we taken this action of the children into account, we should have been able to devise a systemic intervention involving the whole family, and aimed at the crucial problem: the parents' marital problem—an intervention of the type: "Antonella and Fabrizio are willing to put up with the discomfort of having their grandmother live with them because they are convinced that if ever they leave home, their parents will have nothing to say to each other. Their parents are badly in need of someone to speak to, who will break the silence." Having said this, the therapists should have reserved the next session for the parents. Had they done so, besides ratifying the nascent alliance between the two members of the younger generation, they would have effected a *de facto* redefinition: the "patient" was no longer Antonella but the married couple, or rather the relationship between husband and wife.

Once we had swallowed our disappointment at having missed the bus, we calmly decided our next move. (The idea of making good the mistake by telephoning the parents and asking them to come by themselves was quickly discarded. Such attempts are invariably doomed.)

If the mother were to telephone to tell us that Antonella refused to come to the next session, we should not insist and content ourselves with the parents and Fabrizio. Appreciation of the mistake we had made thus helped us to regain control of the situation.

The Fifth Session

In the interval the family made no telephone call to the Center, and the whole Sala family turned up for the fifth session.

The team saw through the mirror that they had adopted the following seating arrangement:

```
                              mother    father
Antonella
           Fabrizio
```

This time Fabrizio did not isolate himself, as he had done in the fourth session, but sat down close to his sister. Antonella, who had put on several more pounds (one might say she was now of standard weight), did not look as elegant and well groomed as she had in the last session. For the first time she had put on a skirt and was wearing flat shoes and an unassuming little gray sweater. Desiderata, by contrast, was in splendid array. Fresh from the hairdresser, she wore a vivid floral dress, drop earrings, and a gold necklace that glittered with every one of her movements. She did not, however, look overdressed and common but had a vital and gypsy-like presence that contrasted sharply with the pallid and dull appearance of the man sitting by her side.

During the presession, we agreed on the strategy to be used. We were very pleased that our prediction had not come true and that Antonella had turned up. This would give us a better chance of repairing our mistake. It was agreed not to go into the concluding remarks of the last session. Instead we would try to focus attention on the relationship of the parents with the help of a remark Antonella and Fabrizio had made during the fourth session ("The obvious thing is to take Grandmother into our house"). We would ask what each of the two children proposed to do to implement this idea.

But once the therapists had entered the room and had been greeted with warm smiles, the mother asked straightaway for permission to explain Antonella's reaction to the last session. Antonella had been very disturbed by the therapists' concluding remarks and, once back at home, had uttered the mysterious, "I am mad and I shall remain mad, but Mother will be cured."

Desiderata had been quite unable to make any sense of it, and Antonella had refused to explain. The father, asked by the therapists to tell them what he had felt about his daughter's statement, said that he had countered with, "But they [the therapists] said they were satisfied with you because you are so cooperative." Antonella kept quiet until the therapists turned to her and asked her what she had meant. "No more and no less than what I said," she replied calmly, "that Mamma is happy now and has stopped crying, and that I am mad." On the last "mad" the mother broke in to tell us that, two or three days after that mysterious phrase, Antonella had done something very wicked, very wicked indeed. Returning home from work one evening, while no one was at home, she had taken her slacks, dresses, and blouses from the wardrobe, put them on the kitchen table, and cut them into tiny pieces. She had saved just one summer dress, one winter dress, and the between-seasons dress she was wearing now. And the only explanation she gave was that they were too tight—when all of them could easily have been let out! . . .

At this point one of the therapists, turning to Fabrizio, asked if he did not think Antonella had had great fun doing these things. Fabrizio hesitated, clearly taken aback. The supervisors behind the mirror were sure that the therapist's question had been a mistake and called him out.

In their view, their colleague had reacted symmetrically to Antonella's apparent provocation. According to them, Antonella's mysterious phrase and her *wicked* cutting up of her dresses had had a quite different meaning: it had been a message of disapproval (addressed to all and sundry but particularly to the therapeutic team) following the team's mistake at the last session. The message, according to the supervisors, was, "Seeing that you persist in worrying about no one but Mother and leave me to cope with all her unresolved problems, it is small wonder that she is smiling and all decked out. I by contrast am badly dressed and mad." In the monitoring room we agreed that our colleague should immediately say what had been agreed during the presession. He returned to the family to enquire into the relationship of the couple, taking as his first question the children's project during the last session: why exactly did they want to take their grandmother into the house?

The rightness of this change of tack was quickly confirmed by the feedbacks. Fabrizio, who at first argued how much the grandmother would benefit from this move, finished by admitting that he himself needed his grandmother because no one was ever at home. His mother used every excuse to go out: she liked to go shopping at lunchtime, always forgot something, and then went out again for hours on end.

When Father returned from work he always complained because Mother was out, but as soon as she came back he went to the barber's or to play cards. If Grandmother were there she would keep Antonella company when she came home from the factory.

"But wouldn't you like Grandmother to keep your mother company also?" asked the therapist. "Bah!" objected Fabrizio, "they are always quarreling. . . ." Antonella, for her part, was quite explicit: she wanted her grandmother in the house to keep her mother company. Papa and Mamma spend very little time together. It's not that they quarrel; they just don't talk to each other. If Father is in, Mother is out, and the other way around. It almost looks as if they avoid each other. . . .

The supervisors were struck by the amazing change that had taken place: an almost complete reversal of the hierarchic relationships. The parents had been put on the carpet; they looked embarrassed, like naughty children, while the therapists and the "children-parents" spoke about *them* in worried tones. Antonella, instead of absenting herself from the session, had offered us a last chance to read her message.

But what precisely did she want to tell us with her cryptic phrase and with the destruction of her dresses when she came back from work to an empty house? After much discussion, we postulated that she wanted to tell us, "Just look at your wonderful work! Now that Mother, with your support, has managed to get rid of Grandmother, she leaves us alone even more than she used to. Papa is incapable of controlling her and keeps going out himself. It's up to me to change all that. My anorexia and now my madness are the only way I can force Mother to stay at home, to think of me, because Mother now doesn't think of me as Antonella, but as a madwoman. If I stay I shall at least be able to nail her down physically."

There seemed no doubt, moreover, that Antonella and Fabrizio had entered into an alliance to keep their mother at home. The father's attitude was unclear. It was impossible to detect the least evidence of a coalition between him and the children.

However, the information elicited from the children during the session made it clear that the couple were competing about who could stay away from home most.

On the basis of these hypotheses the team decided its therapeutic intervention. They would give a positive connotation to the children's behavior: it reflected a purely unselfish concern with their parents' unhappiness. The real "patient," it would be suggested, was the unhappy couple who left their children alone at home. The therapists would shoulder the task of helping the married couple.

The closing of the session was entrusted to the female therapist.

Female Therapist (sitting down opposite the parents and addressing them in a warm and affectionate tone): What we have seen today is how worried Antonella and Fabrizio are about you. They feel that you, Signor Rino, are an unhappy man, and that you, Desiderata, are an unhappy woman. They have described your comings and goings, your empty house, how you escape from it all. They feel that the two of you have serious problems that you have been quite unable to resolve. And they keep thinking of the future: what will Father and Mother do once we have left home? Those two have nothing to say to each other, do nothing together. They know perfectly well that none of it is your fault, that something much stronger than yourselves stops you from being happy together. (*The two parents, tears in their eyes, stare at the therapist and nod.*) Differences in character, perhaps, differences in temperament. . . . The children, especially Antonella, have done everything they can to help you. . . . But we think that's not really their business. We believe that it's our business; we, the therapists, must try to help you solve your problems. And so, at the next session, we expect just the two of you. Antonella and Fabrizio will stay at home.

The date of the next session was arranged. The couple, deeply agitated, shook the therapists' hands without saying a word, while Antonella and Fabrizio did so with broad smiles. In the brief confusion of the handshaking ceremony at the door, Antonella realized that she was shaking the woman therapist's hand for the second time. She said, "I'm very happy to do it again, doctor."

In the team discussion following the session, it was agreed that we had done well, as witness the parents' agitation and the children's smiles.

However, we also noted one worrying point that might jeopardize subsequent developments: Antonella's possible jealousy of us.

The Sixth Session

During the interval between the fifth and sixth sessions, Desiderata telephoned one of the therapists. Two weeks had passed since the last session. She said that Antonella wanted to come to the next session because "she had things she would tell no one but you." In a mysterious voice, she added that she had no idea what it was all about. The therapist asked her to call back again in a week's time, to give her time to consult her colleagues. The team, after having discussed the matter, decided to allow Antonella to attend the session. If our suspicion that Antonella was jealous and wanted to control our relationship with her mother was correct, our refusal to see her would have been a grave mistake and might initiate an uncontrollable spiral of hostility. We realized, of course, that we were acquiescing to being manipulated and hence running a risk. However, we felt that it was worth the trouble; apart from avoiding a possible escalation of hostile reactions, we would be gathering fundamental information.[8]

Punctually on the appointed day Desiderata called back. The therapist then told her that the team had no objection to Antonella's presence. Desiderata said that she was happy because Antonella really wanted to come.

In the presession it was agreed to make the telephone call the central issue. We had to discover who had decided on it (though it was Desiderata who had made the actual call) and following what occasion. As at the beginning of every session, we left the family alone for some time. In the mirror, we observed the threesome seat themselves as follows:

                    mother   father
         Antonella

[8]In connection with our discussion, it is only right to let the reader know an important fact. Precisely because we had focused our attention on Antonella, we had failed to arrive at the obvious hypothesis that there was a joint resistance to our treating the parents without the children. The therapeutic road of anyone using the intrapsychic approach is full of such blind spots.

Antonella had turned into a very beautiful girl; she looked radiant, bronzed, vivacious, with a touch of adolescent arrogance. The parents kept eying her, the mother with anxious eyes, almost furtively, the father with a satisfied air of finding himself in the company of so beautiful a daughter.

As soon as the two therapists entered, Desiderata immediately burst into a chaotic babble; terrible things had happened, Antonella was being wicked with Franco, she was worried about their relationship, expected the worst. . . . While saying these things, she kept whimpering like a little child. After a while, a therapist turned to Antonella, who had kept quiet and seemed in no way bothered, and asked her what her secret reasons had been for wanting to attend the session. She looked completely taken aback. She had not wanted it, in fact. . . . Mamma had told her that the therapist to whom she had spoken on the telephone had insisted on Antonella's presence. Desiderata broke in with a great jumble of words, alleging that she had told the therapist that Antonella *ought* to come to explain certain things to them. . . . The therapists, certain that Desiderata had told them that the girl *wanted* to come, did not insist and took the blame for the misunderstanding. They asked Desiderata why she had thought that her daughter *ought* to attend.

Not at a loss for words, Desiderata poured out another torrent, occasionally interrupted by questions from the therapists. The "terrible things" she had mentioned were: Three weeks earlier Franco, Antonella's boyfriend, had consulted a fortune-teller, who had told him to be careful, because there had been another man in his girlfriend's past, and now there was a middle-aged woman who was giving him the evil eye. Pressed by Franco, Antonella had confessed that, as a little girl, when she took her shoes to the local cobbler, the old man had touched her, and she had let him do it. This had gone on for some time until the cobbler moved away. As for the middle-aged woman who gave Franco the evil eye, Antonella suggested that it might be her mother, Desiderata. This had leaked out, and an argument had started between daughter and mother. Antonella had insisted that she had only been joking, but her mother had turned the whole thing into a big drama. "But why do you get so cross about it all?" the therapists asked. Desiderata's answer was confused. Antonella, she said, was wicked; she was leading Franco by the nose. Unlike her, he was a good person, but everything was bound to end in disaster. One day Franco would pay Antonella back; he might be a dog that merely barks, but one day he would turn on her for sure. Who knows if he had even forgiven her for that ugly business with the cobbler. . . . Noticing that Antonella looked amused, one of the therapists asked her if it didn't bother her that her mother kept interfering. Antonella said quietly that it didn't bother her one bit. All she wanted was for her mother to stop contradicting herself with all this nonsense about good and wicked behavior. She was certain that Franco loved her. Throughout this long transaction, the father, as usual, had kept quiet and looked unruffled. Asked for his views, he played everything down.

During the *team discussion* we remarked on the fact that there had been no mention at all of the parents' relationship. What had come out instead was this comedy with soothsayers and people casting evil eyes. Moreover, Antonella had discovered that she had other than anorectic powers and now took pleasure in provoking her mother. Desiderata for her part wanted nothing better. So what had we really discovered? A fine bag of conjuring tricks!

The therapists had called in a married couple, Desiderata and Mario, to discuss their problems. But, presto, out of a conjurer's hat a different couple—Antonella and Franco—had emerged. The discussion had been about *their* amorous quarrel, about the anguish Mamma suffered because of *them.*

What we had witnessed, therefore, was a maneuver to keep the "old" couple out of the discussion. That Desiderata had hatched this plot seemed beyond doubt, but it was equally indubitable that the others had lent a hand. Had we then come up against some kind of collective fear, or an attempt to evade our challenge?

We decided to focus attention on their fears, describing them with sympathetic understanding. The couple would be asked tentatively to come back without Antonella, and their immediate reactions would be carefully noted. The task of closing the session was delegated to the female therapist, who had also closed the last session with great empathy.

Female Therapist (goodnaturedly, turning to the parents): We have had quite a lengthy discussion trying to figure out what has been happening. The other day we invited you two to come here by yourselves to speak about the trouble between you, about your problem of living happily together. And it seemed you were glad about our offer. And yet today all we did was talk about Antonella and Franco. . . . This has made us think that you may not yet be ready to talk about yourselves, about your troubles as husband and wife. (*At this point, the father, with an agitated expression, held out his hands palm upward as if to show that he would be only too willing. . . . The wife kept her eyes cast down.*) Perhaps you feel a bit discouraged, some lack of confidence . . . the whole thing seems hopeless to you. . . . We should certainly understand, but we nevertheless still believe it would be a good thing for us to work together. But let's give it a bit of time . . . say, after the summer. We'll fix the next appointment for two months from now. Who knows? After that period you might feel ready (fixes the date). You, Antonella, won't be coming along.

Antonella (brightly): Oh, at long last I needn't come here any longer!

When they took their leave, Antonella went out first, with a satisfied expression. The father smiled at us, while the mother, very disturbed, buttonholed the therapist and whispered, "And Antonella, what am I to do with her?" The therapist replied with a smile, "Antonella seems quite capable of looking after herself."

Once the family had left, the team discussed the end of the session and made its predictions. Next time the couple would have to turn up by themselves, but it seemed quite certain that Desiderata would try new diversionary tactics and would, in any case, express her total disbelief in the possibility that *her husband* might change.

The Seventh Session

The married couple presented themselves at the appointed date and sat down side by side, with an embarrassed expression. Asked for news, they said that Antonella was extremely well, worked in a factory, and in her free time was always out and about "with her young friend." The therapist moved on to ask about the relationship between the two of them. Unexpectedly it was the husband who first spoke, and uncharacteristically, he had more to say than his wife. In a calm, decisive tone, he said that he had long ago hit upon a solution that suited him down to the ground: to stay out of the house as much as possible. "Because I am no good to you if I stay in, because I fall asleep on the couch in front of the television, and I'm no good if I go out because I go out." Desiderata, a little less calmly, reproved her husband for always grumbling, for swearing, or returning home late at night. Asked about their sexual relations, Mario said briefly that, as far as he was concerned, they were "normal." Desiderata, with a girlish blush, said "he has the bad habit of waking me up for that thing when he comes back home, and I get absolutely furious." Mario, turning to the therapist, said that this was news to him, because they had never discussed the matter. . . .

Enlarging the enquiry to take in the extended family, it became clear that Desiderata had no contacts with her mother-in-law. It was the husband who visited her. However, since their marriage he had never stayed for a meal with his mother. As for Grandmother Teresa, Mario, after their move, had never once gone to look her up. When his wife stayed with her for a meal, he preferred to eat in a restaurant. But when the old lady came to visit them in their house he always treated her with respect.

During the *team discussion*, we took cognizance of the rather desolate picture the two had drawn of their home life. In substance both had communicated that they considered change impossible. They had apparently grown used to this type of relationship and had expressed no wish to change it. For a long time we remained uncertain how to conclude the session. We had the clear impression that we were dealing with a type of relationship that is fairly common among people of their social background. Afraid of reverting to bourgeois stereotypes, we decided to abstain from any comment, limiting ourselves to fixing an appointment in six months' time. It seemed quite an achievement, as it was, (1) that they should have turned up for the session; (2) that they should have said things they had never said before; (3) that the children should have known that their parents had come to the session to discuss their relationship with us.

The couple agreed to the next appointment and took their leave of us with a great deal of cordiality. On the doorstep, Desiderata turned around and asked with a malicious expression, "And what about the children? Don't you really want them?" Then she burst out laughing, together with the therapists.

Eight days before the appointed date, Desiderata called and spoke to a member of our team. She told him that her husband was in the hospital with an inguinal hernia. He had had it for a long time but recently it had been giving him trouble. He was about to be discharged, but it wasn't certain at all if he would be able to come to the session. "Not that I'm saying that we won't come, no. . . . I'm only calling to let you know that we may not be able to turn up. It depends on whether he feels well enough. It's only a few days from now. . . ." The therapist asked for other news. Antonella was extremely well, she was working and was always with Franco. Desiderata added, "All the blame was put on Franco, and yet he is a good boy. He was just a little bit upset by his disappointment that Antonella was in the hospital. . . ."

The therapist asked Desiderata to call back after he had been able to consult the team about what was to be done.

During the team discussion, we agreed to cancel the next appointment for practical reasons: there was a risk of wasting a session. We also discussed whether to make a later appointment. The prevailing view was to leave the initiative to the couple. The female therapist told Desiderata the next day that the appointment had been canceled. She also asked her to wish her husband a speedy recovery and get in touch again after Christmas. At the end of January, Desiderata called and spoke to a member of the team. "We want to know whether we should come or not." Asked how things were with the family, she replied, "Very bad! Antonella is wicked. She does just what she wants, and always with that Franco. . . . No one can keep those two apart." "But how is Antonella?" "Very well, she eats, she goes to her factory, but she's wicked, wicked. She is no longer what she used to be." "And Fabrizio?" "He is well. He is always out playing with his mates." "And how are things with your husband?" "As usual, not too good, not too bad. . . ." Desiderata then asked if they should come for a session, because Antonella was so wicked. The therapist replied that it certainly was a serious problem, but it seemed doubtful if the team could do anything about it. "That's what I thought as well," Desiderata said with conviction. The therapist said good-bye and invited Desiderata to call with news in six months. "Certainly,

certainly, with great pleasure," she said warmly, "and meanwhile many, many thanks to all of you."[9]

Sala Family Follow-up Record

Selvini called at 1:00 P.M. on October 27, 1984. Desiderata answered the telephone.

Selvini gave her name and mentioned her purpose.

"Antonella has been well since the last session. She married her Franco in 1979. After a year in Milan, they bought a bakery shop in Corsico. He works at the oven, and she serves in the shop. Franco is a good boy, and they are happy. In 1983, they had a little boy who is now 20 months old and who is very well. Antonella is still very slender because she eats too little, but woe betide you if you tell her to eat more! She is now 25 years old. Grandmother Teresa died in 1980.

She went to call her husband and asked him to say hello. "Antonella is still thin but she is very well. The two of them get on well together. The little boy is beautiful and strong. Fabrizio is well, and we are very pleased with him."

He thanked us warmly for all we had done.

[9]The presentation of this case allows me to raise a very important, but infrequently discussed, subject: the *coherence* of successive interventions in a psychotherapeutic process.

This subject is highly relevant to all therapeutic models. Here I shall limit myself to some observations on the interventionist-paradoxical model. In the more verbal phase of interventionism (1972–1977), every session was treated as a self-contained episode. From the first to the tenth session the therapists kept looking for the great "sleight-of-hand," the paradoxical intervention that would change the entire situation. That was the logic behind the entire *Paradox and Counterparadox* period. Boscolo and Cecchin seem to have stuck to this approach, contending that all interventions, however different (i.e., however incoherent), nevertheless introduce different punctuations and thus help to shake rigid family convictions and to suggest a more elastic and circular outlook (Telfener 1983).

Mara Selvini, by contrast, even in this paper, written in 1977, anticipated her future conception of the therapeutic process: a strategy based on a logical and coherent sequence of moves.

In fact, in the Sala case, the successive interventions were far from incoherent and tended to bring all the actors in the system into the picture, the therapists' various "moves" being punctuated responses to the family's reactions. Of particular interest is the intervention made during the third session, namely the ritualization of a triple challenge addressed to the patient by every member of her family in turn, and couched in appreciative terms. Such ritualized challenges were specifically designed for this particular ongoing game [Ed.].

PART SIX

MAKING HYPOTHESES: RESEARCH INTO FAMILY GAMES

CHAPTER 27

Why a Long Interval between Sessions?

Mara Selvini Palazzoli

This paper gives a theoretical account of our normal practice—
which has proved successful—of cutting our connection with the
family after each session for a period of about one month.

The object of this analysis is the family-therapist suprasystem, i.e., the system of interactions between these two subsystems
in the treatment context.

We shall describe the successive hypotheses we framed to
interpret the empirical data our research revealed.

Our present hypothesis, suggested by a great many clinical
observations—especially by some peculiar resistance patterns in
families—derives from the cybernetic model, and in particular
from a number of hypotheses formulated by Ashby (1954). We are
convinced that the greatest threat to the goal of change pursued
by the family-therapist suprasystem is that it may organize itself as
a "too richly joined" system. The practice we have adopted seems
to us to counteract this danger by means of two concurrent opera-

The first version of this article was published in *Terapia familiare*, June 3,
1978, pp. 67–74. The first English translation was published in *Dimensions of
Family Therapy*, ed. M. Andolfi and I. Zwerling, New York: Guilford Press, pp. 161–
169, 1980.

tions by the therapists: (1) introducing into the family system therapeutic inputs that, never varying, act as continuous disturbances of the ongoing organization; (2) interrupting the family-therapist interaction for fairly long intervals, which is essential for accumulating observable reactions.

At the beginning of 1972, our team drew up a plan for research into family therapy with anorectic and schizophrenic patients. Having adopted the systemic model, we made it our chief aim to apply it rigorously. We were determined to avoid at all costs any eclectic contamination by other conceptual models. As to the rhythm of the sessions, we did not consider this a methodological problem. For some time, we continued with our weekly sessions.

It was only by chance that we were confronted with a highly interesting phenomenon: some families, who out of necessity were invited to meet us less frequently, were showing from one session to the next markedly greater changes than families attending weekly sessions. They were families living in southern and central Italy who could not afford many long and expensive journeys. This observation required an explanation.

The most obvious explanation was that these families were more motivated to change: braving the discomfort of the journey (which sometimes meant traveling by night on crowded trains where no sleeping cars were provided) was a clear test of strong motivation and seemed to explain the positive results.

To test the validity of this hypothesis, we decided to prolong the interval between the sessions with families living in Milan as well. The results were similar and forced us to discard the original explanation; being prepared to put up with an uncomfortable journey was no indication of the wish to change.

We then proceeded to frame a second hypothesis: we had reached better results because we had worked better. Confronting a family we were about to leave for a comparatively long period of time, we obviously felt obliged to concentrate more on observation and to call more on our imagination so as to devise original interventions.

This was the starting point of a phase in our work that I shall call *interventive*: we had to devise increasingly "powerful" interventions. It was during that period (1972–1975) that we devised family rituals and systemic paradoxical prescriptions.

However, as we later realized, there was a conceptual error underlying this effort. Although intellectually we knew perfectly well that in the therapeutic treatment context, family and therapists cannot be considered independent entities, underneath we *actually* continued to maintain a separation. We were working exclusively with tightly interlocked and mechanically autocorrective families, and we believed that the long intervals required in order to obtain a change were specific conditions for treating that type of family organization.

Finally certain phenomena, occurring repeatedly with less rigidly organized families as well, compelled us to reconsider the matter. These phenomena were the following:

1. If, after a paradoxical intervention at the end of a session, we did not immediately take leave of the families but lingered on, allowing the members to discuss the session with us, the intervention was weakened and lost its efficacy.
2. If, instead, after "the bomb had been dropped," we took our leave immediately, fixing the date of the following session, quite often we were called on the telephone a few days later and were asked, on this or that pretext (for instance, a worsening in the condition of the identified patient), to agree to a session at an earlier date.
3. If, giving up our "interventive fury," we terminated a session without making any comment or imparting any prescription—just setting the date for the following appointment—this unexpected and cryptic termination stimulated the family to make important changes that could be observed in the following session.

This sequence of empirical verifications helped us to reconsider the treatment context as a suprasystem, the control of which—for the purpose of change—must be kept firmly in hand by the therapists.

First of all, we had to explain why the families' resistance was expressed either through the attempt to prolong the *direct interaction* with the therapists or through the urgent desire to go back to it as soon as possible. Clearly, we thought, in this way the family was aiming at *suppressing* the effects of our intervention; and, in fact, they had been successful when, after one of these telephone calls, we naively agreed to name an earlier date for the appointment.[1] *We had realized that to grant an earlier session was tantamount to our disqualifying our intervention.* The tactic of the family that succeeded in obtaining an earlier appointment was actually that of meeting us again in order to raise completely different problems from the one focused upon in the preceding session. But even when the family did not go as far as that, another form of redundant behavior emerged. Families that, on first negotiating the treatment contract, had shown relief at the prospect of only ten monthly sessions and had commented on how expensive the sessions were, after a therapeutic "uppercut" suddenly inverted their attitude: very graciously they begged us not to be concerned about them . . . they would be pleased to come to many more sessions, and they did not care a bit about the expense!

In order to clarify the matter, we started again, in a sense, from the very beginning: during several team meetings, we reexamined the therapist's peculiar position in the treatment context. It was clear to us that the therapists, if they are up to their task, must enter the suprasystem as accepted and accepting members. But, as we had discovered, it was equally essential that they should firmly hold in their own hands the control of the context and of the definition of the relationship. They must discover as soon as possible certain rules of the ongoing family game without submitting to it, avoiding being caught up in the same organizational pattern. The family game, on the contrary, is geared to enmeshing the therapists, subjecting them to its own rules so as to establish *with them too* the same prevalently homeostatic, tightly interlocked, autocorrective system.

An interesting article by Lynn Hoffman (1975) offered new hints for our theoretical elaboration. In this article, going back to Ashby and particularly to his classic *Design for a Brain*, Hoffman suggested that dysfunctioning families are too richly joined sys-

---

[1]Later, experience taught us to exploit the telephone calls for greater clarification. This generally helped us to discover the pretext hidden under the urgency to see us and enabled us to avoid getting involved in family maneuvers.

tems that, in a way, reproduce the mechanism and the slowness of adaptation of the homeostat's functioning. Still, in therapy, these families may change, and even rapidly:

> Adaptiveness to change in such a system will depend on the possibility for the joints between parts to become temporarily inactive. This observation supports maneuvers in family therapy that emphasize the creation of boundaries between subsystems differentiating individuals from one another, and blocking customary sequences of interaction [p. 457].

In our case, such a hypothesis must include the therapists. Since we had come to regard the family-therapist system as a suprasystemic unity, we were bound to explain in cybernetic terms both our therapeutic maneuver and the family's countermaneuvers.

The hypothesis was supplied by Ashby. As is known, he had devised his homeostat as a model: a starting point for understanding how the human brain functions. Yet the homeostat, as an ultrastable, fully joined system, requires a period of adaptation, and therefore of learning, infinitely longer than that required by the human brain. In order to explain the enormously quicker adaptation of the brain, Ashby formulated two hypotheses:

1. There may be moments during which a partial dynamic disconnection between parts of the brain occurs. In these temporarily disconnected parts, partial changes take place, with possibly an accumulation of these changes.
2. Such disconnections are obtained by introducing in the interactive sequence *constancies* or *null-functions*, designed to temporarily interrupt the flow of information. This may be illustrated by a device used in experimental neurophysiology: the congealing of a segment of the spinal cord acts like the introduction of a constancy or null-function, since the congealed segment, by not interacting with the upper segment, prevents the passing on of information to the lower segment. Thus the spinal cord

becomes temporarily disconnected, separated into two independent subsystems, each compelled to undergo independent adaptations.

If, provided with these hypotheses, we go back to the problem of family therapy mentioned above, we must first of all regard the family-therapist suprasystem as a cybernetic apparatus *in which the chief danger, in connection with the aim of change, is that of becoming organized as a too richly joined system, making it difficult, if not impossible, for the therapists to maintain a metaposition of control.*

We shall now try to explain our therapeutic maneuvers on the strength of these hypotheses.

The first maneuver consists of introducing into the family system some information, or input, having a negentropic effect. Such input, in fact—although it is shaped, as we shall see, in different modalities—always represents *alternative* information and therefore a possibility of learning. A case in point is the prescription of family rituals that tacitly substitutes new rules for those perpetuating the dysfunction. The family that performs such rituals is experimenting on the action level with *behavioral alternatives* formerly excluded from its learning context. In the same way, the concluding move of a session, which reverses the punctuations in order to redefine beliefs and relationships paradoxically, establishes itself as an *alternative epistemology* that overturns the ontological and perceptive universe of the family.

The *second therapeutic maneuver* consists in the therapists' withdrawing immediately after the intervention, cutting off for a longer period of time their direct interaction with the family.

Let us try to analyze the effects of these maneuvers, keeping in mind how difficult it is to describe separately what, in reality, are concomitant phenomena. The effect of the first maneuver, as information, while having an impact on the totality of the system, *cannot* possibly fail to produce a different effect on the various members. Why is this so? Because each member inevitably holds a different position in the network of systemic relationships. Haley (1964) first stated this principle: *it is impossible for two members of one system to occupy an identical position at the same moment.* In this sense, the input introduced by the therapists, by conveying a different meaning to each member of the family, causes each to react in a different way. These different—and differentiating—reactions are merely partial adaptations in answer to the information received. But there is more to it: each partial adaptation of one member becomes for each of the other members of the family a new piece of information, to which it is impossible not to react. Thus an accumulation of partial effects will be reached, provided, as Ashby states, "we allow time for the effects to work round the system," which means that such a sequence of feedbacks to the therapeutic input requires a certain lapse of time to develop and become noticeable. Consequently, if after a therapeutic input we leave the family alone for too short a time, the change will not have developed enough to be observable. An example is the case of an anorectic who, after an intervention, suddenly drops her symptom; the depressive reaction of one or both the parents becomes apparent only after some time has elapsed. Let us consider a more complex case, that of a family of four with an identified schizophrenic boy of 16 and a daughter aged 13, docile and childish in her behavior. If the girl is the first to react to a therapeutic intervention, starting a stormy teenager's rebellion, some time will pass before the mother develops an anguished reaction, to which the identified patient in turn reacts unexpectedly by running away from home.

If the family is left alone for a suitable period, the maelstrom of reciprocal reactions will lead to a conspicuous change. And this change, obviously, happens in connection with the passing of time.

Translating these theoretical reflections into clinical experience, what phenomena are mostly observed in a family left to itself for a month after a therapeutic input?

Very frequently the family *does not say* that there has been a change, and therefore the evidence that there has indeed been a change is expressed by one of the following types of behavior: a pronounced depressive attitude in some member(s), mostly in one or both of the parents; dejection and mistrust towards the therapy; loss of outward control; and intense aggressiveness toward the one who has changed most of all. If the identified patient has dropped his or her symptom, the parents may refer to it almost incidentally as something of minor importance and disqualify it by a jeremiad of reproaches about other forms of his or her behavior. A number of families, with a psychotic member who had been chronically ill for tens of years, have gone as far as to declare that they felt deeply discouraged because the identified patient had not yet recovered by the fourth session!

But the therapeutic process does not operate only in this way. I have mentioned how language, because of its linear and descriptive nature, compels us to describe separately what in reality is concomitant. Everything I have described up to this point, in fact, seems to be a function of the family's subsystem alone. This is not so, inasmuch as our analysis also concerns the family-therapist suprasystem. Thus we realize that the therapists—by withdrawing immediately after the intervention and breaking off interaction with the family for a period of time determined by the therapists— perform a fundamental operation involving them too: they disconnect themselves materially from the suprasystem.

Thus the therapeutic intervention—which by itself has already disconnected the members of the family from their customary connections through the different positions assumed by the various members within the family system—is strengthened by an additional disconnection, this time of a material kind: the therapists cease to interact with the family and exit tangibly, for a time, from the system.

How does this disconnection of the therapists work?

We may say with Ashby that this material disconnection alone is not sufficient to break the system if, at the same time, we do not introduce constancies that are nonfunctional for the former circuit. *These constancies are supplied by the quality of our interventions*—for example, a repetitive ritual, a paradoxical comment delivered in writing, or a systemic prescription, which remains unvaried in the therapist's absence. Constancies, according to Ashby, can cut a system to pieces.

The feedbacks described above pose a terrific risk to the homeostasis of the family subsystem. Disconnected from the therapists, the members of the family are acutely aware of the danger implied in a change of the reciprocal connections. Suddenly nobody knows how the others will react to the "disturbance" introduced by the therapists. Everyone feels alone, separated from the others by a sort of fence. Beyond, there is the unknown. No one, in the meantime, dares to metacommunicate with the others on what has happened. Experience, in fact, has shown us that the members of the family do not discuss among themselves—or, if they do, only perfunctorily—the therapists' comments or prescriptions. When asked, they will show embarrassment and confess that silence has been kept persistently. At most, someone will report some disqualifying comment or sarcastic remark about us uttered by one of the other members. Therefore, once the risk of change has been registered, resistance rises to meet the danger, which means reentering as soon as possible into direct interaction with the therapists, disqualifying, confusing, and neutralizing the intervention.

I am now ready to formulate a few concluding ideas.

The first concerns the length of time necessary for the family-therapist suprasystem to produce a change. We think that this interval, in the first place, varies with the quality of the therapeutic intervention. When interventions "hit the mark," they can enormously shorten the time otherwise required by a family system to develop change.

Nevertheless there is another aspect that militates against haste. A system requires a certain period of time before, in answer to a well-aimed intervention, it can produce the maelstrom of feedbacks that forms an observable change. On the other hand, only an observable change provides the therapists with the information needed for the framing of a further hypothesis and, consequently, for making a further intervention.

However, we are still a long way from being able to establish the optimal interval between a therapeutic intervention and the next session.

In practice, we generally employ intervals of about a month between sessions. We have shortened this interval in only a very few cases. Conversely, and always after we had flung a paradoxical challenge at the family, we have prolonged the intervals for several months, sometimes even for a year, registering positive results. We are gradually reaching the conviction that a very prolonged interval is indicated and perhaps even essential with families presenting chronic schizophrenics as identified patients. The results seem to validate the hypothesis we have formulated.

* * *

THE RELATIONSHIP BETWEEN THE FAMILY AND THE TEAM

"Why a Long Interval between Sessions?" is one of Mara Selvini's most important theoretical papers, one she thought about for a long time and that required a great deal of effort. In fact, even in *Paradox and Counterparadox* (1978, p. 49) we find reference to long intervals between sessions; the reason, however, was not yet fully understood or explained. That took another three years of hard thinking. The belief that therapeutic experience comes first and that the theory follows is a constant thread in Mara Selvini's work. Proceeding by trial and error, framing hypotheses on individual cases, and experimenting with original interventions and prescriptions, the team has accumulated a large amount of experience in the field. Some of these experiments, although more or less improvised to suit a particular case, continue to prove effective and have accordingly been retained.

Then there is the difficult problem of explaining why a certain therapeutic move works, which means elaborating sound theoretical foundations for what may have been a fleeting intuition. The intervals between sessions was a case in point.

The paper is still highly topical; however, there is one important point that, I feel, calls for further comment.

In the first part of the paper, Mara Selvini refers to the family-therapist suprasystem and claims that its dysfunctionality is due to the fact that either the family system or the suprasystem is too closely joined (entanglement). That claim still holds for both the family and the family-therapist relationship. More recently Mara Selvini has clarified matters further and has drawn a fundamental distinction between these two types of systems.

> The failure to consider the family (or the client) as a system-with-a-history that must be distinguished from the therapeutic system leads, as it always has led, to confusion.

In order to analyze therapeutic work for the purpose of generating a theory, we must start out by considering the system-with-a-history that demands our help as a unity *out there*, i.e., separate from the therapist. To that end, we must determine how that system-with-a-history has, over a period of time, elaborated an organization in which certain specific interactive patterns correspond to the emergence and maintenance of symptoms. The setting of family-plus-therapist has no history as such before the beginning of their mutual interaction. Moreover, at the very instant of the first interaction between the two parties, they become (or structure themselves into) an ensemble, that is, a system with mental characteristics in Bateson's sense. Bateson gave the example of a man felling a tree with an axe. Each stroke of the axe is modified or corrected according to the shape of the cut face of the tree left by the previous stroke. Bateson believed that this self-corrective mental process operates by trial and error and has a creative character. Returning to our family-plus-therapist ensemble, at the very moment that they start to interact the two parties constitute a mental system that initiates its own course in time.

But in what way can such a system become and remain creative, that is, therapeutic? In one way only, it seems to me: if the therapist can avoid identifying with any of the specific "historical" patterns that serve to maintain the very conditions for which the family has sought help. This primary duty of the therapist will be simple to perform in some cases and extremely difficult in others, for instance, in the treatment of families with a chronically psychotic member. Discovery of the patterns that sustain the symptom, lest the therapist identify with them, often proves an uphill struggle. Yet it is only by avoiding this trap that the therapist can avoid becoming a part or a piece of the family. I consider it mistaken to assert, as is so often done, that as soon as the therapist makes contact with a family he is already part of it and co-evolving with it. *The therapist is not part of the family, but is a part of the therapeutic system for whose development he is professionally responsible* [Selvini Palazzoli 1984, pp. 282–284].

In the above passage, Mara Selvini highlights the crucial difference between a mental system (or system of communications), which is constructed instantaneously (the moment a transmitter makes contact with a receiver), and a system with a history, the diachronic result of negotiations on the rules.

Initially, the family-therapist suprasystem is qualitatively different from its two constituent subsystems, because it lacks a history and has been based on a precise context marker: a contract for *asymmetrical* collaboration (the client being in a complementary position with respect to the therapist) for a given end.

Defining the precise nature of the therapeutic system is not a mere theoretical exercise but an indispensable analysis of the clinical work. The therapeutic system is devised and put into action in order to exert a particular influence on the client. The control of the game must lie in the hands of the therapists and it is obvious that it is the client alone who must change his behavior. The client contacts the therapist and enters into a clear contract with him. That sort of agreement generates a therapeutic system. This system is justified if, and only if, it facilitates the change the client, in a more or less ambivalent way, requires.

Likening systemic family therapy to a system of communications, although very fruitful in other respects, obscures the basic characteristics of the therapeutic system. In the communications field there are no hierarchies[2]: messages can be more or less informative, but senders and receivers interact and continuously change roles in a completely synchronic and egalitarian way. The communicationalist model is derived from a telephone network: *there is absolute equivalence between the users*. Interhuman relationships, by contrast, are governed by a negotiation of the *differences* between the actors.

Applying the telephone model to human systems therefore means committing another typical communicationalist error, namely, assuming that the effects are completely circular, equal, and reciprocal. The whole thing is a "quantitative" deformation of the "bits" of the messages, based on a failure to appreciate the enormous qualitative complexity of the human system

---

[2]The levels "object," "meta," and "meta-meta" (or content/relationship) are in fact a hierarchy based on the possible interconnection of messages (or parts of one and the same message) but having no links to a hierarchy of senders [Ed.].

in which the internal hierarchization, the genetic premises, the social attribution of roles, and the playing of microsocial games (with relative adaptations and self-fulfilling prophecies) produce decided *inequalities* between the actors and, as an obvious consequence, differences in the weight and sign of the influences. In short, it was impossible to keep propounding the simplistic idea that a higher hierarchic position meant greater power to influence wants. The power is vested in the rules of the game and not in the individual actors or groups. And even when these decisive facts were appreciated, the effects of communicationalism (or the adoption of the telephone-network model) still imposed an oversimplified view, failing as it did to distinguish between the qualitative importance of various factors at work. It is indeed true that, in a system, no one part can hold linear power over the rest, but to understand the game we have to go further than that—we must also appreciate the specificity of the various influences.

With the communicationalist approach, a system of relationships (such as the family) thus wrongly appears to be based on *fully* circular influences, so that no part can have linear power over any other. It was for these reasons that Bateson (1960) with his circular conception of human interactions and the consequent rejection of all hierarchical metaphors (such as "power" or "control") dismissed as an epistemological error the view that psychotherapy is an intervention aimed at changing the patient.

This type of systemic communicationalism, apart from being intrinsically contradictory when it comes to the structural analysis of the family, ignores the highly specific characteristics of the therapeutic system: it is precisely the absence of a common history and the asymmetry of the relationships that allow the therapeutic system to exert an influence on the family system.

Now, it is only when the therapeutic system loses the above characteristics and becomes transformed into a *nonasymmetrical system with a history*, that the change produces great problems, because it is linked to the "natural" and uncontrollable development of the newly constituted living-system-with-a-history. For that very reason, the model of family therapy Mara

Selvini has since adopted involves rules to safeguard the *thera-peutic context.*

The article to the contrary, we must therefore bear in mind that the family and therapeutic systems must be considered both separately and jointly—separately because each had its own history and its own game prior to the therapeutic encounter; jointly because, having established a contract of collaboration, the two parties have thus agreed to a relational game in which the behavior of either party can no longer be linked directly to their own old game but must also be linked to the new game, the one being played in the therapeutic context.

The preservation of a precise and controllable influence of the therapeutic system on the client system is an indispensable feature of the therapeutic contract and aim. This does not deny the fact that the client exerts some influence (of a personal or scientific-professional type) on the therapist. However, the defense of the therapeutic context demands that the reciprocal influences are kept under control by being kept apart.[3]

The therapeutic context thus involves the interaction of two heterogeneous systems. Such interactions are based on two types of rules: *explicit* and *implicit* ones (Viaro and Leonardi 1982).

In conclusion, the therapeutic context has to be planned and run in such a way as to hand the therapist clearly defined control over the nature of the context and of the ongoing game. When there is such control, there is less context shift and hence less therapeutic failure. The therapeutic context implies the maintenance of the collaborative relationship in which the family accepts the complementary "one down" position characteristic of those asking for help and advice.

---

[3]It must be emphasized that this is the main function of the double self-reflective level on which the observational activity of the team is based. The emotional and mental involvement of the supervisor with the client is quite different from that of the direct therapist, who cannot help being conditioned—unbeknown to himself but not to the supervisor—by the looks, smells, postures, and other nonverbal reactions with which the family signals alarm, anguish, or pain when important subjects are broached [Ed.].

THE IMMEDIATE REACTIONS TO
A PARADOXICAL COMMENT

I consider it important also to examine *resistance* to a paradoxical intervention. Are we right to describe as "resistance" the fact that the family challenges the conclusions of a session or, in other cases, tries to continue the interaction by implicitly disqualifying the intervention through switching the discourse to an irrelevant subject?

Should we not rather think that when the intervention is obviously successful inasmuch as it causes surprise (that is, leads to a disorganization of the habitual family epistemology), then the family, because it is startled, is unable to react and to continue the interaction? We need only think of what we have jocularly called "paradoxical faces," that is, of the perplexed looks and dazed silences produced by some "centered" interventions.

On the other hand, if the family responds vigorously or does not seem to be confused, we are entitled to think that the intervention did not upset the old punctuations and perceptions.

Prolonging interactions after the conclusion of the session can be particularly dangerous if the intervention is not "rounded off": some gaps may have been glossed over during the conclusion but will inevitably make themselves felt in the family reaction.

DISORDER AND CHANGE

"Why a Long Interval between Sessions" contains a fundamental idea: the first therapeutic maneuver must be to introduce information with a negentropic effect (i.e., to introduce order).

This idea can, however, be put more succinctly; according to Morin (1977), fresh information will lead to *disorder* in rigid systems (i.e., in systems that are too strictly ordered or are organized in a dysfunctional manner). We need only think of "unexpected" items of information and of all such interventions as, in one way or another, creating *inconsistency* in a system: inconsistency in the premises and in the punctuations (interventions upsetting the philosophy, let alone the specific problems, of the family); inconsistency in behavior, for instance in response to rituals and prescriptions that infringe on the usual family rules.

New order can only spring from disorder; by throwing parts that have long been close to one another into disarray, we create the possibility of new relationships. The change involves two phases: (1) a first phase comprising surprise, disorientation, perplexity, and paralysis (phase of disorder or disorganization); (2) a second phase comprising construction of a new order or of a consistent system of belief and behavior.[4]

[4]I have also postulated—but this matter is still far from clear—that other types of intervention (or some aspects of certain interventions) aim to introduce order directly, in a single phase. I am thinking particularly of structural interventions into the generation gap, of pedagogic interventions, etc. [Ed.].

CHAPTER 28

The Problem of the Referring Person

Mara Selvini Palazzoli, Luigi Boscolo, Gianfranco Cecchin, and Giuliana Prata

The problem of the referring person in family therapy is one of the most insidious and potentially compromising to the success of treatment.[1] However, this problem is overlooked in the literature dealing with family therapy; we have not been able to discover more than its merest mention in publications made to date. During workshops and seminars we have noted occasional allusions to a "hostile referral," but these were sporadic observations, and, while they demonstrate a certain awareness of the existence of this problem, they do not show the full appreciation of its gravity and the consequent need for a detailed analysis.

We did our research in family therapy for years without paying particular attention to this specific problem. Though aware that in certain cases the referring person could constitute a grave problem, and even after establishing (in 1972) that on every fami-

Though not published until January 1980 in the *Journal of Marital and Family Therapy*, this article was written in 1978, during the last year of the Selvini-Boscolo-Cecchin-Prata team.

[1]It is essential to point out that the problem discussed in this paper is based on the experiences of an independent and private center. Family therapy in an institutional context is bound to encounter different problems.

ly's chart, the first question should be, "Who referred the family?," we continued to regard the referring person in the traditional way, *concentrating above all on his relationship with us and underestimating his relationship with the family.*

But certain failures in therapy forced us to go over entire cases in an effort to discover where we had gone wrong. We realized that our error had been basic; *we had failed to build our study of the family upon the systemic model,* for we had been dealing with a family without the member who occupied a nodal homeostatic position in that family, the referring person. Therefore the essential question that we should always ask ourselves is, "What is the present position of the referring person in the family group? Has he/she become involved to the point of becoming an important member in the family system?" Our failure to consider him/her as a member of the family was further aggravated by the fact that the referring person, in not participating in the sessions, had the power of an "absent member."

The problem of the referring person, which may occur in every type of family, reaches maximum intensity and maximum insidiousness when we are dealing with families presenting psychotic patients, particularly, those characterized by the type of communication defined as schizophrenic. We observed that in such families a certain "stickiness" characterizes the various relationships. Wynne and Singer (1963), in their classic work on the disorder of communication in the families of schizophrenics, were the first to observe this phenomenon and speak of it, coining the splendid metaphor *rubber fence.* The "rubber fence" is something that encircles the family, something that absorbs anything or anyone who ventures near it.

The professional who assists the identified patient in such a family is particularly open to this phenomenon. If he passes the family's "entrance exam," the rubber fence silently swallows him whole, and he becomes installed as a full-fledged member of the family. As such, he loses any operative power. Not only this, but having become a member of a family characterized by a highly homeostatic tendency, he will become, paradoxically, an essential prop of the family.

The individual who is absorbed unknowingly by the family commonly passes through three stages. First he feels gratitude and fulfillment for having been welcomed by the family as its helper. However, bit by bit, as all his efforts and urgings towards change in the family go unheeded and, at the same time, his endeavors are met by subtle disqualifications from the family, he enters the second stage, which is characterized by a growing sense of discomfort and unease, by the vague sensation of being trapped. Then in the third stage, pushed to exasperation and seeking some solution, he sends the family to family therapy. We can describe these stages because, in our professional careers, we ourselves have had this experience and are sure that anyone who has worked with schizophrenic families can confirm it.

The reaction of the family bundled off to family therapy is usually one of total obedience. The referring person has become essential to its homeostasis,[2] and he must be kept as a member of the family at all costs. The family will do anything to please him, at least apparently so. If the family therapist inquires into the motive that has led the family into therapy, he will usually receive the following stereotyped, redundant answer: "Well, we've tried everything else. We might as well try this, too." Implicit in this answer is the certainty, "If everything else has failed, this will, too." However, after going to family therapy, they will be able to return to the referring person, their consciences appeased, with an apologetic smile on their lips, in order to resume their idyll where they had left off.

As we said earlier, the problem of the referring person may occur in the most diverse types of families, though it may be less insidious and take place with less frequency in families other than those of the schizophrenic type. Therefore one must consider its possibility in all cases and gather accurate information about it.

WHAT TYPE OF REFERRING PERSON IS MOST SUSPECT?

Those who are most likely to become homeostatic members of the family and are therefore the most to be suspected are:

[2]Rereading these sentences today, one feels rather perplexed. I think it would have been quite enough, and far less abstract, to say that the referring person has stabilized an important relationship with one or more members of the family and hence plays an important part in the game—that is, he increases the number of players and the prestige of the other players—while the game itself has become more rigid and repetitive.

1. Child psychiatrists, neurologists, pediatricians, and family physicians who have been treating one member of the family for years, and have ended up by forming a friendship with him or her.
2. Young psychiatrists and psychologists, so-called "supportive" therapists, who have become involved with the family of the patient, most often with the mother, who maintains contact through long telephone chats, special requests, and invitations. In this case, it is almost always the young therapist who contacts our Center, or else comes personally, with notable anxiety and embarrassment, usually without an appointment, to present his case.
3. More rarely, social workers who are looking after a chronic psychotic or are acting as middlemen between the patient and the family and the patient and the eventual clinic to which he is sent.

HOW DO SUSPECT FAMILIES BEHAVE?

Through observation and careful examination of the relationship between the referring person and the family, we have come to appreciate that when the former occupies a homeostatic position in the family, the latter often displays three different types of behavior patterns in the session, namely:

1. *The smiling family.* This is usually a courteous, good-humored family, without the least anxiety, in spite of the dire relational situation and the serious condition of the designated patient. Its analogical message seems to be, "Here we are at your complete disposition. Now what can we do for you?" This attitude may remind one of the smiling cheerfulness and general helpfulness of the expert public relations person. The information supplied by the family is just as general in that it gives us nothing meaningful. This type of family had adapted itself to the identified patient, who is more of a problem for the referring person than for his family. This family is the most able in sucking in whoever approaches it. A family of this type,

which presented as designated patient a daughter who had been diagnosed as hebephrenic from the age of 10 years, had maintained a close friendship with the referring psychiatrist for years. The young psychiatrist had been a guest in the family's home for long periods of time. During the session with this family, the daughter caricatured the general attitude of the other family members in a curious and redundant manner. Throughout the session she slouched in her chair, with her chin lolling on her chest. It was impossible to see if she was awake or asleep. When, every once in a while, the therapist spoke to her, a tremor passed through her body as if she had heard an alarm bell, and she jerked up her head, with a leering grin on her face.

2. *The angry family.* This type of family appears to be irritated to the point of hostility. The members present a unified front, draw up in ranks, and express in analogical language, especially in body language, the complete exclusion and rejection of the therapist. We had an eloquent example of such behavior in the first session of a family presenting an anorectic patient.

   This family, of a low educational standard but financially well off, came from the countryside, where their village doctor had insisted upon their taking family therapy at our center. The family had agreed to do so out of respect for the doctor, towards whom they felt a long-standing sense of obligation. On our video-tape of the session, it is amusing to observe the following sequence:

   The family is sitting in a line facing the therapist (Selvini). As she speaks to them, the therapist leans slightly forward. She fails to elicit a positive response from them. The family draws closer together. The therapist hitches her chair a bit nearer to them, leans towards them, puts more expression in her face and more empathy into her voice. The family moves back and closer together; the expression on their faces becomes stonier and more impenetrable. The observing members of the team, moved by the obvious frustration of their colleague, repeatedly call her out of the session to give some advice or other, but even when she follows these suggestions she is unable to dent the family's armor.

Within the next few sessions, the identified patient lost weight alarmingly, and her mother consulted two famous local magicians whose magic prescriptions she followed diligently. (They advised her that if her daughter's condition was caused by envy, she would find wood chips in the feather pillows. She opened all the pillows in the house and found wood chips in all the pillows but her own.) In the fifth session, the therapist declared her own impotence and interrupted the family therapy. At that moment, she saw the family members smile for the very first time.

3. *The complaining family.* This family complains about the discomfort it suffers in coming to the session, the length and cost of the trip, the inconvenience of the hour or day, the expense of the therapy, the lack of progress on the part of the designated patient. Characteristically, this type of family does not follow prescriptions. It is in a hurry to finish therapy, to free itself of these pests (the therapists) and return to the referring person to declare that this experiment has been a failure.

WHAT TO DO?

In order to understand the problem of the referring person and to place it in its proper perspective, the family therapist must obtain adequate information concerning him. If the referring person has made contact by telephone, or has come in person to present his case, we try to take into account any information or behavior that bears upon his relationship with the family.

In our experience this occurs only in a minority of cases. More often, it is a member of the family who contacts us and either volunteers the name of the person who has sent him or answers our questions concerning the referral service. At times the situation is immediately clear if the family member says, "Dr. So-and-So sent us, and he's been treating our daughter (son, etc.) for years, and he told us he won't see us anymore if we don't come to see you for family therapy. . . ." Here it is obvious that the therapy cannot begin until the prime importance of that information has been taken into account. In most cases, the referring person who sends the family to therapy with this type of ultimatum rarely makes personal contact with the Center, thus leaving it to the therapists whether or not they should contact him.

We shall now describe what we do in these cases.

The Suspected Referring Person Is Invited to Attend a Session with the Family

We are not speaking of the case of a family therapist who has turned to our center for assistance. In that case, we always make an appointment for a consultation session in which the therapist is also present so that he may eventually continue the therapy on his own. Rather, we are dealing here with a referring person who belongs to one of the categories previously described, who has ordered the family to come to our Center.

The first session with the family is devoted to gathering information about the reasons for which he has sent the family to our Center. If it appears that the relationship has existed over a significant period of time and/or that it is an intense relationship, we can take it that the referring person has become a homeostatic member of the family. At the end of this session, we state that we can continue the therapy only if the referring person is willing to attend personally in order to help us, given his profound knowledge and understanding of the family. We decline any suggestion made by the family to substitute the physical presence of the referring person with records, charts, or letters from his office. We insist that he come in person, the more so as he has shown so much understanding and concern.

In the next session, which is attended by the family and the referring person, we work mainly with the latter, turning to him as a colleague who has been invited to supply essential information. By using this approach, we are able to see to what extent he has become a member of the family and to what extent he has become exasperated with the total lack of change on the part of the family, in spite of all his efforts and advice. At the conclusion of the session, far from criticizing him, we positively connote the work he has done with the family, and actually congratulate him on his failure. Here it is essential to avoid any sarcasm or irony, but rather to express our understanding of the feeling of frustration he must experience. During the session we have been careful to gather data that can now be presented as so many reasons for preventing any changes in the family system, stressing the dangers such changes would entail.

At this point, whether we decide to delay the next session for an appreciable period of time so that everyone involved can reflect upon the dangers of family therapy, or whether we accept the family in therapy by fixing an appointment for the next session, *we no longer make the mistake of advising or prescribing the interruption of the relationship between the family and the referring person.* In dealing with this fundamental point, we are careful to use the "prescription of the symptom," advising, even insisting upon, the continuation of that friendship that has revealed itself as being so comforting and necessary for the cohesion and stability of the family. In this way, the position of the referring person as a member of the family group is implicitly pointed out.

The termination of the game between the referring person and the family, and thus the solution of the problem, should be the result of a session that has been efficiently handled. Then, and only then, can the therapists begin their work of treating the family.

The Suspected Referring Person Is Not Asked to Participate in the Session

In the first meeting with the family, we inquire closely into the family's relationship with the referring person. We are careful not to strike the least note of judgment or disapproval. If anything, we adopt an attitude of acceptance and friendliness. We ask in detail about the length of the relationship, the frequency of meetings and telephone calls, possible gifts on holidays or on particular occasions. Above all, we seek information with which we can construct a graduated scale showing the position of each family member in the relationship with the referring person, beginning with the member who has the strongest links and working down to the member who has the weakest. (This inquiry is not always carried out at the beginning of a course of therapy. At times we are compelled to make this detailed examination in a more advanced phase of the therapy, when we first begin to observe behavior in the family such as we have already described earlier in this paper. In such cases, we discover that the family has minimized or held back significant information concerning its relationship with the referring person.) Once this has been accomplished, and, basing our tactics upon the information obtained, we choose the intervention most likely to surmount the first obstacle in our path.

As an example, we shall mention the case of a family of three: mother, father, and a 15-year-old daughter, Christina. The mother had called the center for a meeting because of Christina, who, from the age of 2, after an attack of meningitis, had been in treatment with a well-known children's neurologist, Dr. Maria Finzi (a fictitious name). The mother explained that they had been sent by Dr. Finzi because Christina was going through a difficult period: she was rebellious, kept making scenes, and refused to take the pills prescribed. However, Christina was doing well at school, and, in our opinion at the time, seemed to show no particular signs of being gravely disturbed.

In the discussion preceding the first session, we decided that the first problem to examine was that of the neurologist who had been treating Christina for the past thirteen years and who, it appeared, had sent the family to our center because Christina refused to take the medication she had prescribed (an antiepileptic).

In response to our questions concerning the family's relationship with the neurologist, we learned that the mother maintained an intimate friendship with her, with frequent visits, chats, and presents. The neurologist, besides taking Christina's EEGs and prescribing sedatives, also concerned herself with the girl's education, discussing it frequently with the mother and less frequently with the father (who, during the session, showed a marked disagreement with his wife on several points, especially those concerning the way of dealing with Christina).

When we tried to discover the reasons why the neurologist had referred the family to family therapy, we encountered a powerful resistance, which indicated that we had hit upon a vital issue. By insisting, we were able to learn that approximately six months earlier the family, which had been paying the neurologist rather high fees for years, had by accident discovered that they had the right to free medical assistance for Christina at a regional neurological clinic. It was the father who was interested in taking the girl to the clinic for examination and later returned for the results of these examinations. He had come home full of enthusiasm, having had a "marvelous" discussion with the specialist who had examined Christina. The results had been normal, and all medication had been suspended.

The mother, not at all convinced, had immediately made an appointment with Dr. Finzi. The moment they entered the office, Christina had declared petulantly that she had been examined by another doctor who had found her normal and who had said she should not take any more medicine. "From that moment," sighed the mother, "even though I tried to explain how it had happened, Dr. Finzi ignored me completely and only talked to the child. She told her to stop taking the medicine if she wanted to, but that after the summer holidays (it was June) she wouldn't see us any more unless we came to your Center. She said that you would have to study our family in order to discover why Christina is so unbearable, and then tell us what to do. I'm waiting for you to do that, so that I can call Dr. Finzi."

Until this point, Christina had maintained an air of complete disinterest in everything that was being said. She kept glancing at her watch, and would answer in monosyllables or with the irritating phrase, "I don't know," whenever she was asked a question.

During the team discussion before the end of the session, we decided unanimously not to offer treatment. The family as a whole was not at all interested in treatment; it had been the mother who had dragged them to the Center in order to obtain, *expressis verbis*, an appointment with the neurologist. As for the neurologist, it seemed evident that she had sent the family to our center because she felt powerless and professionally disqualified as well as entangled in the competition and internal conflicts of the family. We finally agreed upon a paradoxical conclusion that had as its target the relationship of the mother with the neurologist. Here follows our conclusion of the session:

Therapist: Our team is in complete agreement in ruling out family therapy for Christina, because Christina is not sick. She does everything she does for a reason, even if she isn't aware of it. She is trying to maintain the relationship between her mother and Dr. Finzi, and she's trying to keep it in balance. Christina has known for years that her father isn't enough for her mother, that her mother needs someone she can confide in, depend on, and she knows that she has found that person in Dr. Finzi. But then Christina became afraid that her father was beginning to feel left out. So Christina was naughty with Dr. Finzi, who got angry enough to send you all here to us. But, when you arrived here today, Christina began to worry again. If you really started family therapy, there was the danger that her mother would lose her dear Dr. Finzi. That's why Christina didn't co-operate today, why she was always looking at her watch, why she never answered our questions—to discourage us from taking you into therapy! (*Turning towards Christina.*) In fact, Christina, we're not going to do family therapy with you. But you have to keep on doing what you've been doing until now, even if you get fed up, even if you decide you don't want to any more! Keep on behaving in exactly the same way so that your mother can stay friends with Dr. Finzi, but with the right balance! Not too little, or your mother will suffer and feel alone, and not too much, or your father will feel left out.

In other cases where family relationships appeared seriously dysfunctional, for instance in families with a schizophrenic member, we dealt with the problem of the referring person through systemic interventions that, while exposing the ongoing family game by connoting it positively, at the same time included, in an elusive and implicit manner, the referring person, paradoxically encouraging and prescribing the continuation of the relationship.

CONCLUSIONS

The systemic model provides the therapist with adequate means of defining and solving the problem of the referring person. The systemic model, being logically superior to the linear-causal model, allows the therapist to place and to maintain himself in a metalevel with respect to the family and the referring person. Moreover, it seems quite important that the systemic model should provide solutions without creating friction with the referring person, especially when the professional situation is touchy.

Obviously we ought to have consulted all the files and records of the families treated at our center over the ten years of its existence. Unfortunately this proved impossible, since for many years we had underevaluated this aspect of family therapy, and therefore the necessary information was totally or partly missing. From now on we shall systematically collect all data on the referring person.

All the same, we felt it useful to report these observations because they show how serious the problem can be.

* * *

ECOLOGICAL APPROACH VERSUS
FAMILY REDUCTIONISM

"The Problem of the Referring Person" clearly reflected the influence of two factors on Mara Selvini, namely (1) epistemological considerations and (2) research into macro-organizations.

These factors helped her to avoid the blind alleys into which so many family therapists have strayed, people who have become (or rather who have always been) incapable of seeing beyond the family. Progressing from individual to family therapy has, in fact, not helped many therapists to think systemically—all that has changed is the "pathological object": previously the individual, now the family. This has led to reductionism, to the error of not looking beyond the family. Systemic thinking, by contrast, means enlarging the field of vision not necessarily to the family but to any subsystem in significant interaction with the object of the study and of the therapy.[3] In that sense, we can speak of an *ecological outlook, i.e., of an overall approach to all systemic levels, be they external*

---

[3]See, for example, the interaction between designated patient, family, and school in the case of Lisa, p. 107 ff. [Ed.].

to the family or internal to it. In the case of the external levels, this means focusing attention on the extended family, the school, the workplace, the peer group, and, as we saw in "The Problem of the Referring Person," on the relationship between the family and the referring specialist.

In "Why a Long Interval between Sessions?" the object of our research and therapy is clearly defined in terms of the relationship between the family and the therapeutic team.

When dealing with the internal levels, we pay special attention to the genetic inputs, the individual strategies, and the subsystems (the parent couple, the sibling group, and so on).

Only an ecological approach makes it possible to grasp certain types of family behavior unrelated to the family's internal game or to the game they play with the therapist. That, rather than intrapsychic considerations, explains Mara Selvini's interest in the expectations and motivations of the family consulting a therapist. In the preface to the German edition of *The Hidden Games of Organizations* (Selvini Palazzoli et al. 1981) Mara Selvini makes some very interesting comments on this subject:

> As time goes on, I become more and more convinced that the original contribution of this volume is that it centers attention on the first contact between the psychologist and the organization. . . . The analysis of these first contacts has become increasingly important to me, both in trying to understand the ongoing game, and also to avoid dangerous errors. I should like to stress how much this progress in research on big organizations strikes me, in retrospect, to be a repetition of what happened in my family-therapy research. Let me give a concrete illustration. For a long time, I devoted the first session to discovering what game the various members of that family were playing amongst themselves. I did not realize that I should first of all have tried to understand what game the family had started to play *with me.* In other words, when a family turns to a therapist they are already playing a game, either within the family or with their surroundings. Human relationships, as we know, are strategic by nature: they proceed by alternate moves. Hence the very fact that a family asks for help from a therapist at a given moment is nothing but a

move in a game. The appeal to any expert is a move: moreover, and this is what counts, it is the *last* move, because it takes place in the present. It follows that the best moment to understand in what manner a family functions is the moment when they call on us for help. Let me try to explain with an analogy. Imagine the family game as a tangled skein from which one end fortunately dangles out. That end is the appeal to the therapist. To grasp it, to start with it, is the best way of untangling the skein, of "mapping" the type of family organization involved. For that reason, I usually pay a great deal of attention to family motivations even in the first session. One of my tools is a series of questions asked in a good-natured way. Who first thought of consulting me? How did everyone else react to this idea? Who came most willingly or with the greatest expectations? Who came most reluctantly, or with few expectations? And so on. A comparison of the motivations and expectations of the various members of the family provides the therapist with a host of implicit data that are all the more illuminating for being implicit. Thus it is a near certainty that the member who has been most reluctant to turn up is the one who believes he is in a "position of power."

Similarly, in making contact with an organization, the therapist should always remember that the act of consulting or of engaging a psychologist is an important move by that organization, indeed, a highly informative move. For that reason tactics must be devised to elicit information on this crucial matter. Who first thought of consulting or engaging a psychologist? Who first made contact with him? What important messages were implicit in this first encounter?

In family therapy, it is usually one of the parents who makes contact with the expert; in big organizations it is more generally someone at the highest hierarchic level. This should be the expert's invariable starting point: he must observe carefully and gather what information may throw light on the why and wherefores of the original contact. But he must take care: *this is not an* easy task. No one will go out of his way to provide such information. More often than not, the expert will be forced to make up his mind on the basis of reluctant, contradictory, or indeed mendacious material. However, this task, difficult though it is, is also fundamental. To discover the hidden conflict in time, to foil the offer of a dangerous coalition, to accept and neutralize a hostile provocation is tantamount to avoiding a false start that could ruin even the best of projects.

In *The Hidden Games of Organizations* (Selvini Palazzoli et al. 1981), the authors highlight a redundancy: the initiative of calling in a psychologist (or a consultant) by *a loser*, with an implicit offer of a coalition against somebody (op. cit., p. 115 ff.). This redundancy is also present in many requests for family therapy: the treatment has a different meaning for each of the different actors, depending on his attitude to the person who first suggested this kind of therapy. In the case of the overconfident parents of an anorectic child,[4] there is the risk that the therapist may implicitly become the parents' ally in their symmetrical conflict with the identified patient (in which case that game is given a fresh impetus by the alleged powers of the therapist, "a magician who does not miss a trick"). Another common case is that of the brother of the identified patient, who forcibly drives the whole family into therapy.[5]

Matters are quite different when the request for therapy takes the form of an appeal for mediation in a conflict of which the contenders have grown tired. They then appeal to an acknowledged outside authority. This is the most propitious case; therapy is requested for all, and there is maximum collaboration. In terms of games metaphor, inquiring into their expectations and motivations means making an ecological study of the last move: the request for family therapy.

[4]See the case of Elisa, described on pp. 102 ff. [Ed.].
[5]Mara Selvini and her collaborators are currently working with the families of identified psychotics (see Selvini Palazzoli 1985).

CHAPTER 29

Hypothesizing-Circularity-Neutrality: Three Guidelines for the Conductor of the Session

Mara Selvini Palazzoli, Luigi Boscolo, Gianfranco Cecchin, and Giuliana Prata

Our research in family therapy has recently been directed at the most correct and fruitful procedure for interviewing the family. Not that we have been unaware of the great importance of this problem in the past, but, as any reader of our book *Paradox and Counter-paradox* will tell you, the impression often remains that our interventions at the end of the session have come out of the blue. Indeed, we have received letters from many readers in various parts of the world, all asking substantially the same question, "But how did you hit upon that particular intervention?"

That is why, shortly after the first publication of *Paradox and Counterparadox* (in Italian in 1975), we decided to focus our attention and efforts upon this problem. Our primary goal was to isolate and elaborate certain fundamental principles of conducting the interview that would be coherent with the systemic epistemology we have adopted. From these principles we would then be able to develop precise methodologies that would serve as a detailed

First English translation published in *Family Process*, vol. 19, no. 1, 1980. This is the last paper Mara Selvini produced in collaboration with Boscolo, Cecchin, and Prata.

guide for any therapist venturing into the labyrinth of the family session. Our secondary goal was to discard certain conceptually unclarified stereotypes that for decades have been passed on from one professional generation to another in our field—the stereotypes that endow the therapist with those intangible, personal qualities of "intuition," "charisma," and "concern," all of which, by definition, cannot be taught.

After some years of work, we succeeded in establishing three principles that we consider indispensable to interviewing the family correctly. We have tentatively called these principles *hypothesizing*, *circularity*, and *neutrality*. We shall discuss each, first giving its definition and theoretical conceptualization, then its description, with examples and practical applications.

HYPOTHESIZING

By hypothesizing we refer to the framing by the therapist of a hypothesis based on what information he has on the family he is interviewing. The hypothesis establishes a starting point for his investigation as well as his verification of the validity of this hypothesis with specific methods and skills. If the hypothesis is proven false, the therapist must form a second hypothesis based on the information gathered during the testing of the first.

It should be remembered that all family therapy sessions begin with the therapist's having a certain amount of information about the family. In our practice at the Milan Family Center we have at our disposition, even before the first session, certain standard data recorded during the initial contact with either the family or the referring doctor. Even in contexts different from ours, the therapist will always have a modicum of information on which an initial hypothesis can be based. Let us take an example.

A short time ago, we were invited by an institute specializing in family therapy to give a live demonstration of our style of work with families. Our first session was with a small family of two members, a divorced 37-year-old mother and her 13-year-old son. The information registered at the time of the family's initial contact with the institute was sparse: the mother had called several months earlier, just before the summer holidays, requesting a consultation about her son, who, in her words, was difficult to control, rebellious, rude, and prone to delinquent behavior (he had stolen change from her purse). On the basis of this scanty information, our team formulated a hypothesis during our standard presession discussion: the behavior of the boy could be a way of trying to get the father to come back to the family. In accordance with this hypothesis we decided to spend little time listening to the mother's complaints about the boy's misbehavior and instead to focus our questions on their relationship with the absent father. During the interview, our hypothesis was rapidly disproved, but we were able to formulate a second hypothesis: the mother was an attractive and charming woman, and, after all those years of maternal dedication, she may have met "another man," and perhaps her son was jealous and angry and was showing it through his misbehavior.

Our second hypothesis was right on target. For the past few months, the mother had been dating a "friend." While she was telling us this, the boy, quiet until that point, began to get restless and seemed on the verge of tears. When questioned, he said, "Mom isn't the same with me any more—she's all wrapped up in herself—she really doesn't listen to me like she used to. . . ." While her son gave vent to these complaints, the mother remained silent and looked confused and somewhat guilty. The therapeutic conclusion to this session was by now clear to us: both of them were having growing pains and should expect to suffer for some time to come. They needed time to accept the prospect of a separation without feeling abandoned or guilty.

This example demonstrates how the two hypotheses formulated by the therapists and the questions asked in order to verify them led to the information essential for the choice of a therapeutic intervention.

What do we mean, therefore, by hypothesis? And what is its function?

General Definition of a Hypothesis

The etymological meaning of hypothesis is "what underlies," or rather, the proposition on which a conceptual construction is founded. According to the *Abridged Oxford Dictionary*, a hypothesis is "a proposition or principle put forth or stated merely as a basis for reasoning or argument, or as a premise from which to draw a conclusion." In the terminology of experimental science, a hypothesis is an unproved supposition tentatively accepted to provide a basis for further investigation, from which a verification or refutation can be obtained.

The hypotheses framed by family therapists in order to elicit responses that can be verified by the therapist during the session define his activity as experimental. The data of such experimentation derive from immediate (verbal and nonverbal) feedbacks as well as from delayed feedbacks resulting from the prescriptions and rituals given by the therapist at the end of the session. Their object is the further verification of a hypothesis that has so far proved plausible.

As we know, the classic procedure of the experimental method involves three activities or phases: observation, formulation of a hypothesis, and experimentation. The greatest mental effort is needed in the second phase: it is then that the mind must organize the observations it has gathered. A hypothesis can sum up in a few lines a series of empirical facts whose catalogue might take up an entire volume. It is obvious that the soundness (or lack of it) of any piece of research depends on the soundness of the hypothesis.

This definition of "hypothesis" reflects the fundamental etymological meaning of the term: a hypothesis is a *supposition*, regardless of whether it be true or false.

Functional Value of the Hypothesis in General

The hypothesis, as such, is neither true nor false, but rather, *more or less useful.* Even a hypothesis that proves to be false contributes information in that it eliminates a certain number of variables that until that moment had appeared possible. For exactly this function of categorizing information and experience, the hypothesis occupies a central position among the means with which we discipline our investigative work. The essential function of the hypothesis consists therefore in the guide it furnishes to new information, by which it will be confirmed, refuted or modified.

Functional Role of Hypotheses in Family Interviews

The functional role of hypotheses in family interviews is substantially that of guiding the therapist's activity in tracking relational patterns. It is quite likely that such patterns are elicited by the therapist's behavior. Were he to behave in a passive manner, as an observer rather than a "mover," then the family, conforming to its own linear hypothesis, would impose its own script, dedicated exclusively to laying down who is "crazy" and who is "guilty," and resulting in zero information for the therapist. The therapist's hypothesis, by contrast, introduces the powerful input of *unexpected* and *improbable* elements into the family system and for that reason helps to avoid breakdowns and disorder.[1] We shall try to explain this idea in greater detail.

Hypothesis, Information, and Negentropy

Gregory Bateson (1972) says, in his "Why Do Things Get in a Muddle?": "I know that there are infinitely many muddled ways, so things will always go toward muddle and mixedness."

If we apply this universal assertion to the restricted sphere of a family-therapy session, we can by experience confirm its validity. Had we no hypotheses, then our family sessions would tend towards a discouraging increase in disorder and muddle. But what exactly is disorder? Perhaps the clearest definition is that given by Schafroth (1960):

> It is, in fact, no trivial matter to define "disorder." Scientists exist who have the habit of piling up papers and books in a seemingly random fashion on their desks, yet know all the time how to find a given thing. If someone brings apparent "order" to such desks, the poor owner may be unable to find anything. In that case, it is obvious that the apparent "disorder" is, in fact, order and *vice versa*. You will easily see that in this sense the order in the desk

[1] It is important to stress the relativity of the concepts of order and disorder. Here *disorder* is defined as the result of the nondirective passivity on the therapist's part, and *order* in terms of the repetitivity/rigidity of family interaction patterns. From the therapist's point of view, however, order means running the sessions with a program that explodes (that is, brings disorder into) the old rules of the family game [Ed.].

can be measured by the information the owner has about its state. This example illustrates that, by trying to define "disorder" more precisely we return to the previous definition in terms of "lack of information. . . ."

The disorder, disorganization, lack of pattern, or randomness of organization of a system is known as its *entropy.* The decrease in entropy can be taken as a measure of the amount of information. It was noted by Wiener and Shannon that the statistical measure for the negative of entropy is the same as that for information, which Schrödinger has called *negentropy.* Wiener has demonstrated that the concepts of "information" and "negentropy" are synonymous.

However, De Beauregard (1961) has given a more precise definition of the relationship between the two concepts of negative entropy and information with the help of two concepts highly relevant to our research.

Cybernetics tends to define "negentropy" and "information" as a kind of subjective redoubling and to assume the possibility of a double transformation, viz.:

$$\text{negentropy} \leftrightarrows \text{information}$$

Let us note that the meaning of the word information is not the same in the two senses: in the direct transformation *negentropy → information,* "information" signifies acquisition of knowledge. . . . In the inverse transformation *information → negentropy,* information signifies power of organization.

The Hypothesis Must Be Systemic

A fundamental point to emphasize is that every hypothesis must be systemic, must, therefore, include all components of the family, and must provide a supposition about the entire relational function. Let us take an example.

A mother telephoned our Center asking for a consultation. The family was working-class and lived on the periphery of Milan. It was made up of six members: the parents, both in their fifties; a 20-year-old boy, Paolino, who worked as a plumber; a 17-year-old girl, Francesca, who had recently received a secretarial diploma and was looking for a job; a 12-year-old schoolboy, Stefano, and the 14-year-old identified patient, Regina.

Regina, blind since birth, had started to show signs of psychotic behavior from about the age of 4 years, a condition that became so marked that it later prevented her admission to a local school for blind children. For that reason, at the age of 6, she had been sent to an institution in central Italy that cared for a mixture of psychotic, organically impaired, retarded, and handicapped children. Despite the long trip, the mother had visited Regina nearly every month, bringing her home during Christmas and summer vacations. The periods Regina spent at home, however, rendered family life a virtual hell. During the previous summer, Regina, still behaving psychotically, had become very attached to her mother and no longer wanted to leave her. She made no further progress in the institution. In fact, after an initial period of adaptation over a number of years, during which she had reached a certain rapport with the nuns and the other children and had reached the third grade, she had gradually isolated herself more and more. After the last summer vacation she had wrapped herself in a blanket of negativism. During one of the mother's monthly visits, the psychologist at the institute had apparently opposed Regina's further stay and had given the mother the address of our Center. The mother knew neither the name of the psychologist nor why he had suggested our Center. However, she formulated the following explicit demand: "When we turn up, we must decide if it's better for Regina to stay at the institute or come home to stay with us."

This was the information entered on the family's chart at the time of the telephone contact, and an appointment was made for the Christmas holidays, when Regina would be home.

During the meeting preceding the session, our group reviewed the chart and discussed the information already received, with the purpose of formulating a hypothesis. The fundamental question was: What was the systemic game started by Regina's return to the family, with her psychotic behavior unchanged, after years of seclusion in a distant institution? And further: In what way had some change in institutional politics, represented by the unknown psychologist who had advised the mother, converged with a change in the politics of the family that had led to the posing of the dramatic (and sudden) question: "Is it better for Regina to come home to stay with us?"?

We agreed on the hypothesis of a convergence of two different motivations deriving from two subsystems. One was that of the institution. Italy, at that time, was in the midst of a sociopolitical and anti-institutional trend culminating in the conviction that the return to the family is *always* the best solution. To us, however, it seemed that the institution's wish to have Regina removed would have been resisted had it not coincided in some way with the homeostatic imperatives of a family system in danger of change. It was essential to make a hypothesis about the nature of this danger. From the family chart, we knew that Regina had two elder siblings: Paolino, 20 years old and at work, and Francesca, 17 years old, just graduated and in search of a job, a step that would end her dependence on the family. Regina's return to the family at this moment would be the most effective way of ensuring its cohesion. Because of her blindness, not to mention her psychotic behavior, Regina would require constant care and watching. Francesca would probably have to give up her plans for a job and stay at home to help her mother. There would be additional expenses and another mouth to feed, and most likely Paolino would have to contribute more heavily to the maintenance of the family, perhaps sacrificing plans for vacations, girl friends, outings, and so on. The team thus agreed on the formulation of the following systemic hypothesis: the family, having realized that this was a dangerous moment for its homeostasis, "discovered" the duty of taking Regina back home. This return could be a key factor in keeping Francesca or Paolino, or both, from leaving home.

In accordance with this hypothesis, we decided that the session must, above all, involve Francesca and Paolino, their relationships with the various members of the family, their possible projects, their views about Regina's possible return, and the effects they thought this return would have upon their lives. The hypothesis was confirmed by a feedback during the interview: the family crisis was, in fact, about the adolescence of Francesca, who seemed to be just as afraid of it as the others. The problem, therefore, was quite different from the one expounded by the mother.

The kind of hypothesis we have been describing, in addition to being consistent with our systemic epistemology, is suggested by two types of information:

1. Data collected during research into families presenting psychotic members. Often the schizophrenic crisis of one member coincides with the threat that one of the other members, often an adolescent, is about to leave the family. This development can be postulated, as in the above case, when we observe a sudden change in family politics.
2. Specific information about the family under observation. Arriving for the session armed with a hypothesis, the therapist can take the initiative, proceed in orderly fashion, control, interrupt, guide, and elicit transactions, all the time avoiding attempts to inundate him with a flood of meaningless chatter.

CIRCULARITY

By *circularity* we mean the therapist's ability to conduct his investigation on the basis of family feedback in response to what information he solicits about relationships and, therefore, about differences and changes.

The acquisition of that ability demands that therapists free themselves from the linguistic and cultural conditioning that makes them believe they are capable of thinking in terms of "things" and rediscover "the deeper truth that we still think only in terms of relationships" (Bateson).

In 1968 Ruesch and Bateson had already explained and demonstrated this concept:

The same general truth—that all knowledge of external events is derived from the relationships between them—is recognizable in the fact that to achieve more accurate perception, a human being will always resort to change in the relationship between himself and the external object. If he is inspecting a rough spot on some surface by means of touch he moves his finger over the spot, thus creating a shower of neural impulses with definite sequential structure, from which he can derive the static shape and other characteristics of the thing investigated. . . . In this sense, our initial sensory data are always "first derivatives," statements about *differences* which exist among external objects or statements about *changes* which occur either in them or in our relationship to them. . . . What we perceive easily is difference and change—and difference is a relationship.

What we call circularity is therefore our consciousness, or rather, our conviction that we can only obtain authentic information from the family if we work with the following fundamental ideas: (1) information is a difference; (2) difference is a relationship (or a change in the relationship).

This is not enough, however. Yet another device is needed to help the therapist face the complexities of the family: every member of the family is invited to tell us how he sees the relationship between two other members of the family. Here we are dealing with the investigation of a dyadic relationship as it is seen by a third person. One will readily agree that it is far more fruitful, in that it is effective in overcoming resistance, to ask a son, "Tell us how you see the relationship between your sister and your mother," than to ask the mother directly about *her* relationship with her daughter. What is perhaps less obvious is the extreme effectiveness of this technique in initiating a stream of responses in the family that greatly illuminate the various triadic relationships. In fact, by formally inviting one member of the family to metacommunicate about the relationship of two others *in their presence*, we are not only breaking one of the ubiquitous rules of dysfunctional families, but we are also conforming to the first axiom of the pragmatics of human communication: in an interaction, the various participants, try as they may, cannot avoid communicating.

Consider the case of an identified patient invited by the therapist to describe her perception of the relationship between her father and her younger sister. Suppose she shows disapproval of certain forms of behavior by the father toward the sister. It would make a big difference to the information about the triadic relationship (that is, including the person questioned) if the other two became confused, or if each reacted in the same manner, or if only the father were to protest in indignation while the sister remained cryptically silent or showed a marked hostility or scorn.

In one of our cases the identified patient, describing her view of the relationship between her father and her sister, Marina, mentioned a recent, significant episode. She ended by turning to her father with the following accusation, "I had the impression that you made her miserable, and that you do it often." The contrast between the biblical indignation of the father and the expressionless silence of Marina, who neither agreed nor contradicted her sister, allowed us to make certain observations and hence to formulate new hypotheses about the relationship between the two sisters (who, until then, had appeared friendly towards each other), the relationship of each with the father, and the relationship of the father with each of them. At the same time, the therapists, and, even more so, the observers of the session, took notice of the behavior of the mother, who, with shakings of her head and disapproving glances towards the girl, showed her allegiance to her husband in his anger. Needless to say, the next sequence of questions involved the mother: "And now, Marina, how do you see the relationship between your sister and your mother?"

In this way, regardless of the limitations imposed on us by language and cultural conditioning, we can go beyond the triad and the sum of the various triads within the family. Thus the warp will come through the woof, until the design appears in the fabric, without the necessity of posing the most expected, and therefore the most feared and avoided question: "But Marina, how do you see the relationship between your mother and father?"

Other Practical Methods for Collecting Information

In respect of the triadic method of studying relationships and the fundamental principle that information is a difference and that the difference is a relationship (or a change in the relationship), we shall now present some of the practical methods we have found to be extremely valuable in eliciting information:

1. In terms of specific interactive behavior in specific circumstances (and not in terms of feelings or interpretations)—

for example, the transaction initiated by the therapist with the elder son of a family of four, in which the younger son, Lorenzo, presented a violent crisis and struck his mother.

Therapist: When Lorenzo begins to lose control and pushes your mother, what does your father do? And how does your mother react to what he does (or doesn't) do? And what do you do? . . .

2. In terms of differences in behavior and not in terms of alleged intrinsic qualities—for example, a conversation between therapist and child concerning the paternal grandparents who live with the family.

Son: We live together with my grandparents, and they're real naggers.
Therapist: What do they *do* that makes them naggers?
Son: They keep interfering with our parents, telling them what to do with us.
Therapist: Who interferes most, your grandfather or your grandmother?
Son: Grandpa.
Therapist: Whom does he interfere with most, your mother or your father?
Son: With my father.
Therapist: And who gets most annoyed when our grandfather interferes, your father or your mother?
Son: Oh, Mom of course! She wants Dad to tell him off. . . .

3. In terms of ranking by various members of the family of a specific form of behavior or a specific interaction. This invitation to make a classification should be offered to more than one member of the family.

Therapist: Classify the various members of your family in terms of their tendency to stay at home on Sundays. Begin with whoever stays at home most.

or else:

Therapist: It seems that your mother cries a lot at home, that she's very unhappy. Emily, tell me who can cheer her up most when she's sad—your grandmother, father, brother, or you? Draw up a scale.

This method of classification by the members of the family serves as an important source of information in that it not only reveals the position of the various members in the "family game" but may also show up interesting discrepancies among the various classifications.

4. In terms of change in the relationship (or rather in behavior indicative of change in the relationship) before and after a precise event (diachronic investigation).

The following example is taken from the first session with a family of four. The mother had asked for help with the rebellious and aggressive behavior of her 12-year-old son, Marco. There was also a younger sister, Sissy. Nearly every day, violent fights erupted between mother and son. The precise event the therapist began to ask about was the father's heart attack, after which he had left his job and obtained an invalid's pension.

Therapist (to Sissy): Your mother said that Marco has always been a difficult child. But did your mother and brother fight more before or after Father got sick?

Sissy: Oh, after, after. Mommy gets much angrier, and she's more nervous too. . . . It's just that at a certain point she has to stop . . . when Daddy puts his hand over his heart.

5. In terms of differences in respect to hypothetical circumstances.

Therapist: If one of you children should have to stay at home, without getting married, which one do you think would be the best for your father? Which one do you think would be the best for your mother?

We use all these approaches during the investigation of the symptom, even in the first session. Rather than become involved in tedious lists of symptomatic behavior, the therapist focuses attention on *how* each member of the family reacts to the symptom. The model is triadic—a member of the family is invited to describe in what manner another member reacts to the symptom and in what way yet another family member reacts to that reaction.

The following example is taken from the first session with a family presenting an anorectic son, Marcello.

Therapist (to Ornella, the sister): When your mother tries to get Marcello to eat and he refuses the food, what does your father do?
Ornella: For a while he holds himself back, but eventually he gets furious and starts to yell.
Therapist: At whom?
Ornella: At Marcello.
Therapist: And when he yells at Marcello, what does your mother do?
Ornella: She gets mad at Daddy. She says that he's ruining everything, that he doesn't have any patience, that he's just making everything worse.
Therapist (to the father): And while all this is going on, what does Ornella do?
Father (smiling at his daughter with open admiration): She just goes on eating as if nothing were happening!

The Gradual Enlargement of the Field of Observation

Another important method of gathering information during the family interview is to begin with the investigation of the subgroups. An example follows.

A young couple with two sons, Paolo and Alessandro, 6 and 4 years old, respectively, consulted our center because they had great difficulty in controlling Paolo. In the period prior to the session, his spiteful behavior had become unbearable; for example, he had flooded the house and had hammered nails into an expensive piece of furniture.

During the team discussion preceding the first session, we decided to investigate the family relationships beginning with the various subgroups. If, as is often the case, the father was absent at work all day and the mother remained at home with the children, our inquiry would begin with the subgroup mother–children, using the terms we have already described:

1. In terms of differences:

Therapist (to the father): Who is more attached to his mother, Paolo or Alessandro?

2. In terms of specific interactive behavior in specific circum- stances:

Therapist: Paolo, when you get Alessandro mad, what does your Mommy do? Alessandro, when you get Paolo mad, what does your Mommy do?

We would then proceed to the entire family, always following the standard procedure.

Therapist: When Daddy's home in the evening, is Paolo more naughty with Mommy or less naughty? If he's naughty with Mommy, what does Daddy do?

Only after forming a well-articulated picture of the nuclear family can we enlarge the investigation to include relationships with the families of origin of the parents, dwelling in detail upon the relations between grandparents and grandchildren—i.e., "Who is Grandmother's pet?"—always keeping to the above-mentioned methods for obtaining information.

NEUTRALITY

By therapeutic neutrality we refer to the specific pragmatic effect of the therapist's overall behavior during the session on the family (and not to his intrapsychic attitude).

We shall try to explain exactly what this pragmatic effect is by describing a hypothetical situation. Let us imagine that one of our team members has just terminated his interview with the family, has gone to discuss the information he has gathered with the rest of the team, and that an interviewer approaches the family and asks the various members for their impressions of the therapist. If the session has been conducted in accordance with the rules of systemic epistemology, the various members of the family will have plenty to say about the personality of the therapist (his possession or lack of intelligence, human warmth, agreeability, style). However, if they are asked to state whom he had supported or sided with or what judgment he had made concerning one or another individual or his respective behavior or of the entire family, they will seem puzzled and uncertain.

In fact, as long as the therapist invites one member to comment upon the relationship of two other members, he seems to be allied to that person. However, this alliance shifts the moment he asks *another* family member and yet another to do the same. The end result of the successive alliances is that the therapist is allied with everyone and no one at the same time.

Furthermore, the more familiar the therapist is with systemic epistemology, the more interested he is in provoking feedbacks and collecting information, and the less likely to make moral judgments of any kind. The expression of any judgment, be it one of approval[2] or of disapproval, implicitly and inevitably allies the therapist with one of the individuals or groups within the family and must be avoided.[3] At the same time, we try to observe and neutralize as early as possible any attempt towards coalition, seduction, or privileged relationships with the therapist made by any member or subgroup of the family.

[2]Positive connotation, that is, the approval of symptomatic behavior, may also be used at the end of the session as a paradoxical intervention.

[3]What has here been implicitly subsumed under the heading of neutrality can also be defined as "avoidance of disapproval." It is obvious that, for instance, with a family presenting an infantile patient, the act of blaming the family for having a problem child has two consequences. To begin with, it reflects an alliance with the identified patient by casting him in the role of a poor victim of wicked parents. Secondly, it militates against the involvement and collaboration of the parents and sometimes also of the so-called healthy children who, faced with the therapists' criticism, can adopt a protective "parental" attitude towards their father and mother [Ed.].

In fact, it is our belief that the therapist can be effective only to the extent that he is able to reach and maintain a different level (metalevel) from that of the family.

Conducting the interview in accordance with the principles and methods discussed above effectively helps the therapist to gather information and therefore aids him in his therapeutic work. By information we chiefly refer to the increase in the therapist's knowledge of the ensemble of the relational modes at work in the family. Upon this awareness the therapist will base his possible therapeutic interventions, comments, simple prescriptions, ritualized prescriptions, or family rituals.

The present phase of our research has brought us face to face with a new problem. Can family therapy produce change solely through the negentropic effect of our present method of conducting the interview, i.e., without the need of a final intervention?

We hope that this question will be answered after a significant number of family therapies have been conducted on the basis of the above-mentioned method of interviewing and of omitting any final intervention.

CHAPTER 30

The Turning Point

Matteo Selvini

"Hypothesizing-Circularity-Neutrality" was a turning point in Mara Selvini's research work. It closed the "interventionist" phase, during which the major effort was concentrated on the final intervention at the end of the session. The focus of attention was now shifted to what happens *during* the session, to the interviewing techniques and to the strategies and tactics of conducting the session. The therapeutic effectiveness of the entire course of the therapy, during and between the sessions, was being taken into account, when the earlier view had been that all the team's work was a mere preliminary to the elaboration of the final intervention, of the resolving counterparadox.

With this transformation, the therapeutic atmosphere, too, became changed: it was now less "athletic" and competitive.

Again, while the therapists had contented themselves with understanding some aspects of the ongoing game, and then devoted themselves to designing an appropriate intervention, now, with the concept of hypothesis-making, they entered more deeply into the whole nature of the game.

Circular research into the relationships came to be seen not as a mere preparation for, but as an integral part of, effecting change; by reducing anxiety about interventions, it left the therapists much more energy for reflecting about the game.

REALITY OR RELATIVITY OF HYPOTHESES

The paper mentioned the functional role of hypotheses: they are neither true nor false, but simply more or less useful. This assertion, which has profound implications not examined here in depth, has given rise to many discussions and also to theoretical differences between Mara Selvini and Luigi Boscolo–Gianfranco Cecchin.

As for the reality or relativity of hypotheses (subjectivity), many authors insist on the absolute dependence of hypotheses on the belief or premises of the therapist (constructivism or relativism). First and foremost among these were Boscolo and Cecchin themselves: "There is no truth; there is only punctuation. That is, when it comes to assessing the meaning of behavior there are only different punctuations, or points of view, no certainties or absolutes" (Tomm 1980).

Others have adopted a rigidly pragmatic and relativist position. Keeney (1982) states, "Punctuating or mapping a world follows from how an observer chooses to see" (p. 157).

Fisch and colleagues (1982) write:

> We are talking *only* of views, not of reality or truth, because we believe that views are all we have, or ever will have. It is not a question of views that are more or less real or true, or progressively approaching the truth. Some views may be more useful or effective than others in accomplishing one's chosen end but this is a pragmatic criterion, not one of "reality" [p. 11].

These interpretations are based on the unknowability of reality (we only know maps, never the territory, or "the thing in itself"), and, since there can be no criterion for judging the truth, usefulness is said to be our only criterion for distinguishing and choosing between possible hypotheses.

True, reality is reconstructed with the help of the observer's beliefs and prejudices: this explains why a Kleinian "sees" an unresolved depressive position, a biomedical psychiatrist "sees" a dysfunction of the neurotransmitters, while a systemic therapist "sees" a move in a dysfunctional relational game. The constructivists undoubtedly have an important point, but they exaggerate it to the point of absurdity. According to them, the formulation of a hypothesis is completely independent of the ongoing processes within a given family and also of the interaction between the family and the therapeutic team. Everything takes place in the therapist's mind and is stamped by his prejudices.

In that case *any* relational hypothesis whatsoever leads to change (inasmuch as it introduces circularity into the family epistemology). Now this is belied by therapeutic experience: an intervention that produces brilliant results in one situation will prove totally useless in another. A new circular epistemology only proves its worth if the resulting intervention is based strictly on information supplied by the family and if it helps in rearranging the various pieces of the puzzle in a new, that is, in a convincing and consistent, way.

In fact, even if it is true that any hypothesis is useful in the sense that it stimulates the therapist's activity and hence helps him to learn from his mistakes as well as to keep control of the context, we cannot ignore the way in which the therapist constructs his hypotheses, not only because he is guided by his own maps, but also because these maps are based on specific information elicited from the family, that is, by means of an interactive and self-reflective process within the therapeutic context.

Every family-therapy hypothesis is the result of a *negotiation* (interaction) between the therapist's "prejudices" (or his experience, his store of hypotheses, the most "fashionable" ideas) and the factual information elicited from the family.

Indeed, Mara Selvini (as we have already seen) in the course of therapy with a single family, often sheds a hypothesis that has proved wrong and, on the basis of the in-session feedback, develops new ones.

Some maps are clearly more accurate than others, and it is precisely on this accuracy that their usefulness depends. If we read Korzybski's (1933) famous dictum in full we shall find that it goes as follows: "A map is not the territory it represents, but, if correct, it has a *similar structure* to the territory, which accounts for its usefulness."

We can therefore say that one (family-) therapeutic hypothesis is more useful than another because it reflects the game of a given family more accurately than another. A hypothesis is abandoned in the absence of enough "justifying pieces" (confirmations). As Bebe Speed (1984), who calls himself a co-constructivist, has put it in his brilliant "How Really Real Is Real?" a paper that reflects the views of Mara Selvini and her current collaborators, "Our ideas and hypotheses about the world are not unrelated to that world, they are *not* arbitrary; they are in a mutual ongoing and changing relationship with it."

Mara Selvini has now clarified her own epistemological position, taking the rather "realistic" view that a hypothesis can approximate a family game more or less well.

As her research has developed, there has been a growing attempt to *type* a number of games leading to psychosis. If a hypothesis is found to apply in one family, and is also found to apply in other situations, then it acquires a larger dimension and hence raises hopes of a broader classification.

In that sense hypotheses do not have a merely pragmatic or functional importance; their importance increases as they *approximate* the ongoing game of a particular family system.

THE THERAPIST'S "MODES" AND MAPS

This does not mean belittling the importance and the relative independence of the therapist's convictions (maps). In reexamining, for the preparation of this collection, the clinical papers written by Mara Selvini over the past twelve years, I have noticed certain phenomena with a resemblance to modes. I have already referred to this fact in my commentary, "The therapists abandon the parental role and prescribe it paradoxically to the members of the last generation."

Every time a new idea on a possible dysfunctional game is advanced and produces striking therapeutic results, there is a marked tendency to apply that hypothesis (or intervention) to other situations, even if they seem quite different. Obviously, the hypothesis may not be confirmed in the other cases, and a new idea will arise that will help to restart the whole process; it is, however, unlikely that the earlier mode will vanish without a trace: the old hypothesis will remain a valuable item in the arsenal of the team s maps (or experiences).

THE THERAPIST'S ACTIVITY AND THE CONTROL OF THE RELATIONSHIP

Similarly, I do not deny the usefulness of false hypotheses inasmuch as they can stimulate the therapist's activity and supply important information. If the therapist were to remain completely passive, he would be allowing the family to impose its own rules and to repeat its old game, neutralizing what effects he might have had on that game.

The implicit rules of active control of the therapeutic process are essential to the construction of a therapeutic context. Such control *does not have any therapeutic value in itself* but is a prerequisite of any application of the delicate and particular demands of the therapeutic situation.

The creation of a therapeutic context can allow the projection and insertion into dysfunctioning family systems of "inputs" for change, or of new information and unexpected or unpredictable experiences.

Here I want to stress the following nexus:

> *hypothesis-making—therapist's activity—*
> *control—implicit rules*

which has not been stressed in "Hypothesizing-Circularity-Neutrality," a paper that concentrates on hypothesis-making as a means of introducing information and as an instrument (through the activity of the therapist) needed for maintaining order during the session and for preventing chaos.

THE SPLIT-UP OF THE SELVINI-BOSCOLO-CECCHIN-PRATA TEAM

"Hypothesizing-Circularity-Neutrality," apart from being a turning point in the work of Mara Selvini and her collaborators, can also be considered a point of arrival: the creation of a new school of family therapy. It was in 1978 that Luigi Boscolo and Gianfranco Cecchin began to abandon the research approach that had prevailed throughout the period under review and to devote their energies to teaching and training instead.

That decision, in fact, led to the break-up of the old research team: Selvini and Prata, though by no means opposed to their colleagues' new activity, decided to continue along the old road.

For a better understanding of these events, the reader is referred to Mara Selvini's "Present Imperfect," which I have quoted elsewhere in this book.[1] While there is no explicit reference to the break-up, of which very few people were aware at the time, the echoes are unmistakable.

In 1979 and 1980 the split came about in stages; for a time the two groups continued to collaborate for one half-day a week until, at the end of 1980, all common research came to an end. The use of the Center, too, was divided: half a week for each of the two stumps of the old team.

In time, Mara Selvini came to realize that this kind of "cohabitation," quite apart from the technical problem of not being able to use the Center at all times, created a great deal of confusion. Keeping up a common image (the name and address of the Center) was a source of many misunderstandings: Boscolo and Cecchin were no longer abreast of Selvini's and Prata's latest projects, nor did Selvini and Prata know what Boscolo and Cecchin were teaching in Italy and abroad. (See, for example, the debate on the "reality" of hypotheses.)

In Italy and abroad people continued to speak of the Milan team as if it were still in existence, when in fact it had ceased to

[1]See Preface.

be. The misunderstanding was cleared when the split was publicly and formally announced in 1982, and Selvini and Prata transferred to a new center in the Viale Vittorio Veneto. Then they began to work with new collaborators and founded the New Center for Family Studies.

EPILOGUE

The story of Mara Selvini's research from 1967 to 1978 ended at the same time as the end of her collaboration with Luigi Boscolo and Gianfranco Cecchin. I have tried to present the milestones along this adventurous road: the abandonment of psychoanalysis, and later of communicationalism, in the theoretical realm, and the abandonment of analytical and pedagogical techniques, and hence also of purely interventionist-paradoxical methods, in the practical field. They pointed Mara Selvini toward her current research into games and the associated problems.

I have attempted to tell the reader that story "from within." In the last six years Mara Selvini has developed new ideas and experiments that, in part, are still to be written or published. This is particularly true of her research at the New Center for Family Studies with two teams (one with Giuliana Prata, an association that ended in June 1985, and the other with Stefano Cirillo, Anna Maria Sorrentino, and myself) and involving a particular prescriptive method that, structuring the therapeutic context in a relatively invariable way, allows a host of confrontations that would have been unthinkable with the old therapeutic methods. Mara Selvini is currently writing a book devoted to these studies.

At the same time, she is indirectly supervising a number of other research projects by Maurizio Viaro, whose contributions I have mentioned several times, and by Innocenzo Pisano and Lucia D'Ettore.

She is likewise directly involved in the reorganization of the Corsico Psycho-Social Center, a project described in several articles and in a book (Covini et al. 1984).

Some of these new research projects and ideas have been touched upon in my comments, but they will be treated more fully and organically in a forthcoming publication similar to the present one. It will review the work of Mara Selvini and her collaborators since 1980. As the reader can see from the bibliography that follows, this work is already quite considerable.

APPENDIX

Writings of Mara Selvini Palazzoli and Collaborators since 1980

Selvini Palazzoli, M., and Prata, G. (1980). Die Macht der Ohnmacht. In *Der Familienmensch*, ed. D. V. Wedt and R. W. Enderlin. Stuttgart: Klett-Cotta.

Viaro, M. (1980). Case report. Smuggling family therapy through. *Family Process* 1:35–44.

Selvini Palazzoli, M., Anolli, L., Di Blasio, P., Giossi, L., et al. (1981). *Sul Fronte dell'Organizzazione*. Milan: Feltrinelli. See particularly the last chapter, "Beyond the Dyad," reelaborated and published by Ricci and Selvini Palazzoli (1984) in *Family Process* 25:169–176, under the title "Interactional Complexity and Communication." See also the Preface to the French edition (1984): *Dans les Coulisses de l'Organization*. Paris: E.S.F. English ed., *The Hidden Games of Organizations*, New York: Pantheon Books, 1987.

Barrows, S. E. (1982). Interview with Mara Selvini Palazzoli and Giuliana Prata. *American Journal of Family Therapy* 10:60–69.

Selvini Palazzoli, M. (1982). On the front of organization. In *Zusammenhänge*, vol. 3, Zurich: Institut für Ehe und Familie, pp. 40–50.

Selvini Palazzoli, M., and Prata, G. (1982). Snares in family therapy. *Journal of Marital and Family Therapy* 8:443–450.

Selvini, M., Covini, A., Fiocchi, E., and Pasquino, R. (1982). Al di là della terapia familiare: esperienze di ristrutturazione sistemica di un centro psichiatrico territoriale. *Terapia Familiare* 12:19-39.

Viaro, M., and Leonardi, P. (1982). Le insubordinazioni. *Terapia Familiare* 12:41-63.

Malagoli Togliatti, M. (1983). Sul fronte dei servizi: interview with Mara Selvini Palazzoli. In *La Terapia Sistemica*. Rome: Astrolobio.

Prata, G. (1983). Conflit conjugal avec tentative de suicide du mari. *Thérapie Familiale* (Geneva) 4:149-170.

Selvini Palazzoli, M. (1983). The emergence of a comprehensive systems approach. *Journal of Family Therapy* 5:165-177.

Selvini Palazzoli, M., and Prata, G. (1983). A new method for therapy and research in the treatment of schizophrenic families. In *Psychosocial Intervention in Schizophrenia. An International View*, ed. H. Stierlin, L. C. Wynne, and M. Wirsching. Berlin: Springer.

Viaro, M., and Leonardi, P. (1983). Getting and giving information. Analysis of a family interview strategy. *Family Process* 22:27-42.

Cirillo, S., and Sorrentino, A. M. (1984). La terapia della famiglio con paziente handicappato. In *Handicap in Movimento*, ed. S. Panzera, Milan: F. Angeli, pp. 62-75. English trans. Handicap and rehabilitation: two types of information upsetting family organization. *Family Process* 24:283-292, 1986.

Covini, A., Fiocchi, E., Pasquino, R., and Selvini M. (1984). *Alla Conquista del Territorio*, preface by Mara Selvini Palazzoli. Rome: La Nuova Italia Scientifica.

Pisano, I. (1984). Sous-systèmes scolaires. Effet catalysant du psychologue sur la communication. Address to the Colloque International des Psychologues scolaires, Orleans, 2-6 July.

Prata, G., and Masson, O. (1984). Resolution d'une syndrome de Gilles de Tourette par une séance de consultation familiale. *Thérapie Familiale* 5:101-119.

Selvini Palazzoli, M. (1984). Behind the scenes of the organization. Some guidelines for the expert in human relations. *Journal of Family Therapy* 6:299-307.

—— (1984). Review of *Aesthetics of Change* (B. Keeney, New York: Guilford Press, 1983). *Family Process* 23:282-284.

Selvini Palazzoli, M. (1985). Anorexia nervosa: a syndrome of the affluent society. *Journal of Strategic and Systemic Therapies* 4:12-16.

—— (1985). The emergence of a comprehensive systems approach: supervisor and team problems in a district psychiatric centre. *Journal of Family Therapy* 7:135-146.

—— (1985). The problem of the sibling as the referring person. *Journal of Marital and Family Therapy* 11:21-34.

Selvini Palazzoli, M., Cirillo, S., Selvini, M., and Sorrentino, A. M. (1985). L'individuo nel gioco. *Terapia Familiare* 19:65-73.

Cirillo, S. (1986). *Famiglie in Crisi e Affido Familiare*. Rome: La Nuova Italia Scientifica.

Selvini Palazzoli, M. (1986). Toward a general model of psychotic family games. *Journal of Marital and Family Therapy* 12.

Viaro, M., and Leonardi, P. (1986). The evolution of the interview technique: a comparison between former and present strategy. *Journal of Strategic and Systemic Therapies* 5:14-30.

Selvini, M., Covini, A., Fiocchi, E., and Pasquino, R. (1987). I veterani della psichiatria. *Ecologia della Mente* 4:in press.

Sorrentino, A. M. (1987). *Handicap e Reabilitazione*. Rome: La Nuova Italia Scientifica.

References

Abeles, G. (1976). Researching the unresearchable: experimentation on the double bind. In *Double Bind: The Foundation of the Communicational Approach to the Family*, ed. C. E. Sluzki and D. C. Ransom, pp. 113–151. New York: Grune & Stratton.

Alberti, L. B. (1969). *I Libri della Famiglia*. Turin: Einaudi.

Anolli, L. (1981). *Anche lo psicologo deve fare i conti son se stesso* (The psychologist, too, must square accounts with himself). In *Sul Fronte dell'Organizzazione*, ed. M. S. Palazzoli et al. Milan: Feltrinelli. English trans., *The Hidden Games of Organizations*. New York: Pantheon, 1987.

Ashby, W. R. (1954). *Design for a Brain*. New York: John Wiley & Sons.

Barcai, A. (1971). Family therapy in the treatment of anorexia nervosa. *American Journal of Psychiatry* 3:286–290.

Bateson, G. (1958). The new conceptual frames for behavioral research. In *Acts of the Sixth Annual Psychiatric Institute*, pp. 54–71. Princeton: Princeton University Press.

—— (1960). Minimal requirements for a theory of schizophrenia. *Archives of General Psychiatry* 2:477–491. Reprinted in *Steps to an Ecology of Mind*, pp. 215–241.

—— (1972). *Steps to an Ecology of Mind.* San Francisco: Chandler.
—— (1979). *Mind and Nature.* London: Wildwood House.
Bateson, G., Jackson, D. D., Haley, J., and Weakland, J. H. (1956). Towards a theory of schizophrenia. *Behavioral Science* 1:251–264. Republished in *Double Bind: The Foundation of the Communicational Approach to the Family,* ed. C. E. Sluzki and D. C. Ransom, pp. 3–23. New York: Grune & Stratton.
Benedetti, G. (1969). *Neuropsicologia.* Milan: Feltrinelli.
Berne, E. (1964). *Games People Play.* New York: Grove.
Bibring, E. (1953). The mechanism of depression. In *Affective Disorders,* ed. P. Greenacre. New York: International Universities Press.
Binswanger, H. (1959). The case of Ellen West. In *Existence,* ed. R. May et al. New York: Basic Books.
Boss, M. (1955). *Introduction à la Médicine Psychosomatique.* Paris: PUF.
Bott, E. (1971). *Family and Social Network.* London: Tavistock.
Bruch, H. (1961). Transformation of oral impulses in eating disorders. *Psychiatric Quarterly* 35:458.

Caillois, R. (1967). *Les Jeux et les Hommes.* Paris: Gallimard.
Covini, A., Fiocchi, E., Pasquino, R., and Selvini M. (1984). *Alla Conquista del Territorio,* preface by Mara Selvini Palazzoli. Rome: La Nuova Italia Scientifica.
Crozier, M., and Friedberg, E. (1977). *L'acteur et la Système.* Paris: Seuil.

de Beauregard, O. C. (1961). Sur l'équivalence entre information et entropie. *Sciences* 11:51.
Dell, P. (1981). Some irreverent thoughts on paradox. *Family Process* 20:37–42.
Di Blasio, P. (1981). Le coalizioni negate. In *Sul Fronte dell'Organizzazione,* ed. M. S. Palazzoli et al., pp. 205–212. Milan: Feltrinelli. English trans., *The Hidden Games of Organizations.* New York: Pantheon, 1987.

English and English. (1958). *A Comprehensive Dictionary of Psychological and Psychoanalytical Terms.* London: Longman, Green.

Fairbairn, W. R. D. (1962). *An Object Relation Theory of the Personality.* New York: Basic Books.
Ferraresi, P. (1970). Psicoterapia, pedagogia, fisioterapia. Address to the Socio-psychiatric and Socio-therapeutic Seminar, Milan, May 16–17.

Ferreira, A. (1963). Family myth and homeostasis. *Archives of General Psychiatry* 9:457–463.

—— (1966). Family myths. *Psychiatric Research Report* 20.

Fisch, R., Weakland, J., and Segal, L. (1982). *The Tactics of Change: Doing Therapy Briefly*. San Francisco: Jossey Bass.

Greenberg, G. (1977). The family interactional perspective: a study and examination of the work of Don D. Jackson. *Family Process* 16:385–412.

Haley, J. (1959). The family of the schizophrenic: a model system. *Journal of Nervous and Mental Diseases* 129:357–374.

—— (1961). Development of a theory: a history of a research project. In *Double Bind: The Foundation of the Communicational Approach to the Family*, ed. C. E. Sluzki and D. C. Ransom. New York: Grune & Stratton, 1976.

—— (1962). Family experiments: a new type of experimentation. *Family Process* 1:265–293.

—— (1964). Towards a theory of pathological systems. Address to a meeting of the Eastern Pennsylvania Psychiatric Institute, October. Republished in *Family Therapy and Disturbed Families*, ed. G. H. Zuk and B. Nagy. Palo Alto, Calif.: Science and Behavior Books, 1967.

—— (1971). *Changing Families: A Family Therapy Reader*, pp. 227–236. New York: Grune & Stratton.

Hoffman, L. (1975). Enmeshment and the too richly cross-joined system. *Family Process* 14:457–469.

—— (1981). *Foundations of Family Therapy*. New York: Basic Books.

Jackson, D. (1957). The question of family homeostasis. *Psychiatric Quarterly Supplement* 31:79–90.

Keeney, B. (1982). What is the epistemology of family therapy? *Family Process* 21:155–168.

Korzybski, A. (1933). *Science and Sanity*. New York: Scientific Press.

Lederer, W. J., and Jackson, D. D. (1968). *The Mirages of Marriage*. New York: W. W. Norton.

Lewin, K. (1945). The research center for group dynamics of MIT. *Sociometry* 11:126–136.

Minuchin, S. (1970). Treatment of a case of anorexia nervosa. Fourth International Congress of Child Psychiatry, Jerusalem, August 3–7.

Montalvo, B., and Haley, J. (1973). In defense of child therapy. *Family Process* 12:227–244.

Morin, E. (1977). *La Méthode.* Paris: Editions de Seuil.

Morris, G. D., and Wynne, L. C. (1965). Schizophrenic offspring and parental styles of communication. *Psychiatry* 28:1.

Rosman, B. L., Minuchin, S., and Liebman, R. (1975). "Family-lunch": an introduction to family therapy in anorexia nervosa. *American Journal of Orthopsychiatry* 45:846–853.

Ruesch, J., and Bateson, G. (1968). *Communication: The Social Matrix of Psychiatry.* New York: W. W. Norton.

Rusconi, S., and Selvini Palazzoli, M. (1967). La prima seduta di una terapia familiare congiunta. *Psicoterapia e scienze umane* 4:15–19.

——— (1970). Il transfert nella coterapia intensiva della famiglia. *Rivista di Psicologia Analitica* 1:157–177.

Satir, V. (1964). *Conjoint Family Therapy.* Palo Alto, Calif.: Science and Behavior Books.

Schafroth, M. T. (1960). The concept of temperature. In *Selected Lectures in Modern Physics,* ed. H. Messel. London: Macmillan.

Selvini, M., Covini, A., Fiocchi, E., and Pasquino, R. (1982). Al di là della terapia familiare: experienze di ristrutturazione sistemica di un centro psichiatrico territoriale. *Terapia Familiare* 12:19–39.

Selvini Palazzoli, M. (1963). *L'anoressia mentale.* Milan: Feltrinelli. Republished as *Self-Starvation: From the Intrapsychic to the Transpersonal Approach to Anorexia Nervosa.* London: Chaucer, 1974. American ed. New York: Jason Aronson, 1981.

——— (1967). Disordini del pensiero e relazioni familiari degli schizofrenici (Thought disorders and family relationships of schizophrenics). *Archivio Neur. Psic. Psich.* 38:306–319.

——— (1968). Preface to N. W. Ackerman, *Psicodinamica della Vita Familiare (Psychodynamics of Family Life).* Turin: Boringhieri.

——— (1969a). Preface to *Psicoterapia Intensive della Famiglia: Aspetti Teorici e Practici,* ed. J. Boszormenyi-Nagy and J. Framo. Turin: Boringhieri.

——— (1969b). Psicoterapia dell'anoressia mentale. *Medicina Psicosomatica* March 14.

——— (1970). The families of patients with anorexia nervosa. In *The Child in His Family,* ed. J. Anthony and C. Koupernik. New York: John Wiley & Sons.

——— (1971). Preface to the Italian edition of Gerhild Von Staabs, *Der Sceno-Test.* Florence: Edizione OS.

—— (1972). The family of the anorectic patient: a model system. *Archivio Psic. Neurol. Psich.* 4:311–342. Reprinted in *Self-Starvation*, American ed. New York: Jason Aronson, 1981, pp. 202–216.

—— (1975). The family of the anorectic and the family of the schizophrenic: a transactional study. First published in German in *Ehe. Zentralblatt für Ehe und Familienkunde* 3:107–116. Read at the Fourth Family Therapy Symposium, Zurich, October 1975.

—— (1977). Un avvenimento culturale: la traduzione italiana dell-'opera di Gregory Bateson (A cultural event: the Italian translation of the works of Gregory Bateson). *Archivio Psic. Neur. Psich.* 4.

—— (1978). Interview in *Socialmagazin* 3:32–41.

—— (1979). Present imperfect. Address delivered to mark the fourth Don Jackson Memorial Day, San Francisco.

—— (1981). Comments on Dell's paper. *Family Process* 20:44–45.

—— (1984). Review of *Aesthetics of Change* (B. Keeney, New York: Guilford Press, 1983). *Family Process* 23:282–284.

—— (1985). The problem of the sibling as the referring person. *Journal of Marriage and Family Therapy* 11:21–34.

Selvini Palazzoli, M., Boscolo, L., Cecchin, G., and Prata, G. (1972). The family of the anorectic patient: a model system. In *Archivio Psic. Neur. Psich.* 4:311–342. Republished in Selvini Palazzoli, M. (1981). *Self-Starvation*. New York: Jason Aronson, pp. 202–216.

—— (1977). La prima seduta di una terapia familiare sistemica. *Terapia Familiare* 2:5–13.

—— (1978). *Paradox and Counterparadox.* New York: Jason Aronson.

Selvini Palazzoli, M., Cirillo, S., D'Ettorre, L., Garbellini, M., et al. (1976). Come si interviene su una coalizione negata in un istituto per minori handicappati: un successo istruttivo. In *Il Mago Smagato*, p. 155. Milan: Feltrinelli.

—— (1981). *Sul Fronte dell'Organizzazione*, pp. 205–212. Milan: Feltrinelli. English trans., *The Hidden Games of Organizations.* New York: Pantheon, 1987

Selvini Palazzoli, M., and Ferraresi, P. (1972). L'obsédé et son conjoint. *Social Psychiatry* 7:90–97, 111.

Shands, H. C. (1971). *The War with Words.* The Hague-Paris: Mouton.

Sluzki, C., and Verón, E. (1976). The double bind as a universal pathogenic situation. In *Double Bind: The Foundation of the Communicational Approach to the Family*, ed. C. Sluzki and D. C. Ransom, pp. 251–263. New York: Grune & Stratton.

Speed, B. (1984). How really real is real? *Family Process* 23:511–530.
Spiegel, J. P., and Bell, N. W. (1959). Family of the psychotic patient. In *American Handbook of Psychiatry*, vol. I, ed. S. Arieti, pp. 114–149. New York: Basic Books.
Sullivan, H. S. (1955). *Conceptions of Modern Psychiatry*. London: Tavistock.

Telfener, U. (1983). *La Terapia Sistemica*, pp. 89–96. Rome: Astrolabio.
Thomä, H. (1961). *Anorexia Nervosa*. Stuttgart: Klett.
Tomm, K. (1980). Statement at the Calgary Seminar (Canada). Quoted in: The Milan approach: a tentative report. In *Treating Families with Special Needs*, ed. D. S. Freeman and B. Trute, Ottawa, 1982.

Viaro, M., and Leonardi, P. (1982). Le insubordinazzioni. *Terapia Familiare* 12:41–62.
——— (1983). Getting and giving information: analysis of a family-interview strategy. *Family Process* 22:27–42.

Watzlawick, P., Beavin, J., and Jackson, D. D. (1967). *Pragmatics of Human Communication*. New York: W. W. Norton.
Watzlawick, P., Weakland, J. H., and Fisch, R. (1974). *Change. Principles of Problem Formation and Problem Resolution*. New York: W. W. Norton.
Wynne, L. C., and Singer, M. T. (1963). Thought disorders in the family relations of schizophrenics. *Archives of General Psychiatry* 9:191–206.

Index